Building User-Friendly DSLs

Get the eBook FREE!

(PDF, ePub, Kindle, and liveBook all included)

We believe that once you buy a book from us, you should be able to read it in any format we have available. To get electronic versions of this book at no additional cost to you, purchase and then register this book at the Manning website.

Go to https://www.manning.com/freebook and follow the instructions to complete your pBook registration.

That's it!
Thanks from Manning!

Building
User-Friendly DSLs

MEINTE BOERSMA
FOREWORD BY FEDERICO TOMASSETTI

MANNING
SHELTER ISLAND

For online information and ordering of this and other Manning books, please visit
www.manning.com. The publisher offers discounts on this book when ordered in quantity.
For more information, please contact

> Special Sales Department
> Manning Publications Co.
> 20 Baldwin Road
> PO Box 761
> Shelter Island, NY 11964
> Email: orders@manning.com

Manning Publications Co.	Development editors: Heidi Nobles and Karen Miller
20 Baldwin Road	Technical development editor: Mark Elston
PO Box 761	Review editor: Mihaela Batinić
Shelter Island, NY 11964	Production editor: Andy Marinkovich
	Copy editor: Andy Carroll
	Proofreader: Katie Tennant
	Technical proofreader: David Cabrero Souto
	Typesetter: Dennis Dalinnik
	Cover designer: Marija Tudor

ISBN: 9781617296475
Printed in the United States of America

To my family, for supporting me throughout the long process of writing this book

brief contents

contents

foreword

DSLs seem like a very well-kept secret because of our failures as a community to explain them in simple words. Personally, it took getting a PhD and working many years in the field to understand what can be achieved with a DSL, and it was not very tempting for others to follow. Meinte draws another path with this book. He presents the clearness of thought you would expect from a mathematician, but he spares us the complications. We, as a community, needed a pragmatic mathematician to show us the way.

I always admired the elegance of Meinte's thoughts when he was sharing his experience on projects like ALEF (a DSL built for the Dutch Tax and Custom Agency), or his experience designing Más, his own Language Workbench, or what he learned at Mendix, a company later acquired by Siemens. Naturally, when I learned he was working on this book, I took the opportunity to interview him, to learn more about it. Since then, I have been waiting patiently for this book to be in your hands.

So, what can you expect to get from this book?

The book throws away the historical baggage of building DSLs and traditional approaches, which are better suited to create heavy IDEs. Meinte instead adapts those ideas to a world where lightweight solutions running in the browser are the norm.

You will learn everything that is necessary to understand what DSLs are for and how they can be concretely built. While keeping things simple, Meinte manages to cover the basic and advanced topics. For example, you'll really appreciate the discussion of mechanisms for managing change.

Reading this book will give you a deep understanding of what scenarios DSLs open and how they work, without leaving any mysteries or dark corners. This understanding will serve you well, as the principles will still be valid even when the implementation techniques change. In this sense, reading this book is highly likely to prove an excellent investment for you.

I genuinely envy you, as this book will save you a lot of trouble learning this topic. I am also sure you will enjoy reading it.

Have fun, and welcome to the DSL community!

—FEDERICO TOMASSETTI, Software Architect & Founder at Strumenta

preface

Domain-specific languages (DSLs) have existed essentially since the beginning of programming and software development, in various shapes and forms. Many DSLs have been implemented, and they've been used, often with great success, to drive software development. It's therefore surprising that hardly any standard, go-to textbooks (specifically) on DSLs exist. Even fewer can be considered to be entry-level, in the sense that they don't assume the reader has prior knowledge about several aspects of software language engineering.

Despite their longevity and their usefulness, DSLs still occupy a relatively small niche in software development. In fact, plenty of software developers are not aware of their benefits or even their existence. Those who are aware often find themselves unable to adopt a DSL-based approach in their daily job precisely because of its obscurity. Moreover, software developers are a hard crowd to "sell to": they tend to be strongly opinionated and are used to an abundance of readily available open source tooling.

That is why I eagerly accepted when Manning Publications asked me to write a book on DSLs. I was glad to learn that they asked me specifically because of my focus on *projectional editing*. Projectional editing does not rely on parsing textual DSL content. Instead, it takes DSL content, represented as structured data, and *projects* it in a syntax that also serves as a UI to change the DSL content. This approach allows for a very straightforward learning path across the fundamentals of DSLs.

I've been implementing DSLs based on projectional editing for more than a decade. In that time, tooling has improved significantly, especially on the web side of things. It's now entirely possible to implement a fully functional DSL without relying on language engineering–specific tools, libraries, or frameworks, instead of just using mainstream, open source web technology. That makes for an ideal starting point for learning to implement DSLs without getting locked in to any particular framework.

For many, the COVID-19 pandemic offered an ideal opportunity to achieve focus-intensive projects like writing a book. For those like me, having a family of three young children who had to be entertained and home-schooled throughout lockdowns, that was decidedly less true. This explains in part why this book took a "tad" longer than anyone could originally anticipate.

Another reason is that I had to learn that it's better to take the time and space to explain one thing well than to explain many things too quickly. Because of that, about half of the proposed table of contents got slashed. At the same time, the number of pages, listings, and figures ended up being a lot higher than originally projected. I'm convinced all of that has made for a much better and more useful book that's focused on bringing the power of projectional editing to non-software development businesses.

The final reason is that I grossly underestimated the amount of work that goes into a book of this size and detail. Over the course of this book, we'll evolve an entire codebase, continuously adding new, but also changing existing, code. This means that changing something anywhere in the book often had a cascading effect that was error-prone to address.

For me, the result was well worth the effort. I hope the same will be true for you.

acknowledgments

First, I want to thank Nadine for supporting me emotionally, logistically, and financially throughout this "somewhat" prolonged endeavor, and for serving as my primary "hot off the press" proofreader.

Many other people have contributed in some way to this book. Special mentions:

- Marjan Bace and Michael Stephens at Manning Publications for getting in touch with me and providing me with this opportunity.
- Bert Bates for challenging me on the assumptions underlying the book, thereby improving its contents and potential manifold—a process I like to call "Bertification."
- Jos Warmer for advising me to *not* write this book, but nevertheless supporting me through proofreading, sparring about the contents, and making me aware of existing teaching material.
- Mark Elston for proofreading and checking every single bit of code: you've done a wonderfully thorough job. Any bugs that remain are entirely my own fault.
- All my model-driven friends/colleagues/"partners in crime" for their continued support, with a special mention of Federico Tomassetti.
- Joris van Aart for the support, not in the least by suggesting I take a sabbatical.
- Everyone else at Manning Publications involved in some way with this book: senior development editor Karen Miller, development assistant Melissa Ice, project coordinator Malena Selic, MEAP producer Ivan Martinovic, production

manager Aleksandar Dragosavljevic, production editor Andy Marinkovich, copyeditor Andy Carroll, and proofreader Katie Tennant.

- All of the reviewers who took the time to provide feedback on the manuscript: Adhir Ramjiawan, Alain Lompo, Arjan van Eersel, Brent Honadel, Burk Hufnagel, Cameron Presley, Chris Viner, Conor Redmond, David Cabrero, David Paccoud, Dhivya Sivasubramanian, Emmanouil Chardalas, Erik Vullings, Evyatar Kafkafi, Frans Oilinki, Fred Heath, Gary Pollice, George Thomas, Giampiero Granatella, Goetz Heller, Gustavo Filipe Ramos Gomes, Hilde Van Gysel, Hugo Cruz, Jeremy Chen, Johannes Lochmann, John Pantoja, Jort Rodenburg, Joseph Perenia, Julien Pohie, Kathik Rajendran, Kelum Prabath Senanayake, Kumar Unnikrishnan, Marc-Anthony Taylor, Michael Kumm, Mikael Byström, Mike Hewitson, NaveenKumar Namachivayam, Patrice Maldague, Ryan Barrett, Sambasiva Andaluri, Samvid Mistry, Satej Kumar Sahu, Simone Sguazza, Suhasa Krishnayya, Sujith Surendranatha, Thomas Fischer, Tim van Deurzen, Tobias Kaatz, and Vinicius Morais Dutra.
- Everyone who commented on the MEAP liveBook for taking the trouble to point out typos, bugs in the code, inconsistencies, and whatnot, and making suggestions.
- All my friends and family for using "Is it done yet?" as a recurring conversation starter.
- Everyone who bought the book during the MEAP for providing me with the impetus to keep going whenever the going was tough.

Finally, we turn to the one who has done more for this book than anyone else—possibly including myself. I've often noticed that writers profusely thank their editors in the acknowledgments. With the limited understanding of the book production process I had before, that always left me a bit puzzled.

Now I understand.

Heidi: Thank you *so much* for teaching me how to write books, helping me every step of the way on this journey, and fighting for this book fearsomely. This book wouldn't have existed, and certainly not in this form, without you. I loved using our weekly touch-bases to compare notes on international politics, toddlers and their many antics, and the merits of regional delicacies. Your students probably don't fully appreciate how lucky they are to have you as their teacher.

about this book

In this book, you'll learn how to implement and use DSLs that are user friendly, using mainstream web technology. User-friendly DSLs are targeted to, and implemented for, people who are not software developers or programmers themselves, but are subject matter experts (SMEs) in their *business domain*—I'll refer to such SMEs as *domain experts* from now on.

Software developers empower domain experts by implementing DSLs with which the domain experts can capture the business knowledge or subject matter expertise that should go into a desired software system. This is a win for the software developers because this approach scales: the tedious, repetitive, and monotonous parts of software development are relegated to the domain experts, who can handle those parts efficiently using the DSLs at their disposal. You can see this approach in action with *no/low-code software development platforms*. Such platforms rely heavily on languages that are specific to the domain of specifying some type of application. These no/low-code languages are often visually oriented and implemented through projectional editing.

Who should read this book?

Building User-Friendly DSLs is written for readers interested in

- Learning the basics of software language engineering
- Implementing DSLs using projectional editing, using mainstream web technology
- Adopting a DSL-based approach to software development in a business-oriented context (business domains)

This book offers the following takeaway skills:

- Recognizing the potential for user-friendly DSLs in business domains
- Adopting a DSL-based approach through implementing a Domain IDE that exposes a DSL
- Being able to work with ASTs in code
- Implementing a basic web editor for the DSL, including content assist and validation (constraints checking)
- Implementing expressions and business rules
- Implementing a type system and code generator as part of a DSL

The reader should possess the following skills:

- *JavaScript (medium)*—The reader *should* be able to code nontrivial programs using JavaScript. I'll explain the JavaScript idiom we'll be using in detail in appendix B, which includes some features introduced in recent years. It should be feasible for a reader to understand this book and the code in it despite not knowing JavaScript if they are familiar with another modern general-purpose programming language (GPL). In principle, it's also possible to port all the code and do all the exercises using another GPL and its ecosystem—in particular, its backend and UI frameworks/libraries and development tooling.
- *Web development (basic)*—It's *not required* that the reader already be able to code complete web applications on their own, because I'll be providing step-by-step instructions, but it would be beneficial. We'll touch on the following aspects of web development:
  - *Node.js, npm, command-line interface (CLI) (basic)*—The reader must be able to (follow instructions to) install Node.js (https://nodejs.org) and to use either npm or Yarn from the command line to do dependency management and web bundling. The latter really boils down to being able to execute commands like `npm install --save-dev parcel`, `npm start`, and such. I'll provide the commands to execute.
  - *HTML (basic)*—The reader should have an understanding of HTML, and more specifically, the existence of the DOM and Event APIs. I'll be using the most common tags (`<div>`, `<span>`, `<input>`, etc.) and the event handlers that can be attached to these (`onChange`, etc.). We'll use React and the JSX syntax for this.

The following skills are optional, as the relevant required knowledge will be explained in appendix B:

- *React (basic, optional)*—It would be beneficial if the reader already has some knowledge of and skill with React and its JSX syntax, and more generally, Reactive programming. However, I'll be using, and explaining, React in a very formulaic style in combination with the state management library MobX, so this is not a hard prerequisite. For more in-depth knowledge about React, I recommend reading *React Quickly, Second Edition*, by Morten Barklund and Azat Mardan (Manning, 2023).

- *Web bundling (basic, optional)*—I'll be using Parcel to do web bundling. I'll explain how to do it, what goes into this process, and why it's necessary.
- *CSS (basic, optional)*—It's not necessary for the reader to have knowledge of and skill with CSS to do a smidgen of basic styling, as I'll provide all the styling required.

How this book is organized: A roadmap

This book has 15 chapters and 2 appendixes:

- Chapter 1 explains what DSLs are, what their key aspects are, and more importantly, what the benefits of adopting a DSL-based approach can be. This chapter has no code, and can—and *should*—be read by anyone who is involved in software development.
- Chapter 2 explains how to represent DSL content as structured data, using a notation for object-relation diagrams that we'll use throughout the rest of the book. We call DSL content represented this way an abstract syntax tree (AST). This chapter also has no code.
- Chapter 3 explains how to encode ASTs (represented as object-relation diagrams) as JavaScript values in code, how to interact with them, and how to traverse them algorithmically. The code in this chapter forms the basis for everything else we'll do in this book.
- Chapter 4 explains the concept of projectional editing: an AST representing content according to a DSL is projected as a visualization in the form of an HTML DOM. This projection is built on and extended throughout the rest of the book until chapter 15.
- Chapter 5 explains how to modify the projection to turn it into a DSL editor with which domain experts can manipulate individual values in the projected AST.
- Chapter 6 explains how to modify the projection so the domain experts can interact with and manipulate the AST on an object level.
- Chapter 7 explains how to turn ASTs into JSON and back again, so that we can transport and store/persist them.
- Chapter 8 explains how to turn an AST into a working software system by generating code from it and integrating that in a codebase.
- Chapter 9 explains how we can avoid generating failing code by adding constraints to the DSL.
- Chapter 10 explains how to manage changes to the DSL content and the DSL itself.
- Chapter 11 explains how to add expressions, particularly binary operations like 1 + 1, to a DSL.

- Chapter 12 explains how to deal with the peculiarities of expressions—in particular, the order of operations—when using projectional editing.
- Chapter 13 explains how to add a type system to a DSL.
- Chapter 14 explains how to add business rules to a DSL, including how to generate the code that runs these.
- Chapter 15 discusses a number of topics that we didn't cover in earlier chapters, but that are important to touch on. This chapter can be read separately.
- Appendix A explains how to set up the development environment used to implement the example DSL in chapters 3 through 14, and how to use it. This is probably the daily "bread-and-butter" for many readers, who can skim through this appendix, or potentially skip it entirely.
- Appendix B details the JavaScript idiom we'll be using to implement the example DSL. This includes how we use React, in combination with the MobX state management framework, to implement a frontend according to a coding style that achieves *Transparent Functional Reactive Programming* (TFRP). We'll rely on that coding style from chapter 5 onwards.

Chapters 3 through 14 evolve a complete codebase. Whenever a chapter uses knowledge from an appendix, an explicit reference is made.

A reader already familiar with DSLs, software language engineering, or model-driven software development should be able to read this book according to this alternative organization:

- Appendixes A and B: JavaScript development of web apps
- Chapters 2, 3, 7, 10: Fundamentals of ASTs, *structure*
- Chapters 4–6: Projectional DSL editor, *notation*
- Chapter 8: Code generation, *meaning*
- Chapters 9 and 13: *Constraints*
- Chapters 11–12: Expressions
- Chapter 14: Business rules
- Chapter 15: Miscellaneous

All of the contents in this book have been produced by a human—me—and not by an LLM such as ChatGPT.

About the code

You can get executable snippets of code from the liveBook (online) version of this book at https://livebook.manning.com/book/building-user-friendly-dsls. All source code in this book is available for download from the Manning website at https://www.manning.com and from GitHub at https://github.com/dslmeinte/Building-User-Friendly-DSLs-code. Each of chapters 3 through 15 and appendix B have their own directory/folder containing the relevant code. Each of those directories contains a

README.md file explaining what exactly is in that directory and how to run the code in it.

To be able to run it, you'll need to have a development environment set up—see appendix A for details on that. Any personal computer that's moderately recent should suffice. Thanks to the existence of web IDEs (see also section B.3), a computing device such as a tablet or even a large mobile phone might be enough.

This book contains many examples of source code both in numbered listings and in line with normal text. In both cases, source code is formatted in a fixed-width font `like this` to separate it from ordinary text. Sometimes, some of the code is typeset in **bold** to highlight code that has changed from previous steps in the chapter, such as when a feature is added to an existing line of code.

In many cases, the original source code has been reformatted; we've added line breaks and reworked indentation to accommodate the available page space in the book. In some cases, even this was not enough, and listings include line-continuation markers (➥). Additionally, comments in the source code have often been removed from the listings when the code is described in the text. Code annotations accompany many of the listings, highlighting important concepts.

Why JavaScript (and not TypeScript)

It's been obvious to me for a long time that DSL implementation should target the web: domain experts should not need more than a browser—and probably a working internet/intranet connection—to use DSLs. This almost evidently means that I'd be using a JavaScript-based development environment.

With a heavy heart, I decided against using TypeScript. TypeScript is an extension of JavaScript that primarily adds optional strong static typing to JavaScript. Leaning on TypeScript's type system to determine whether your code will break at run time helps tremendously with writing good code efficiently.

So why not use it? There are a few reasons:

- It adds complexity to the toolchain in the form of a "transpiler" (a compiler that produces *source* code instead of bytecode). This transpiler has to be integrated into the build process, including with the web bundling framework we use—see section B.2. Using something like the Deno runtime (https://deno .land/) would help a lot here, but Deno is not as mainstream as Node.js (yet).
- Not everyone knows TypeScript, which narrows the potential reader base of this book. I could explain every TypeScript feature I used explicitly, but that would cost extra time and space, and the book is heavy enough as it is.
- TypeScript is especially helpful while changing existing, and writing new, code. The payoff for the code in the book, which is already written, would be limited.

Nevertheless, I strongly advise anyone implementing a JavaScript application to use TypeScript on top of JavaScript. The return on investment (ROI) of leaning on the support you can get from TypeScript's type system is huge. To learn how to use Type-

Script, you could pick up the book *TypeScript Quickly* by Yakov Fain and Anton Moiseev (Manning, 2020).

Why projectional editing (and not parsing)

This book focuses exclusively on using the paradigm of *projectional editing* to implement a DSL. There are three reasons for that choice:

- Plenty of books and other kinds of resources exist that explain using parsing to implement software languages, of which DSLs are a subfamily. See section 15.1 for references, and some explanation about, parsing.
- No books exist that explain projectional editing in general, without being tied to a particular tool that specifically helps with implementing software languages and DSLs. See section 15.4.1 for more explanation about such tools, which are called *language workbenches*.
- Projectional editing has many advantages over a parsing-based approach—see section 15.1 for a discussion of these. Projectional editing also has a few disadvantages, but in my experience, those are outweighed by the advantages, especially in the context of DSLs for business domains and their domain experts.

We're not going to discuss anything about parsing, grammars, syntax highlighting, and all these things that are only intrinsically relevant for textual DSLs. If you expected this book to be about those topics, then I hope you can turn that disappointment around and learn about projectional editing instead.

liveBook discussion forum

Purchase of *Building User-Friendly DSLs* includes free access to liveBook, Manning's online reading platform. Using liveBook's exclusive discussion features, you can attach comments to the book globally or to specific sections or paragraphs. It's a snap to make notes for yourself, ask and answer technical questions, and receive help from the author and other users. To access the forum, go to https://livebook.manning.com/book/building-user-friendly-dsls/discussion. You can also learn more about Manning's forums and the rules of conduct at https://livebook.manning.com/discussion.

Manning's commitment to our readers is to provide a venue where a meaningful dialogue between individual readers and between readers and the author can take place. It is not a commitment to any specific amount of participation on the part of the author, whose contribution to the forum remains voluntary (and unpaid). We suggest you try asking the author some challenging questions lest their interest stray! The forum and the archives of previous discussions will be accessible from the publisher's website for as long as the book is in print.

about the author

MEINTE BOERSMA has been an active practitioner of model-driven software development and DSL engineering since 2007. He designs, implements, and deploys DSLs for various companies and organizations, using a multitude of technologies. Furthermore, he speaks at conferences, publishes blogs, participates in the development of open source standards and frameworks for DSL engineering, and is actively involved with the software language/DSL engineering community.

about the cover illustration

The figure on the cover of *Building User-Friendly DSLs* is captioned "Marchand Juif à Constantinople," or "a Jewish tradesman in the city now known as Istanbul." He is holding a couple of bolts—rolls of fabric—woven on a loom. The fabric shows figures or patterns introduced by the weaving.

Even though this person predates the advent of computers by centuries, textile weaving and DSLs are connected through the Jacquard loom (or machine).[1] The Jacquard machine can be thought of as a rudimentary computer executing "programs" that are fed to it in the form of punch cards. The language that those "programs" are written in is far from general-purpose: it's rather closer to a domain-specific language. The connection between textiles and DSLs doesn't stop there: *knitting patterns* are typically described using a DSL.

The cover image is taken from a collection by Jacques Grasset de Saint-Sauveur, published in 1797. Each illustration is finely drawn and colored by hand. In those days, it was easy to identify where people lived and what their trade or station in life was just by their dress. Manning celebrates the inventiveness and initiative of the computer business with book covers based on the rich diversity of regional culture centuries ago, brought back to life by pictures from collections such as this one.

---

[1] See the Wikipedia article at https://en.wikipedia.org/wiki/Jacquard_machine, or the more colorful exposé by the Science and Industry Museum in Manchester (https://mng.bz/PNrP).

What is a domain-specific language?

This chapter covers

- What a domain-specific language is
- What adopting a DSL-based approach does for an organization
- When to use a DSL
- What the key aspects of a DSL are

If you're reading this book, you've probably already heard about domain-specific languages (DSLs). You might even have realized that you may need to use one. But do you really? And what *is* a DSL, and how would you build one?

Teaching about DSLs is tricky because it's a very broad topic and is interconnected with other topics in both software development and computer science. This book will *not* try to teach you *everything* about DSLs or overwhelm you with myriad details. Instead, it will take you on a carefully planned route through a set of connected topics that cover all the basics and skills you'll need to craft your own DSLs. This learning path will be example driven, quite literally going from the concrete to the abstract.

This book will also focus on *business*-oriented DSLs to empower domain experts, who are first and foremost business stakeholders and who generally don't have backgrounds as software developers. The "user-friendly" part of this book's title is meant to encompass qualities like "easy to understand and learn," "practical," etc. To that end, we'll start by sketching out an example business case for which we'll build a complete DSL throughout the course of this book.

1.1   *A business case: A car rental company*

In this section, I'll introduce a concrete and representative business case in some detail. We'll use this business case throughout the book as a running example, to keep our discussions concrete and grounded.

Imagine a local car rental company that is in the business of renting vehicles to individuals. The company has a sizable fleet of cars of different types, makes, and configurations. Consider a prospective customer interested in renting a car from this company. They would input parameters like the rental period, type of car, and contract type into the company's website, or in an app on a mobile device, and ask it to produce a price quote (see figure 1.1). Once they find a combination of parameters that produces a favorable outcome, they can continue and reserve a vehicle with those parameters. You've probably done this a couple of times yourself.

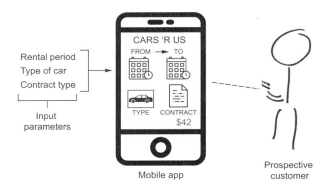

Figure 1.1   A prospective customer uses a car rental company's app to get a price quote for a rental

Let's take a closer look at how this piece of software (web or native app) computes a price based on the input parameters: rental period, type of car, and contract type. A few factors go into computing the price:

- Discounts may apply, based on the length of the rental period or the presence of holidays within the date range.
- Each type of car has its specific rate.
- The contract type determines whether there's a flat rate per day, a rate based on the distance driven, or a combination of those, possibly with a mileage cap.
- Discounts may be given for other reasons, like marketing campaigns.

Determining a car rental price based on the input parameters involves a lot of *business knowledge*, which often takes the form of *business logic*. If we were to look at the code that computes the price quote, it would probably be quite complicated, with a lot of nested conditional logic in the form of `if` or similar statements. We'd probably also see some intermediate state in the form of variables that are initialized, set, or manipulated based on certain conditions. How did the developers who wrote the code know what they should be writing? Let's assume that the developers weren't already experts on car rentals—they must have been handed some kind of *specification* by the people in the company who set rules for these things.

But how would the business's experts write that specification down? Typically, you'd expect a collection of documents that use natural language to describe business knowledge. For example, table 1.1 could be part of the specification for how to compute a price quote.

Table 1.1   Natural language expressing car rental business knowledge

If the rental period contains a national holiday, then a surcharge rate of 10% is applied to the rental price for that holiday.
If the length of the rental period exceeds a whole week, then a discount rate of 5% is applied to the per-day rate.
If the car is a genuine gas guzzler, then an additional environmental fee of $10/day is applied.

These business rules take the form "If <condition>, then <consequence>." The *condition* part specifies when the rule should trigger, or *fire*, and the *consequence* part specifies what should happen in that case. Business rules interact with each other to determine the various price components, and, subsequently, the total price, based on the input parameters. This is an often-used format for specifying business knowledge that's useful for, and usable by, business experts. We'll look at a more precise definition of business rules in chapter 14.

Computing a price for a prospective customer constitutes a very small part of all software-based business processes within the car rental company. Other business processes could include

- Confirming a reservation with the customer
- Having the customer change or cancel their reservation
- Processing a customer who is coming in to pick up their rental
- Processing a car after it's been dropped off by the customer
- Invoicing
- Doing administrative chores for the cars in the fleet

Translating a specification of all of an organization's business knowledge and processes into working code is a lot of work. It's not just that there's a lot of business knowledge. The specification itself must be checked for completeness, consistency, and ambiguities. That requires plenty of back and forth between the software developers and the business experts. Implementing business knowledge in this way is therefore usually time consuming, tedious, and expensive.

Software development is like this, in part, because business experts normally don't have the background, knowledge, or skills to develop software themselves. Even though they tend to be highly educated, they typically have had no education in programming. Business experts may be great at specifying the *what*, but they're usually not great at specifying the *how*. Wouldn't it be great if they didn't have to learn all about software development and could just write down their business knowledge using helpful tools?

In this book, we're going to explore how we can develop software tools for business experts that will allow them to write down their business knowledge in a way that's both understandable for them and that can be *automatically* translated into working software. This puts the business experts, rather than the software developers, at the center of software development. Our goal isn't just to make the business experts feel more important—we'll look at all the advantages (and some disadvantages) of this approach in section 1.3.

DSLs vs. programming languages

We call the form in which experts can write their business knowledge a *domain-specific language*, or DSL for short. It's a software language that's specifically crafted for the domain that the business experts inhabit, or own.

A *software language* is an artificial language that exists through software. It's very precisely defined (usually through some kind of "grammar"), and "prose" written in it has a precise meaning—we say that it's a *formal* language. A software language has a clear "notation" or "syntax": a system of writing that's readily understood by its readers and writers. This notation can (and often does) look like text, or even like natural language. However, even if the language looks like a natural one, it doesn't allow ambiguity like natural languages typically do. A software language comes with a set of software tools that allow users of the language to write it down and process it further.

All programming and modeling languages are software languages, but the converse is not true, which leaves space for DSLs, as well as a couple of other kinds of software languages. A DSL is not a genuine programming language, nor is it a general modeling language, but it shares a lot of characteristics with those types of languages. We'll go into what makes a software language domain-specific in section 1.4.

In the course of this book, we're going to develop DSL tools for the car rental company's business experts so they can specify their business knowledge. Along the way, you will learn how to create original DSLs to meet your own needs. The next section explains more precisely what DSL tools we're going to be creating.

1.2   *Using a DSL-based approach for software development*

We're going to break up software development to put business experts at the center. Our key enabler in doing this is a DSL. Instead of having the business experts write their business knowledge in documents using natural language, the experts will use a tool called the *Domain IDE* to write down their business knowledge as *DSL content*.

Typically, software developers use an *integrated development environment* (IDE) to write software in one or more programming languages. Our Domain IDE will target business experts, so it won't include most of the bells and whistles that software developers are used to. Instead, it will provide the business experts with enough functionality to empower them to write the desired DSL content. If we design the DSL and the Domain IDE properly, this DSL content will not only be understandable, writable, and maintainable by business experts, but it will be precise enough to serve as a specification. We'll call this a *DSL-based approach for software development*.

> **NOTE**   To keep our naming aligned with the term *DSL*, we'll talk about *domain experts* rather than *business experts*. We can consider all businesses to be domains in their own right. We'll come back to this in section 1.4.

Instead of implementing the required business software by translating a specification to code, we, as software developers, will primarily develop a Domain IDE that the domain experts will use. We will also make sure that the Domain IDE builds working software, *generating* code directly and automatically from the DSL content. We'll also build any parts of the working software that can't be specified by the domain experts.

To avoid getting bogged down in whether a piece of software should be called an "app" or "application," or whether it's even really running, we'll call our entire desired software system the *Runtime*. This Runtime (with a capital "R") is not to be confused with runtimes like the JVM, .NET, Node.js, etc. Those runtimes operate on a level much closer to the OS and are just technology—they're not business-centric or domain-specific at all. In the case of our car rental company, the Runtime will consist of both the app that customers use to arrange a rental, and the point-of-sale systems that employees use to execute the business processes. Both the customers and the employees are *business stakeholders*. We won't call them domain stakeholders, since not all of them are really inhabitants of the domain: customers, in particular, are just serviced by the domain.

The Domain IDE is a separate application that the domain experts use to write down their business knowledge. These days, it makes sense that the Domain IDE should be a web app, running in a browser. That not only avoids domain experts having to install and update an application, but web apps are also easier to make work on multiple types of computing devices. Developing web apps is a mainstream skill, so a lot of software developers already have that skill. Finally, implementing a Transparent Functional Reactive frontend (see appendix B) is well understood in the web world.

> **NOTE**   If you're already familiar with DSLs, chances are that you expect to be implementing a *textual* DSL as part of the Domain IDE. Doing that would involve coming up with a grammar, generating a parser from it, and so on. This book uses a different approach, called *projectional editing*. It works directly with and on the abstract syntax tree (AST). For a textual DSL, the AST would be produced by a parser as an intermediate representation of the DSL content. I'll explain this choice more later on, in sections 1.2.3 and 15.1.

The DSL-based approach for software development is summarized in figure 1.2.

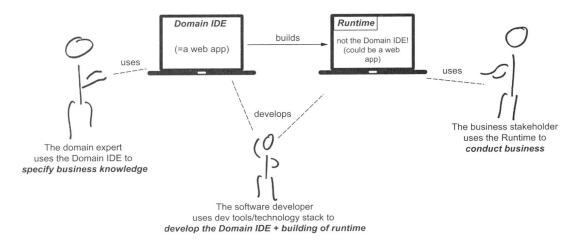

Figure 1.2   **Using a DSL-based approach to develop a Runtime using a Domain IDE**

1.2.1   *The design of the Domain IDE*

To get an idea of what a Domain IDE looks like, I'm going to cheat and use my prescient crystal ball to take some screenshots of the Domain IDE for the car rental company.

> **NOTE**   The Domain IDE that we'll be building over the course of this book will differ from the screenshots that follow. The Domain IDE we'll build will be as lean as possible and will focus exclusively on editing the DSL content. The parts of the Domain IDE that are necessary but aren't specifically DSL-based will be left as an exercise for you to explore.

Domain experts should be able to express the following kinds of business knowledge in the Domain IDE (as noted previously in table 1.1):

- If the rental period contains a national holiday, then a surcharge rate of 10% is applied to the rental price for that holiday.
- If the length of the rental period exceeds a whole week, then a discount rate of 5% is applied to the per-day rate.
- If the car is a genuine gas guzzler, then an additional environmental fee of $10/day is applied.

Domain experts should be able to create, change, update, and maintain DSL content that truthfully represents this business knowledge in the Domain IDE. Let's look in my crystal ball to see what a similar set of rules could look like. Figure 1.3 shows two business rules that are a bit simpler than the preceding ones, but they're still actual business rules.

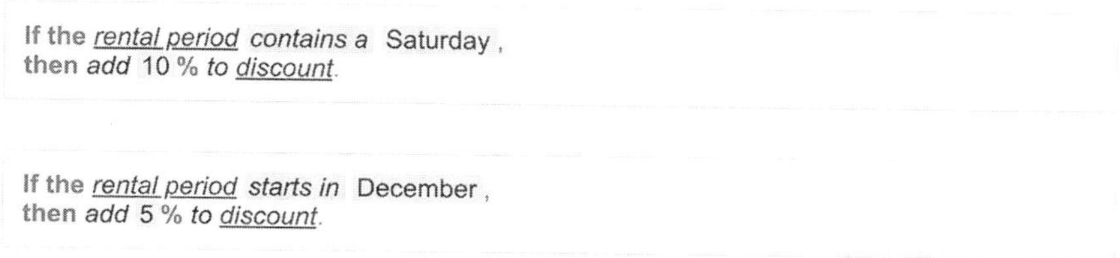

If the *rental period* contains a Saturday ,
then *add* 10 % *to discount*.

If the *rental period* starts in December ,
then *add* 5 % *to discount*.

Figure 1.3   Two simple business rules, as seen in the Domain IDE

These rules check the date range of the intended rental and apply discounts if their conditions hold. For example, if the rental period lasts from December 4 until December 10, 2020, the customer should be given a discount of 15%, because that date range contains both a Saturday *and* it starts in December.

As you can see in figure 1.4, these business rules are not just text: different parts of the sentences have different font styles, colors, and backgrounds. Not only are the business rules nicely rendered in the browser, the domain experts can edit them. They don't do this by adding or deleting individual characters, like they would in a text editor. Instead, domain experts can interact with the DSL content in precise ways that will make sense to them. This might seem restrictive, but it also serves as guidance, making it difficult to input DSL content that is patently wrong.

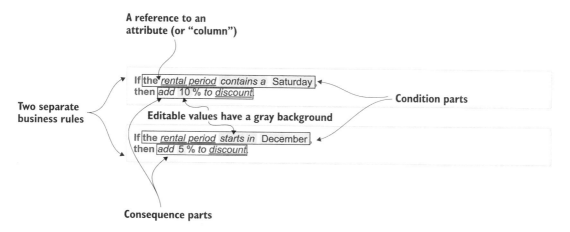

Figure 1.4   The same two business rules, with explanatory annotations

Here are some examples of how this is different from textual editing:

- Since we know we're dealing with business rules, it doesn't make sense to edit the If and then text, or the punctuation (the comma separating the if and then parts of the sentence, and the period ending it).

- We don't force the domain experts to type `the` or the `%` symbol after the percentage. Such adornments are rendered automatically.
- When adding content, the domain expert is guided such that they can only input content that makes sense at that place. For example, we provide the domain expert with a drop-down menu for choosing the day after the `contains a` text (see figure 1.5).

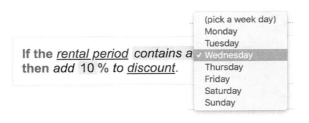

Figure 1.5   Choosing a weekday for a `contains a` operation

- Likewise, when adding or changing the condition of a business rule, the domain expert can choose from a limited number of constructs that make sense there (see figure 1.6).

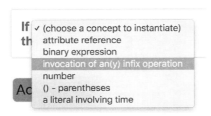

Figure 1.6   Choosing a construct when editing the condition of a business rule

- The `then` text in a business rule should always be followed by an action, so it doesn't make sense to allow conditions (like `rental period starts in December`) there.
- If the domain expert tries to add `peanuts` to the discount, they are greeted with an error message (see figure 1.7).

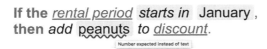

Figure 1.7   A business rule with an error

To be useful, the Domain IDE has to do more than just show the business rules on the screen. Figure 1.8 zooms out with the crystal ball a bit. This part of the Domain IDE is called the *editor*, and it shows all the DSL content we're focusing on in editable form.

Business rules section: *Standard*
  Valid from: 01/01/2020
  Context: *Rental*

If the *rental period* contains a Saturday ,
then add 10 % to *discount*.

If the *rental period* starts in December ,
then add 5 % to *discount*.

Add new rule

Figure 1.8   The same two business rules, shown inside the Domain IDE editor

Figure 1.9 explains these new parts of the editor.

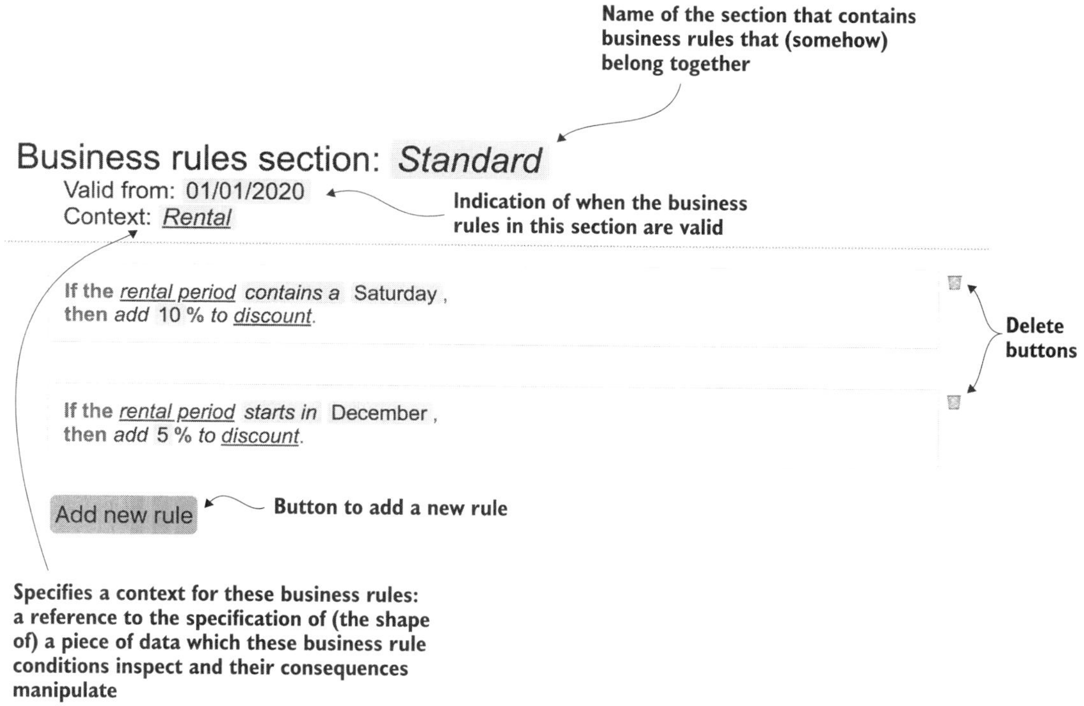

Name of the section that contains business rules that (somehow) belong together

Business rules section: *Standard*
  Valid from: 01/01/2020
  Context: *Rental*

Indication of when the business rules in this section are valid

If the *rental period* contains a Saturday ,
then add 10 % to *discount*.

If the *rental period* starts in December ,
then add 5 % to *discount*.

Delete buttons

Add new rule   **Button to add a new rule**

Specifies a context for these business rules: a reference to the specification of (the shape of) a piece of data which these business rule conditions inspect and their consequences manipulate

Figure 1.9   The same two business rules in the editor, with explanatory annotations

At this point, you should wonder where the `rental period` referenced in the business rules comes from. It seems to point to a piece of data in the context of a rental. It stands to reason that the domain experts will have to say something about what data the Runtime will be dealing with. Could that have something to do with the `Rental` context referenced at the top? It sure does, as you're about to see.

Let's take another look in my crystal ball and see what defining a data structure could look like in the Domain IDE (figure 1.10).

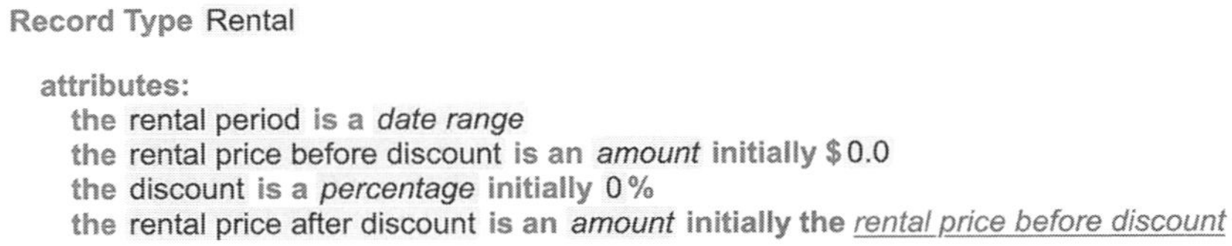

Record Type Rental
attributes:
the rental period is a *date range*
the rental price before discount is an *amount* initially $0.0
the discount is a *percentage* initially 0 %
the rental price after discount is an *amount* initially the rental price before discount

Figure 1.10 Origin of the referenced `rental period`: the `Rental` record type

This is a different kind of DSL content that doesn't specify conditional business logic, but rather defines the shapes of pieces of data. Figure 1.11 provides some more explanation.

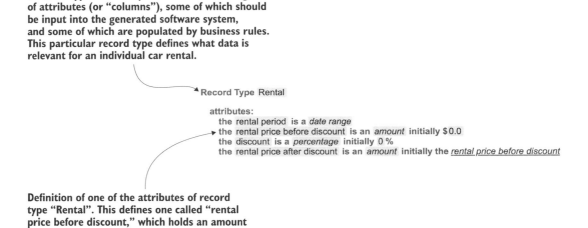

A record type defines a piece of data consisting of attributes (or "columns"), some of which should be input into the generated software system, and some of which are populated by business rules. This particular record type defines what data is relevant for an individual car rental.
Record Type Rental
attributes:
the rental period is a *date range*
the rental price before discount is an *amount* initially $0.0
the discount is a *percentage* initially 0 %
the rental price after discount is an *amount* initially the rental price before discount
Definition of one of the attributes of record type "Rental". This defines one called "rental price before discount," which holds an amount that could change over time, but initially holds the value "$0.0."

Figure 1.11 The same `Rental` record type, with explanatory annotations

This definition conveys the following information:

- It specifies a *record type*, meaning that the Runtime will be able to store data conforming to this record type's specification. In particular, such a record holds the data associated with an intended car rental, as suggested by the name "Rental." The

record type *describes* such records, but it doesn't store any of the Runtime data. This description could correspond to any number of things in the Runtime, such as
- Tables in the database
- Classes used in the code for the business rules' execution
- Forms in the UI

- The `Rental` record type has four attributes, laid out in an indented section suggestively captioned "attributes." These could correspond to multiple things in the Runtime, such as
  - Columns in a table in the database
  - Fields on a class or object
  - Fields on a form in the UI
- Each attribute consists of one line with the following form:

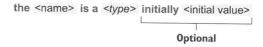

Optional

In other words, an attribute has a *name*, a *type*, and, optionally, an *initial value*. The value of the attribute in a newly created record is initialized to that initial value, provided it's specified.

- The name of an attribute is human readable. In particular, it's allowed to contain whitespace.
- The type of an attribute determines what values are stored in the database column corresponding to the attribute, and how these values are presented and processed by the Runtime. The type of an attribute can be
  - A `date range` consisting of from and to dates
  - A monetary `amount` in dollars
  - A `percentage`
- The optional initial value of an attribute is an *expression* that produces a value of the attribute's type, which the attribute in a newly created record will be initialized to.

As you can see, the DSL content isn't simple text, so the Domain IDE editor can't be a regular text editor. We've already seen at least two kinds of DSL content: business rules and record types. That implies that the Domain IDE must let domain experts organize and navigate around the various kinds of content. The Domain IDE must also provide a way to delete or rearrange content, or to input and change section metadata. This aspect of the UI is generally called the *chrome* of the IDE: the part of the IDE's UI that doesn't show actual DSL content but that is nevertheless necessary to be able to work with the IDE.

So far, we've only seen the editor part of the IDE, with some chrome in the form of buttons for creating or deleting content. Figure 1.12 zooms out even more and shows the whole Domain IDE.

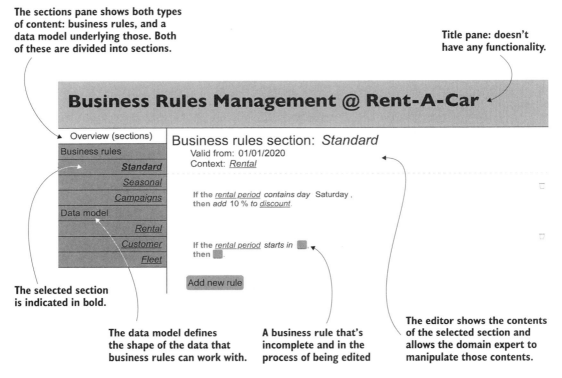

Figure 1.12   A view of the whole Domain IDE, again focused on the Standard section containing business rules

For completeness' sake, figure 1.13 focuses the editor on the Rental section

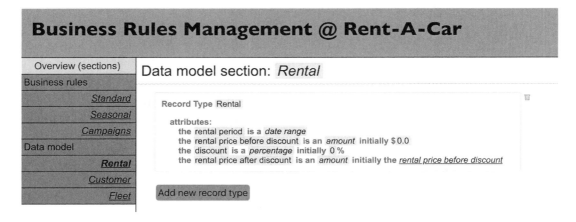

Figure 1.13   A view of the whole Domain IDE, now focused on the Rental section containing the `Rental` record type

To summarize, the Domain IDE's design consists of the following:

- *An editor*—A pane that shows DSL content (business rules or record types) in editable form. This pane also shows editable section metadata, such as the name of the section, a date range for when the business rules are valid or active, and a referred context in the case of the business rules section. The editor is not a text editor: this editor allows only DSL content to be input, and it assists and guides the domain experts.
- *IDE chrome*—This includes
  - A title pane
  - A sections pane that provides an overview of both kinds of DSL content
  - Buttons in the editor for creating new items (business rules or record types) or for deleting existing ones in the DSL content

1.2.2   The architecture of the Domain IDE

Having outlined *what* we should be implementing for the domain experts, we can now start to think about *how* we'll do that. Since we've already decided that the Domain IDE will be a web app, much of the architecture is going to be pretty standard—we'll at least have the components illustrated in figure 1.14.

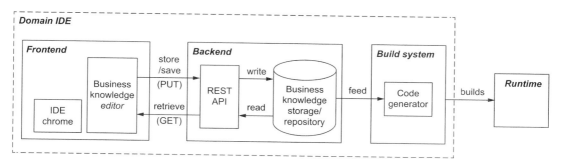

Figure 1.14   The architecture of the Domain IDE

First there is a *frontend*, which domain experts interact with through a browser. We laid out the desired functionality of the frontend in the previous section.

The frontend receives data representing the DSL content from the backend, visualizes it in an appropriate way, and allows domain experts to manipulate it. The most important part of the frontend is the editor for the DSL content. You've already seen in section 1.2.1 that the editor is not a plain text editor but rather a UI for the data representing the DSL content. This sort of editor is called a *projectional* editor, because it *projects* the data representing the DSL content without losing its underlying structure. Alternatively, it's called a *structured* editor because it works directly on the structure of the data representing the DSL content, rather than manipulating plain text on a character-by-character basis. We call a DSL with a projectional editor a *projectional DSL*.

The *backend* of the Domain IDE consists of an API for the frontend to communicate with and a storage facility, or repository, where the business knowledge is stored.

The *build system* has a code generator at its heart. The business knowledge stored in the repository is fed into the generator, which uses it to generate code for the Runtime. The build system then combines the generated code with nongenerated, manually crafted code and configuration, and completely builds the Runtime. This generation process can be triggered from the Domain IDE, from the command line, or through Continuous Integration (CI).

Later, we'll discuss which technology stack we're going to use to create the Domain IDE. For now, I'll just say that the stack is going to be based on JavaScript with mainstream tools, frameworks, and packages from the JavaScript world.

1.2.3   What we'll be doing in this book

In this book, we'll be developing the Domain IDE I've outlined in the previous sections. I won't assume you have prior knowledge of anything directly related to DSLs or software language engineering. Instead, we'll draw on mainstream technologies, knowledge, and skills to teach you just enough language engineering to craft an actual DSL.

"Just enough" here means that I'll teach as few topics as possible, but I'll teach those thoroughly, with plenty of examples and context. That, unfortunately, also means that I won't cover many topics that should be part of a broader understanding of DSLs. This will keep the book focused, so you can work through it alongside a demanding day job and still learn enough to apply your new skills immediately. In chapter 15, I'll point out a number of topics that I don't cover in this book, and I'll provide references to outside material so you can follow up on those topics if you're interested.

The following fundamental topics of language engineering will be among those I do cover in this book:

- *Abstract syntax trees (ASTs)*—What they are and how to work with them.
- *Projectional editing*
- *Code generation*
- *Expressions with binary operators*—This includes the treatment of precedence and priority, and left-, right-, and no-associativity.
- *Type systems*
- *DSL evolution*

These are some things we *won't* be covering in this book:

- *We won't be learning about textual DSLs*—In particular, we won't be learning about parsing, grammars, syntax highlighting, and other things that are only relevant for textual DSLs. This is not an oversight but completely intentional. I'll provide a *very* brief introduction to textual DSLs in section 15.1, and I'll also explain there why I chose projectional editing over a parsing-based approach.

- *We won't be learning about internal DSLs*—Internal DSLs are DSLs that live inside a host language by piggybacking on the syntax of an existing language. That makes them hard to use in a high-quality Domain IDE intended for business experts who aren't software developers.
- *We won't specify the DSL itself using a DSL*—We'll implement the DSL, but we won't be eating our own dog food. We will touch on this topic again in section 15.4.1, when we discuss *language workbenches.*
- *We won't fully develop the Runtime*—We'll only generate the parts of the Runtime's code that can be described in the developed Domain IDE.
- *We won't target business-rules engines*—The DSL-based approach tends to be really effective for specifying business logic using business rules, but we'll generate Java-Script code that runs on its own, without using an existing business-rules engine.
- *We won't build an interpreter for DSL content*—Instead of generating code from DSL content as part of the Runtime, we could implement the Runtime to directly *interpret* the DSL content. Both approaches have their pros and cons. I chose to explain code generation, because the result is tangible and should be close to what you'd build using a traditional software development approach.

1.3 Why use a DSL-based approach for software development?

Adopting a DSL-based approach should have several positive effects on the software development process. I say "should," because adopting a DSL-based approach is not always the right choice. We'll get back to that later, in section 1.3.4.

Let's look at a few broad categories of positive effects.

1.3.1 Empowering the domain experts

Having a DSL empowers domain experts:

- *Domain experts can write a precise specification themselves, using the Domain IDE.* They don't have to rely on software developers to manually translate every detail to the Runtime. Instead, the build system component of the Domain IDE will automatically generate and build a Runtime from the specification the domain experts write in the Domain IDE. This improves their effectiveness considerably. It also improves their efficiency, because the DSL editor assists and guides them in efficiently writing valid DSL content.

  Another way to say this is that the DSL approach makes software development much more agile for domain experts, since they can add or change features of the Runtime and test them on their own.

- *There are usually more domain experts than software developers around, so "scaling out," or scaling horizontally, is a viable way to increase productivity.* This is compounded by the fact that the domain experts are already—by definition—knowledgeable about the domain.

The same is not true for most software developers. Software developers are experts in specifying the *how* using general programming languages, but they're rarely experts in any specific domain. They will have to learn the domain well enough to start translating the specification written by the domain experts into working code. That learning process takes time, which translates to costs and longer running times for the entire software development effort.

1.3.2 Improving the efficiency of the software development process

Using a DSL improves efficiency:

- *Large parts of the Runtime code are automatically derived by the build system from the DSL content.* This relieves software developers of the more tedious aspects of software development. How often have you had to add a field to a form, a column to a database table, a field to a class, and all kinds of handling just because someone added a single item to a specification? That kind of work takes time and energy, so eliminating it not only improves efficiency, it leaves more time to do more interesting things, like work on the Domain IDE.
- *Because the specification is turned into working code automatically, it should be possible to verify changes almost instantly.* It should also be possible to deploy changes really quickly—essentially at the touch of a button. Again, this improves the agility of the Runtime development.
- *The specification in the Domain IDE becomes the center of communications for the whole development, with the DSL acting as a common language.* You could say that expressing the specification as DSL content *captures* the domain and builds understanding between domain experts and software developers at the same time.

1.3.3 New possibilities

A DSL-based approach also opens up new possibilities that don't exist in a traditional software development approach:

- *Because the specification is machine processable, it also becomes machine checkable.* This means that you can automatically verify whether the specification is complete, unambiguous, and satisfies other desirable properties. This is not something you can really do with a non-formal specification, because that would involve a lot of people and time.
- *The specification can be extended with tests that are written by the domain experts themselves.* Such tests reside "near" the specification of the business knowledge that the tests are meant to validate. They can even be executed on the fly in the Domain IDE, giving domain experts immediate feedback on the correctness and completeness of their specification. This builds confidence across the software development process, and it saves a lot of time and effort.

- *The core of the business domain is encoded precisely, unambiguously, and independently of the technology used to implement the Runtime in a DSL, making it quite future proof.* It requires much less effort, and it's much less tedious, error prone, and risky, to
  - Change the architecture, technology stack, or overall design of the Runtime
  - Reuse the business knowledge for another Runtime, or for some other purpose

1.3.4   *Criteria for adopting a DSL-based approach*

Does this mean you should *always* use a DSL? The simple answer is "No." As always, "it depends," and unfortunately not in the hard science way. The trick—or rather, the knack—lies in recognizing the potential of a DSL in a given situation, and gauging whether it would be a sensible idea.

In this book, we'll be focusing on domains that I like to call *business domains*. A business domain is a domain that's not really computer dependent. The car rental business—especially computing rental prices and such—is a good example of a business domain: in theory, you don't even need software for it. Often, there are ulterior reasons for developing software for the domain, such as cost effectiveness, efficiency, or regulatory compliance. The software itself (which we call the Runtime) is not the domain's core business–it's just something you need, and it preferably doesn't get in the way and doesn't cost too much.

Business domains are often good targets for a DSL-based approach. Developing software for business domains usually has two main challenges:

- There are not enough on-site software developers to initiate a software development project and follow it through to the end. This means outsourcing at least part of the development effort, which means extra time, costs, and risks. A DSL-based approach can mitigate this by being more time- and cost-effective.
- Communicating business knowledge in the domain (in any form) to software developers is difficult and error prone, as illustrated in figure 1.15. Even if the domain experts are able to write precise enough specifications in free-form documents—and this is a big if—the software developers still have to learn enough about the domain to properly read and understand them. Often, software developers unintentionally end up being domain experts by the end of the development. A DSL-based approach can mitigate this in two ways:
  - With a Domain IDE, domain experts can effectively take over a large part of the software development effort by writing DSL content that serves as a specification for the Runtime.
  - The DSL serves as a common, shared language between domain experts and software developers. This improves the efficiency and effectiveness of that communication considerably, which usually translates into improved time- and cost-effectiveness.

None of this is quantifiable up front, so we could do with some criteria to help us make the right decisions. Table 1.2 lists some helpful criteria. The more boxes you

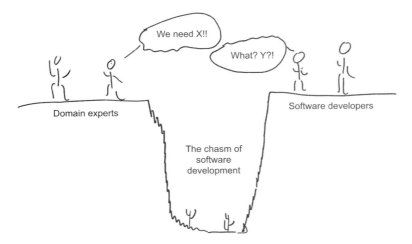

Figure 1.15   The chasm of software development

can confidently tick, the likelier it is that you could—or *should*—use a DSL-based approach.

Table 1.2   Criteria for judging when a DSL-based approach could be helpful

■ The domain is a business domain.
■ The business knowledge to be specified is of considerable size.
■ Any piece of knowledge has plenty of detail, with complicated relationships and connections between pieces.
■ The specification will be written by more than one person.
■ The specification will be based on a set of clearly identifiable *concepts* that are applied consistently. A concept is a construct with a specific and clearly defined meaning. In our car rental example, we already have the following concepts: business rule, condition, action, record type, and attribute.
■ The specification contains a lot of expressive business logic, along the lines of "When the customer has paid interest in every of the last 12 months, they are eligible for a discount of 10% on the interest of the next month." Award bonus points if this business logic is naturally or comfortably expressible using business rules.
■ The specification is dynamic: it changes often, and these changes must be propagated to the Runtime quickly.
■ There's a potentially complicated, but clear, path from pieces of the specification to pieces of code for the Runtime. This implies it's possible to implement a generator.

There's no such thing as a free lunch. Apart from the advantages of having a DSL, implementing and using one comes with certain costs and accompanying risks.

- *Implementing a Domain IDE takes time and effort, for both the software developers and the domain experts.* The software developers will craft the Domain IDE, which requires understanding the domain. The domain experts will clarify the domain as much as is needed for the software developers to create the Domain IDE.

- *Implementing a DSL requires additional skills and knowledge on the part of the software developers.* This is precisely why you should be reading this book, of course. However, even having read this book and sticking as much as possible to mainstream technologies, implementing a Domain IDE is never going to be as easy as implementing a regular software system.

- *The domain experts need to transition to using the Domain IDE.* They'll have to change their old way of working that captures their business knowledge in free-form documents. This requires education and migration, as well as support from the software developers that crafted the Domain IDE.

- *Using a DSL complicates software development technologically.*
  - It's necessary to keep the Domain IDE working in order to use the Runtime.
  - The build system part of the Domain IDE must be integrated with the rest of the project. Some aspects that need to be integrated are versioning, Continuous Integration/Continuous Delivery (CI/CD), and release management.

As always, these disadvantages must be weighed against the advantages.

> **Exercise 1.1**
> - For every criterion in table 1.2, discuss whether and to what extent it applies to the case of the car rental company.
> - Do the same for a project from your daily working life.

1.4   What is a DSL?

I have already stated that DSL is short for *domain-specific language*, and that a DSL is a software language. In this section, we'll dive deeper into what makes a software language a domain-specific one, and what key aspects it has.

Let's decipher all the elements in figure 1.16. As a first step, let's see what the *D* stands for. A domain is a *particular, focused area of knowledge*. It comes with a group of *domain experts* who *inhabit* or *own* the domain: they are people who possess, shape, and extend that area's knowledge, and they share it with business stakeholders and other interested parties. In the case of our example car rental company, the domain experts are the employees responsible for formulating all business knowledge around computing price quotes, executing business processes, safeguarding regulatory compliance, etc.

Domain experts typically converse with each other using a *domain-specific ubiquitous language*. This language is usually based on a natural language, but it's enriched with

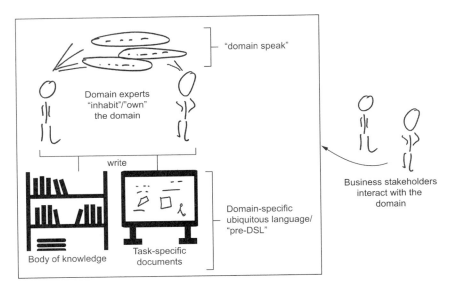

Figure 1.16   What is a *domain*?

domain-specific terms and notations that are given precise, domain-specific meanings. Even if domain experts aren't aware they're doing it, their way of speaking, working, and reasoning tends to converge over time.

Such a domain-specific ubiquitous language is not a proper DSL yet—it generally comes in both a verbal and a written form. The written form is used for the domain's body of knowledge and for task-specific documents, such as the specification of a Runtime. The verbal form I like to call "domain speak," and it's used by the domain experts to discuss the body of knowledge and task-specific documents. This ubiquitous language is not a software language because it lacks a solid definition, as well as software tools. It's certainly a precursor to a software language, though: you could call it a "pre-DSL."

Once you've decided to use a DSL-based approach to undertake a particular software development project, it becomes your job to *extract* a proper DSL from this pre-DSL, as illustrated in figure 1.17. This means you have to identify the core principles, concepts, and constructs in the pre-DSL, provide precise definitions for them, determine how to notate them suitably, and give them precise meanings. You also have to create software tools so the domain experts can work with the extracted DSL—in our case, that's the Domain IDE.

Central to figure 1.18 is the actual DSL content, which is what the domain experts will see and manipulate. The other elements of this diagram illustrate the *key aspects* of any DSL, and the relations between them.

Let's take a look at each of these key aspects and see what they entail in general, as well as how they relate to our car rental example specifically.

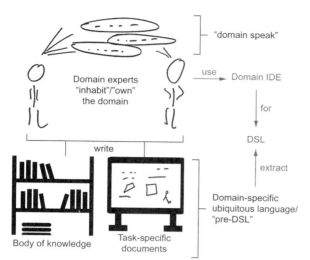

Figure 1.17   Extracting a DSL from the pre-DSL

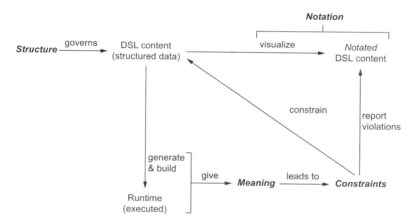

Figure 1.18   The key aspects of a DSL

1.4.1   *A DSL's notation*

The most immediate and captivating part of a DSL is undoubtedly its notation: a system of writing that visually represents the DSL content so it can be understood by the domain experts. For most intents and purposes, a notation *is* the DSL. Figure 1.19 zooms in on the relation between DSL content and its visualization using a notation.

The notation can be anything. Often, it is "boxology": boxes containing text and sub-boxes, with lines or arrows between them. Sometimes there are graphical elements that are not boxes, but icons (or other symbology) or tables.

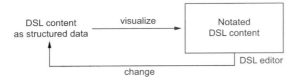

Figure 1.19   **Zooming in on the notation aspect of a DSL**

The DSL notation doesn't need to be graphical: many DSLs are purely textual. It doesn't need to look like code in a `monospaced font`, though we can leverage good typesetting to improve readability, or even to convey specific meanings and to make it look like a well-designed document. This is certainly the case for our car rental DSL.

Sometimes, rarely, the notation is something else entirely.

Regardless of its type, a DSL's notation is typically built from a small set of visual building blocks. For textual DSLs, these building blocks would be keywords, identifiers, strings, and numbers—various categories of text, each with their specific meaning, often typeset in a specific style to help convey that meaning. An example in the car rental scenario is the way references to attributes are typeset as web links. For graphical DSLs, these building blocks would be boxes, slots in those boxes, lines or arrows, labels next to the arrows, and so on. Keeping the number of visual building blocks small makes the language easier to parse visually, and therefore to understand.

We're going to give our DSL a notation by implementing a *projection* for our DSL content. This is a software component that takes the DSL content as input and outputs a visualization of it—in our context, as content rendered in a web browser. In chapters 5 and 6, you'll learn how to turn that projection into an *editor*, so the DSL content is more than just a pretty picture. In chapters 11 and 12, you'll learn how to extend the editor to make it work nicely for expressions, such as `1 + 2 * 3`.

1.4.2   A DSL's structure

Notation is not thrown together happenstance—every DSL has a certain fixed *structure*. This structure makes it possible for the domain experts to understand the DSL, but also for a computer to process it automatically.

The starting point of the structure is the notion of a *concept*. A concept is the blueprint for a fundamental construct in the DSL. It has a name and a collection of *properties*, each of which also has a name as well as a *type*. A property's type determines what can be stored as that property's value.

We'll see in chapter 2 how to represent DSL content entirely using *instances* of concepts. Instances assign values that occur in the DSL content to properties as *settings*.

It's often quite easy to discern instances and their settings in the notated DSL content because of distinctive visual cues. In the car rental example, we can readily identify the following concepts and their properties:

- The instances of the business rule concept look like this:

In this example, "condition" and "consequence" correspond to the concept's properties. The visual cues are "If the" and "then," respectively.

- Instances of the record type concept look like this:

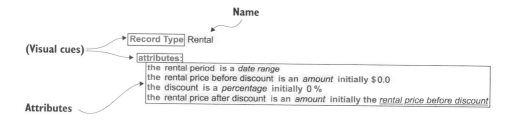

This concept has properties representing its name and its attributes. The instance as a whole is cued by the text "Record Type," and the location of the attributes is cued by the text "attributes." An instance of this or any such concept groups data together that intrinsically belongs to that instance.

- Instances of the attribute concept look like this:

This concept has properties representing its name, its type, and, optionally, an initial value. The visual cues are "the," "is a," and "initially," respectively.

Instances of concepts don't live in isolation but work together through *relations*. For example, an instance of the record type concept holds instances of the attribute concept as values of its "attributes" property. In general, relations between instances are represented by settings.

The DSL's structure is governed by the concepts and their properties. The properties' types govern how instances can relate to each other. Figure 1.20 summarizes what a DSL's structure is made of and how it relates to DSL content. In chapter 2, you'll learn how to represent DSL content as structured data, and we'll discover the structure of the car rental company's DSL in the process.

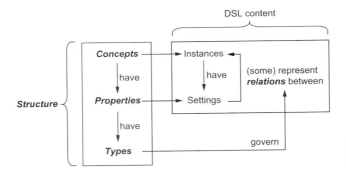

Figure 1.20   Zooming in on the structure aspect of a DSL

1.4.3   A DSL's meaning

A DSL has to *mean* something. A much-used synonym for meaning is *semantics,* but what that word really means is hotly debated among software language practitioners. Personally, I like to keep it simple: the meaning of a DSL is what it produces from DSL content. In our case, we're generating code for the Runtime from the DSL content, building the Runtime, and running it—see figure 1.21. As far as I'm concerned, the runtime behavior of the Runtime as it ranges over all possible DSL content *is* the meaning (or semantics) of the DSL.

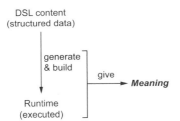

Figure 1.21   Zooming in on the meaning aspect of a DSL

In chapters 8 and 14, you'll learn how to use *templates* to implement a code generator for the two kinds of DSL content that we saw: record types and business rules.

1.4.4   A DSL's constraints

Not everything you can write down in accordance with a DSL's structure makes sense. Even if the DSL's structure allows the domain expert to add dollar amounts to dates, the build system would probably object to that. In the worst case, the Runtime will choke on it during execution.

We can prevent the build system or Runtime from failing as a result of nonsensical DSL content by augmenting the DSL's structure with a set of *constraints.* In this sense, giving the DSL meaning *leads to* a DSL having constraints. A constraint runs queries against the DSL content to check for patterns that would cause problems in the build system or Runtime. If such a pattern is found, the Domain IDE warns the domain expert about it with a meaningful message that highlights the offensive DSL content. Figure 1.22 summarizes this.

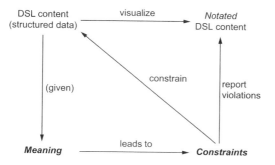

Figure 1.22 Zooming in on the constraints aspect of a DSL

In the car rental Domain IDE, this would look like the following:

If the *rental period* *starts in* January ,
then *add* peanuts *to* *discount*.

In chapter 9, we'll find constraints for our car rental DSL, and we'll implement them.

In this chapter, we've explored what a DSL is, what key aspects it's made up of, why you should (or shouldn't) use one, and how you would use one. We've also seen a design for a Domain IDE for domain experts in a car rental company. In most of the rest of the book, you'll learn how to build that Domain IDE.

Summary

- A *domain-specific language* (DSL) is a software language that targets a specific domain. That domain is "inhabited" or "owned" by domain experts. The DSL, and the software tools supporting it, typically empowers these domain experts and assists them in achieving greater effectiveness and efficiency.
- Within *business domains*, domain experts produce a specification of the software system (the *Runtime*) they require. In a DSL-based approach, software developers provide domain experts with a Domain IDE that allows them to author this specification as precise *DSL content* that can be used to generate much of the Runtime.
- A *Domain IDE* is a piece of software that consists of a frontend and a backend. The frontend primarily provides a *DSL editor* that allows domain experts to author DSL content. The backend provides an API, a repository for DSL content, and a *build system* that generates and builds the Runtime from that DSL content.

- One style of DSL editor is the *projectional* kind: the editor *projects* the DSL content to a UI used by the domain experts to manipulate it in accordance with the allowed structure.
- A DSL has four *key aspects*:
  - A DSL's *notation* is the system of writing used to visually represent the DSL content. The notation is implemented through the *projection*, which typically presents DSL content in a web browser. By adding editing functionality to the projection, it becomes a DSL *editor*.
  - A DSL's *structure* determines what can be expressed in the DSL by defining *concepts*, which have properties, each of which has a *type*. Concepts can be *instantiated*, and *settings* on an instance hold the values of the properties the instance was instantiated from. Some settings represent *relations* between instances; this is governed by the type of their properties.
  - A DSL is given *meaning* by what is produced from the DSL content and what that content does. In our case, the DSL's meaning is the way that the Runtime—built from code generated from DSL content—behaves when it's executing.
  - A violation of a *constraint* warns the domain expert about DSL content that will cause problems for the build system—specifically its code generator—or for the Runtime.
- Adopting a DSL-based approach can empower domain experts by giving them the tools to develop large parts of the Runtime themselves, without needing traditional software developers as much. It also means that the core of the business domain is encoded precisely, unambiguously, and independently of the technology in a DSL, making it much more future proof.
- Using a DSL can look like a "silver bullet," but there are ramp-up costs for implementing the DSL and risks in transitioning to a DSL-based software development process. Domain experts need to be aware of these and to weigh them against the benefits. For many business domains, the benefits of crafting a DSL start to outweigh the costs only in the longer run.
- A number of criteria (or "tells"), listed in table 1.2, can help you determine whether it's worth implementing a DSL for your (business) domain.

Representing DSL content as structured data

This chapter covers

- Learning to represent structured data using a notation for object-relation diagrams
- Representing the details in DSL content as tree-like structured data
- Learning common terms for the new things we encounter

In the previous chapter, we showed that one of the key aspects of a DSL is its *structure*, which underlies all DSL content. In this chapter, we're going to make that structure explicitly visible, as shown in figure 2.1. More precisely, we're going to represent DSL content as *structured data*. Data is good, data we can handle, right? This will allow us to start writing code for that structure in the next chapter.

In section 2.1, you'll learn how to write down structured data precisely, using the *object-relation diagram* (ORD) notation. This notation will be used throughout the book to graphically represent DSL content in an *abstract syntax*. In section 2.2, we'll extract ORDs from example DSL content. This extraction process works for all notated DSL content, producing what software language engineers call *abstract syntax trees* (ASTs). Later, in chapter 4, we'll reverse this process: given an AST represented in code, we'll reconstruct the notated DSL content in what is also known

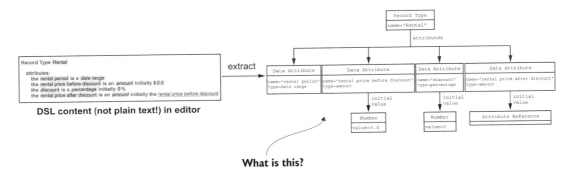

Figure 2.1 What we're going to do in this chapter

as *concrete syntax*. The projection we'll implement for this will be the basis for our DSL editor. In chapters 5 and 6, we'll make this visualization editable.

2.1 *Establishing an object-relation diagram notation for structured data*

Before we can represent the details in DSL content as structured data, let's agree on a representation for structured data. Many notations for structured data already exist, but I'll use my own flavor of *object-relation diagrams* (ORDs). (You can think of this notation as a super-simplified variant of UML's object diagrams.)

ORD and ERD

An ORD is not the same thing as an *entity-relationship diagram* (ERD). An ORD *describes* actual objects, including the data they hold and relations they have with other objects in the diagram. An ERD, on the other hand, *prescribes* what data *can* be present in objects—as instances of entities—and what relations *may* exist between instances. So an ERD describes the range of all ORDs you might encounter in a certain context, instead of capturing one particular piece of structured data.

For this book, however, you can forget I ever mentioned ERDs.

It probably comes as no surprise that the fundamental building block of ORDs is the *object*. An object groups data in a meaningful way, and it's visually represented as a box, as shown in figure 2.2.

Figure 2.2 A simple ORD containing only one object

The object's box has two compartments:

- The upper compartment holds the *concept label*, indicating what concept the object represents—in this case, `Thing`. You can think of the concept label as the object's *type*, but the word "type" is used so often that it easily causes confusion.

  We say that an object with the concept label `Thing` is "an *instance* of `Thing`." We'll almost always leave the "instance of" part out entirely, saying, "this is a `Thing`." Likewise, we'll favor the term "object" over "instance" from here on.

- The lower compartment holds any number (including zero) of *simple settings*. Each simple setting assigns a *simple value* to a particular *property*: `<property's name> = <value>`. A simple value can be a string, a number, a Boolean, or an enumerated value.

  The first simple setting on our object reads `name="Foo"`, meaning that the property called `name` is assigned (and holds) the value `Foo`. This is quite likely meant to convey that this object's name is `Foo`. We'll use that as a convention: if an object has a `name` property with a value of `Foo`, we'll say "the object named `Foo`," or "the `Foo` object."

  (The adjective "simple" implies that other kinds of settings might exist. Later on, we'll encounter an additional kind.)

For clarity, let's annotate figure 2.2—see figure 2.3.

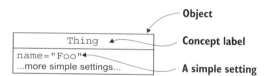

Figure 2.3   A simple ORD containing only one object, with annotations

We haven't stated what it means for a value to be simple. Any value that's not an object or collection of objects is considered to be simple. In particular, strings (text), numbers, and Booleans (`true` or `false`) are simple values. Paradoxically, we consider the absence of a value to be a simple value as well. It's customary to denote that value as `null`, or `undefined` if you're a JavaScript purist. This value is typically used to represent missing or optional content.

Let's make things a little bit more complex. Figure 2.4 contains the following things:

- The first object (the upper box) is again (an instance of) a `Thing`, and it's named `Foo`.

- The second object (the lower box) has `Something else` as its concept label, and it's named `Bar`.

- There's a new diagram element in the form of a solid arrow going from the object named `Foo` to the object named `Bar`. This element indicates a *relation*

from the first object to the second. The arrow is labeled with the property name
`other`. All relations have a direction, going from a *source* object to a *target* object.

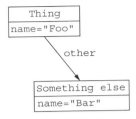

Figure 2.4 A slightly more complex ORD containing two objects with a relation

A relation such as the one in figure 2.4 has a certain *kind*; this one is of the *containment* kind, indicated visually by the arrow being solid. This means that this relation expresses that the `Foo` object *contains* the `Bar` object through a property named `other`. Containment is a form of ownership—any object can be contained by at most one other object. To avoid any existential crises, self-containment is not allowed. Let's annotate figure 2.4 a bit—see figure 2.5.

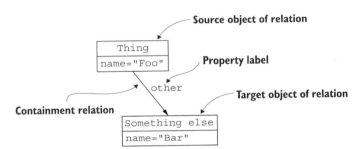

Figure 2.5 Annotating the containment relation

Containment relations are limited in the sense that any object can have at most one incoming containment relation. We're going to need an additional, more permissive, kind of relation to work around this and represent general structured data: the *reference* relation. Let's extend figure 2.4 with a reference relation; figure 2.6 expresses that the source object `Bar` *references* the target object `Foo` through the `back` property whose name labels the arrow. To distinguish between the containment and reference kinds of relations, the arrow of a reference relation is dashed.

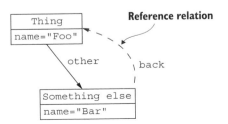

Figure 2.6 Adding and annotating a reference relation

It's convenient to view any relation as a setting on its source object. We can do that as shown in figure 2.7.

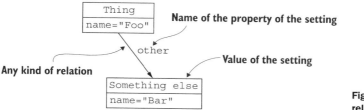

Figure 2.7   Viewing a relation as a setting

The property that the relation is labeled with is also the property of the setting, and the target object is the value it's assigned. A setting that corresponds to a relation is not a simple setting, because simple settings appear in the lower compartment of an object's box. In effect, the settings of an object are the simple settings of that object plus all the relations originating in that object.

Finally, we'll add two rules to prevent confusion:

- A property's name must be unique among all the properties of a concept. It's OK for properties of *different* concepts to share a name, though.
- A property can be used for exactly one kind of value: a containment relation, a reference relation, or a simple setting. You can't have a setting on one object for a `something` property with a string value, and another setting on the same object for `something` that contains some other object, or that references yet another object.

Disregarding the reference relations, an ORD can be arranged as a tree, because an object can be contained by at most one other object.

ORD rules

To recap, ORDs play by the following rules:

- An object is represented by a box. The box has two compartments:
  - The upper compartment of the box only holds the *concept label*, identifying what *concept* the object is an instance of. It's OK to have multiple objects with the same *concept label*. These are then separate instances of that concept.
  - The lower compartment of the box holds any number (including zero) of *simple settings*. Each simple setting assigns a *simple value* to one particular *property*, which occurs uniquely among the simple settings of the object: `<property name> = <value>`. Any value that's not an object or collection of objects is considered simple: strings (text), numbers, Booleans (`true` or `false`), and `null` are simple values. The latter represents missing or optional content.

(continued)

- Any two objects can have a *relation*, which is represented as an arrow labeled with a property (name).
  - There are two kinds of relations:
    - Containment, with a solid arrow
    - Reference, with a dashed arrow
  - Any object can be contained, meaning it's the *target* of a containment relation, by at most one object regardless of the property through which it is contained. No object can contain, or be contained by, itself. Self-references are OK.
  - There's no limit on how many relations have a certain object as their *source*. In particular, a source object can have relations to multiple target objects, even through the same property. In this sense, relations are different from simple settings, but we still regard a relation as a setting on its source object. The property the relation is labeled with is also the property of the setting, and the target object is the value it's assigned.
- A property's name must be unique among all properties of a concept.
- A concept's property can be used for exactly one kind of value: containment relation, reference relation, or simple setting.
- The settings of an object are the simple settings of that object plus all the relations originating in that object.

This style of ORD will allow us to represent the data present in DSL content in a structured way. We'll make use of that throughout this book to visualize ASTs more conveniently and clearly than we can through code. Relations between objects are much more visible in an ORD than they are in code.

Exercise 2.1
- Pick some data from your daily work life, and represent it as an ORD.
- Concepts and their properties so far seem to exist through the use of their names and the properties' apparent types. Do you feel it's necessary to make this more explicit? (There are no wrong answers here.)
- I haven't introduced any kind of relations between *concepts*, such as inheritance or mixins. Do you feel that's necessary to have? (There are no wrong answers here, either.)

2.2 Going from concrete to abstract syntax

Notated DSL content is often called *concrete syntax*. We can say that figure 2.8 is a piece of concrete syntax, or we can talk about this DSL content's concrete syntax. The adjective "concrete" implies—by symmetry—the existence of an *abstract syntax*, and such a syntax does exist. The structured data we're going to extract from the DSL content's concrete syntax is typically called "the abstract syntax of the concrete syntax." The abstract syntax is intended to represent the DSL content abstractly, with all the essential pieces of information found in the notation, but independent of the notational details of the concrete syntax.

Record Type Rental

> **attributes:**
> the rental period is a *date range*
> the rental price before discount is an *amount* initially $ 0.0
> the discount is a *percentage* initially 0 %
> the rental price after discount is an *amount* initially the *rental price before discount*

Figure 2.8   The DSL content defining the `Rental` record type

Consider the DSL content in figure 2.8, defining the `Rental` record type from the car rental example. This DSL content *describes* the data found in any `Rental` record. In chapter 8, we'll turn such descriptions into code that works with actual data. Before we do that, however, we should be able to work with these descriptions themselves, in the form of structured data. Let's reduce the DSL content in this figure to structured data using an ORD. In other words, let's take the concrete syntax in figure 2.8 and extract its abstract syntax.

We'll rely on *visual cues* in the example's concrete syntax to guide us. Such visual cues can be keywords, symbols, or other visual markers such as boxes, arrows, etc. We'll start by looking at the "thing" as a whole. We seem to be dealing with a `Record Type` that happens to be called `Rental`. There doesn't seem to be a sensible way to divide up the information in it: both the name and attributes clearly belong to it. Let's do the obvious thing and represent the `Rental` record type as a whole using one object.

What concept label shall we put on this object? Since it evidently represents a *record type*, we might as well use `Record Type`, as shown in figure 2.9.

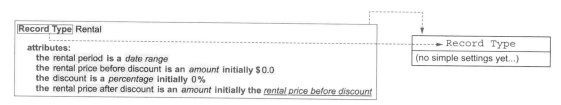

Figure 2.9   Extracting only the outline of the `Rental` record type

The next piece of data is the name of the record type: `Rental`. Let's add a simple setting for a property called `name` with a value of `Rental` (see figure 2.10).

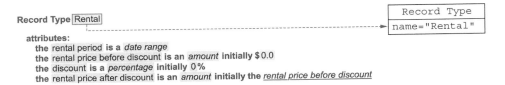

Figure 2.10   Extracting the name of the `Rental` record type

The next piece of DSL content we'll tackle are the attributes, of which `Rental` has four, laid out in an indented section suggestively captioned `attributes`. Each attribute consists of one line of the following form:

the *<name>* **is a** *<type>* **initially** *<initial value>*

$$\underbrace{\qquad\qquad\qquad}_{\textbf{Optional}}$$

In other words, each attribute has a *name*, a *type*, and, optionally, an *initial value*, to which the value of the attribute in a newly created record is initialized. A record type can have any number of attributes, so it makes sense to represent each attribute by its own object. Let's first create the outlines of the attributes (see figure 2.11).

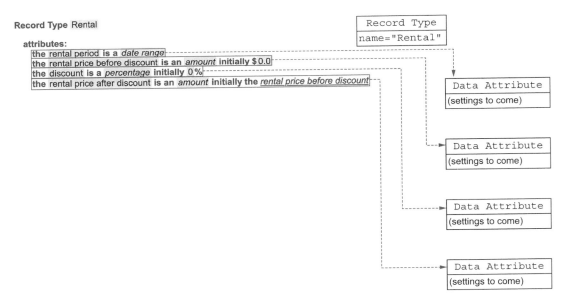

Figure 2.11   Sketching the outlines of the objects representing attributes

Now we have an object for each attribute, but without details in the form of settings. Also, I've left these attribute objects dangling in this diagram. Let's fix this by having the `Rental` object contain all of the attributes through containment relations. The rules for ORDs say that such relations are labeled with a property's name. It seems obvious to use the name `attributes` for that. We can justify this by pointing to the visual cue `attributes` (see figure 2.12).

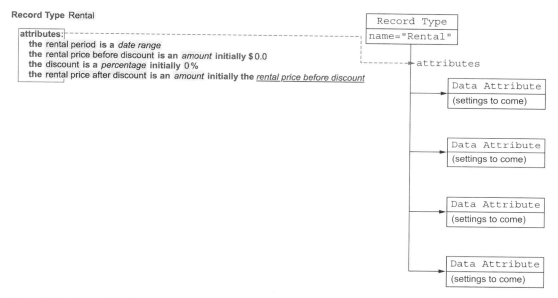

Figure 2.12   Connecting the `attributes` objects to the `Record Type` object through containment relations

Having taken care of the containment, let's add the names of each attribute. The names are simple, free text. This means we can represent them as simple settings for a property called `name` on their corresponding attribute objects (see figure 2.13).

The types of the attributes are a different matter. The italic typesetting of the `type` data could be taken to suggest that these are not free text. It seems reasonable that an attribute's `type` comes from a limited choice of options. Maybe the values we see here (`date range`, `amount`, and `percentage`) are all the possible values? Without further information we can't make a more informed decision.

For now, let's treat the `type` simply as text. To make it look a bit less free-form, we won't put double quotes around the values, though. Figure 2.14 adds the settings for the `type` property and shows how they're derived from visual cues.

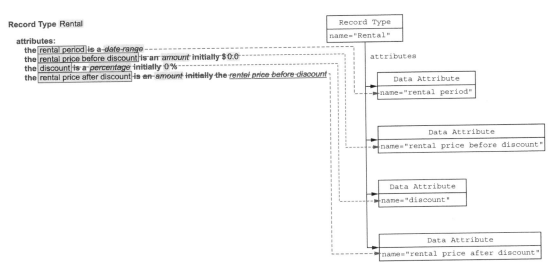

Figure 2.13 Adding simple settings for the `name` property of the attribute objects

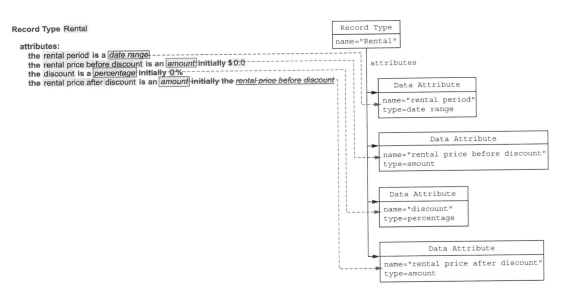

Figure 2.14 Adding simple settings for the `type` property of the attribute objects

Next up are the initial values of the attributes. Consider the following:

- Not all attributes have an initial value. This strongly suggests that we should be making use of optional properties.

- We already have at least two quite different forms of initial values:
  - Numbers in some precision and with a presentation conforming to the attributes' types: `$0.0` and `0%`. We could represent this with a simple setting on the attribute object holding an optional numeric value. But if we go that route, wouldn't we end up with lots of optional properties on the attribute object?
  - The name of an attribute typeset as a link that you should be able to click to navigate to, such as the `rental price before discount` attribute. This suggests the presence of a reference relation to an attribute, but where would we put the property for the reference relation?
- Maybe the domain experts need to express even more complicated formulas for an initial value?

To capture all this variation in an attribute's initial value, it makes sense to represent initial values through separate objects. These will be contained by their attributes' objects through a property named `initial value`.

Let's take the number values first. We need to represent these as objects, so we need to come up with a suitable concept label. Let's keep things obvious and choose `Number` as our label.

We'll assume that the `type` of an attribute will also dictate how initial values of that attribute will be presented. In particular,

- The `rental price before discount` and `rental price after discount` attributes having `amount` as their `type` means that their initial values are going to be presented as dollar amounts.
- The `discount` attribute having `percentage` as its `type` means that its initial value is going to be presented with a trailing `%`.

Such assumptions should not be made lightly; they place a burden on the visualization of the structured data as DSL content. We'll come back to this assumption later on, in chapters 4 and 8, where we'll back up this assumption through implementation. For now, this assumption means that we can represent the numbers through a property `value` on a `Number` object. Since numbers are anything but free-form text, we'll omit the double quotes around the value of the simple setting of the `value` property. We're now ready to represent the initial values of two of the three attribute objects that define one.

Figure 2.15 illustrates how these values are extracted:

- The content after each of the first two `initially` visual cues maps to corresponding `Number` objects.
- The `initially` visual cues justify these `Number` objects being contained by their corresponding attribute objects (the second and third ones respectively) through a property called `initial value`.
- The numeric values `$0.0` and `0%` are stored in the settings for a property called `value`.

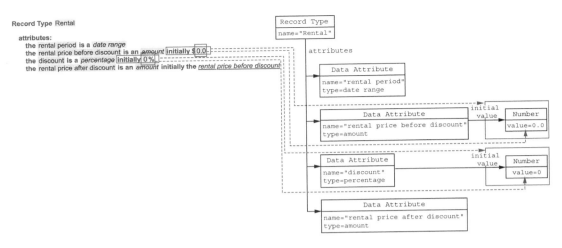

Figure 2.15   Extracting the initial values that are numbers

That leaves us with just one piece of data that's so far gone unrepresented: the initial value of `rental price after discount`. We already saw that this a reference to the `rental price before discount` attribute.

Let's first add an object with an `Attribute Reference` concept label. We can now finally use the other kind of relation: the reference relation. Let's add a reference relation labeled with an `attribute` property, starting at the `Attribute Reference` object and targeting the `rental price before discount` attribute object.

You'll see this in figure 2.16:

- The content after the third `initially` visual cue maps to an `Attribute Reference` object.
- This `Attribute Reference` object is contained by the fourth attribute object, through the `initial value` property.
- The `rental price before discount` text maps to a reference to the `rental price before discount` attribute, through the `attribute` property of the `Attribute Reference` object.

Let's strip away the DSL content and focus on the structured data only, as shown in figure 2.17.

In the next chapter, you'll learn how to encode the structured data represented by diagrams such as these. Then, in chapter 4, you'll learn how to visualize encoded structured data as DSL content.

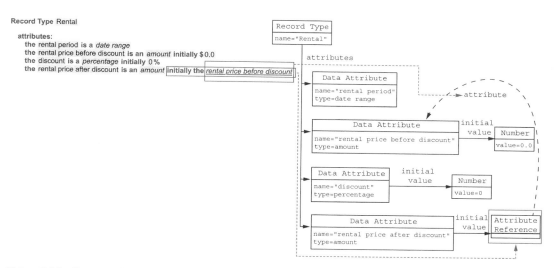

Figure 2.16   Representing an initial value that is a reference

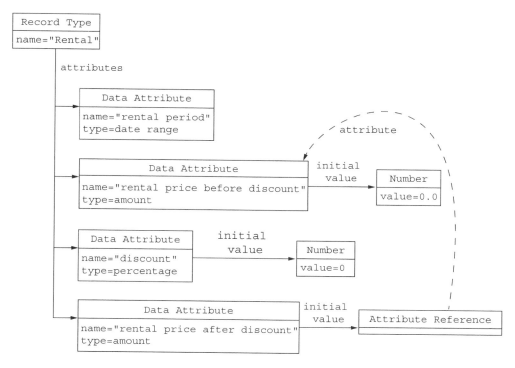

Figure 2.17   The end result of the extraction process

Before we go on, let's disregard the one reference relation in figure 2.17 and rearrange the objects a bit so we end up with figure 2.18. This looks suspiciously like a tree of the computer sciencey kind—technically an *n-ary tree*. Indeed it is a tree, and this is true for any ORD extracted from any DSL content. Because of the restrictive nature of the containment kind of relations, each object has at most one arrow corresponding to a containment relation pointing to it. For that reason, and because such diagrams represent the abstract syntax of (the concrete syntax of) DSL content, we call these *abstract syntax trees*, or ASTs. From here on, we're going to use the term AST all the time.

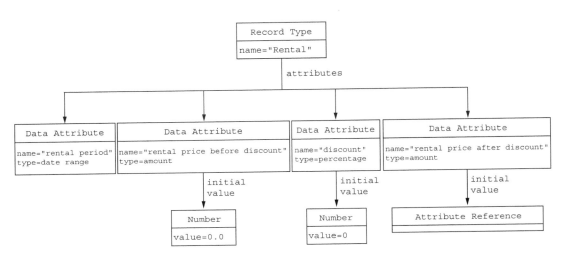

Figure 2.18   The extracted ORD (without the reference relation) laid out as a tree

NOTE   Wait a minute, didn't we have to forget the reference relations to see an ORD as a tree? That's true, and it's why some people refer to ASTs as *abstract syntax graphs* (ASGs). Technically, ASG is the more accurate term, but AST is much more common, and has evolved to mean the same thing.

Although we've only represented one piece of DSL content so far, this process works for *all* DSL content in the same way. That means that DSL content is, in the end, just structured data. Along the way, we've seen the structure of the DSL (the concept, properties, and relations) come tumbling out. Starting in the next chapter, we'll look at DSL content from the "just data" viewpoint. DSL content is, in the first place, structured data, and everything else is derived or computed from that. In particular, a DSL's notation is just a visualization of the DSL content as structured data.

Our path in the upcoming chapters is shown in figure 2.19. In chapter 3, we'll be turning extracted structured data into code so we can start writing code for the DSL's implementation. In chapter 4, we'll visualize that structured data as proper DSL

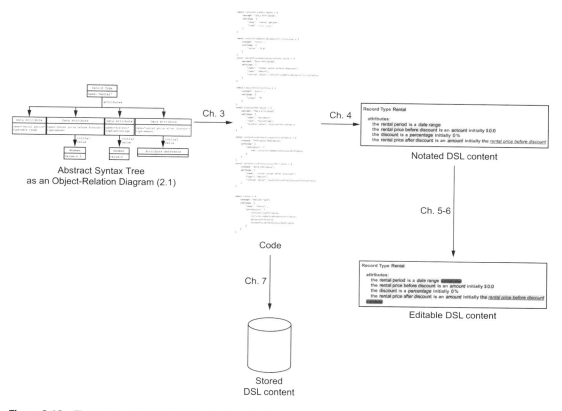

Figure 2.19 The path we'll be taking in chapters 3 through 7

content, and in chapters 5 and 6 we'll make that content editable. In chapter 7, we'll store that structured data somewhere and read it back from that storage.

Exercise 2.2

- Write down all the concept labels in figure 2.17, together with their properties.
  - How many do you count? Do you think this number will scale linearly with the size of the DSL content?
  - Make the structure of these concepts explicit, including their properties.
- We assumed earlier that we could always derive a type to govern the presentation of number values in the DSL content. Modify the extracted `Number` objects to not rely on that assumption.
- Extract an ORD from either of the two examples of business rules we saw in figure 1.3. Can you reuse any of the concept labels from figure 2.17? Hint: You could cheat by leafing through the rest of the book.

Summary

- The notation of a DSL is called its *concrete syntax*. Notated DSL content can also be referred to as *content in (its) concrete syntax*.
- Using a process of annotating visual cues and extraction, the concrete syntax of DSL content can be reduced to structured data. This structured data is the *abstract syntax* of that DSL content, which can be notated as an *object-relation diagram* (ORD).
- When reference relations are disregarded, the ORDs of the abstract syntax can be laid out in a tree shape. Such tree-shaped ORDs are called *abstract syntax trees* (ASTs).

3

Working
with ASTs in code

This chapter covers

- Encoding ASTs (represented as ORDs) as values in code
- Using Node.js interactively to construct ASTs in code
- Interacting with an encoded AST
- Traversing encoded ASTs algorithmically

In the previous chapter, you learned what an abstract syntax tree (AST) is and how to represent one using an object-relation diagram (ORD). In this chapter, you'll learn how to put this representation into code, as in-memory data, and how to work with that encoded AST: inspect it, alter it, and traverse it. These skills will form the basis of the Domain IDE's codebase. You'll probably also encounter these notions outside of this book.

3.1 Turning ASTs into code

In this section, you'll learn how to turn ASTs, which are notated in the ORD style we introduced in chapter 2, into data that a computer can work with. As announced in chapter 1, we're going to implement our Domain IDE in JavaScript, so we'll turn the AST into a JavaScript value. This process is called *encoding*: the AST is turned into JavaScript code that produces a JavaScript value that faithfully represents the AST.

Let's turn the AST for our example DSL content, describing the Rental record type, into code that produces a JavaScript value representing it. For convenience, let's reiterate our example DSL content: the specification of a record type called Rental that captures the details of a single car rental (see figure 3.1). As you learned in chapter 2, figure 3.2 shows the AST for this fragment of DSL content.

Record Type Rental

    attributes:
       the rental period **is a** *date range*
       the rental price before discount **is an** *amount* **initially** $ 0.0
       the discount **is a** *percentage* **initially** 0 %
       the rental price after discount **is an** *amount* **initially the** *rental price before discount*

Figure 3.1   Our example DSL content: the specification of a Rental record type

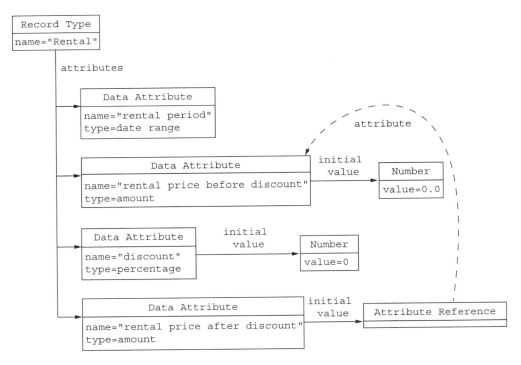

Figure 3.2   The full AST for the example DSL content

We're going to encode this AST in (or as) JavaScript code. To do so, I'm going to assume you have set up a suitable development environment that lets you play around with JavaScript. Appendix A explains how to set one up.

Let's start at the top, the root of the AST, which is an object labeled as a `Record Type`. We'll encode that as a JavaScript object with key-value pairs. We'll also encode the concept label of that object as `Record Type`. We use JavaScript's object literal notation as follows.

Listing 3.1   Encoding the root of the AST as a JavaScript object

```
const rental = {
    concept: "Record Type"
}
```

JavaScript object encoding the AST object. The object is assigned to a constant called rental.

The key-value pair inside the object encoding the concept label "Record Type".

The easiest way to check this code, and the code listings that follow, is to use Node.js (see appendix A), instead of trying to run things in a browser. You can test this code by using Node.js's REPL functionality, which is explained in section A.5.

Testing the execution of listing 3.1 should look like this:

```
$ node
> const rental = {
...       concept: "Record Type"
... }
undefined
> rental
{ concept: 'Record Type' }
>
(To exit, press ^C again or type .exit)
>
```

Copy and paste the code listing.

Defining a constant is an assignment that returns undefined.

To exit Node.js's REPL and return to the command-line prompt, press Ctrl-C twice, Ctrl-D once, or type .exit.

Note that you'll have to restart Node.js for each listing to avoid the following wholly reasonable error:

```
Thrown:
SyntaxError: Identifier 'rental' has already been declared
```

Alternatively, you can save the code listing in a separate JavaScript file, such as src/listingX.js, and run it as follows:

```
$ node src/listingX.js
```

That command executes the code in that file and then immediately exits Node.js again, without entering REPL mode. This way of calling Node.js doesn't produce any REPL-like output; it only produces output when the invoked code executes `console.log(…)` or `console.dir(…)`.

To print the entire AST, create a new file, such as src/print-pretty.js, with the contents of listing 3.2.

Listing 3.2 `print-pretty.js`

```
module.exports = (value) => {
    console.log(JSON.stringify(value, null, 2))
}
```

This exposes a function that prints a JavaScript value in a pretty way to the JavaScript console (the command-line window in Node.js). Next, add the following line to listingX.js:

```
require("./print-pretty")(rental)
```

Rerunning $ `node src/listingX.js` will produce a pretty-printing of the AST:

```
$ node src/listingX.js
{
  "concept": "Record Type"
}
```

As we continue, I'll assume that you have established your favorite way to execute the code snippets we'll discuss.

Next, we'll encode the name of the `Record Type`, which is `Rental`. More precisely, we want to encode that the `name` property is set to the value `Rental`. To do that, we'll introduce a new key-value pair to the `Rental` object. The key of that pair is going to be `settings`, and its value is going to be another JavaScript object that will store all the settings:

```
const rental = {
    concept: "Record Type",
    settings: {              ⟵──  The key-value pair
        "name": "Rental"           holding all the settings
    }                        ⟵──  The key-value pair encoding the
}                                  setting for the name property, with
                                   the name being a JavaScript string
```

In the preceding code, we put the key's name in double quotes: `"name"`. For strings that are valid JavaScript identifiers, this isn't strictly necessary, but we'll have properties with names that are not valid JavaScript identifiers, like `initial value`, which has a space in it. To keep the look consistent throughout, we'll put double quotes around all property names in the `settings` object, even if they technically don't need it.

Figure 3.3 shows how far we have got in encoding the entire example AST:

1 An AST object becomes a JavaScript object.
2 The concept label—the contents of the upper compartment of the object's box in the diagram—becomes the value of a key-value pair with `concept` as the key.
3 The settings—the contents of the lower compartment of the box—become key-value pairs on a subobject that's stored as the value of a key-value pair with `settings` as the key.

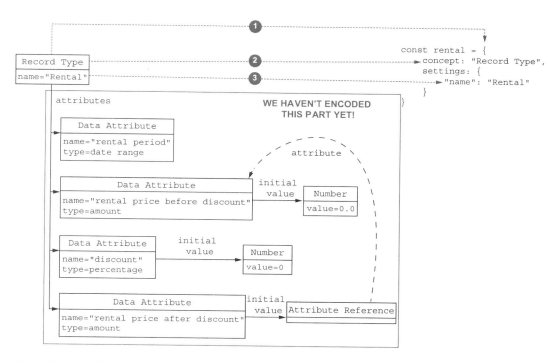

Figure 3.3   Encoding the `Rental` AST object in code, including its name but none of the other details yet

3.1.1   Encoding containment relations

We haven't encoded all the details of the `Rental` object yet. We haven't encoded any of its contained objects or any of the objects contained by them. The `Rental` object contains four objects of the `Data Attribute` concept through the `attributes` containment relation. Three of those contained objects contain objects themselves, through a containment relation called `initial value`. Let's encode the `Data Attribute` objects and see how we can encode their contained objects through the `attributes` relation.

First, let's encode the first attribute object as a separate JavaScript object, in the same way we did for the `Rental` object:

```
const rentalPeriodAttribute = {
    concept: "Data Attribute",
    settings: {
        "name": "rental period",
        "type": "date range"
    }
}
```

A JavaScript object encoding the first attribute is created and assigned to a constant called rentalPeriodAttribute so we can refer back to this object in later code.

Then we can go back to how we encoded the `Record Type` and patch that code as follows:

```
const rental = {
    concept: "Record Type",
```

```
settings: {
    "name": "Rental",
    "attributes": [ rentalPeriodAttribute ]        ⟵
}
}
```

> The attributes property of the Rental object is multivalued, and we encode that using a JavaScript array value for the corresponding key-value pair.

NOTE   Because the code that defines the `rental` constant references `rental-PeriodAttribute`, the code defining `rentalPeriodAttribute` must precede it.

The preceding patching of the code encodes the containment relations between the `Rental` object and the first attribute object, whose name is `rental period`. Figure 3.4 shows the AST after this code change.

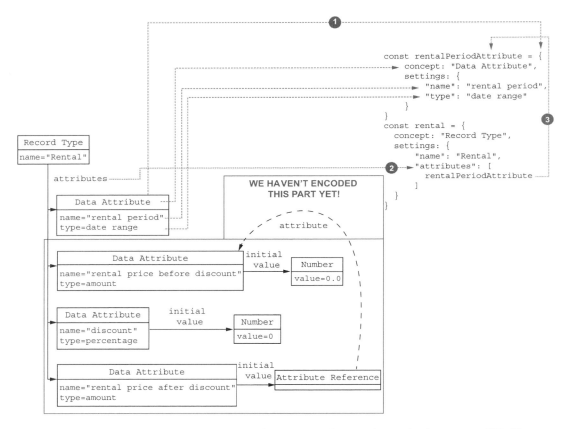

Figure 3.4   Encoding the first `Data Attribute` AST object and its containment by the `Rental` AST object.

We've now added the following:

❶   The first attribute object becomes a JavaScript object, assigned to the `rental-PeriodAttribute` constant so we can refer to it in later code.

2 The relation containing the first attribute object in the `Rental` object becomes a
value in the JavaScript array, which in turn is the value of the key-value pair
encoding the `attributes` property.

3 The value in the JavaScript array refers back to the `rentalPeriodAttribute`
constant we created earlier.

Let's do the same for the other attribute objects, but still without the initial value
objects they contain:

```
const rentalPeriodAttribute = {
    concept: "Data Attribute",
    settings: {
        "name": "rental period",
        "type": "date range"
    }
}
const rentalPriceBeforeDiscountAttribute = {
    concept: "Data Attribute",
    settings: {
        "name": "rental price before discount",
        "type": "amount"
    }
}
const discountAttribute = {
    concept: "Data Attribute",
    settings: {
        "name": "discount",
        "type": "percentage"
    }
}
const rentalPriceAfterDiscountAttribute = {
    concept: "Data Attribute",
    settings: {
        "name": "rental price after discount",
        "type": "amount"
    }
}

const rental = {                      ◁───┐  Create the root object last,
    concept: "Record Type",                │  after all the attributes'
    settings: {                            │  objects.
        "name": "Rental",
        "attributes": [
            rentalPeriodAttribute,
            rentalPriceBeforeDiscountAttribute,
            discountAttribute,
            rentalPriceAfterDiscountAttribute
        ]
    }
}
```

Figure 3.5 shows the AST after this code change.

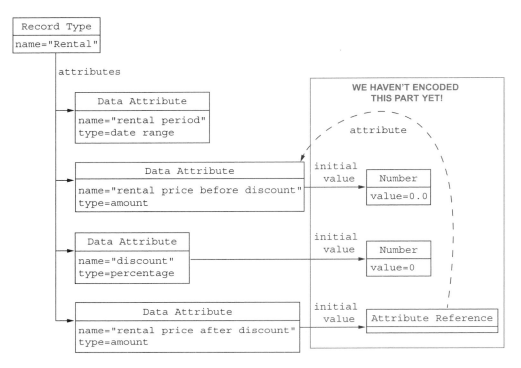

Figure 3.5   Encoding all of the `Data Attribute` AST objects and their containment by the `Rental` AST object

Now let's add the objects for the initial values of the second and third attributes in the same way:

```
const rentalPriceBeforeDiscountInitialValue = {
    concept: "Number",
    settings: {
        "value": "0.0"
    }
}
const rentalPriceBeforeDiscountAttribute = {
    concept: "Data Attribute",
    settings: {
        "name": "rental price before discount",
        "type": "amount",
        "initial value":
            rentalPriceBeforeDiscountInitialValue
    }
}

const discountInitialValue = {
    concept: "Number",
    settings: {
```

Creates a separate JavaScript object for the initial value object belonging to the second attribute, and assigns it to a **rentalPriceBeforeDiscountInitialValue** constant.

Adds a key-value pair for the initial value property, containing the appropriate initial value object, which we can reference through the **rentalPriceBeforeDiscountInitialValue** constant.

```
            "value": "0"
        }
    }
}
const discountAttribute = {
    concept: "Data Attribute",
    settings: {
        "name": "discount",
        "type": "percentage",
        "initial value": discountInitialValue
    }
}
```

The situation is now as shown in figure 3.6.

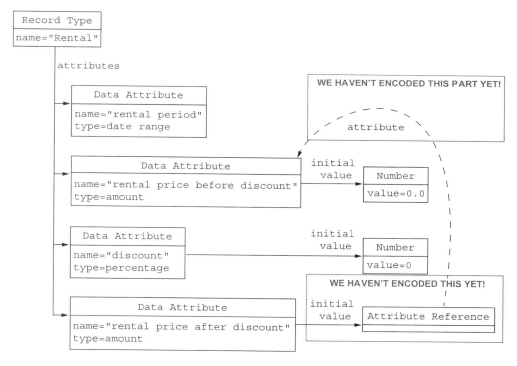

Figure 3.6 Encoding all of the `Data Attribute` AST objects, as well as the initial value objects for the attributes named `rental price before discount` and `discount`

3.1.2 Encoding reference relations

So far, so good, but this encoding isn't complete yet. We haven't taken care of the attribute reference relation. This relation specifies that the `rental price after discount` attribute is to be initialized to the initial value of the `rental price before discount` attribute. Let's find out how we can encode reference relations such as this.

Let's try adding a key-value pair to the object stored in the `rentalPriceAfter-DiscountInitialValue` constant as follows:

```
const rentalPriceAfterDiscountInitialValue = {
    concept: "Attribute Reference",
    settings: {
        "attribute": {
            ref: rentalPriceBeforeDiscountAttribute
        }
    }
}
```

This causes a problem: the value of the key-value pair with the `attribute` key in this JavaScript object looks—for all intents and purposes—like a *contained* object instead of a *referred* object. Without additional knowledge, how could we see that this value is actually the target of a reference relation?

A straightforward way around this problem is to *wrap* all references in separate *wrapper objects*. Such wrapper objects are JavaScript objects that should be easily distinguishable from encoded AST objects. Let's wrap `rentalPriceBeforeDiscountAttribute` in a suitable way:

```
const rentalPriceAfterDiscountInitialValue = {
    concept: "Attribute Reference",
    settings: {
        "attribute": {
            ref: rentalPriceBeforeDiscountAttribute
        }
    }
}
```

We can now immediately recognize that the value of `attribute` is a wrapper object for a reference, not an AST or settings object. It has one key-value pair with the `ref` key, but none with the `concept` or `settings` keys. Also, because `ref` is not the name of a property in the ORD, we don't put it in double quotes. The target of the reference can now be retrieved as follows: `rentalPriceAfterDiscountInitialValue.settings["attribute"].ref`.

We can now safely patch the code for the `rentalPriceAfterDiscountAttribute` constant:

```
const rentalPriceAfterDiscountAttribute = {
    concept: "Data Attribute",
    settings: {
        "name": "rental price after discount",
        "type": "amount",
        "initial value": rentalPriceAfterDiscountInitialValue
    }
}
```

Figure 3.7 summarizes how this relates to the example AST.

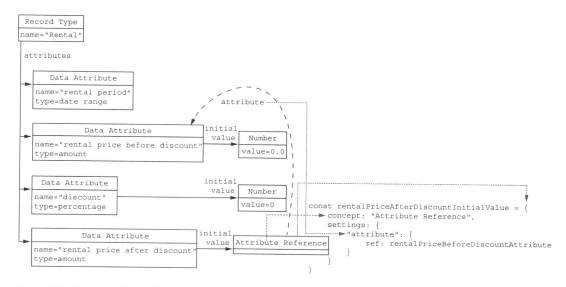

Figure 3.7 Encoding the setting for the `initial value` property on the fourth `Data Attribute` AST object

Why not use ID-based references?

You might be wondering, "Why not encode a reference through some ID that AST objects might (or should) have?" Instead, we chose to encode a reference relation through a JavaScript *object reference*. The only reason we wrap such a reference in a separate object is to recognize the reference for what it is. Navigating over the reference relation is then a simple matter of evaluating the expression `astObject.settings[<property name>].ref`, which is simple and fast. Obtaining the target of a relation reference like this also goes by the name *dereferencing*.

We haven't given our AST objects IDs yet because we haven't needed them. Since a JavaScript object reference is really just a memory address in disguise, you can think of that address as the ID for now. We *will* need to retrofit an actual object ID in chapter 6, when we serialize ASTs to, and deserialize them from, JSON.

Using IDs to point to the target of a reference relation has the disadvantage that we'd have to look up an AST object through its ID, instead of just dereferencing it. Obtaining the target of a relation reference like this is also referred to as *resolving the reference*. Looking up stuff in the AST is expensive: the referenced AST object could be anywhere in the AST. Without additional infrastructure, we might have to traverse the entire AST before we found the right AST object. There are ways to optimize this by caching lookup tables, but that would require us to add lots of code just to get the references working. It's alright to have to do this during deserialization, but not during normal interactions with the AST.

Now that we've encoded all the details of the example AST, let's see all of that code together.

Listing 3.3 Encoding the entire example AST (src/ch03/rental-AST.js)

```
const rentalPeriodAttribute = {
    concept: "Data Attribute",
    settings: {
        "name": "rental period",
        "type": "date range"
    }
}
const rentalPriceBeforeDiscountInitialValue = {
    concept: "Number",
    settings: {
        "value": "0.0"
    }
}
const rentalPriceBeforeDiscountAttribute = {
    concept: "Data Attribute",
    settings: {
        "name": "rental price before discount",
        "type": "amount",
        "initial value": rentalPriceBeforeDiscountInitialValue
    }
}
const discountInitialValue = {
    concept: "Number",
    settings: {
        "value": "0"
    }
}
const discountAttribute = {
    concept: "Data Attribute",
    settings: {
        "name": "discount",
        "type": "percentage",
        "initial value": discountInitialValue
    }
}
const rentalPriceAfterDiscountInitialValue = {
    concept: "Attribute Reference",
    settings: {
        "attribute": {
            ref: rentalPriceBeforeDiscountAttribute
        }
    }
}
const rentalPriceAfterDiscountAttribute = {
    concept: "Data Attribute",
    settings: {
        "name": "rental price after discount",
        "type": "amount",
        "initial value": rentalPriceAfterDiscountInitialValue
    }
}
const rental = {
    concept: "Record Type",
```

```
settings: {
    "name": "Rental",
    "attributes": [
        rentalPeriodAttribute, rentalPriceBeforeDiscountAttribute,
        discountAttribute, rentalPriceAfterDiscountAttribute
    ]
  }
}
```

Let's summarize the process of encoding an AST as a JavaScript value generically:

- An AST object is encoded as a JavaScript object { } having certain key-value pairs.
- The concept label is encoded as a key-value pair on the encoding object with `concept` as the key and the concept label as the value.
- All settings are stored in a JavaScript object that's the value in a key-value pair with `settings` as the key. We'll assume that this `settings` subobject will exist (and be equal to {}) even if no property settings exist on the AST object.
- A setting, whether it's a simple setting or any kind of relation, is encoded as a key-value pair on that second `settings` subobject. The key will be the name of the setting's property, and the value will be the value of the setting. That value is encoded using the following rules:
  - A multivalued setting is encoded as an array […] that is the value of the key-value pair.
  - The contain*ed* object in a containment relation is the value, or one of the values, of the corresponding key-value pair on the contain*ing* object.
  - The target of a reference relation is wrapped in a JavaScript object of the following form:

    ```
    {
        ref: <a JavaScript object reference
            ⇒ to the target of the reference relation>
    }
    ```

  - A value for a setting that's not a relation is encoded as a JavaScript string, Boolean, or number.

Figure 3.8 represents that generic process graphically.

3.2 Interacting with ASTs

In the previous section, you learned how to encode an AST. But how can we interact with that encoded AST? Suppose that we have been given an encoded AST, such as through running the code in listing 3.3. How can we inspect its settings and change them?

First, let's make sure we can play around with the example AST. I find it convenient to use the Node.js REPL for that. As before, we can start the Node.js REPL by

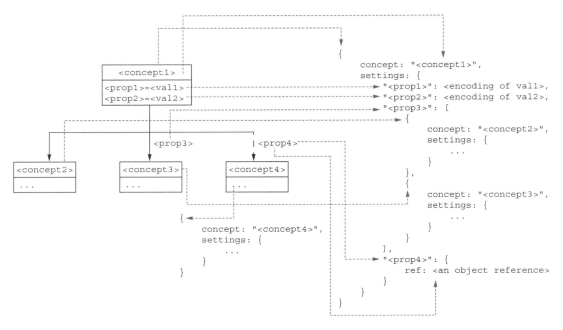

Figure 3.8   Encoding an AST generically

executing the `node` command on the command line. We can now copy and paste listing 3.3 into the Node.js REPL.

In order to use that code more often, we can put it in a file. Create a new src/ch03/rental-AST.js file, and copy the contents of listing 3.3 into it. Make sure you add the following line at the end of the code:

```
module.exports = rental
```

We can now read this file into the REPL by executing the following command:

```
> const rental = require(<path to file>)
undefined
```

We have created a constant called `rental` that contains the example AST. (As before, the creation of a constant evaluates to `undefined`.) Let's see what's stored in `rental`:

```
> rental
{
  concept: 'Record Type',
  settings: {
    name: 'Rental',
    attributes: [ [Object], [Object], [Object], [Object] ]
  }
}
```

This seems to work, although we can't see inside the values of the `attributes` setting. We'll access those and other data in the next subsection.

3.2.1 *Accessing concept labels and settings' values*

For starters, let's try to access the `concept` label of the encoded AST object stored in `rental`:

```
> rental.concept
'Record Type'
```

Now let's access its `name`, remembering that we put the settings on every AST object in a `settings` subobject:

```
> rental.settings["name"]
'Rental'
```

All fine! I've chosen to always use the array accessor style to access the values of key-value pairs in a `settings` subobject: `….settings["<property name>"]`. You can use the usual property access style, `….settings.<property name>`, provided the property name is a valid JavaScript identifier, but this is not the case for a property name like `initial value`, which has a space in it. We simply use the style that consistently works. The `concept` label is not a setting, however, so I prefer to access that with the usual property access style: `<AST object>.concept`.

Let's now try to look up the fourth attribute:

```
> rental.settings["attributes"][3]
{
  concept: 'Data Attribute',
  settings: {
    name: 'rental price after discount',
    type: 'amount',
    'initial value': { concept: 'Attribute Reference', settings: [Object] }
  }
}
```

The `rental.settings["attributes"][3]` expression might look weird for two reasons. First, there's a double pair of square brackets. To help in decoding the meaning of this expression, you can add extra parentheses as follows: `(rental.settings ["attributes"])[3]`. Because the `attributes` property is a multivalued containment relation, we know that the parenthesized subexpression `rental.settings ["attributes"]` must evaluate to an array.

Second, why do we say `[3]` when we want to access the fourth attribute? That's because JavaScript arrays number their members from 0; we say that these arrays are *0-indexed*. The first member has index 0, the second is index 1, etc. Just remember that index = position - 1.

It would be interesting to see whether we can verify that the one reference relation we have behaves as we would expect it to. More precisely, the setting for `attribute` on the object reachable through the setting for `initial value` on the fourth attribute object should be the second attribute object. Let's first put the value of that `attribute` setting into a separate constant:

```
> const attributeRefSetting = rental.settings["attributes"][3]
    ⇒ .settings["initial value"]
    ⇒ .settings["attribute"]
undefined
```

Now we should be able to navigate to the target end of the reference relation using `attributeRefSetting.ref`:

```
> attributeRefSetting.ref
{
  concept: 'Data Attribute',
  settings: {
    name: 'rental price before discount',
    type: 'amount',
    'initial value': { concept: 'Number', settings: [Object] }
  }
}
```

The evaluation result looks suspiciously like the second attribute object. We can verify that as follows:

```
> attributeRefSetting.ref === rental.settings["attributes"][1]
true
```

Finally, we can try to modify some settings' values. Let's change the initial value of the `discount` attribute to 10%:

```
> rental.settings["attributes"][2].settings["initial value"]
    ⇒ .settings["value"] = 10
10
```

3.2.2   *Recognizing AST and reference objects*

The code in the previous subsection works because we know what properties we can expect settings for and what the shapes of their values can be. We know beforehand that a `Data Attribute` object has a setting for a `name` property, and that its value will be a string. We also know that a `Record Type` object has a setting for an `attributes` property, and that the value of that setting is an array. Finally, we know that the setting for the `attribute` property on an `Attribute Reference` object is a reference object, { `ref: <target>` }, and that the target is an encoded AST object.

But let's say we didn't have that knowledge, or we couldn't or don't want to rely on it. How can we recognize encoded AST objects and reference objects, and how can we distinguish them from each other and from other types of JavaScript values?

Here's an idea: let's use JavaScript's built-in `typeof` operation:

```
> typeof rental
'object'
> typeof rental.settings["name"]
'string'
```

Promising! Now let's see whether the `typeof` operator can properly recognize the values of settings for multivalued properties:

```
> typeof rental.settings["attributes"]
'object'
```

That's not really helpful, since this doesn't allow us to distinguish AST and reference relation objects from multivalued properties' values. Luckily, JavaScript also has an `Array.isArray` function, so let's try that:

```
> Array.isArray(rental.settings["attributes"])
true
```

Also,

```
> Array.isArray('foo')
false
> Array.isArray(42)
false
> Array.isArray({})
false
```

We conclude that we can use the `Array.isArray` function to reliably recognize arrays as values of multivalued properties' settings.

Now we need a way to recognize AST and reference relation objects. Let's see if we can use the `typeof` operator to recognize such objects:

```
> typeof rental
'object'
> typeof {}
'object'
```

This is as expected, but we have to be wary of the following behavior:

```
> typeof null
'object'
```

Let's create a helper function.

Listing 3.4   Helper function to identify "true" JavaScript objects

```
const isObject = (value) => (!!value) && (typeof value === "object")
     => && !Array.isArray(value)
```

This function first checks whether `value` is "not nothing" through the expression `!!value`. This expression coerces *truthy* JavaScript values to `true` and *falsy* values to `false`. In particular, `undefined` and `null` are falsy values. Then it checks whether `typeof` returns `object`. Last, it checks whether it's not an array.

> **Truthy, falsy, and !!**
>
> Follow these links for more information on
>
> - Truthy and falsy: https://developer.mozilla.org/en-US/docs/Glossary/Truthy and https://developer.mozilla.org/en-US/docs/Glossary/Falsy
> - The `!!` operator: https://stackoverflow.com/questions/29312123/how-does-the-double-exclamation-work-in-javascript

Let's test it:

```
> isObject(undefined)
false
> isObject('foo')
false
> isObject(42)
false
> isObject([ 1, 2, 3 ])
false
> isObject({})
true
```

We can conclude that the `isObject` function reliably distinguishes "true" JavaScript objects from other JavaScript values, including arrays, even though JavaScript itself deems these quite object-like.

Now, how can we recognize an encoded AST object? We know that it's a JavaScript object and that it should have two key-value pairs with the keys `concept` and `settings`. We can reliably check for the presence of such key-value pairs using JavaScript's `in` operator:

```
> "concept" in rental
true
> "settings" in rental
true
> "concept" in attributeRefSetting
false
> "settings" in attributeRefSetting
false
```

Looks good! Let's put that knowledge in another helper function.

Listing 3.5   Helper function to identify encoded AST objects

```
const isAstObject = (value) => isObject(value) && ("concept" in value)
    ⟹ && ("settings" in value)
```

We could even go so far as to check whether `value.concept` is a string and `value.settings` is an object, but I'll leave that to you as an exercise. Let's test this function:

```
> isAstObject(rental)
true
> isAstObject(rental.settings["attributes"])
false
> isAstObject(rental.settings["attributes"][0])
true
> isAstObject(attributeRefSetting)
false
```

Now we just need to find a way to recognize encoded reference relations as such. We can do this the same way as for encoded AST objects, since a single reference relation is encoded as a reference object of the form { ref: <target> }. Let's implement a function to recognize reference objects.

Listing 3.6   Helper function to identify reference objects

```
const isAstReferenceObject = (value) => isObject(value) && ("ref" in value)
```

We can now recognize an encoded reference relation as a reference object that has an AST object as the value under the `ref` key. Let's implement another function for that.

Listing 3.7   Helper function to recognize reference relations

```
const isAstReference = (value) => isAstReferenceObject(value)
    ⟹ && isAstObject(value.ref)
```

Let's test this `isAstReference` function:

```
> isAstReference(attributeRefSetting)
true
> isAstReference(rental)
false
```

All good! Finally, let's create a file called ast.js in the src/common path in our development environment—we'll put our helper functions in this file.

Listing 3.8   Initial contents of the src/common/ast.js file

```
const isObject = (value) => (!!value) && (typeof value === "object")
    ⟹ && !Array.isArray(value)
```

```
const isAstObject = (value) => isObject(value) && ("concept" in value)
    ⇨ && ("settings" in value)
module.exports.isAstObject = isAstObject

const isAstReferenceObject = (value) => isObject(value) && ("ref" in value)
const isAstReference = (value) => isAstReferenceObject(value)
    ⇨ && isAstObject(value.ref)
module.exports.isAstReference = isAstReference
```

Export the isAstObject and isAstReference functions so we can import them in other files. The isObject and isAstReferenceObject functions are only used within this file, so we don't have to export them.

We can now import the helper functions in other files as follows:

```
const { isAstObject, isAstReference } = require("__<relative path to ast.js>__")
```

See section B.1.7 on how to use `require`. The correct relative path from a file directly in the src directory would be ./common/ast.

I chose to put the ast.js file in the src/common path for the following reasons:

- We'll place all code that we're going to evolve throughout the book in the src/ directory.
- We'll place code that will be common to the frontend, backend, and code generator in the common/ subdirectory.

We can now reliably recognize encoded AST objects and reference objects, and we can distinguish them from each other and from other types of JavaScript values. These other types can only be simple data types: string, Boolean, number, or "void," meaning `null` or `undefined`.

Exercise 3.1
Adapt the `isAstObject` function to also check that `concept` is a string and `settings` is an object.

3.3   *Traversing ASTs*

An AST that's stored in memory is not very useful in its own right: you need to be able to do something with it, which generally means going over *all* the objects in the AST in an organized fashion. A useful, common, and well-known way to do that is *depth-first tree traversal* (DFTT). This approach visits all the objects in an AST, as well as their settings, in an orderly fashion. In this section, we'll look at how a depth-first tree traversal works, and how to implement one. Instead of trying to traverse our full example AST, let's traverse a smaller version of the same AST (see figure 3.9).

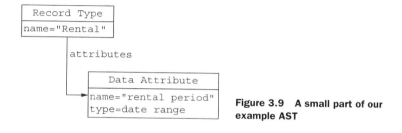

Figure 3.9 A small part of our example AST

Figure 3.10 showcases how we'll traverse this AST in an orderly depth-first fashion.

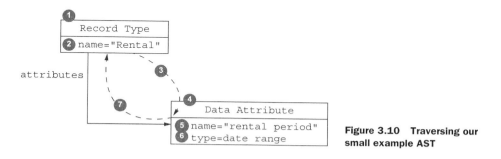

Figure 3.10 Traversing our small example AST

Let's lay out the steps of this traversal:

1 We start at the root object of the tree and visit the Record Type object.

2 We visit the first setting on the Record Type object, which is the setting for the name property.

3 We visit the second setting on the Record Type object, which happens to be the first (and, in this diagram, only) member of the attributes containment relation.

4 We visit the object at the target end of that relation, which is the first (and, in this diagram, only) Data Attribute object.

5 We visit the first setting on that Data Attribute object, which is the setting for the name property.

6 We visit the second setting on the Data Attribute object, which happens to be the one for the type property.

7 We've now finished visiting all the settings for the Data Attribute object, so we backtrack to the Record Type object to see whether we've got any more work to do there. We conclude that we've finished visiting all the settings for the Record Type object, which means we're finished with the whole AST.

What we actually *do* when we visit a particular object or setting on the AST depends on what we want to achieve by executing the depth-first tree traversal. We may want to search for something in the AST, change things in the AST, or make a copy of the entire AST. In any case, the DFTT pattern only prescribes how all objects and settings in the AST are visited; it doesn't really say much more. This offers great flexibility, but it also means that it's entirely up to us to make the right thing happen. We'll get back to that later.

Let's enlarge the AST a little bit and traverse it (see figure 3.11).

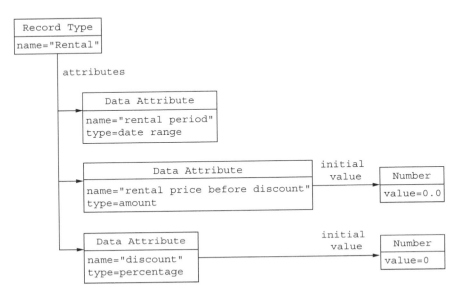

Figure 3.11   A slightly larger part of the example AST

We'd traverse this one as shown in figure 3.12. Steps 1 to 7 are exactly the same in both approaches (figures 3.10 and 3.12). Let's look at the new steps, 8 to 16.

8   We visit the second member of the `attributes` containment relation (now that it's in the diagram).

9   We visit the object at the target end of that relation, which is the second `Data Attribute` object.

10   We visit the first setting on that `Data Attribute` object, which is for the `name` property.

11   We visit the second setting on the `Data Attribute` object, which is for the `type` property.

12   We visit the third setting on the third `Data Attribute` object, which holds the `initial value` containment relation.

13   We visit the first `Number` object, which is the target object of that containment relation.

14   We visit the only setting on that object, which happens to be for the `value` property.

15 We backtrack to the `Data Attribute` with the name `rental price before discount` and conclude that we visited all its settings.

16 We backtrack to the `Record Type` object again.

Steps 17 to 25 are essentially the same as steps 8 to 16, and I'll let you explore those on your own.

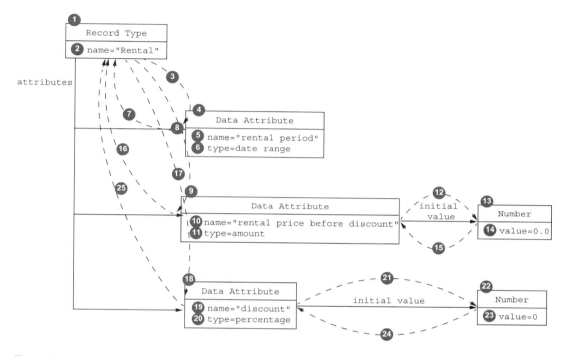

Figure 3.12   Traversing the bigger example AST

Both of the slimmed-down ASTs we've traversed so far lack reference relations. How are those dealt with in a DFTT? Let's drop the first and third `Data Attribute` objects from the full AST and try traversing the remaining AST (see figure 3.13).

The new phenomenon in this traversal is where we visit the reference relation, which is the value for the setting for the `attribute` property (see step 18 in figure 3.14). It's different from visiting a containment relation, like we do in step 16, because we don't actually traverse to the target object and continue traversing from there. That's because we're sure to visit that object through another route. In our case, the `rental price before discount` object was visited in step 4, as a result of traversing over one of the `attributes` containment relations in step 3. Instead of visiting the target object, we can just *look* at it and make decisions based on that. Just looking at the target object also prevents us from ending up in an infinite loop.

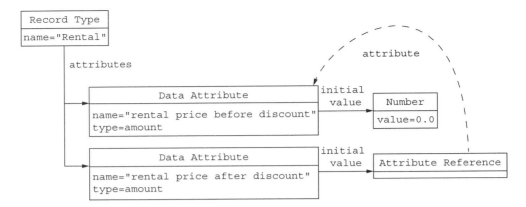

Figure 3.13   Most of the example AST

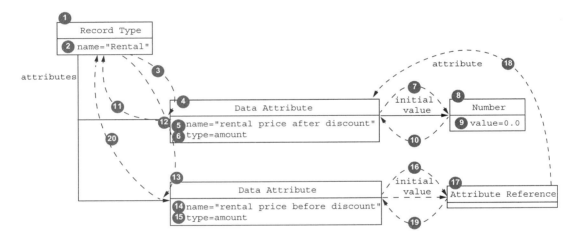

Figure 3.14   Traversing most of the example AST, including visiting a reference relation

3.3.1   *The general recipe for DFTT*

In general, a DFTT does the following for every AST object, starting with the root object of the AST:

1 We visit the object as a whole, and do with it whatever we need to do. That often means looking at the concept label.

2 Then we visit all the settings we find on the object, in any fixed order that makes sense. This could be the order in which the settings were put on the object, or alphanumerically by the names of the settings' properties. For every setting, we inspect its value and do the following:

- If it's an AST object, we're apparently dealing with the contained part of a containment relation. In that case, we traverse to that contained object to visit it.
- If it's a reference object, `value.ref` references the targeted AST object. We *look* at the target object, but we don't traverse to it.
- If it's an array, meaning that the setting is multivalued, we traverse to all items in the array separately. There, we first traverse into the first item, and visit that, before moving on to the later items. In other words, we stick to the array's order.
- If it's anything else—let's say a "simple" JavaScript data type, such as a string or a number—we can choose to inspect that value, but there's nothing to traverse to after that.

3 Every time we finish with visiting all the settings on an object, we backtrack to the last object where we might have some work to do. Backtracking means that we traverse backward from the target to the source of the last containment relation we traversed.

The preceding recipe is illustrated in figure 3.15. In the next section we'll use this recipe to implement a function that counts the number of leaves in an AST.

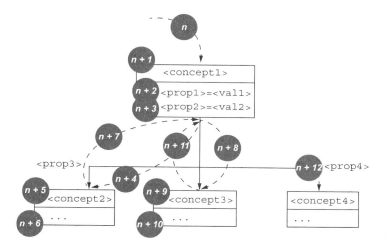

Figure 3.15 Traversing an AST generically

You probably noticed the word *first* used a couple of times: that is why this is a *depth-first* tree traversal. It always goes to a deeper or lower part of the tree first, before visiting anything on the same or a higher level. Also note that we traverse over all containment relations, twice even: both forward and backward.

A DFTT can be conveniently implemented using *recursion*. This is because the JavaScript execution engine keeps track of the traversal for us, through a call tree. Backtracking is done simply by executing the `return` statement.

The preceding recipe only relies on the generic shape of AST objects. It does not rely at all on knowing anything specific about the concepts in the DSL we're building. In other words, *it's generic for all ASTs*. This is convenient; it means we don't have to provide any information from the outside.

If you're interested in what the traversal looks like for the full example AST, it's illustrated in figure 3.16. I won't tire anyone—including myself—by writing the traversal out as text.

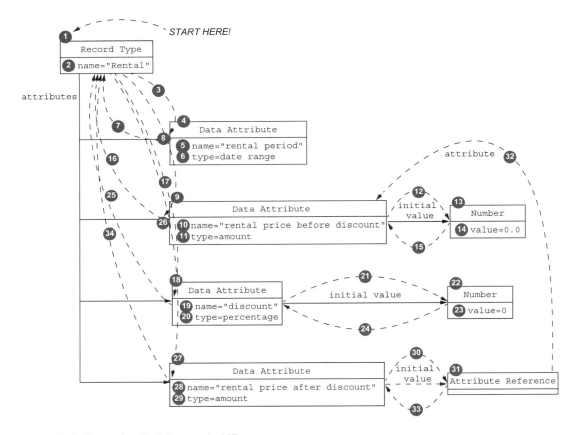

Figure 3.16 **Traversing the full example AST**

Eating your own dogfood

You might have been looking at the traversal diagrams and wondering how much effort went into them. I can assure you that it goes against my lazy nature to make those diagrams by hand. Instead, I *generated* them with a little bit of JavaScript code that takes an actual AST and computes the paths that the traversals take. Visualizing the path that a DFTT takes is itself a DFTT!

3.3.2   Example: Counting the leaves of an AST

We'll implement a relatively simple example of a traversal. It won't seem to do anything useful right now, but that will allow us to focus on the traversal itself.

Let's say we've been handed an AST encoded as a JavaScript value, as we've been doing so far, and we need to count the number of leaf objects in it. A *leaf object* is an AST object that has no children, so, in other words, no outgoing containment relations. We'll implement a JavaScript function called `numberOfLeaves` in the ast.js file. This function should take an AST and return an integer: the number of leaf objects in that AST.

The DFTT recipe is written from the viewpoint of being handed an AST object. However, changing this viewpoint slightly makes the recursion simpler to write down. Let's say you're handed *some value* without knowing beforehand whether it's an AST object or any other kind of value represented in the AST. For every possible kind of value, we look up in the recipe what should be done with that value.

Let's write a recursive function, called `numberOfLeaves`, that takes *any* JavaScript value. We'll use the `isAstObject` and `isAstReference` helper functions we defined in ast.js, as well as the built-in `Array.isArray` function, to decide what to do with the given value. By calling this function on the AST's root, we can then compute the number of leaves in the entire AST: `numberOfLeaves(astRoot)`.

Import the usual helper functions from ast.js (assuming the code resides in src/ch03/).

Define a numberOfLeaves function using the arrow function idiom. This works even when the function is recursive.

```
const { isAstObject, isAstReference } =
    require("../common/ast")

const numberOfLeaves = (value) => {
    if (isAstObject(value)) {
        const sub = sum(Object.values(value.settings)
            .map(numberOfLeaves))
        return sub === 0 ? 1 : sub
    }
    if (isAstReference(value)) {
        return 0
    }
    if (Array.isArray(value)) {
        return sum(value.map(numberOfLeaves))
    }
    return 0
}
```

Check whether the value is an encoded AST object.

If the value is an encoded AST object, sum the number of leaves on all the values of all the settings in the AST object, and put the result in the sub constant.

If sub equals 0, the AST object can't contain anything and so must be a leaf, so return a value of 1.

If the value is a reference, we don't follow it, and return 0.

Check whether the value is an array, and sum the integer values in it if it is.

If the value is anything else, return 0.

In the preceding listing, the constant `sub` is called that because it counts the number of leaves in the *sub*tree, starting at the AST object but excluding that object itself.

The sum function sums an array of integers. JavaScript doesn't have that function built in, so we need to define it ourselves:

```
const sum = (numbers) => numbers
    .reduce((currentSum, currentNumber) => currentSum + currentNumber, 0)
```

> **NOTE** The numbers we'll be summing will be integers, but that doesn't make a difference for the implementation. JavaScript doesn't have different types for integers and other numeric types, such as floats.

The preceding code uses the reduce function defined on arrays, which reduces an array in a left-to-right fashion. (In functional programming languages, this function is often called foldLeft.) The reduce function takes two arguments:

- A reducer, which is a function taking two arguments: an accumulated value, and a current value. For the purpose of summing numbers, we'll simply add the accumulated value to the current value.
- A default value that is returned when the array is empty. Because the sum of an empty array is 0, this default value should be 0.

We'll put this definition in the same file as numberOfLeaves. Now let's test the number-OfLeaves function on our Rental record type AST:

```
> numberOfLeaves(rental)
4
```

Counting leaves in an AST may not seem to be very useful. However, the code pattern for DFTT is already peeking out of the preceding code. Let's try to make that pattern more explicit by generalizing the code of numberOfLeaves somewhat.

Listing 3.9   Code pattern for DFTTs

```
const myDepthFirstTreeTraversalFunction = (value) => {
    if (isAstObject(value)) {
        ...initialization...
        for (const propertyName in value.settings) {
            ...do something involving value.settings[propertyName]
            ➡ - most likely call myDepthFirstTreeTraversalFunction
            ➡ recursively on it...
            ...at this point, we can still make decisions
                ➡ based on the property's name...
        }
        return ...the sensible thing when value is an encoded AST object...
    }
    if (isAstReference(value)) {
        return ...the sensible thing when value is a reference object,
            ➡ probably something involving value.ref...
    }
```

```
    if (Array.isArray(value)) {
        return ...some transformation of
            ➥ value.map(myDepthFirstTreeTraversalFunction)...
    }
    return ...the sensible thing when value is the value of a setting...
}
```

For clarity, I put some extra emphasis on the `myDepthFirstTreeTraversalFunction` name because you'll have to replace that name a number of times. This really is only a pattern, which we'll have to fit to any specific purpose.

> **NOTE** You could try to make a generic function for DFTT and pass functions to it to perform the real work. This is hard to do properly for all uses of the pattern, and the resulting code is not more readable, so I choose to just repeat the pattern.

As was the case for the DFTT recipe at the beginning of section 3.3.1, this code pattern doesn't rely at all on the specifics of the DSL. Instead, it's generic for all ASTs that are encoded in the way we agreed to in section 3.1.

Exercise 3.2

- Modify the `numberOfLeaves` function such that it prints a *trace* of what it's doing, using `console.log(...)` or `console.dir(...)`.
- Simulate executing the `numberOfLeaves` function on the `Rental` example AST from figure 3.2 by annotating figure 3.16. Write down the value of `sub` for every visit of an AST object, and write down the return value on the backtracking arrows.
- Implement a `leaves` function that returns an array of all the leaves, rather than just counting them.
  - Consider using the `flatMap` function defined on arrays.
  - In what order would you expect the leaves to appear in this function's results? Verify your reasoning using the `Rental` example AST.
- Implement a function called `weight` that "weighs" a given AST by assigning a weight of 1 to every AST object, as well as to every separate, non-void value in a setting on an AST object.
  - Use the pattern for DFTT.
  - The weight of the full example AST, as encoded in listing 3.3, should evaluate to 20.
- Implement a function called `findByName` that tries to find an AST object by name in a given AST.
  - It should visit every AST object and check whether it has a setting for a property called `name` and whether it matches the given name.
  - The first AST object to satisfy these criteria should be the only value returned. If no AST object can be found, you should return `undefined`.

(continued)
  – Use the pattern for DFTT.
  – Check your code by searching for various names in the full example, as encoded in listing 3.3.
  – Think about how `findByName` is different from `weight`. Does `findByName` always visit every object in the AST?

3.3.3 More about ASTs

In chapter 4, we'll code a projection for this type of AST. The projection will also perform a DFTT of sorts, even though it won't follow the previous code pattern exactly. In chapters 5 and 6, we'll turn this projection into a proper DSL editor. In chapter 7, we'll look at more DFTTs that serialize ASTs as JSON and deserialize JSON back into ASTs. In chapter 9, we'll use a DFTT to check the AST using constraints.

Why explain ORDs?

At this point, you might be wondering, "Why do we need ORDs at all? We could have gone straight from DSL content to encoding ASTs! Why did you make me read chapter 2?"

The answer is, we *could* have made that leap, but the resulting textual representation in code would not have been as clear as an ORD is. Furthermore, we're going to use ORDs throughout the book to help visualize various aspects of, and algorithms for, working with ASTs.

Using textual representations would also make our discussion very dependent on the chosen programming language. ORDs function as an *abstract* syntax for structured data. You could argue that the ORD notation forms a DSL for the domain of representing structured data. This is another instance of "dogfooding": we're using a DSL to help learn about DSLs.

Summary

- Any AST can be encoded as a JavaScript value.
- An AST object is encoded as a JavaScript object with the following structure: `{ concept: <concept label>, settings: <a JavaScript object encoding this AST object's settings> }`.
- A setting for a property on an AST object is encoded as a key-value pair in the `settings` subobject: `settings: { <property's name>: <setting's encoded value>, … other encoded settings… }`.
- A simple setting or a containment relation is encoded as is.
- A reference relation is encoded as a JavaScript object called a *reference object*. It has the following structure: `{ ref: <JavaScript object reference to the target object of the reference relation> }`.

- A multivalued setting is encoded as a JavaScript array, with each member of the setting encoded as an array item.
- After encoding an AST as a JavaScript value, it can be interacted with.
- An AST object can be recognized as such by checking whether it's a JavaScript object with the specific structure shown above.
- A setting for a property on an AST object can be accessed through a JavaScript expression of the form `<encoded AST object>.settings["<property name>"]`.
- A containment relation can be navigated over or followed simply by looking at the corresponding setting's value.
- A reference object encoding a reference relation can be recognized by checking that it's a JavaScript object with the specific structure shown above.
- A reference relation can be navigated over or followed through a JavaScript expression of the form `<corresponding setting's value>.<reference object>.ref`.
- A *depth-first tree traversal* (DFTT) is a useful algorithm for traversing encoded ASTs, and it's easy to implement using recursion.

Projecting the AST

This chapter covers

- Projecting an AST to a visualization as an HTML DOM
- Using a polymorphic, stateless React component to implement the projection iteratively

In chapter 2, we showed how to reduce notated DSL content to abstract syntax trees (ASTs) represented as object-relation diagrams (ORDs). In chapter 3, you learned how to encode ASTs in ORD format, so we have a representation of them in memory as a JavaScript value. In this chapter, we're going to reverse that process: given an AST in memory, we'll visualize it as notated DSL content (see figure 4.1). We call this reverse process *projection*: we *project* the AST as notated DSL content.

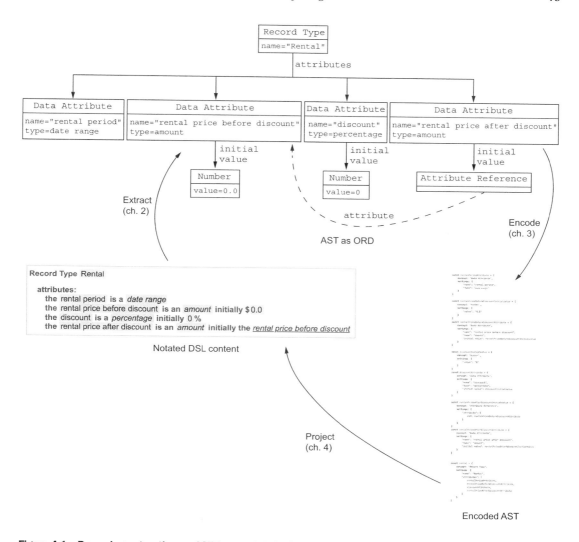

Figure 4.1   Reversing extracting an AST from notated DSL content and encoding it is *projecting*.

Figure 4.2 illustrates the projection's implementation in more technological detail. First, we have to get hold of an AST: loading an encoding of it gives us an in-memory representation that we can project. Then, we hand that in-memory representation off to a projection function, which returns an HTML document object model (DOM). Finally, the browser renders that DOM, which gives the domain expert their notated DSL content.

As usual, we'll be using the `RentalRecord Type` example, shown again in figure 4.3. The extracted AST for this is shown in figure 2.17, and it's encoded as listing 3.3. In other words, we're going to reconstitute figure 4.3 from listing 3.3.

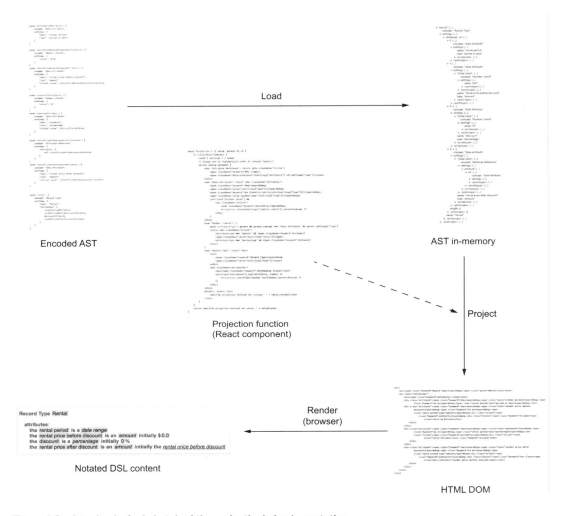

Load

Encoded AST

Projection function
(React component)

AST in-memory

Project

Render
(browser)

HTML DOM

Record Type Rental

attributes:
the rental period is a *date range*
the rental price before discount is an *amount* initially $0.0
the discount is a *percentage* initially 0 %
the rental price after discount is an *amount* initially the *rental price before discount*

Notated DSL content

Figure 4.2   A technological sketch of the projection's implementation

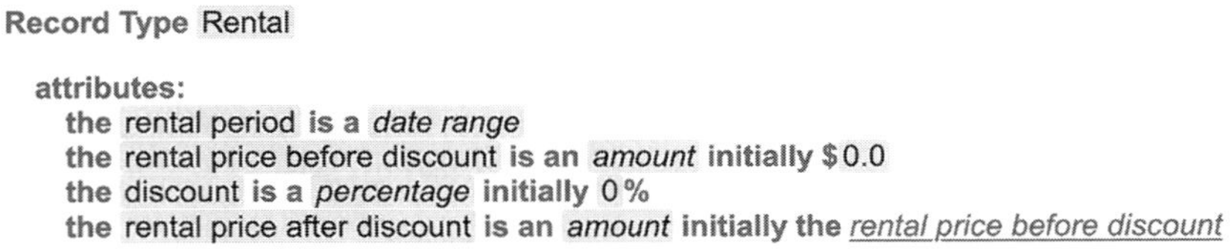

Record Type Rental

attributes:
the rental period **is a** *date range*
the rental price before discount **is an** *amount* **initially** $0.0
the discount **is a** *percentage* **initially** 0 %
the rental price after discount **is an** *amount* **initially the** *rental price before discount*

Figure 4.3   The example DSL content: the specification of a record type called Rental

The way we'll implement this particular projection will serve as a good template for implementing projections for any DSL. We'll do this in a way that's iterative—primarily on a per-concept basis. We'll be relying on the techniques we developed in the second half of chapter 3 to interact with an AST and extract information from it. Later, in chapter 5, we'll expand our implementation of the projection to make the resulting notated DSL content *editable*, turning the projection into an *editor*.

> **TIP** For this and the following chapters, I'm going to assume that you've set up a suitable development environment, and that you know how to implement a frontend using an appropriate framework and tools. If necessary, please take some time to go through appendixes A and B—specifically, section A.2 and sections B.2 through B.4.

> **NOTE** In this and subsequent chapters, I'll use the term "HTML DOM" to mean "the React DOM that's rendered as an HTML DOM," even though they're different things. This difference is explained in appendixes B and C for the sake of completeness and accuracy. To produce an HTML DOM, we'll be using JSX syntax, which looks a lot like real HTML. The only apparent difference is that attribute names sometimes differ: HTML is less restrictive in attributes' names, whereas React demands these to be valid JavaScript identifiers.

4.1 Preparing the implementation of the projection

Let's set up a basic frontend for our Domain IDE. We'll do the following:

1. Set up a development environment—see section A.2 or A.3.
2. Initialize a code repository.
3. Set that repository up for JavaScript development—see section A.4.
4. Copy the files index.html, index.js, and styling.css from listings B.2, B.3, and B.4 into a src/frontend folder.

Figure B.3 looks nothing like figure 4.3, but that's not surprising since we haven't even got hold of an AST yet. Let's retrieve the example AST from listing 3.2, so we'll have something to project. I'll assume that all the code from chapter 3 resides in the src/ch03 directory, so that listing 3.3 resides in the src/ch03/rental-AST.js file. I'll also assume that the following line was added to the end of that file:

```
module.exports = rental
```

We can import the exported value into src/frontend/index.jsx by means of the following import statement:

```
import rental from "../ch03/rental-AST"
```

The `rental` constant now contains the AST for the `RentalRecord` Type. Let's add the preceding statement to the src/frontend/index.jsx file, directly before the call to `render`.

Now let's take another look at the call to React's `render` function. This is the first argument of that call:

```
<span>Projection goes here!</span>
```

Let's replace that with a call to a *stateless React component*. Stateless React components, and how to use them, are explained in section B.3. Let's create a new src/frontend/projection.jsx file to hold a function that implements a React component that, in turn, implements the projection.

Listing 4.1   The initial contents of src/frontend/projection.jsx

```
import React from "react"                    ⬅──── Import the HTML tags part
                                                   of the React framework.
export const Projection = () =>             ⬅────
  ➥  <span>Projection goes here!</span>
```

Export a function that defines a stateless React component, naming it Projection.

NOTE   React insists on giving a React component a name that starts with an uppercase character.

Now we can use this `Projection` React component in index.jsx, replacing the `<span>Frontend goes here!</span>` code (which was the argument of the call to `render`) with a call to the `Projection` React component as if it were an HTML element.

Listing 4.2   src/frontend/index.jsx—using `Projection`

```
import React from "react"
import { createRoot } from "react-dom/client"

require("./styling.css")

import rental from "../ch03/rental-AST"           Import the
import { Projection } from "./projection"    ⬅──  Projection function.

createRoot(document.getElementById("root"))
  .render(
      <Projection />                  ⬅───── Call it.
  )
```

The `rental` value isn't used anywhere yet, so let's change that as well. We can pass an argument to a call to a React component in JSX syntax through an attribute. Let's change the call as follows:

```
<Projection astObject={rental} />
```

In this case, the `Projection` function will receive the following object:

```
{
    "astObject": rental
}
```

We can *destructure* this object in the `Projection` function as follows:

```
export const Projection = ({ astObject }) =>
    <span>Projection goes here!</span>
```

See sections B.3.1 and B.1.6 for an explanation of destructuring. The parameter specification, `({ astObject })`, means that this function expects one argument, `{ astObject }`, which happens to be an object with a key-value pair with key `astObject`. When called, the value of that key-value pair ends up in a local variable named `astObject`. We're still not doing anything with that value, so let's rectify that in the next section.

4.2 Implementing the projection iteratively

We have prepared a tiny codebase with a vestigial React component to implement the projection in and an actual AST to project. Let's implement a projection to HTML that reconstitutes figure 4.3 from the example AST.

We'll do this in an iterative way, on a per-concept basis. We'll also use a couple of code patterns—or "tricks," if you will—that are helpful in implementing a projection for any DSL. This genericity will help us implement the projection in a way that's loosely coupled to the DSL's particular structure.

Let's change the `Projection` component function so that it returns a hint that will help and guide the developer implementing this projection:

Use the generic astObject as the parameter's name to not make assumptions about the kind of value this function receives.

The JavaScript expression between curly braces is evaluated, and the result becomes the textual content of an <em> element.

```
export const Projection = ({ astObject }) => {
    return <em>{"No projection defined for value: "
        + astObject}</em>
}
```

The result of this change looks a bit ungainly and only slightly helpful, as shown in figure 4.4.

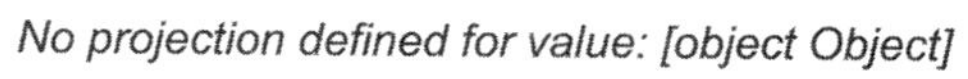

No projection defined for value: [object Object]

Figure 4.4 **The browser showing the `Projection` component function producing a generic hint**

It's about time we started making use of the fact that we're dealing with an AST, and that `rental` is an AST object. We'll use the techniques from chapter 3 for that. We can start by recognizing that a value is an AST object and producing a more focused hint:

**Import the isAstObject function we wrote
in chapter 3, again using destructuring.**

```
import { isAstObject } from "../common/ast"      ◁──────   Check whether the value
                                                            passed is an AST object.
export const Projection = ({ astObject }) => {
    if (isAstObject(astObject)) {                    ◁──    Switch on the concept
        switch (astObject.concept) {             ◁──        label of the AST object.
            default: return <em>                 ◁──
                ⇒ {"No projection defined for concept: "        Define a default case so we
                ⇒ + astObject.concept}</em>                     can return a hint stating which
        }                                                       concept isn't handled yet.
    }
    return <em>{"No projection defined for value: "
        ⇒ + astObject}</em>               ◁──────   If astObject is not an AST object,
}                                                   produce the hint for a generic value.
```

The result is shown in figure 4.5. This is already more helpful. We'll now take the hint
and implement the projection of AST objects with the concept `Record Type`.

No projection defined for concept: Record Type

**Figure 4.5   The `Projection` component
function producing a more focused hint for
AST objects**

4.2.1   *Projecting record types*

Let's project the one instance of the `Record Type` concept in our example AST, but
without its attributes. If we were to do this in HTML, it would look like the following
listing.

Listing 4.3   The partial HTML for our example record type

```
<div>                             Style Record Type appropriately
    <div>                         with the "keyword" CSS class.       Style the record type's name
        <span className="keyword ws-right">                          with the "value" CSS class.
            ⇒ Record Type</span>           ◁──
        <span className="value">Rental</span>    ◁──    Style the part of the record
    </div>                                              type's projection with attributes
    <div className="section">               ◁──         with the "section" CSS class.
        <div><span className="keyword">attributes:</span></div>
        <!-- ...attributes... -->        ◁──
    </div>                                       HTML that visualizes the record type's
</div>                                           attributes should be added here.
```

NOTE   In listing 4.3, we used a `ws-right` CSS class to make sure that an
HTML element is visually separated from the contents on its right by some
whitespace ("ws" is short for *whitespace*). Later on, we'll use the `ws-left` and
`ws-both` CSS classes to visually separate an HTML element from the contents
on its left side and both sides, respectively.

The HTML in listing 4.3 references some CSS classes, so let's define those. We'll add them to src/frontend/styling.css:

```css
span.keyword {
    font-weight: bolder;
    color: rgb(100, 100, 100);
}

.ws-right {
    margin-right: 0.5rem;
}

.ws-left {
    margin-left: 0.5rem;
}

.ws-both {
    margin-right: 0.5rem;
    margin-left: 0.5rem;
}

span.value {
    padding-left: 0.15em;
    padding-right: 0.15em;
    border-radius: 5px;
    background-color: rgb(228, 228, 228);
}

div.section {
    margin-top: 1em;
    margin-left: 1em;
}
```

> **NOTE** Styling a DSL's notation is important: good design and layout don't just look nice; they play an important role in making the DSL content understandable to the domain experts. Moreover, the look and feel of editing interactions determines, to a large extent, how well the domain experts can manipulate the DSL content. For those reasons, I choose to style the DSL's projection minimally, but somewhat decently, using CSS.

Let's put the HTML code from listing 4.3 in our `Projection` React component by adding the following `case` to the `switch` statement:

```html
case "Record Type": return <div>
    <div>
        <span className="keyword ws-right">Record Type</span>
        <span className="value">Rental</span>
    </div>
    <div className="section">
        <div><span className="keyword">attributes:</span></div>
        <!-- ...attributes... -->
    </div>
</div>
```

In listing 4.3, I highlighted in bold the pieces of information we should extract from the AST, and I did the same in the preceding JSX code. We'll replace the text `Rental` in listing 4.3 with an expression that extracts the record type's name from its AST object, and inserts it at that place:

```
<span className="value">{astObject.settings["name"]}</span>
```

We're using an effective two-part technique here:

1　We create an HTML mockup of some of the notated DSL content, including correct styling using CSS.
2　We replace pieces of information in the HTML mockup that can be derived from the AST with suitable JSX expressions.

This technique is often referred to as *templating*. We'll use it often throughout the book.

Now we'll project the individual attributes. We can extract these from the AST object as `astObject.settings["attributes"]`, which is an array. We have to call the `Projection` component for every array member (section B.3.4 explains how to do this):

```
{astObject.settings["attributes"]
    .map((attribute, index) =>
        <Projection astObject={attribute} key={index} />
)}
```

Replacing the `...attributes...` HTML comment in the `Record Type` case with the preceding code has the effect you see in figure 4.6.

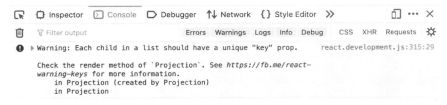

Record Type Rental

attributes:
*No projection defined for concept: Data
AttributeNo projection defined for concept: Data
AttributeNo projection defined for concept: Data
AttributeNo projection defined for concept: Data
Attribute*

Figure 4.6　A screenshot of the browser after implementing the projection of record types, with hints for their attributes, and a React warning

The next problem is that the hints about the `Data Attribute` concept not being handled aren't lined up properly. We can fix that by wrapping the `<em>` element that produces the hint in a `<div>` element:

```
default: return <div>
    <em>{"No projection defined for concept: " + astObject.concept}</em>
</div>
```

This change ensures that each `<em>` element is displayed on a separate line. The entire `Projection` component function—as it currently stands—is shown in the following listing.

Listing 4.4 The `Projection` function after section 4.2.1

```
export const Projection = ({ astObject }) => {
    if (isAstObject(astObject)) {
        switch (astObject.concept) {

            case "Record Type": return <div>
                <div>
                    <span className="keyword ws-right">Record Type</span>
                    <span className="value">
                        {astObject.settings["name"]}</span>
                </div>
                <div className="section">
                    <div><span className="keyword">attributes:</span></div>
                    {astObject.settings["attributes"].map((attribute, index)
                        => <Projection
                        astObject={attribute} key={index} />
                    )}
                </div>
            </div>

            default: return <div>
                <em>{"No projection defined for concept: "
                    + astObject.concept}</em>
            </div>
        }
    }

    return <em>{"No projection defined for value: " + astObject}</em>
}
```

The result of this code change is shown in figure 4.7.

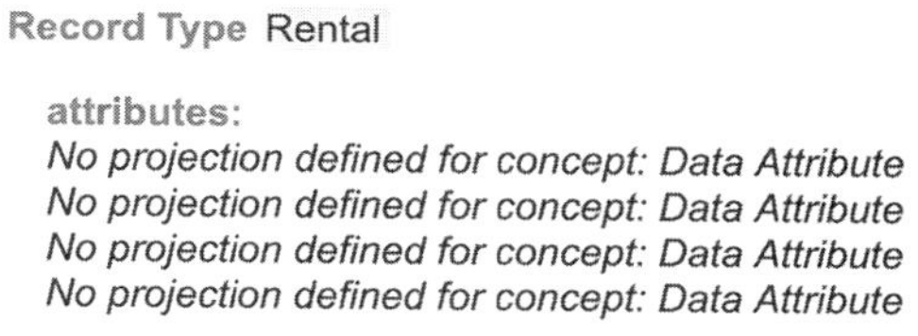

Record Type Rental

attributes:
No projection defined for concept: Data Attribute
No projection defined for concept: Data Attribute
No projection defined for concept: Data Attribute
No projection defined for concept: Data Attribute

Figure 4.7   The browser's display after implementing the projection of record types, with hints for their attributes and fixes for the React warning and alignment

NOTE The `Projection` component function is essentially a big `switch` statement that switches on the concept of AST objects. A fancy word for that code pattern is *polymorphism*, which stems from the Greek words "poly"/ "πολυ" meaning "many" and "morphé"/"μόρφή`" meaning "form." A polymorphic function is a function that is able to handle arguments of multiple different forms.

Exercise 4.1

- The `Projection` component function is starting to look a bit like a depth-first tree traversal. What are the differences?
- Projecting the attributes of a record type is now handled explicitly by the case for `Record Type`. We could also hand the *entire* `astObject.settings` `["attributes"]` array value over to the `Projection` component function, and let it decide how to handle multivalued properties. Change the code accordingly, and consider the following questions:
  - Do you feel the resulting code is more readable?
  - If so, is that just because it looks more like listing 3.9?
  - Do you think we'll lose some flexibility by handling arrays generically?

4.2.2 *Projecting attributes*

Let's take the hint in figure 4.7 and implement the projection of individual attributes. As before, let's start with what the HTML for the first attribute would look like:

Make sure the keyword text "is a" is separated both from the attribute's name on the left and the attribute's type on the right, using the whitespace CSS class ws-both.

```
<div className="attribute">
    <span className="keyword ws-right">the</span>
    <span className="value">rental period</span>
    <span className="keyword ws-both">is a</span>
    <span className="value enum-like">date range</span>
</div>
```

Style the attribute's type appropriately using both the "value" and "enum-like" CSS classes.

I styled the bits that we can derive from the AST object for this attribute in bold.

We now need to define the new `attribute` and `enum-like` CSS classes and add these definitions to src/frontend/styling.css:

```
div.attribute {
    margin-left: 1em;
}

span.enum-like {
    font-style: italic;
}
```

Let's add the following case to the switch statement in the Projection component function:

```
case "Data Attribute": return <div className="attribute">
    <span className="keyword ws-right">the</span>
    <span className="value">{astObject.settings["name"]}</span>
    <span className="keyword ws-both">is a</span>
    <span className="value enum-like ws-right">
        {astObject.settings["type"]}</span>
</div>
```

I took the liberty of replacing the derivable bits with JSX expressions that perform the derivations, which are rather straightforward. Those are shown in bold for your convenience.

> **NOTE**   I tend to put the cases of the switch statement in alphabetical order of their labels—in our case, these are the concepts' labels. This is a matter of personal preference, but I find it a convenient way of organizing the cases that keeps the code searchable and stable.

Next, we have to take care of the optional initial value, whose value can be accessed as astObject.settings["initial value"]. Section B.3.5 explains a common React code pattern for rendering HTML conditionally. Let's use this pattern in the completely new case for Data Attribute:

Use the React code pattern to only project the initial value when it's present.

```
case "Data Attribute": return <div className="attribute">
    <span className="keyword ws-right">the</span>
    <span className="value">{astObject.settings["name"]}</span>
    <span className="keyword ws-both">is a</span>
    <span className="value enum-like ws-right">
        {astObject.settings["type"]}</span>
    {astObject.settings["initial value"] &&
        <div>
            <span className="keyword ws-right">
                initially</span>
            <Projection
                astObject={astObject.settings["initial value"]} />
        </div>
    }
</div>
```

Wrap the actual projection in a <div> element, because we must return one element from this expression.

Call to Projection to project the initial value

Project the keyword for the initial value part of an attribute.

This yields the result shown in figure 4.8.

Let's project the correct indefinite article first: a type whose name starts with a vowel should be preceded by "an," while all other type names should be preceded by "a." We'll put this in a separate function:

```
const indefiniteArticleFor = (nextWord) => "a"
    + (nextWord.toLowerCase().match(/^[aeiou]/) ? "n" : "")
```

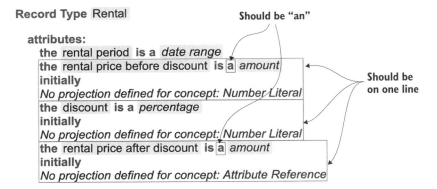

Figure 4.8   The browser after implementing the projection of attributes, with some problems indicated

This function uses the regular expression /^[aeiou]/ to determine whether the next word starts with any of the five vowels in English and adds an "n" to the "a" if that's the case. To make this work when the next word happens to start with an uppercase character, we first lowercase nextWord before matching it against the regular expression.

We can now adjust the third <span> element in the case for Data Attribute to use that function:

```
<span className="keyword ws-both">is
   ⇒ {indefiniteArticleFor(astObject.settings["type"])}</span>
```

The problem with the attributes having an initial value spanning three lines instead of one is caused by us having to use a wrapping <div> element for both the optional initial value part of an attribute's projection and the hint produced for an unhandled concept. By default, before any CSS shenanigans, a <div> element is rendered by the browser on a "new line," meaning below the previous content and on the left side of its containing box. We can fix this problem by setting the CSS display property to inline-block on the wrapping <div> elements.

We'll introduce a proper CSS definition for that, and add it to src/frontend/styling.css:

```
div.inline {
    display: inline-block;
}
```

Then we can reference the "inline" CSS class on those elements:

```
...
{astObject.settings["initial value"] &&
    <div className="inline">
```

```
            <span className="keyword ws-right">initially</span>
            <Projection astObject={astObject.settings["initial value"]} />
        </div>
    }
    ...
    default: return <div className="inline">
    ...
```

The result of these manipulations is shown in figure 4.9.

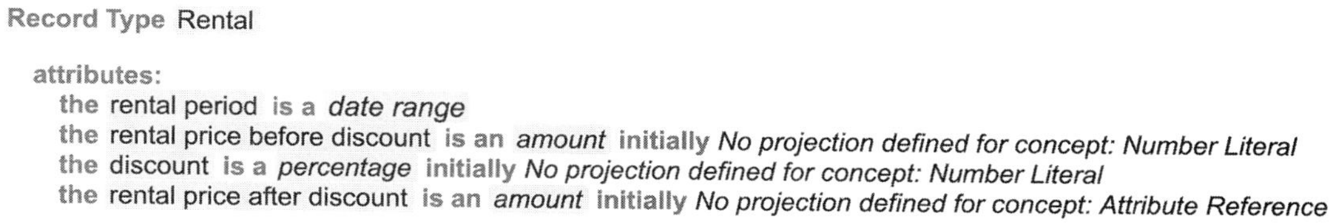

Record Type Rental

attributes:
  the rental period is a *date range*
  the rental price before discount is an *amount* initially *No projection defined for concept: Number Literal*
  the discount is a *percentage* initially *No projection defined for concept: Number Literal*
  the rental price after discount is an *amount* initially *No projection defined for concept: Attribute Reference*

Figure 4.9   A screenshot of the browser after implementing the projection of attributes, after fixing the problems

Apart from the missing projections of initial values, I have another gripe with this code. I find it a bit tedious to have to type `astObject.settings["<property name>"]` everywhere. To remedy that, I'd like to assign `astObject.settings` to a local constant named `settings` via object destructuring:

```
const { settings } = value
```

If we put this statement directly after the test for whether `value` is an AST object, we can access properties' values on the AST object without needing to type `astObject.` every time. The resulting code for the projection's implementation is as follows.

Listing 4.5   The `Projection` component function as it currently is

```
export const Projection = ({ astObject }) => {
    if (isAstObject(astObject)) {
        const { settings } = astObject
        // (cases are in alphabetical order of concept labels:)
        switch (astObject.concept) {

            case "Data Attribute": return <div className="attribute">
                <span className="keyword ws-right">the</span>
                <span className="value">{settings["name"]}</span>
                <span className="keyword ws-both">is
                    ⇨ {indefiniteArticleFor(settings["type"])}</span>
                <span className="value enum-like ws-right">
                    ⇨ {settings["type"]}</span>
                {settings["initial value"] &&
                    <div className="inline">
                        <span className="keyword ws-right">initially</span>
                        <Projection astObject={settings["initial value"]} />
```

```
                            </div>
                        }
                    </div>

                    case "Record Type": return <div>
                        <div>
                            <span className="keyword ws-right">Record Type</span>
                            <span className="value">{settings["name"]}</span>
                        </div>
                        <div className="section">
                            <div><span className="keyword">attributes:</span></div>
                            {settings["attributes"].map((attribute, index) =>
                                <Projection astObject={attribute} key={index} />
                            )}
                        </div>
                    </div>

                    default: return <div className="inline">
                        <em>{"No projection defined for concept: "
                            ➥ + astObject.concept}</em>
                    </div>
                }
            }

            return <em>{"No projection defined for value: " + astObject}</em>
        }
```

4.2.3   *Projecting the initial values*

Let's implement the projection of the two remaining, unhandled concepts: Number (on the second and third attributes), and Attribute Reference (on the fourth, last attribute). The easier one of the two is Attribute Reference. The HTML for it looks like this:

```
<div className="inline">
    <span className="keyword ws-right">the</span>
    <span className="reference">rental price before discount</span>
</div>
```

As usual, I highlighted the bit of text that we ought to derive from the Attribute Reference instance. We saw in chapter 2 that the value of an attribute property of an Attribute Reference instance is a reference to a Data Attribute instance. We can gain access to the name of the targeted AST object inside the projection code for Attribute Reference as follows:

```
settings["attribute"].ref.settings["name"]
```

Let's also add a definition for the "reference" CSS class in src/frontend/styling.css:

```
span.reference {
    font-style: italic;
```

```
    color: blue;
    text-decoration: underline;
}
```

Let's add the corresponding case to the `Projection` component function:

```
case "Attribute Reference": return <div className="inline">
    <span className="keyword ws-right">the</span>
    <span className="reference">
        {settings["attribute"].ref.settings["name"]}</span>
</div>
```

Projecting a `Number` seems like it should be easy enough, if it weren't for the presence of that pesky `$` prefix for the `amount` type value, and the `%` postfix for a `percentage` type value. Without those, the implementation would simply be as follows:

```
case "Number": return <div className="inline">
    <span className="value">{settings["value"]}</span>
</div>
```

The big question here is how to determine whether a value is supposed to be an amount, a percentage, or something else. Figure 4.10 will help to explain how we can do that.

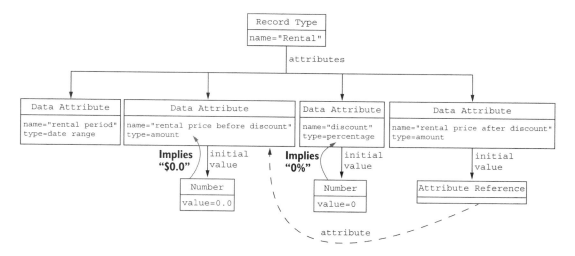

Figure 4.10   **Traversing up the example AST to determine how to present `Number` objects**

From one of the `Number` objects, we just have to go up one level of the tree to get to an attribute's AST object, where we can easily read off the type. The problem is that we currently have no way of traversing back over the `initial value` containment relation to the `Number` object's parent. The simplest way to work around that is to pass the parent as an extra argument to the `Projection` component function. Let's change the declaration of, and calls to, the `Projection` component function first. (I've added some extra indentation in the following code to aid with readability.)

```
...
export const Projection = ({ astObject, parent }) => {        ⟵  Change the declaration
...                                                               of Projection to add a
<Projection                                                       parent argument.
    astObject={settings["initial value"]}
    parent={astObject}                    ⟵  Inside the case for Data
/>                                            Attribute, specify the
...                                           parent argument.
<Projection
    astObject={attribute}
    parent={astObject}          ⟵  Inside the case for
    key={index}                     Record Type, specify
/>                                  the parent argument.
...
```

We won't change the initial call to `Projection` in the first argument to the `render` function. This will pass an empty value for `parent`, which is something we will need to check for.

To determine the type for a `Number` object, we first check whether the value of `parent` is a `Data Attribute`. We can determine that from the value of that attribute's `type` property: `parent.settings["type"]`. We can now determine the attribute's type as follows:

```
const type = parent && parent.concept === "Data Attribute"
    ⮕ && parent.settings["type"]
```

This code relies on the handy shortcut `&&` operator again:

1 We check whether `parent` is "something" before proceeding. If it is "something," it can only be an AST object. If it's nothing, we're apparently dealing with the root of the AST.

2 We check whether the `parent` AST object happens to be an attribute before proceeding.

3 Provided the evaluation of the assigned expression hasn't yet returned a falsy value, we return the (presumably truthy) value of its `type` property.

We can now expect the contents of `type` to be the name of the type of the attribute. (We won't explicitly handle the unexpected case where it's a falsy, and potentially non-stringy, value.) Armed with that knowledge, we can conditionally add `<span>` elements for the `$` prefix or a `%` postfix:

```
case "Number": {
    const type = parent && parent.concept === "Data Attribute"
        ⮕ && parent.settings["type"]
```

```
      return <div className="inline">
          {type === "amount" && <span className="keyword">$</span>}
          <span className="value">{settings["value"]}</span>
          {type === "percentage"
              ➥ && <span className="keyword">%</span>}
      </div>
}
```

With that, we've reconstructed figure 4.3 from the example AST.

For the sake of this overview, I'll reproduce the entire contents of src/frontend/ index.jsx, src/frontend/projection.jsx and src/frontend/styling.css in the following listings.

Listing 4.6   Final version of src/frontend/index.jsx

```
import React from "react"
import { createRoot } from "react-dom/client"

require("./styling.css")

import rental from "../ch03/rental-AST"

import { Projection } from "./projection"

createRoot(document.getElementById("root"))
    .render(
        <Projection
            astObject={rental}
        />
    )
```

Because of its length, I've split up the final code of src/frontend/projection.jsx into two listings: first the "outside" part of the code, and then the "inner" part consisting of cases of the switch statement corresponding to the concepts.

Listing 4.7   Final version of src/frontend/projection.jsx—the "outside" part

```
import React from "react"

import { isAstObject } from "../common/ast"


const indefiniteArticleFor = (nextWord) => "a"
    ➥ + (nextWord.toLowerCase().match(/^[aeiou]/) ? "n" : "")


export const Projection = ({ astObject, parent }) => {
    if (isAstObject(astObject)) {
        const { settings } = astObject
        // (cases are in alphabetical order of concept labels:)
        switch (astObject.concept) {

            // ...cases corresponding to concepts...        ⟵  The cases corresponding
                                                                to concepts are in
                                                                listing 4.8.
```

```
            default: return <div className="inline">
                <em>{"No projection defined for concept: "
                    ➥ + astObject.concept}</em>
            </div>
        }
    }

    return <em>{"No projection defined for value: " + astObject}</em>
}
```

```
case "Attribute Reference": return <div className="inline">
    <span className="keyword ws-right">the</span>
    <span className="reference">
        ➥ {settings["attribute"].ref.settings["name"]}</span>
</div>

case "Data Attribute": return <div className="attribute">
    <span className="keyword ws-right">the</span>
    <span className="value">{settings["name"]}</span>
    <span className="keyword ws-both">is
        ➥ {indefiniteArticleFor(settings["type"])}</span>
    <span className="value enum-like ws-right">
        ➥ {settings["type"]}</span>
    {settings["initial value"] &&
        <div className="inline">
            <span className="keyword ws-right">initially</span>
            <Projection
                astObject={settings["initial value"]}
                parent={astObject}
            />
        </div>
    }
</div>

case "Number": {
    const type = parent
        ➥ && parent.concept === "Data Attribute"
        ➥ && parent.settings["type"]
    return <div className="inline">
        {type === "amount" &&
            ➥ <span className="keyword">$</span>}
        <span className="value">{settings["value"]}</span>
        {type === "percentage" &&
            ➥ <span className="keyword">%</span>}
    </div>
}

case "Record Type": return <div>
    <div>
        <span className="keyword ws-right">Record Type</span>
        <span className="value">{settings["name"]}</span>
    </div>
```

```
    <div className="section">
        <div><span className="keyword">attributes:</span></div>
        {settings["attributes"].map((attribute, index) =>
            <Projection
                astObject={attribute}
                parent={astObject}
                key={index}
            />
        )}
    </div>
</div>
```

Listing 4.9   Final version of src/frontend/styling.css

```
body {
    font-family: Arial, Helvetica, sans-serif;
    font-size: 24pt;
}

span.keyword {
    font-weight: bolder;
    color: rgb(100, 100, 100);
}

.ws-right {
    margin-right: 0.5rem;
}

.ws-left {
    margin-left: 0.5rem;
}

.ws-both {
    margin-right: 0.5rem;
    margin-left: 0.5rem;
}

span.value {
    padding-left: 0.15em;
    padding-right: 0.15em;
    border-radius: 5px;
    background-color: rgb(228, 228, 228);
}

div.section {
    margin-top: 1em;
    margin-left: 1em;
}

div.attribute {
    margin-left: 1em;
}
```

```
span.enum-like {
    font-style: italic;
}

div.inline {
    display: inline-block;
}

span.reference {
    font-style: italic;
    color: blue;
    text-decoration: underline;
}
```

In this chapter, you learned how to project an in-memory AST to a visualization in HTML. In the next chapter, we're going to expand the projection to support *editing*.

Exercise 4.2

If you're familiar with web frontend development, especially using React, you might consider the preceding approach—using a polymorphic function—weird. Normally—insofar as anything is "normal" about web development—you'd create separate components for each individual concept. A `<RecordType>` component would project `Record Type` AST objects, while a `<DataAttribute>` component would project attribute AST objects, etc. In other words, the organization of the projection's implementation code would be *strongly coupled* to the DSL's structure. The separate components would closely match the DSL's structure on a concept level.

Try reimplementing the projection in this way, and ponder the following questions:

- Do you feel the code is clearer, more readable, or more maintainable this way?
- Suppose you wanted to reuse the projection of concepts like `Number` and `Attribute Reference` elsewhere. What would you need to do to make that possible?
- Suppose you wanted to provide the same level of guidance to the developer implementing the projection as the iterative approach in combination with a polymorphic function does. What would you need to do to make that possible?

This is an experiment. You can discard the resulting code.

Summary

- A *projection* projects an (encoded) AST as DSL content in a concrete syntax. A projection can be implemented as a function that produces an HTML DOM by using React and the JSX syntax.
- A projection function is typically a *polymorphic* function. The polymorphism can be used to implement the projection function as a single stateless React component.

- *Templating* is a technique for iteratively implementing a projection.
  - It starts from a static HTML mockup, which is the projection of a piece of example DSL content. Specific pieces of information in the HTML mockup that can be derived are gradually replaced with suitable JSX expressions that are parameterized by an AST's content. This is typically organized in a concept-by-concept fashion.
  - A generic fallback case will alert the software developer of the Domain IDE to concepts or values for which no projection has been implemented.

Editing values in the projection

This chapter covers

- Changing values in existing DSL content
- Introducing *edit state* in React component functions to implement editability

In chapter 4, we implemented a projection that visualizes an AST as projected DSL content in the DSL's notation. That AST isn't going to produce itself, though: we'll have to extend the Domain IDE so that domain experts can create and change ASTs. To that end, we're going to turn the projection from chapter 4 into a true *editor* over the course of this chapter. We're going to look at how the projection's current implementation projects each piece of data in the AST and decide how to make that editable piece by piece.

In chapter 6, we'll see how to add and delete whole AST objects. In the current chapter, we'll first figure out how to make the individual values of properties' settings in the AST editable. There are a few different kinds of such property values:

- Free-format textual values, such as the names of record types or their attributes
- Number values, such as the initial value of an attribute
- Values from a fixed set, such as the type of an attribute

- Reference values, such as which attribute is referenced from an `Attribute Reference` AST object

We're going to rely in particular on section B.4 in appendix B. It explains how we'll use the MobX state management library to be able to use the idea of *Transparent Functional Reactive Programming* (TFRP) to make the projection function *reactive*.

Figure 5.1 shows what property values can be encountered in a record type and what their kinds are. We're going to make these property values editable.

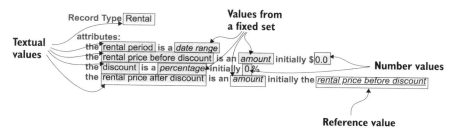

Figure 5.1   A catalog of the kinds of property values encountered in a record type

Figure 5.2 shows how the values in figure 5.1 and editing them relate to the AST. The lower part of this image gives a preview of what editing the values will look like. Textual and number values are editable through a regular input box. Fixed set and reference values are editable through a drop-down menu.

To make all of this work, we'll have to add various bits of new machinery. These mechanisms will be reusable in implementing an editor for *any* DSL.

We'll continue coding with (the latest versions of) the src/common/ast.js, src/frontend/index.html, src/frontend/index.jsx, src/frontend/projection.jsx, and src/frontend/styling.css files from chapter 4. We'll adapt and expand these to edit the kinds of property values listed above. We'll also be using the MobX framework to make the projection *transparently reactive*, keeping its implementation clean and tidy. To that end, if you aren't already familiar with MobX, please review section B.4, which explains what you'll need to know for this chapter.

5.1   *Changing names*

Let's make textual values editable, so we can change the name of a record type, or one of its attributes. Until now, we've projected such names using the following piece of JSX code:

```
<span className="value">{astObject.settings["name"]}</span>
```

Because we'll have to expand this code quite a bit, we'll start by refactoring it into a separate React component function:

```
const TextValue = ({ value }) => <span className="value">{value}</span>
```

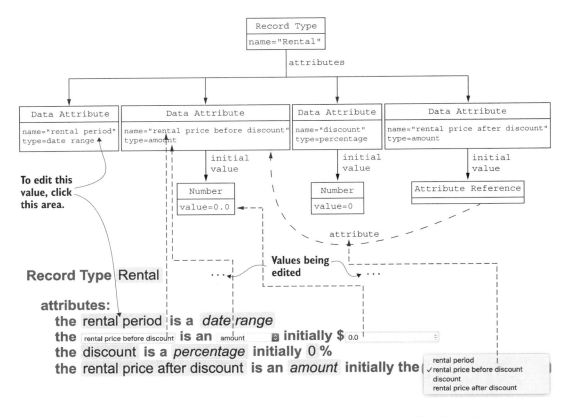

Figure 5.2   Editing capabilities at the value level that we're going to extend the DSL editor with

The first piece of JSX code can then be rewritten as follows:

```
<TextValue value={astObject.settings["name"]} />
```

Let's put this `TextValue` value component in a separate file, src/frontend/value-components.jsx, as follows.

Listing 5.1   The `TextValue` React component function after refactoring

```
import React from "react"          ⟵  Import React's definition        Define an exported React
                                       for HTML tags.                   component function
export const TextValue = ({ value }) =>    ⟵                           using closure and
    <span className="value">{value}</span>                             destructuring syntax.
```

We now have a React component that we can pass a string value into, and which then gets projected as a textual value. To use this exported React component, we have to import it into src/frontend/projection.jsx:

```
import { TextValue } from "./value-components"
```

We'll put this code before the `Projection` function so we can use it there. Now we'll replace the two occurrences of

```
<span className="value">{settings["name"]}</span>
```

inside the `Projection` function with the following:

```
<TextValue value={settings["name"]} />
```

There's also a line that projects the value of a number object:

```
<span className="value">{settings["value"]}</span>
```

For the moment, we'll leave that line alone, but we'll come back to it later in this chapter.

5.1.1 Starting the editing

The grey background of name values is meant to distinguish those values from other non-editable DSL content (like keywords), while still looking like part of the running text. Let's allow the domain expert to click anywhere on the grey area to start editing.

To do that, we'll need to put an *event handler* that handles mouse click events on the `<span>` element. We'll do that by adding an attribute called `onClick` to the `<span>` element. Its value is a function that receives an *event object*: an object that contains information about the event that was fired as a result of the domain expert's actions:

```
export const TextValue = ({ value }) =>
    <span className="value"
        onClick={(_) => {
            alert(
                `Editing of text value "${value}" started!`)
        }}
    >{value}</span>
```

Put a mouse click event handler on the `<span>` element through the onClick attribute.

Use the reviled alert function to annoy yourself with a pop-up box indicating that you've clicked a name value area on the screen.

I use plenty of "unnecessary" whitespace and tend to break to a new line early: that makes the code more readable and easier to expand.

Exercise 5.1

Make the required changes to the code in src/frontend/projection.jsx yourself, run it, and try it out.

Remember that you run the Parcel web bundler (see section B.2) as follows from command line:

```
$ npx parcel src/frontend/index.html
```

This will start serving the bundled and hot-reloading implementation of the projection on http://localhost:1234.

5.1.2   *Using edit state*

We should allow the domain expert to edit the textual value by putting that value in *edit mode* as easily as possible. The fact that a particular textual value is being edited should not change the AST, so we have to store that information somewhere outside the AST. Such data is *edit state* that keeps track of whether the domain expert is currently editing a particular value found in the AST. It also contains the original value while it's being edited, before the new, changed value is written back into the AST.

We're going to introduce edit state for a textual value, in the form of a plain JavaScript object with (for the moment) two key-value pairs:

```
{
    value: "...",
    inEdit: false
}
```

The textual value that's being edited, initially copied from the AST and to be written back to the AST again

A Boolean value indicating whether the value is being edited

This edit state object holds all the state necessary to keep track of the editing of a particular textual value. Changing the `inEdit` value to `true` should put the `TextValue` component into edit mode, once we've finished changing the component's code.

We're now going to change the `TextValue` component function to use and manipulate this edit state object:

```
export const TextValue = ({ editState }) =>
    <span className="value"
        onClick={(_) => {
            editState.inEdit = true
        }}
    >{editState.value}</span>
```

Replace the call to alert(...) with an assignment setting the inEdit property of the edit state object to true.

Get the value from the edit state object.

Now we'll change the calls to `TextValue`:

```
<TextValue editState={{ value: settings["name"], inEdit: false }} />
```

Note the double pair of curly braces in the preceding code: the outer pair is for delimiting the attribute, and the inner pair is for object construction.

Clicking any name value area still has no effect, because we haven't done anything with the value of `inEdit` yet. Let's change that:

Produce a projection depending on the value of editState.inEdit.

```
export const TextValue = ({ editState }) =>
    editState.inEdit
        ? <input type="text"
            defaultValue={editState.value}
            autoFocus={true}
        />
        : <span className="value"
            onClick={(_) => {
```

Produce an HTML <input> text input box when in edit mode.

This is the React way of stating what the initial value of the input box should be.

Specify that the input box must receive focus as soon as it is created.

Produce the same <span> element as before, when in the default, view-only mode.

```
            editState.inEdit = true
        }}
    >{editState.value}</span>
```

The preceding code uses JavaScript's *ternary operator* with the following syntax: `<condition> ? <true-branch> : <false-branch>`.

NOTE   In the preceding code, the spelling is `autoFocus`, instead of `autofocus` with a lowercase "f" as we'd expect from HTML. React takes care of "respelling" the attribute when mapping to HTML.

Exercise 5.2

Apply the preceding code changes and test the result. What happens when you click on a name value? Did you expect that result? Can you explain why?

Figure 5.3 visualizes what happens when the `Projection` function is called with an AST node containing a property with a textual value. It pays special attention to the roles of the edit state object and the `TextValue` component.

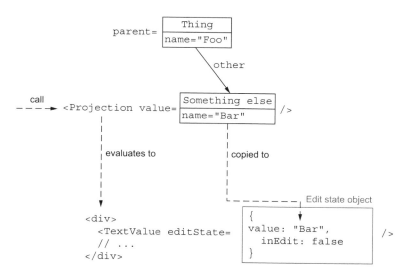

Figure 5.3   Visualization of a call to `Projection` creating an edit state object, and calling `TextValue` with it

In this figure, we're calling `Projection` with a `Something else` named `Bar` for the `value` attribute. We also pass `Bar`'s parent `Thing`, named `Foo` via the `parent` attribute to comply with the signature of the `Projection` function. The call to `Projection` produces an HTML DOM using JSX syntax. Part of that HTML DOM is the result of calling our new `TextValue` component with an edit state object. The `value` property of that edit state object is initially assigned the value `Bar`, which is the value of the `name` property on the `Something else` object.

Edit state objects are constructed *during* the projection of the AST, but they are nevertheless part of the state. When the `Projection` function is called for an AST object, exactly one edit state object is constructed for every setting on that AST object.

5.1.3   *A reactive architecture for projectional editors*

Figure 5.4 recaps what we've done since the beginning of chapter 3. We made a React component function, `Projection`, that projects an AST to an HTML DOM. This HTML DOM is then rendered by the browser: this is our projected DSL content. When the domain expert does something like clicking a certain part of that projection with the mouse, or pressing a key, an event is fired. This event is subsequently handled by an event handler. Such an event handler typically inspects the event to decide whether further action needs to be taken. A typical action would be to modify the AST.

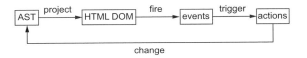

Figure 5.4   **A reactive architecture for projectional editors (before introducing edit state)**

This cycle should be restarted automatically after modifying the AST. This type of infinite loop is called *reactiveness*: the projection function automatically *reacts* to (changes to) the AST.

Unfortunately, the `Projection` React component function isn't reactive out of the box. As announced earlier, we're going to use MobX to make `Projection` reactive with a minimum number of code changes. For an explanation of MobX (including how to add it to the codebase's dependencies), see section B.4.

In our case, "application state" not only means "the data in the AST" but also edit state. An updated architecture diagram is shown in figure 5.5.

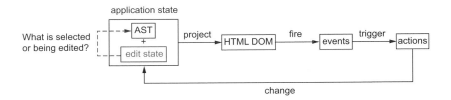

Figure 5.5   **A reactive architecture for projectional editors, with application data split up into AST and edit state**

In the next chapter, I'll introduce another form of edit state that tracks selection.

5.1.4 Reacting to change with MobX

Clicking a name value area currently has no effect, because we haven't made the projection function reactive yet. We'll mark our stateless React components as reactive, starting with the `TextValue` component:

```
import { observer } from "mobx-react"            ⟵┤ Import the observer function from
                                                    MobX's React-specific package.
export const TextValue = observer(({ editState }) =>     ⟵┐ Wrap the entire
    editState.inEdit                                        function body of
        ? // ...the rest of the code                        TextValue with
            ⟹ from the previous version of TextValue...     observer.
)
```

Setting `editState.inEdit` to `true` changes the application's state: MobX calls this an *action* that we'll have to mark explicitly. The function that acts as the mouse click event handler is marked as an action by wrapping it with the MobX `action` function:

```
import React from "react"
import { action } from "mobx"              ⟵┤ Import MobX's
import { observer } from "mobx-react"           action function.

export const TextValue = observer(({ editState }) =>
    editState.inEdit
        ? <input type="text"
            defaultValue={editState.value}
            autoFocus={true}
        />
        : <span className="value"              ┐ Wrap the mouse click
            onClick={action((_) => {           │ event handler with
                editState.inEdit = true        ┘ MobX's action function.
            })}
        >{editState.value}</span>
)
```

The preceding code showcases a ubiquitous pattern in reactive components. Most event handlers will look like the following:

```
on<SomeEvent>={action((event) => {
    // ...all code changing state goes here...
})}
```

Unfortunately, clicking a name value area *still* has no visible effect. That's because the `TextValue` component can only react to *observable* state, but we're not passing it such state yet. Before handing off the edit state object to `TextValue`, we have to make it observable. We do this using the MobX `observable` function. First, we import that function into src/frontend/projection.jsx, somewhere before the `Projection` function:

```
import { observable } from "mobx"
```

Then we change the calls to `TextValue` to wrap the edit state object with the `observable` function:

```
<TextValue editState={observable({ value: settings["name"],
    ➥ inEdit: false })
} />
```

Now, clicking on a name value area *finally* has an effect (figure 5.6).

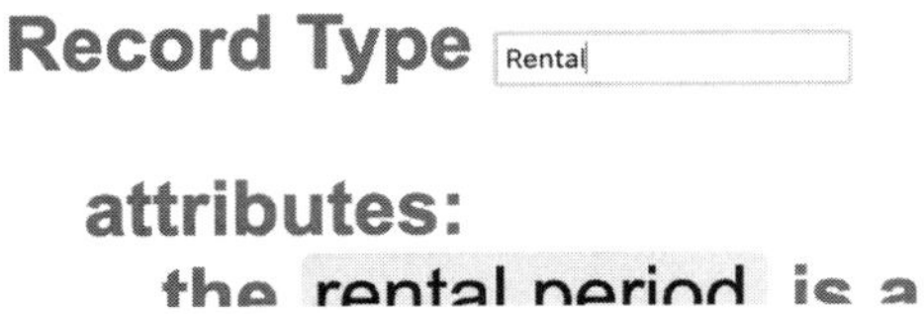

Record Type `Rental`

attributes:
the rental period is a

Figure 5.6   A name value area being edited using the `TextValue` component

This looks rather ugly, so let's add some styling to src/frontend/styling.css:

```
input {
    font-size: 12pt;
    border-radius: 5px;
    border: 3px solid yellow;
    background-color: lightyellow;
    padding-left: 5px;
}

input:focus {
    outline: none;
}
```

Avoids showing the blue border around the input box—see figure 5.6.

Depending on your particular sense of aesthetics, you may consider the result in figure 5.7 an improvement (see the e-book for the full-color version).

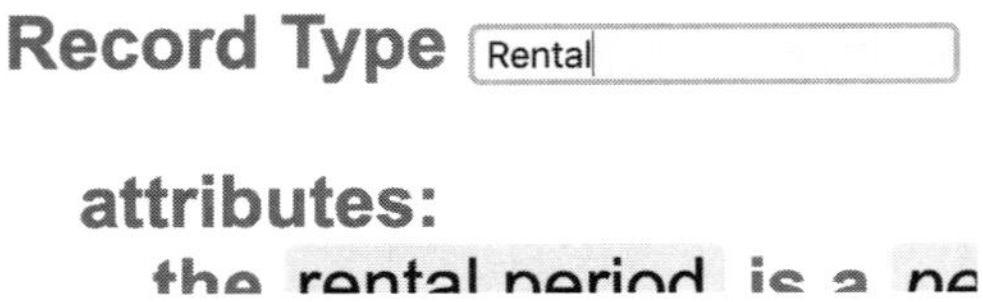

Record Type `Rental`

attributes:
the rental period is a ne

Figure 5.7   A name value area being edited using the `TextValue` component with some styling

---

Exercise 5.3

Apply the preceding code changes. Play around with the editor as it is now.

- What functionality is still missing?
- Is there any weird or unexpected behavior?
- What ways can you see to improve the user experience (UX)?

We'll get around to fixing a number of glaringly obvious issues shortly, so you don't need to immediately start fixing any problems you've found.

5.1.5   *Stopping the editing*

We can now start editing, but we can't stop it in any way. That also means we currently can start editing more than one name value area, as shown in figure 5.8.

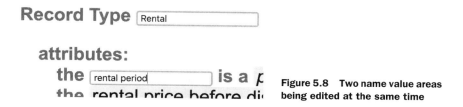

Figure 5.8   Two name value areas being edited at the same time

This behavior is confusing, so let's change it so that the editing of a value is stopped whenever the domain expert shifts focus away from the input box for that value. The domain expert shifts focus either by clicking outside the input box with the mouse or by pressing the Tab key. This ensures that they can edit at most one thing at a time. These user actions trigger "blur" events, which we can react to by adding the following event handler to the `<input>` element:

```
onBlur={action((_) => {
    editState.inEdit = false
})}
```

Next, we also want to stop editing whenever the domain expert presses the Enter or the Escape key. We do that by having the `<input>` element react to key-up events as follows:

```
onKeyUp={action((event) => {
    if (event.key === "Enter"
        || event.key === "Escape") {
        editState.inEdit = false
    }
})}
```

Receive an event object holding all information related to the event that was fired.

Check which key has been pressed by inspecting the value of the key property of the keyboard event object.

Exercise 5.4

Apply the preceding code changes, and test them to see whether editing now works the way you'd expect.

5.1.6 *Updating the AST*

The domain expert can now start and stop editing, but any change to the value in the
`<input>` element is ignored. After editing is stopped, the projection simply returns to
its previous state. That's no surprise: the `<input>` element changes the value of `edit-`
`State.value`, which is only a *copy* of the value of `settings["name"]`. We have to provide the `TextValue` component with a way to change the original `settings["name"]`
value as well.

We can do that by adding a `setValue` property to the edit state object. This property
holds a function that receives the new value as its first and only argument, and which
should update `settings["name"]`. Its corresponding key-value pair looks like this:

```
setValue: (newValue) => { settings["name"] = newValue }
```

The `setValue` property is not part of the application state: it's a function that modifies
state, but because it's not a mutable value, it's not state itself. It's simply convenient to
pass this function as a property of the edit state object.

After inserting some extra whitespace for readability, here is the call to `TextValue`:

```
<TextValue
    editState={observable({
        value: settings["name"],
        inEdit: false,
        setValue: (newValue) => { settings["name"] = newValue }
    })}
/>
```

We don't have to wrap the `setValue` function with `action` because `observable` does
that automatically for property values that are functions.

Next, we're going to call the `setValue` function inside the `TextValue` component.
We'll obtain the contents of the input box by evaluating the expression `event.target`
`.value` inside an event handler of an `<input>` element. For convenience and clarity,
we'll assign this value to a local constant named `newValue`. We'll use the following
code in various places in the `TextValue` component's code in a minute:

```
const newValue = event.target.value
editState.setValue(newValue)
```

We want to execute this code unless the domain expert presses the Escape key to cancel editing, in which case we'll keep the original value in the AST. In all other circum-
stances, the AST will be changed by calling the `setValue` function. This changes the
two event handlers inside the `TextValue` component function as follows:

```
onBlur={action((event) => {
    const newValue = event.target.value
    editState.setValue(newValue)          ◁─┐   Call the setValue function with the new value
    editState.inEdit = false                  │   when the domain expert shifts focus outside
})}                                           │   the input box or when they press the Tab key.
```

```
onKeyUp={action((event) => {
    if (event.key === "Enter") {
        const newValue = event.target.value
        editState.setValue(newValue)
        editState.inEdit = false
    }
    if (event.key === "Escape") {
        editState.inEdit = false
    }
})}
```

◁ **Call the setValue function with the new value when the domain expert presses the Enter key.**

◁ **Don't call the setValue function when the domain expert presses the Escape key.**

With these changes, names still won't update if editing is stopped without pressing the Escape key. That's because *the AST itself* is neither observable nor observed, yet. Let's fix the observability first. We can do this by wrapping `rental` with the `observable` function in the call to `Projection` inside the call to the React `render` function. We'll do this in src/frontend/index.jsx:

```
import { observable } from "mobx"

// ...other existing code...

createRoot(document.getElementById("root"))
    .render(
        <Projection
            astObject={observable(rental)}
        />
    )
```

◁ **Import MobX's wrapper function in this file as well.**

◁ **Wrap the Rental AST with the MobX function before passing it to the projection.**

The `rental` object is not just one object: it's really a whole tree. Luckily, the `observable` function makes any object passed to it not only observable, but even *deeply* observable. Essentially, whatever happens *inside* a deeply observable object is fully observable as well, and it's on display for interested parties that have subscribed as observers.

> **WARNING** An AST is almost always a graph, rather than a tree. Exercise 5.5 shows that this causes a subtle but serious problem, which we won't fix until chapter 7.

Now that we've made the whole `rental` AST observable in one fell swoop, we only have to mark the `Projection` component function as an observer:

```
import { observer } from "mobx-react"

// ...other existing code...

const Projection = observer(({ astObject, parent }) => {
    // ...all other existing code...
})
```

Now you should be able to edit the names of the record type and its attributes.

As you've seen, implementing editability for textual values—arguably one of the simpler kinds of values—takes quite some effort. Luckily, we can reuse the machinery we've developed so far to implement editability for numerous other kinds of values.

Exercise 5.5

What happens when you change the name of the second attribute, `rental price before discount`?

- Is the projection of the `Attribute Reference` instance, which is the initial value of the last attribute, `rental price after discount`, updated?
- Had you expected that behavior? Why (or why not)?

The answer to the last question in exercise 5.5 should have been: "No, I expected the projection of an attribute reference to reflect the change to (the name of) the referred attribute! After all, it's a *reference*, not a *copy*, right?" This is valid reasoning: the name of the referenced attribute is retrieved using the expression `settings["attribute"]` `.ref.settings["name"]`. The `settings["attribute"].ref` part means that we're dealing with an AST object that's the target of a reference relation. Once we have the target object, we can look up its name: `<target object> .settings["name"]`

It turns out there's a fundamental issue with this implementation, and it has everything to do with the nature of references. The problem is that we didn't tell MobX how to distinguish a JavaScript object reference that expresses a parent-child relation from one that expresses a reference relation. We'll fix this problem later, in chapter 7. For now, I'd like to focus on expanding our editing capabilities.

5.2   *Changing the value of a number object*

Changing a measly string value turned out to be quite a journey. Luckily, much of the machinery required is now in place, so things should speed up a bit now. Let's change the value of a number object, such as the initial value of the `rental price before discount` and `discount` attributes.

As we did for textual values, we're going to implement a new value component that, given a suitable edit state object, will provide an editable projection of a number value. This `NumberValue` component looks rather a lot like `TextValue`, so I'll give it to you in its entirety right away. It will go in src/frontend/value-components.jsx.

Listing 5.2   Initial code for the `NumberValue` component

```
const isNumber = (str) => !isNaN(str)        ◁──┐  Define a function that checks whether
    ⇨  && (str.trim().length > 0)                │  a given string represents a number.

export const NumberValue = observer(({ editState }) =>
    editState.inEdit
```

```
? <input type="number"
    defaultValue={editState.value}
    autoFocus={true}
    onBlur={action((event) => {
        const newValue = event.target.value
        if (isNumber(newValue)) {
            editState.setValue(newValue)
        }
        editState.inEdit = false
    })}
    onKeyUp={action((event) => {
        if (event.key === "Enter") {
            const newValue = event.target.value
            if (isNumber(newValue)) {
                editState.setValue(newValue)
                editState.inEdit = false
            }
        }
        if (event.key === "Escape") {
            editState.inEdit = false
        }
    })}
/>
: <span className="value"
    onClick={action((_) => {
        editState.inEdit = true
    })}
>{editState.value}</span>
)
```

> Give the <input> element the type "number".

> Validate the new value before manipulating the edit state.

> The AST is only updated with the new value if it's really a number. Otherwise, we let the domain expert continue to edit so they can fix the problem.

The preceding code validates the contents of the input box by checking whether it's a number, using the isNumber function. The AST is only updated with the new value—using the editState.setValue function—if it's a number.

Recognizing numbers in JavaScript

JavaScript often makes things more difficult than seems necessary. An example of this is determining whether something is a number. The built-in isNaN function is *almost* exactly what we need: !isNaN(str) returns true for strings with numbers and false for anything other than pure whitespace strings.

JavaScript is under the impression that a string purely consisting of whitespace is a number; e.g., isNaN(" ") yields false. We recognize such a string by removing all whitespace from the left and right of it using the built-in String.trim function, and checking that the remaining string isn't empty.

We can now replace the following code that appears inside the Number case in the Projection function,

```
<span className="value">{settings["value"]}</span>
```

with the following call to the `<NumberValue>` component.

Listing 5.3   Using the `NumberValue` component in the projection of a Number

```
<NumberValue
    editState={observable({
        value: settings["value"],
        inEdit: false,
        setValue: (newValue) => { settings["value"] = newValue }
    })}
/>
```

You'll also have to import the `NumberValue` component into src/frontend/projection.jsx.

Listing 5.4   Importing the `NumberValue` component into src/frontend/projection.jsx

```
import { NumberValue, TextValue } from "./value-components"
```

Exercise 5.6

Apply the code changes in listings 5.2 through 5.4.

Test the editing capability for number objects thoroughly, and ponder the following questions:

- Does the component work as expected, especially when you try to input things that are not numbers, like `123lizard`?
- What happens when you add leading or trailing zeroes (like `0001000`) and try to commit that value? Could you fix that behavior (easily)?
- Is that behavior consistent across different browsers?

The code for the `TextValue` and `NumberValue` components indeed is quite similar. Let's DRY (as in "Don't Repeat Yourself") them to avoid having duplicate code. The upshot is that we could add editing capabilities to both of these components by changing code in one place.

Figure 5.9 shows the code for both components next to each other, with diffing highlighting added. I adjusted some of the indentation in the code for `TextValue` to line up the similarities.

Apart from the names of the components, these are the main differences:

- The type of the `<input>` element.
- `NumberValue` validates the new value using the `isNumber` function before calling the `editState.setValue` function. `TextValue` doesn't do any validation: all input is OK.

```
 1                                                    1+ const isNumber = (str) ⇒ !isNaN(str) && (str.trim().length() > 0)
 2─ export const TextValue = observer(({ editState }) ⇒   2
 3       editState.inEdit                               3+ export const NumberValue = observer(({ editState }) ⇒
 4─         ? <input type="text"                        4       editState.inEdit
 5             defaultValue={editState.value}           5+         ? <input type="number"
 6             autoFocus={true}                         6             defaultValue={editState.value}
 7             onBlur={action((event) ⇒ {               7             autoFocus={true}
 8                 const newValue = event.target.value  8             onBlur={action((event) ⇒ {
 9                                                       9                 const newValue = event.target.value
                                                        10+                if (isNumber(newValue)) {
 9                 editState.setValue(newValue)         11                     editState.setValue(newValue)
                                                        12+                }
10                 editState.inEdit = false             13                 editState.inEdit = false
11             })}                                      14             })}
12             onKeyUp={action((event) ⇒ {             15             onKeyUp={action((event) ⇒ {
13                 if (event.key === "Enter") {         16                 if (event.key === "Enter") {
14                     const newValue = event.target.value  17                     const newValue = event.target.value
                                                        18+                    if (isNumber(newValue)) {
15                     editState.setValue(newValue)     19                         editState.setValue(newValue)
16                     editState.inEdit = false         20                         editState.inEdit = false
17─                                                     21+                    }
18                 }                                    22                 }
19                 if (event.key === "Escape") {        23                 if (event.key === "Escape") {
20                     editState.inEdit = false          24                     editState.inEdit = false
```

Figure 5.9   The `TextValue` (left) and `NumberValue` (right) components

Let's add a function to src/frontend/value-components.jsx that returns a value component function that's parameterized with the following data:

- `inputType`—A string with the type for the `<input>` element
- `isValid`—An optional validation function

Define a function that returns a
stateless React component function.

```
const inputValueComponent = ({ inputType, isValid }) =>
    observer(({ editState }) =>
        editState.inEdit
            ? <input
                type={inputType}
                // ...rest of the code...
    )
```

The code for the actual
component, returned as a result
of calling the HOC, starts here.

The rest of the code we'll extract
from existing components.

Set the type of the `<input>`
element to what's passed.

The `inputValueComponent` function implemented in the preceding code isn't a stateless React component function itself, but returns one. A function that returns a function is called a *higher-order component* (HOC). The `inputValueComponent` function takes an object with key-value pairs, `inputType` and `isValid`, which serve as the parameters. The `inputType` parameter is a string that is a valid value for the `type` attribute of an `<input>` HTML element. The `isValid` parameter is either falsy or a function that determines whether a given string is considered valid.

I like to use an object to pass the parameters, because it resembles how you pass attribute values to components, and it forces us to explicitly use the parameters' names. Once we're done implementing this function, we can change the definitions of the `TextValue` and `NumberValue` component functions to this:

```
export const TextValue = inputValueComponent({ inputType: "text" })

const isNumber = (str) => !isNaN(str) && (str.trim().length > 0)
export const NumberValue = inputValueComponent({ inputType: "number",
    ➥    isValid: isNumber })
```

Even though the `isNumber` function is referenced only once, I keep it separate because the name is an opportunity to clearly express what the function does.

Now, how can we handle the optional validation function? If no validation function is given, then every new value is OK. If a validation function is given, then the new value is deemed to be valid if the validation returns `true` when called with that new value. We can use the short-circuiting behavior of JavaScript's `||` logical OR operator to implement that behavior. If the left-hand side `<lhs>` is truthy, then `<lhs> || <rhs>` returns that truthy value; otherwise, it returns the right-hand side `<rhs>`. We can now check whether `newValue` passes the optional validation by evaluating the following expression:

```
!isValid || isValid(newValue)
```

With this trick up our sleeves, we can complete the rest of the code. Because these two components won't change anymore for the rest of the chapter, I'll list the current full contents of src/frontend/value-components.jsx after refactoring `TextValue` and `NumberValue` into a higher-order component.

Listing 5.5   **src/frontend/value-components.jsx after refactoring**

```
import React from "react"
import { action } from "mobx"
import { observer } from "mobx-react"

const inputValueComponent = ({ inputType, isValid }) =>
    observer((({ editState }) =>
        editState.inEdit
            ? <input
                type={inputType}
                defaultValue={editState.value}
                autoFocus={true}
                onBlur={action((event) => {
                    const newValue = event.target.value
                    if (!isValid || isValid(newValue)) {
                        editState.setValue(newValue)
                    }
                    editState.inEdit = false
                })}
                onKeyUp={action((event) => {
                    if (event.key === "Enter") {
                        const newValue = event.target.value
                        if (!isValid || isValid(newValue)) {
```

```
                                    editState.setValue(newValue)
                                    editState.inEdit = false
                                }
                            }
                            if (event.key === "Escape") {
                                editState.inEdit = false
                            }
                        })}
                    />
                    : <span className="value"
                        onClick={action((_) => {
                            editState.inEdit = true
                        })}
                        >{editState.value}</span>
            )
```

```
export const TextValue = inputValueComponent({ inputType: "text" })

const isNumber = (str) => !isNaN(str) && (str.trim().length > 0)
export const NumberValue = inputValueComponent({ inputType: "number",
    isValid: isNumber })
```

Let's return to src/frontend/projection.jsx. Another opportunity for DRY-ing is formed by the creation of the observable edit state objects as values of an editState attribute. They all look like this:

```
editState={observable({
    value: settings[<property name>],
    inEdit: false,
    setValue: (newValue) => { settings[<property name>] = newValue }
})}
```

Let's write a function that creates an observable edit state object for the property with a given name:

```
const editStateFor = (propertyName) => observable({
    value: settings[propertyName],
    inEdit: false,
    setValue: (newValue) => { settings[propertyName] = newValue }
})
```

We'll put this code right after the line saying const { settings } = value in the Projection function. Now we can change all calls to TextValue to this:

```
<TextValue editState={editStateFor("name")} />
```

Likewise for the NumberValue case:

```
<NumberValue editState={editStateFor("value")} />
```

That tidies up the current code of the `Projection` function a bit, and we can likely use the `editStateFor` function more often.

Exercise 5.7
Apply the preceding code changes, and check that they work.

TIP   DRY-ing frontend code as we've done here not only makes that code shorter and more maintainable. It also makes it easier to keep the UI consistent in behavior and styling.

5.3   *Choosing the type of an attribute*

Now that the editing of text and number values is done through nicely refactored code, let's make the types of attributes editable. We've seen three types so far: `amount`, `date range`, and `percentage`. Typically, such *data types* come from a fairly limited set. We should make choosing a type from this set as easy as possible for the domain expert.

Why not use a simple drop-down menu for this? The well-known `<select>` element is not the fanciest way to implement that, but it always works, and with a small amount of code. A simple drop-down menu that shows all the available possibilities makes it easy for domain experts to discover what they can do.

Let's add a separate component to src/frontend/value-components.jsx to choose from a list of options using a drop-down menu. This component has three required parameters:

- `editState`—The edit state object
- `className`—CSS class names to style the value shown when it's not being edited
- `options`—A list of strings with the available choices

Listing 5.6   The `DropDownValue` component in src/frontend/value-components.jsx

**Specify that the select box must
receive focus as soon as it's created.**

```
export const DropDownValue = observer((({ editState, className, options }) =>
    editState.inEdit
        ? <select
            autoFocus={true}
            value={editState.value}
            style={{ width: Math.max(
                ...options.map((option) => option.length))
                + "ch" }}
```

**Make sure that the select box
has a suitable display width
by computing the maximum
length of the option strings.**

**Specify the selected value. The
`<option>` element whose contents
match this string value is selected.**

```
                              onChange={action((event) => {
                                  editState.setValue(event.target.value)
                                  editState.inEdit = false
                              })}
                              onBlur={action((_) => {
                                  editState.inEdit = false
                              })}
                              onKeyUp={action((event) => {
                                  if (event.key === "Escape") {
                                      editState.inEdit = false
                                  }
                              })}
                              className={className}

                          >
                              {options.map((option, index) =>
                                  <option key={index}>{option}</option>
                              )}
                          </select>
                          : <span className={className}
                              onClick={action((_) => {
                                  editState.inEdit = true
                              })}
                          >{editState.value}</span>
        )
```

Annotations:

- **Stop editing when the domain expert shifts focus away from the select box.** → onBlur
- **A change event is fired when the option selection is changed. The option that's currently selected can be retrieved from the event object as event.target.value.** → onChange
- **Stop editing when the domain expert presses the Escape key.** → onKeyUp
- **Produce a list of <option> elements by mapping over the options list.** → {options.map(...)}
- **Produce an <option> element using the index variable as the value for the special React key attribute.** → <option key={index}>{option}</option>
- **Use the className parameter to style the value when it's not being edited.** → <span className={className}
- **Start editing when the domain expert clicks the value area.** → onClick

To calculate a suitable width for the select box, the expression `Math.max(...)` computes the length of the longest of the option strings. The subexpression `options .map((option) ? option.length)` computes an array containing the lengths of option strings. To determine the maximum of those lengths, we'd like to pass these lengths to the `Math.max` function that's built into JavaScript. This function takes an arbitrary number of number-valued arguments through its one *rest parameter*, but it doesn't take an *array* of numbers. (For details on JavaScript rest parameters, see the Mozilla documentation: https://developer.mozilla.org/en-US/docs/Web/JavaScript/Reference/Functions/rest_parameters.) We can get around that using the ... spread operator: `Math.max(...<array of lengths>)`—also see section B.1.9.

After calculating the maximum length, we append `ch`, which is the CSS unit that represents the width of a regular character in the current font. A value of `14ch` for the CSS `width` property means that "date range" (a string of length 10) should fit inside the select box. Because non-monospace fonts have varying character widths (with some characters being wider than `1ch`), there's no guarantee that the text will fit snugly.

To keep font sizes consistent, we have to add the following to src/frontend/styling.css:

```
select {
    font-size: 12pt;
}
```

In src/frontend/projection.jsx, we first have to import this new component, together with the previous two:

```
import { DropDownValue, NumberValue, TextValue }
    ➥ from "./value-components"
```

We now can rework the projection of an attribute's type,

```
<span className="value enum-like ws-right">{settings["type"]}</span>
```

to the following:

Pass the same class names as before.

Create an edit state object using the editStateFor function.

```
<DropDownValue
    className="value enum-like ws-right"       ◁────────
    editState={editStateFor("type")}           ◁────────
    options={[ "amount", "date range", "percentage" ]}   ◁──
/>
```

Pass the list of types as options (in alphabetical order).

Figure 5.10 shows the result of clicking the type value area once. We have to click once more to be able to select another type (figure 5.11).

Figure 5.10   The type value area projected by the `DropDownValue` component, after clicking it once

Figure 5.11   The type value area projected by the `DropDownValue` component, after clicking it twice

Exercise 5.8
When you change the type of the second or third attribute to another value, what happens with the projection of the number in the initial value of that attribute? In particular, what happens if you change the type to `date range`? Doesn't the result lack something, such as a `days` keyword?

Fix this shortcoming. Hint: This can be a one-line fix, but not inside the `Data Attribute` case in the `Projection` function.

Exercise 5.9 (optional)
It's entirely OK to feel unsatisfied with the way the drop-down menu looks. This book is not about UI styling, and I have to pick my battles. However, feel free to fix the `DropDownValue` component, or even to replace it with something that's more to your liking.

5.4 Choosing an attribute for a reference

The only kind of values that we're not able to change yet are references, so let's make references editable. In our case, that means being able to change the reference setting for the `attribute` property on an `Attribute Reference` object. There's one such object, which is the initial value of the `rental price after discount` attribute, and it points to the `rental price before discount` attribute.

We already have most of what we need, thanks to the other kinds of values we already can edit. In particular, we can reuse the `DropDownValue` component for a drop-down menu. The options in that drop-down menu should consist of all the attributes of the current containing record type.

This is a harder variant of the challenge we encountered in chapter 4, when we projected a number object defining the initial value of an attribute. For that, we needed to determine whether to show the number as `$0.0` or `25%` depending on the type of the attribute containing the number object. In that case, we knew we only had to travel over the `initial value` containment relation in the reverse direction, from the `Number` object back to the attribute object (see figure 5.12). From there, we could inspect the value of the `type` property of that attribute object.

We made traveling back possible by passing an additional `parent` attribute to the `Projection` function. The value of that `parent` attribute is the AST object that contains the AST object that's being projected. That's true anytime except when projecting the AST root: in that case, the `parent` value is undefined.

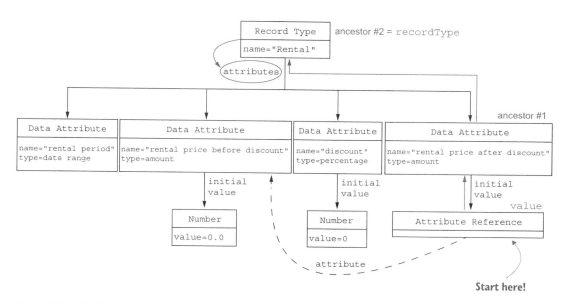

Figure 5.12 Finding all attributes in the record type by traversing up the example AST from the attribute reference

We're going to extend the `parent` mechanism so we can travel back up the AST over the chain of containment relations, as far as we need to go. We'll do that by not only passing the parent, but instead passing an array of *all* ancestors of the AST object currently being projected. To that end, we'll first alter the signature of the `Projection` function, replacing the identifier `parent` with `ancestors`:

```
const Projection = observer(({ astObject, ancestors }) => {
    // ...rest of the code...
})
```

Next, we'll switch our attention back to the `Attribute Reference` case of the `switch` statement. First, we'll change that case from a single `return` statement to a statement block:

```
case "Attribute Reference": {
    return ...
}
```

To find all attributes of the current record type from an `Attribute Reference` object, we'll first look up that record type. To do so, we simply find the AST object with concept label `Record Type` among the members of `ancestors`:

```
const recordType = ancestors.find((ancestor) =>
    ancestor.concept === "Record Type")
```

We'll put this line in the `Attribute Reference` case, before the `return` statement. We can find all attributes reachable from the current attribute reference as follows:

```
const attributes = recordType.settings["attributes"]
```

Put this line in between the `recordType` constant definition and the `return` statement.

To make this mechanism work, we have to alter all calls to the `Projection` function in src/frontend/index.jsx. Let's start with the one kicking things off, from the AST's root down:

```
createRoot(document.getElementById("root"))
    .render(
        <Projection
            astObject={observable(rental)}
            ancestors={[]}
        />
    )
```

Because the AST's root has no ancestors, we pass an empty array. Arguably, that's even better than implicitly passing an `undefined` value by not specifying a value for the `parent` attribute.

Next, we adapt the call to `Projection` for all attributes in the `Record Type` case by adding an `ancestors` attribute:

```
<Projection
    astObject={attribute}
    ancestors={[ astObject, ...ancestors ]}
    key={index}
/>
```

The value expression for the `ancestors` attribute uses the ... spread operator (explained in section B.1.9) as well, but now inside an array construction expression:

```
[ value0, ...[ value1, value2, value3 ], value4 ]
```

The preceding code evaluates to

```
[ value0, value1, value2, value3, value4 ]
```

The expression `[ astObject, ...ancestors ]` evaluates to a new array. This new array has `astObject` (the current AST object to project) as its first member. This is then followed by all the members of the array held in the `ancestors` attribute passed to the `Projection` function.

The resulting array is passed as the value of the `ancestors` attribute of the nested call to `Projection`. This means that the `ancestors` array is always in reverse order: the parent is the first member (with index 0), and the AST's root will be the last member. For our attribute reference, the value of `ancestors` would equal [`rentalPriceAfterDiscount-Attribute`, `rental`].

My preference for the reverse order is based on my experience that you usually don't need to travel far up the AST's containment hierarchy to find the information you need. This way, you don't have to iterate over the ancestors from back to front, which means clearer code. If you do need the AST's root, you know where to find it: in the array's last position, which is easy and fast to look up.

The call to `Projection` that projects the initial value inside the `Data Attribute` case should receive the same treatment:

```
<Projection
    astObject={settings["initial value"]}
    ancestors={[ astObject, ...ancestors ]}
/>
```

With this ancestors mechanism in place, we can start modifying the `Attribute Reference` case in the `Projection` function. The `DropDownValue` component's `options` attribute should be an array of strings, which are shown as the text of options in the drop-down menu, and simultaneously serve as IDs for the options. Let's use the names of the attributes for that:

```
options={attributes.map((attribute) => attribute.settings["name"])}
```

This does mean that we can't reuse the `editStateFor` function, as we did before. After all, passing `editStateFor("attribute")` to `DropDownValue` would result in that component breaking when it tries to use the `settings["attribute"]` reference object as a string value. We'll have to construct an edit state object in the following special way:

```
observable({
    value: settings["attribute"].ref.settings["name"],
    inEdit: false,
    setValue: (newValue) => {
        settings["attribute"].ref =
      attributes.find((attribute) =>
          attribute.settings["name"] === newValue)
    }
})
```

Identify the currently referred attribute by its name.

Look up the attribute in the current record type by the name passed as newValue, and set the ref property of the settings object to that.

The `Attribute Reference` case in the `Projection` function should now read as follows:

```
case "Attribute Reference": {
    const recordType = ancestors.find(
        (ancestor) => ancestor.concept === "Record Type")
    const attributes = recordType.settings["attributes"]
    return <div className="inline">
        <span className="keyword ws-right">the</span>
        <DropDownValue
            editState={observable({
                value: settings["attribute"].ref.settings["name"],
                inEdit: false,
                setValue: (newValue) => {
                    settings["attribute"].ref =
      attributes.find((attribute) =>
          attribute.settings["name"] === newValue)
                }
            })}
            className="reference"
            options={attributes.map(
                (attribute) => attribute.settings["name"])}
        />
    </div>
}
```

Clicking the attribute reference area triggers a drop-down menu with all the attributes of `Rental` as selectable options.

> ## Exercise 5.10
> Play around with editing the attribute reference in the fourth attribute, and consider the following questions:
>
> - Does it make sense to be able to refer to the attribute that contains the attribute reference? Would the universe spontaneously explode if you set the reference to point to the `rental price after discount` attribute? What could

be a good way to prevent this from happening? If you can think of a one-line fix, please implement it!

- Do *any* of the attributes other than `rental price before discount` make sense as values for that attribute reference? Why is (or isn't) that? Can you describe those reasons as code?

- How could you make clear to the domain experts why they can't choose a particular object for a reference? Would they prefer to not see nonsensical reference targets in the drop-down menu? Or would they prefer seeing them, but having them flagged as nonsensical in some way? Or would it be better to only warn them *after* they have selected a nonsensical target?

For completeness' sake, I'll list the full contents of src/frontend/index.jsx and src/frontend/projection.jsx here, with two small improvements.

Listing 5.7 src/frontend/index.jsx—final version in this chapter

```
import React from "react"
import { createRoot } from "react-dom/client"
import { observable } from "mobx"

require("./styling.css")

import rental from "../ch03/rental-AST"

import { Projection } from "./projection"

createRoot(document.getElementById("root"))
    .render(
        <Projection
            astObject={observable(rental)}
            ancestors={[]}
        />
    )
```

As before, I'll split up this chapter's final code of src/frontend/projection.jsx—this time into three listings (listings 5.8 to 5.10).

Listing 5.8 src/frontend/projection.jsx—the outside part

```
import React from "react"
import { observable } from "mobx"
import { observer } from "mobx-react"

import { isAstObject } from "../common/ast"
import { DropDownValue, NumberValue, TextValue } from "./value-components"


const indefiniteArticleFor = (nextWord) => "a"
    + (nextWord.toLowerCase().match(/^[aeiou]/) ? "n" : "")
```

```
export const Projection = observer((({ astObject, ancestors }) => {
    if (isAstObject(astObject)) {

        const { settings } = astObject
        const editStateFor = (propertyName) => observable({
            value: settings[propertyName],
            inEdit: false,
            setValue: (newValue) => { settings[propertyName] = newValue }
        })

        // (cases are in alphabetical order of concept labels:)
        switch (astObject.concept) {

            // ...cases corresponding to concepts...          ◁───┐  The cases corresponding
                                                                  │  to concepts are in
            default: return <div className="inline">             │  listings 5.9 and 5.10.
                <em>{"No projection defined for concept: "
                    ➥ + astObject.concept}</em>
            </div>
        }
    }

    return <em>{"No projection defined for value: " + astObject}</em>
})
```

Listing 5.9   src/frontend/projection.jsx—the first inside part

```
case "Attribute Reference": {
    const recordType = ancestors.find(
        ➥ (ancestor) => ancestor.concept === "Record Type")
    const attributes = recordType.settings["attributes"]
    return <div className="inline">
        <span className="keyword ws-right">the</span>
        <DropDownValue
            editState={observable({
                value:
                ➥ settings["attribute"].ref.settings["name"],
                inEdit: false,
                setValue: (newValue) => {
                    settings["attribute"].ref =
                    ➥ attributes.find(
                    ➥ (attribute) =>
                        ➥ attribute.settings["name"] === newValue)
                }
            })}
            className="reference"
            options={attributes.map((attribute) =>
                ➥ attribute.settings["name"])}
        />
    </div>
}

case "Data Attribute": return <div className="attribute">
    <span className="keyword ws-right">the</span>
```

```
<TextValue editState={editStateFor("name")} />
<span className="keyword ws-both">is
    ➥ {indefiniteArticleFor(settings["type"])}</span>
<DropDownValue
    className="value enum-like ws-right"
    editState={editStateFor("type")}
    options={[ "amount", "date range", "percentage" ]}
/>
{settings["initial value"] &&
    <div className="inline">
        <span className="keyword ws-right">initially</span>
        <Projection
            astObject={settings["initial value"]}
            ancestors={[ astObject, ...ancestors ]}
        />
    </div>
}
</div>
```

Listing 5.10   src/frontend/projection.jsx—the second inside part

```
case "Number": {
    const attribute = ancestors.find(
        ➥ (ancestor) => ancestor.concept === "Data Attribute")
    const type = attribute.settings["type"]
    return <div className="inline">
        {type === "amount"
            ➥ && <span className="keyword">$</span>}
        <NumberValue editState={editStateFor("value")} />
        {type === "date range"
            ➥ && <span className="keyword ws-left">
                ➥ days</span>}
        {type === "percentage"
            ➥ && <span className="keyword">%</span>}
    </div>
}

case "Record Type": return <div>
    <div>
        <span className="keyword ws-right">Record Type</span>
        <TextValue editState={editStateFor("name")} />
    </div>
    <div className="section">
        <div><span className="keyword">attributes:</span></div>
        {settings["attributes"].map((attribute, index) =>
            <Projection
                astObject={attribute}
                ancestors={[ astObject, ...ancestors ]}
                key={index}
            />
        )}
    </div>
</div>
```

Look up the current attribute explicitly, without relying on the number object being directly contained as the initial value of an attribute.

This is the one-line fix alluded to in exercise 5.8.

In this chapter, you learned how to make individual values of properties' settings in the AST editable. In the next chapter, we'll extend our editing reach to the object level, when we add new objects to the AST, select them, and delete them from the AST.

Summary

- Adding editing capabilities to the projection makes it a true *DSL editor*, which is the essential component of a Domain IDE. Particular editing capabilities include
  - Changing a value of a simple setting on an AST object. Such a value can be a textual value, a number value, or a value from a fixed set.
  - Changing the target of a setting that encodes a reference relation.
- To make the projection's code readable and maintainable, these editing capabilities are implemented as React component functions: *value components*. Each value component focuses on a value of a particular kind: text, number, or a fixed set.
- By using a *reactive* architecture based on *Transparent Functional Reactive Programming* (TFRP), the projection will automatically re-render when the AST is changed. This requires very few changes or additions to the code.
- *Edit state* is state that keeps track of whether the domain expert is editing something, and if so, what setting (for which property) on what AST object. It's encoded as an object that's constructed while running the projection, and it's passed to the value components. The value of the key-value pair on an edit state object with the `setValue` key is a function that's called by the value component with the new value for the setting that's being edited.
- The application state for the Domain IDE consists of the AST and the edit state objects. Figure 5.5 illustrates how TFRP is used to implement editing capabilities on top of the projection.
- In addition to an AST object to project, the projection function also receives a list of the ancestors of that AST object. This can be used to extract information from anywhere in the AST—not just from the AST object currently being projected—whenever that information is needed by the projection.

Editing objects in the projection

6

This chapter covers

- Adding new AST objects to the projection
- Selecting AST objects in the projection
- Deleting AST objects from the projection
- Projecting unset properties
- Capturing special keypresses

In chapter 5, you learned how to make property values in the AST editable. That's useful, but it's not enough for domain experts to have complete control over the AST. In this chapter, we'll extend the capabilities of the DSL editor to add new and delete existing AST objects, as outlined in figure 6.1.

We're going to use all of the mechanisms we implemented in chapter 5, and we'll need a couple of new mechanisms too. You'll probably need all of these to implement an editor for any DSL.

To identify which AST object should be deleted, we're going to implement a selection mechanism. We're also going to show how to deal with properties of newly created AST objects that don't have a value set yet. You'll also learn how to handle keyboard events and deal with event propagation. We'll continue with the code from the latest versions of the files under src from chapter 5.

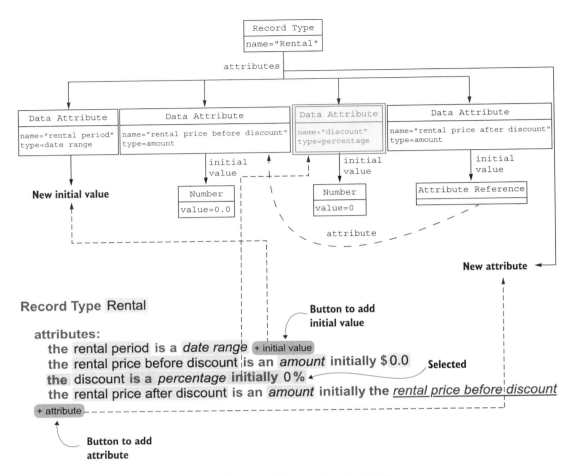

Figure 6.1   Extending the DSL editor's editing capabilities at the object level

6.1   *Adding new objects to the AST*

Let's enable a domain expert to add new AST objects to the example AST—our trusty `Rental` record type. There are two spots where we could add new objects (see figure 6.2):

1   Add a new attribute (of concept `Data Attribute`) to the attributes of a record type.
2   Add a new AST object as an initial value to an attribute that doesn't define one yet. There are currently two choices for the concept: `Attribute Reference` and `Number`. This means we'd also need some way to select which concept to add.

We'll add both of these capabilities.

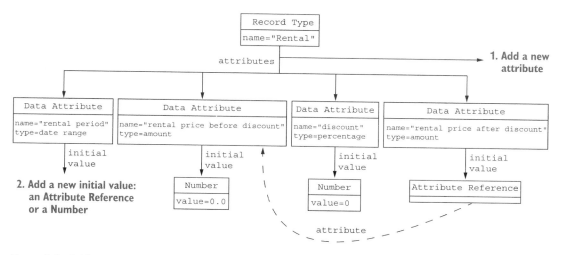

Figure 6.2 Adding new objects to the AST

6.1.1 Adding an attribute

Capturing all the details of a rental with only four attributes seems unlikely. Let's add the option to add a new attribute. For that, the domain expert will need to see a *call to action*: a visual cue inviting the domain expert to trigger some functionality. The simplest thing that will work is a button, so let's add one under the already existing attributes of the record type:

```
// (existing code:)
<div className="section">
    <div><span className="keyword">attributes:</span></div>
    {settings["attributes"].map((attribute, index) =>
        <Projection
            astObject{attribute}
            ancestors={[ astObject, ...ancestors ]}
            key={index}
        />
    )}
    // Add a button:
    <button
        className="add-new"
        tabIndex={-1}
    >+ attribute</button>
// (existing code again:)
</div>
```

We'll define the "add-new" CSS class on the button.

Add this attribute so the domain expert can't inadvertently tab to the button. This will be necessary unless you take the trouble of setting up correct tabbing for all projected DSL content.

This button text is probably as clear to most domain experts as longer text, such as "Add an Attribute."

Let's also style the `<button>` element a bit:

```
button.add-new {
    font-size: 18pt;
```

```
    border-radius: 10px;
    border: 0;
    background-color: rgb(49, 161, 49);
    cursor: pointer;
}
```

The result is shown in figure 6.3.

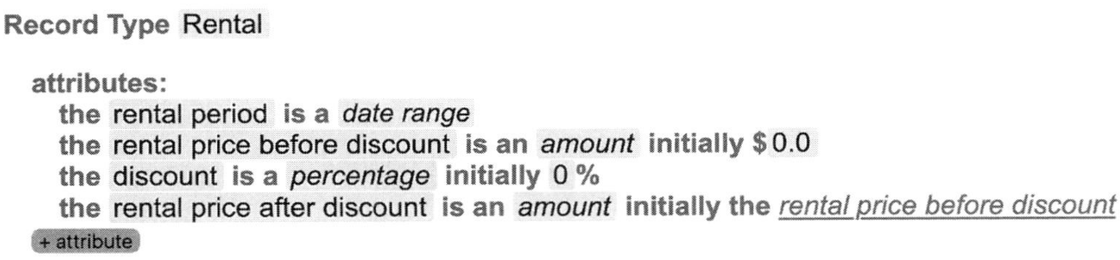

Record Type Rental

    attributes:
      the rental period **is a** *date range*
      the rental price before discount **is an** *amount* **initially** $ 0.0
      the discount **is a** *percentage* **initially** 0 %
      the rental price after discount **is an** *amount* **initially the** *rental price before discount*
    + attribute

Figure 6.3   The `Rental` record type with a button to add a new attribute

The button doesn't do anything yet, so let's make it clickable. As usual, we can do this by adding an attribute to the `<button>` element with a handler for a mouse click event.

Listing 6.1   Code for the mouse click event handler on the "+ attribute" button

```
onClick={action((_) => {            ◁——— Trigger an action when
    settings["attributes"].push({          the button is clicked.
        concept: "Data Attribute",  ◁——— Add a new AST object
        settings: {}  ◁                    to the attributes.
    })           Put a settings object
})}              on the new object.     Put the appropriate concept
                                        label on the new object.
```

Since any AST object passed to the projection is already deeply observable, any new AST object that's added to an existing AST object is automatically deeply observable as well. Because we're now using the MobX `action` function in src/frontend/projection.jsx (again), we have to import that function in this file as well. Make sure that the following line is somewhere at the top of src/frontend/projection.jsx:

```
import { action, observable } from "mobx"
```

Clicking the button now makes the app crash, showing an empty screen. The JavaScript console displays the error shown in figure 6.4.

    We didn't initialize a setting for the `name` property of the new attribute object, so the name value will be `undefined`. We then proceeded to call the `indefiniteArticle-For` function with that value, so its argument, `nextWord`, will be `undefined` as well. We

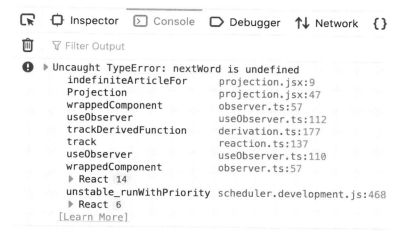

Figure 6.4 **The JavaScript console with a runtime error in the** `indefiniteArticleFor` **function**

can fix this by first testing whether `nextWord` is a string before we try to use string methods on it:

```
const indefiniteArticleFor = (nextWord) => "a"
    + ((typeof nextWord === "string"
        && nextWord.toLowerCase().match(/^[aeiou]/)) ? "n" : "")
```

As you can see in figure 6.5, the app doesn't crash anymore, but the name and type values are missing, and there's no visual indication showing the domain expert how to do something about that. We can improve on that by providing *placeholders* for the missing values. A placeholder is a piece of text that's shown when a value is empty, and it serves as a call to action to provide a value.

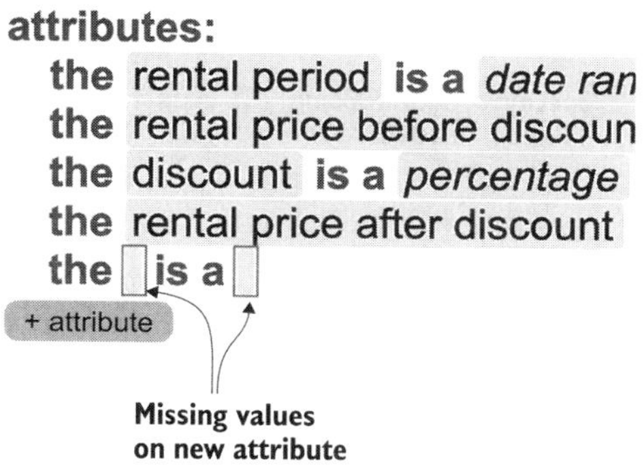

attributes:
    the rental period **is a** *date ran*
    the rental price before discoun
    the discount **is a** *percentage*
    the rental price after discount
    the ☐ **is a** ☐
+ attribute

Missing values
on new attribute

Figure 6.5 **The attributes of the** `Rental`
record type with a new attribute added,
without placeholders

A trick to speed up testing

After every code change you make, you have to manually click the "+ attribute" button to test the functioning of the app. We can emulate this mouse click by executing the statement in the event handler in listing 6.1 beforehand. Add the following code just before the `Projection` to do that:

```
rental.settings["attributes"].push({
    concept: "Data Attribute",
    settings: {}
})
```

Remember to remove this after you're done with the button!

You can use this trick elsewhere to more efficiently check functionality after making code changes.

I like to use placeholder text that includes the name of the property whose value the domain expert is going to edit, surrounded with <...>, and in an appropriate style. The styling should make clear that a value is missing, and the <...> syntax should indicate which property's value is missing. In our case, I'll use <name> and <type> as placeholder text.

Let's implement the placeholder functionality for the textual value of the name of an attribute. The `<TextValue>` component is responsible for projecting editable text values, so it should implement the placeholder functionality. We'll change `input-ValueComponent` in src/frontend/value-components.jsx to pass the placeholder text in as an attribute:

```
const inputValueComponent = ({ inputType, isValid }) =>      Add an attribute to
    observer(({ editState, placeholderText }) =>         the component
        // ...rest of the code...            ⟵          function returned.
    )                                                    This attribute holds
                                                         the placeholder text.
```

Next, we should change the JSX expression that produces the projection when the text value is not being edited. The specified placeholder text should be shown when the value is missing:

Specify a "value-missing" CSS class if the value is
missing, in addition to the regular "value" class.

```
// ...rest of the code in the inputValueComponent function...
: <span
    className={"value"
        ➥ + (isMissing(editState.value) ? " value-missing" : "")}
    onClick={action((_) => {
        editState.inEdit = true
    })}
>{isMissing(editState.value)
    ➥ ? placeholderText : editState.value}</span>
```

Show the value of
placeholderText if the
value is missing, and the
actual value otherwise.

The space in the " value-missing" string in the preceding code ensures that the two CSS class names are properly whitespace separated.

We haven't defined the isMissing function yet. Let's add the following line somewhere at the top of src/frontend/value-components.jsx:

```
const isMissing = (value) => value === null || value === undefined
```

Let's also add a definition for the "value-missing" CSS class to src/frontend/styling.css:

```
span.value-missing {
    background-color: rgb(209, 108, 108);
    color: lightgray;
    text-decoration: underline;
    text-decoration-style: dashed;
    text-decoration-color: rgb(228, 30, 23);
}
```

This CSS class styles the placeholder text with a reddish color to encourage the domain expert to replace the placeholder text with a sensible value. Now we only have to specify the placeholder texts themselves in calls to <TextValue> by adding an attribute:

```
<TextValue editState={editStateFor("name")} placeholderText="<name>" />
```

The projection of a Data Attribute has one such call to modify. The call to <Text-Value> for the name of Record Type should receive the same treatment.

> **Exercise 6.1**
> - Apply the preceding code changes and test them.
> - What happens when you start editing the name of an added attribute but leave it empty? Is this behavior desirable?
> - Try to find a simple way to fix this.

We haven't implemented the placeholder functionality for the attribute's type property yet, so the app looks like what you see in figure 6.6.

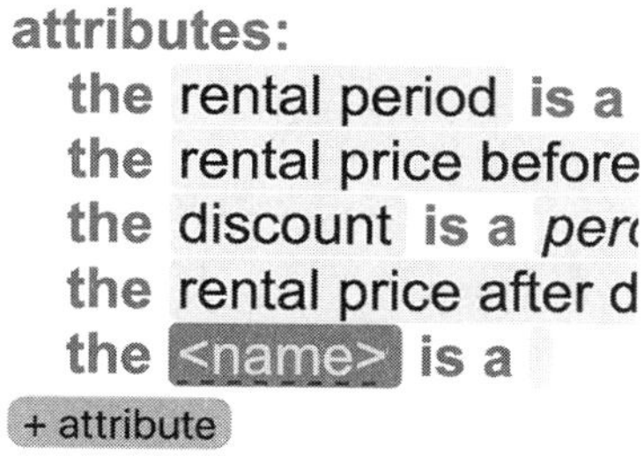

Figure 6.6   The attributes of the Rental record type with a new attribute added, and with placeholders

Let's also implement placeholder functionality on the `<DropDownValue>` value component. Changing `<DropDownValue>` is pretty straightforward now that we've already done it for `inputValueComponent`:

```
export const DropDownValue = observer(({ editState, className, options,
        ➥ placeholderText }) =>
    editState.inEdit
        ? // ...rest of the branch producing a <select>...
        : <span
            className={className
                ➥ + (isMissing(editState.value) ? " value-missing" : "")}
            onClick={action((_) => {
                editState.inEdit = true
            })}
        >{isMissing(editState.value)
                ➥ ? placeholderText
                ➥ : editState.value}</span>
)
```

Finally, we have to specify placeholder text in the call to `<DropDownValue>` for the `type` property of an attribute:

```
<DropDownValue
    className="value enum-like"
    editState={editStateFor("type")}
    options={[ "amount", "date range", "percentage" ]}
    placeholderText="<type>"
/>
```

As you can see in figure 6.7, the app now looks like it makes sense.

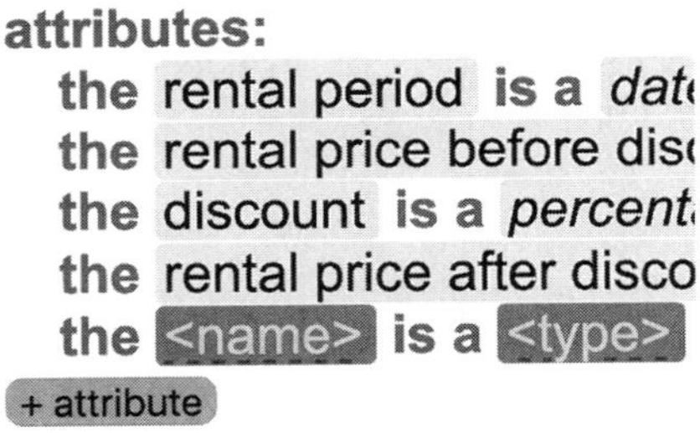

attributes:
    the rental period **is a** *dat(*
    the rental price before dis(
    the discount **is a** *percent(*
    the rental price after disco
    the <name> **is a** <type>
    + attribute

Figure 6.7   The attributes of the
`Rental` **record type with new attributes**
added, and with placeholders

Exercise 6.2
- Apply the preceding code changes and test them.
- Do you notice anything weird when trying to choose a type for the attribute using the drop-down menu? We'll fix this problem in section 6.1.2.

Exercise 6.3

Take a closer look at the code of the `inputValueComponent` and `<DropDownValue>` functions in src/frontend/value-components.jsx. The code for displaying input or drop-down values that are not being edited looks rather similar. It did so before, but now that we've extended that code with placeholder functionality, it becomes even more apparent. Here's a screenshot of the similarity.

Refactor this commonality into a separate React component function called `Display-Value`. Also, replace the code in this screenshot with appropriate calls to `<Display-Value>`. The `<DisplayValue>` component should have three attributes.

Exercise 6.4

Use the tip outlined in the sidebar "A trick to speed up testing" to emulate the domain expert having already added a new attribute. Give this new attribute the name `new attribute` and the type `amount`.

One more thing I'd like to refactor has to do with how we assemble the arguments for React's `className` attribute. When we need to add a CSS class's name conditionally, we currently use some string manipulation.

Listing 6.2 Computing the `className` attribute

```
className={className + (isMissing(editState.value) ? " value-missing" : "")}
```

Section B.3.6 introduces some code that can improve this by using a helper function. This helper function is named `asClassNameArgument`, and it should reside in a src/frontend/css-util.js file—see listing B.7. After importing this function, we can rewrite the code in listing 6.2 as follows:

```
className={asClassNameArgument(className,
    isMissing(editState.value) && "value-missing")}
```

Exercise 6.5

Apply the preceding code changes, and test whether everything works as before.

6.1.2   *Adding an initial value*

We can now add a new attribute and set its name and type, but we can't yet specify an initial value for it. Let's make it possible to add a specification for an initial value to any attribute that doesn't have one yet. There are currently two choices for the concept: `Attribute Reference` and `Number`. This means we also need a way to select which concept to add.

The first thing we need is a call to action. Let's use the same type of button that we used for adding an attribute. Change the `Data Attribute` case of the `Projection` function as follows:

```
case "Data Attribute": return <div className="attribute">
    // ...9 lines of other code in this case...
    {settings["initial value"]
        ? <div className="inline">
            <span className="keyword ws-right">initially</span>
            <Projection
                astObject{settings["initial value"]}
                ancestors={[ astObject, ...ancestors ]}
            />
        </div>
        : <button
            className="add-new"
            tabIndex={-1}
            onClick={action((_) => {
                settings["initial value"] =
                    placeholderAstObject
            })}
        >+ initial value</button>
    }
</div>
```

Use the ternary operator to produce something whether settings["initial value"] is truthy or falsy.

Put the projection that we implemented previously in the true branch of the ternary operator.

Put an add button in the false branch of the ternary operator.

Set the value of the "initial value" property to placeholderAstObject.

We'll define the `placeholderAstObject` value next, but as long as it's truthy, the button should already disappear after it's clicked.

> **Exercise 6.6**
>
> Refactor the two occurrences of `<button ...>` to an `<AddNewButton>` React component in a separate file, src/frontend/support-components.jsx. This component will render a button that creates a new "thing"—typically a new AST object—and adds it to the appropriate location. This component should take two attributes: the button text and an no-argument function that performs the necessary update to the AST. (Don't forget to include the necessary `import` statements in the new file.)

We're going to define the `placeholderAstObject` value as follows, in src/common/ast.js:

```
const placeholderAstObject = "<placeholder for an AST object>"
module.exports.placeholderAstObject = placeholderAstObject
```

We'll also have to import it in src/frontend/projection.jsx by making the following code change:

```
import { isAstObject, placeholderAstObject } from "../common/ast"
```

This constant is not falsy, nor is it recognized as an AST object, so it can serve as a stand-in, or placeholder, AST object without fear of confusion. A setting having this value indicates that the domain expert apparently intends to provide a proper value. The reason for putting it in src/common/ast.js is that we'll have to recognize this value in parts of the codebase other than just the projection.

Let's project this particular value in an editable way, so the domain expert can make good on their intention. Before we change the projection of initial value for that, though, let's first check the effect of the previous code changes. To do that, first create a new attribute named new attribute with type amount, either manually or by means of exercise 6.4.

As shown in figure 6.8, we now have a button for adding an initial value to any attribute that doesn't yet have one. Clicking this button has the effect shown in figure 6.9.

the new attribute is an *amount* + initial value

Figure 6.8   An attribute without an initial value, but with a button to add one

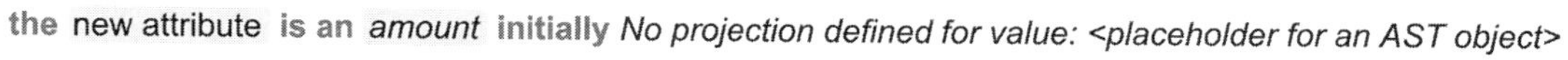

the new attribute is an *amount* initially *No projection defined for value: <placeholder for an AST object>*

Figure 6.9   The effect of clicking the "+ initial value" button, without distinguishing between "no value" and "want to specify a value"

We have to change the projection of initial value to handle the placeholderAst-Object value. Replace the following in the Data Attribute case of the Projection function,

```
<Projection
    astObject{settings["initial value"]}
    ancestors={[ astObject, ...ancestors ]}
/>
```

with the following code in src/frontend/projection.jsx.

Listing 6.3   Choosing a concept to add as an initial value

Call the <DropDownValue> component to let the domain expert choose the right concept.

Compare settings["initial value"] to the placeholderAstObject.

```
{settings["initial value"] === placeholderAstObject
    ? <DropDownValue
```

```
      editState={observable({
          inEdit: true,
          setValue: (newValue) => {
              settings["initial value"] = {
                  concept: newValue,
                  settings: {}
              }
          }
      })}
      options={[
          "Attribute Reference",
          "Number"
      ]}
      placeholderText="<initial value>"
  />
  : <Projection
      astObject={settings["initial value"]}
      ancestors={[ astObject, ...ancestors ]}
  />
}
```

Start editing "initial value" right after the "+ initial value" button has been clicked.

Specify as options the two concepts that make sense as initial values.

Create a new AST object, and assign that to the attribute's "initial value" property.

The new AST object has as a concept the value chosen from the drop-down menu.

An AST object requires a settings subobject, so initialize that to an empty object: {}.

Specify the placeholder text in the same way as before.

Call Projection as when we're not dealing with placeholderAstObject.

Clicking the "+ initial value" button indeed opens the drop-down menu right away, as shown in figure 6.10.

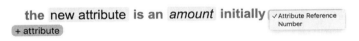

Figure 6.10   The drop-down menu with the two appropriate concepts

The domain expert can now choose the Number option, and a new number object will be created. However, when we're lacking a value *and* a placeholder, it looks weird, as shown in figure 6.11.

Figure 6.11   An attribute without an initial value nor a placeholder for it

the new attribute is an *amount* initially $|

Let's add a placeholder to the projection of a Number (figure 6.12) by passing suitable text to the call to <NumberValue>:

```
<NumberValue editState={editStateFor("value")} placeholderText="<number>" />
```

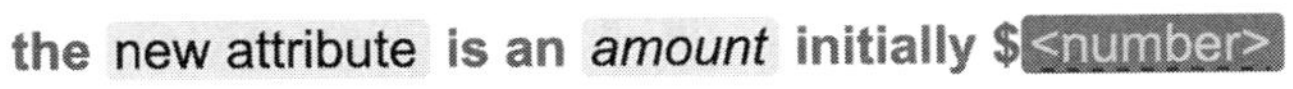

Figure 6.12   An attribute with a placeholder for an initial value

the new attribute is an *amount* initially $<number>

When the domain expert stops editing before specifying a value, a sensible placeholder is displayed, as shown in figure 6.13.

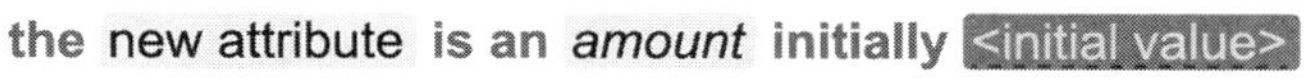

the new attribute is an *amount* initially <initial value>

Figure 6.13   An attribute with a placeholder for the initial value after stopping editing

We'll give the domain expert the means to delete that placeholder in section 6.3.

Unfortunately, there's no way to choose the `Attribute Reference` option. This is the same problem you should have encountered in exercise 6.2.

This is a consequence of how `<select>` works, and because we're listening to a *change*, rather than some other click-like event. We could solve this problem in many ways, but the simplest solution is adding an *action text*. This is an option that can't be chosen, but that provides the domain expert some guidance through an explanation. This is usually the first option, also distinguished from the other options through some specific styling.

Let's specify the action text through an attribute on the call to `<DropDownValue>` in listing 6.3:

```
{settings["initial value"] === placeholderAstObject
    ? <DropDownValue
          // ...attributes to specify editState, options,
          ➥ and placeholderText...
          actionText="(choose concept for initial value)"      ◁─┐  Provide an
      />                                                            action text to
      : <Projection                                                explain to the
          astObject{settings["initial value"]}                     domain expert
          ancestors={[ astObject, ...ancestors ]}                  what they're
      />                                                            choosing.
}
```

Now let's change the `<DropDownValue>` component to receive the value for the action text through an attribute, and to display it:

```
export const DropDownValue = observer(({ editState, className, options,
        ➥ placeholderText, actionText }) =>        ◁──  Receive the value for the
    editState.inEdit                                    action text through an
        ? <select                                       extra attribute.
            autoFocus={true}
            value={editState.value}
            style={{ width: Math.max(
                ...options.map((option) => option.length),
                actionText && actionText.length      ◁──────────┐
            ) + "ch"
        }}                                   Calculate the length of the action
                                             text string (when present) as an
                                             extra argument to Math.max(...).
```

```
onChange={action((event) => {
    const newValue = event.target.value          Assign the chosen option
    if (newValue !== actionText) {                to a newValue constant,
        editState.setValue(newValue)              for convenience.
        editState.inEdit = false
    }
})}
// ...event handlers for onBlur, and onKeyUp as before...

{actionText && <option key={-1}
    className="action">{actionText}</option>}
{options.map((option, index) =>
    <option key={index}>{option}</option>)}
// ...rest of the code as-it-was-before...
```

Check whether the chosen option equals the specified action text. Only set the property's value when an option has been chosen that's not the action text.

Add an option for the action text (when given). This option gets key value −1, because that can never be the index of an element in the options list.

We'll also style the action text option a little, to make it *look* suitably deselectable:

```
select option.action {
    color: lightgray;
    font-style: italic;
}
```

Figure 6.14 shows the initial value with the drop-down menu on the action text, after having clicked the "+ initial value" button. Figure 6.15 shows the result after clicking the drop-down menu to choose one of the options.

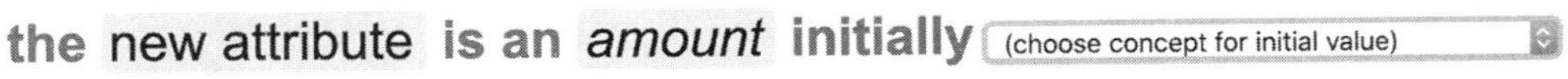

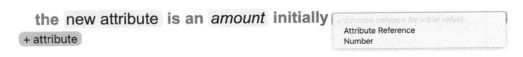

Figure 6.14   The drop-down menu with the action text

Figure 6.15   The drop-down menu after clicking the drop-down menu

Now the domain expert can choose the `Attribute Reference` option. But when they do so, they will be presented with a blank page, and with errors on the JavaScript console, as in figure 6.16.

```
❶ ▶ Uncaught TypeError: settings.attribute is undefined
      Projection                  index.jsx:48
      ▶ MobX 8
      ▶ React 11
      unstable_runWithPriority scheduler.development.js:653
      ▶ React 10
      unstable_runWithPriority scheduler.development.js:653
      ▶ React 4
    [Learn More]
```

Figure 6.16   The JavaScript console with a runtime error in the projection of an `Attribute Reference`

The referenced line in src/frontend/projection.jsx is part of the `Attribute Reference` case in the `Projection` function. This case currently reads as follows:

```
case "Attribute Reference": {
    const recordType = ancestors.find(
        (ancestor) => ancestor.concept === "Record Type")
    const attributes = recordType.settings["attributes"]
    return <div className="inline">
        <span className="keyword ws-right">the</span>
        <DropDownValue
            editState={observable({
                value:
    settings["attribute"].ref.settings["name"],
                inEdit: false,
                setValue: (newValue) => {
                    settings["attribute"].ref =
    attributes.find(
        (attribute) => attribute.settings["name"] === newValue)
                }
            })}
            className="reference"
            options={attributes.map(
                (attribute) => attribute.settings["name"])}
        />
    </div>
}
```

The line on which the runtime error is reported, due to settings["attribute"] being undefined.

This assignment statement also assumes that settings["attribute"] is not undefined, and even that it should be a reference object.

We can expect a runtime error here, since the new AST object that represents an `Attribute Reference` is initialized with `settings` having the value {}. (This is done near the middle of listing 6.3.)

To fix this, we first have to make sure this expression doesn't fail when `settings["attribute"]` is `undefined`. We can do that by prepending the expression with `settings["attribute"] &&`:

```
value: settings["attribute"] && settings["attribute"].ref.settings["name"]
```

This ensures that the expression evaluates to `undefined` when `settings["attribute"]` is `undefined`. Choosing the `Attribute Reference` option now produces a drop-down menu with the options for the target attribute without crashing.

For clarity, we also specify an action text for the drop-down menu with the target attributes. Add the following attribute value to the call to `<DropDownValue>` in the preceding listing, just after the `options` attribute:

```
actionText="(choose an attribute to reference)"
```

We have another code line that assumes `settings["attribute"]` exists and happens to be a reference object:

```
settings["attribute"].ref = attributes.find(
    ➥ (attribute) => attribute.settings["name"] === newValue)
```

With this code line, selecting a target attribute again leads to errors on the JavaScript console. Let's fix that so that the reference object is created every time a target attribute is chosen for the reference:

```
settings["attribute"] = {
    ref: attributes.find(
        ➥ (attribute) => attribute.settings["name"] === newValue)
}
```

This newly created reference object is automatically observable, because any AST object passed to `Projection` is always deeply observable. That's courtesy of wrapping the whole AST with MobX's `observable` function before passing it in the initial call to `Projection`. Because the value assigned to `ref` in the `settings` object is an AST object that's already observable, MobX recognizes that `ref` should be treated as a reference.

Finally, if the domain expert defocuses the drop-down menu for the target attribute, we'd like to show a sensible placeholder. Add the following attribute to the call to `<DropDownValue>`, after the `actionText` attribute:

```
placeholderText="<attribute>"
```

With that last code change, adding an initial value should work as expected.

Exercise 6.7
Apply all the previous code changes, and test them.

In particular, perform the following steps:

1 Create a new attribute.
2 Give it a name and a type.
3 Set the initial value to be an `Attribute Reference`.

4 Choose a target attribute.

5 Change the name of the referenced attribute.

Does the projection of the attribute reference change as well? At the end of chapter 5, I pointed out a problem with references not behaving as references in the projection. Do you concur that this problem doesn't occur for *newly created* references? Can you think of a reason why and how you could solve the reference problem in general?

Now repeat the five steps above, but without giving the new attribute a name during the second step. What happens? What assumptions does the implementation rely on? Are these assumptions violated by incomplete and invalid content?

We'll discuss how to properly deal with invalid content in chapter 9. In the meantime, domain experts should create valid content as much as possible.

The UI and UX of projectional DSLs

Hardly anything we did in this section was specific to implementing DSLs. Most of it was "good ole" user interface (UI) and interaction (UX) design and implementing visualization and editing capabilities for DSL content. Creating and initializing a new AST object and inserting it in the right place in the AST were the only two things that were specific to DSLs.

This state of affairs is pretty common for *projectional DSLs*: the kind of DSL that has an editor using projectional editing. After all, projectional DSLs see content as structured data and provide an editable visualization for that data. UI and UX typically comprise an inordinate part of the total development effort, and it's no different for implementing projectional DSL editors.

6.2   Selecting objects

Before they can delete objects, such as entire attributes, from the AST, the domain expert needs a way to *select* the AST object to delete. Let's add the ability to select an individual AST object for deletion, or potentially for other purposes. We're first going to focus on the special case of selecting an attribute, and then we'll generalize this to making the AST objects of any concept selectable.

6.2.1   Selecting an attribute

We have to somehow keep track of *whether* an attribute or other AST object has been selected, and if so, *which* one. This is another piece of application state that's specific to the editing experience.

Let's use a separate `selection` object for that. This object has only one property, `selected`, whose value is either `undefined` or a reference to an AST object. These values correspond to nothing and to the referenced AST object being selected, respectively.

Add the code in listing 6.4 to src/frontend/projection.jsx anywhere before the `Projection` function.

Listing 6.4   Setting up state to keep track of AST object selection

```
const selection = observable({ selected: undefined })
```

By making the `selection` object observable, we can react transparently to the `selected` property being set. No matter when and from where we set `selection.selected`, the projection should update itself immediately to reflect what object was selected. To achieve that, we'll have to use this `selection` object somewhere and read its `selected` property. Let's change the `<div>` element, which is the outermost DOM element produced by the projection of an attribute, as follows:

```
case "Data Attribute": return <div
    className={asClassNameArgument("attribute",
        (selection.selected === astObject)
        && "selected")}
    onClick={action((_) => {
        selection.selected = astObject
})}>
// ...rest of the existing code...
```

Check whether selection.selected points to astObject (the AST object currently being projected).

If it does, add the "selected" CSS class to the class names of the outermost `<div>` DOM element.

Set selection.selected to astObject, which is the attribute object.

Add a mouse click event handler.

To get the preceding code to work, we have to import the `asClassNameArgument` function from src/frontend/css-util.js. Do that by adding a corresponding `import` statement somewhere at the top of src/frontend/projection.jsx. Because `selection` is observable, MobX recognizes that the new value is already observable and treats the `selected` property as a reference.

To really show that some object was selected, we'll add a definition for the "selected" CSS class at the end of src/frontend/styling.css:

This CSS definition assumes that the projection of any AST object produces a `<div>` as its outermost DOM element.

Set the background color to a shade of yellow that "looks selected."

```
div.selected {
    background-color: khaki;
    width: max-content;
    outline: none;
}
```

Avoid an unwanted outline around the selected area.

Specify that the background color only extends as far as the projected DSL content itself, instead of all the way to the right border.

When the domain expert clicks anywhere on the area of the third attribute, this changes the projection as shown in figure 6.17.

We've now added selection functionality, but we've also gained a problem: starting editing of a particular value also triggers the selection of the AST object the value resides in. In our situation, a value area is a `<span>` element, and clicking that element

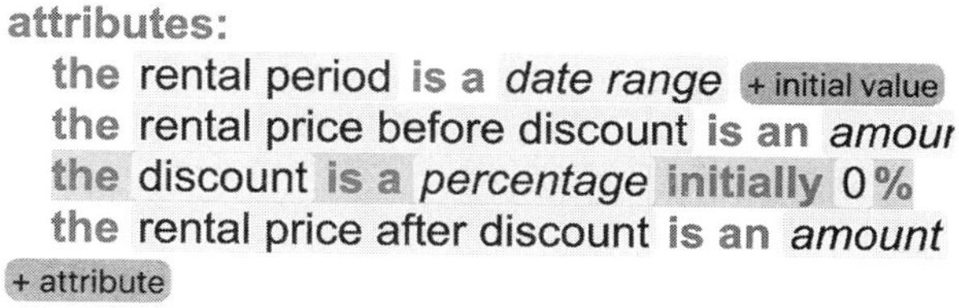

attributes:
the rental period is a *date range* `+ initial value`
the rental price before discount is an *amoun*
the discount is a *percentage* initially 0%
the rental price after discount is an *amount*
`+ attribute`

Figure 6.17 The `Rental` **record type with one of the attributes selected**

fires a mouse click event. The corresponding event object is not only passed to the `onClick` event handler that starts editing, but it also "bubbles" or *propagates* up the HTML DOM tree to all DOM elements surrounding the `<span>`. This means that the `onClick` event handler that selects the attribute object in which the value happens to reside is also called, so the attribute gets selected.

The easiest fix for this problem is to stop propagation using the `stopPropagation()` function on any event object. Change the `<DisplayValue>` component in src/frontend/value-components.jsx as follows.

Listing 6.5 Adding an `onClick` **event handler to** `<DisplayValue>`

Receive the event object by name, instead of ignoring the argument.

```
const DisplayValue = ({ editState, className, placeholderText }) =>
    <span
        className={asClassNameArgument(className,
            isMissing(editState.value) && "value-missing")}
        onClick={action((event) => {
            event.stopPropagation()
            editState.inEdit = true
        })}
    >{isMissing(editState.value) ? placeholderText : editState.value}</span>
```

Stop the propagation of the mouse click event.

This code assumes you completed exercise 6.3 and refactored common code in the `inputValueComponent` and `DropDownValue` functions to a separate `<DisplayValue>` component function.

With some further testing, you might notice that the problem we just solved also occurs when clicking a button to add an AST object. The same fix applies there: make sure that `event.stopPropagation()` is called when an `onClick` event occurs. When that change is made, the `<AddNewButton>` component's code in src/frontend/support-components.jsx looks like this:

```
export const AddNewButton = ({ buttonText, actionFunction }) =>
    <button
        className="add-new"
        tabIndex={-1}
        onClick={action((event) => {
            event.stopPropagation()
            actionFunction()
        })}
    >{buttonText}</button>
```

Clicking an input element of a value that's being edited also selects the AST object that contains that value. We can fix that behavior in the same way, by adding the following event handler to the `<input>` element produced by the `inputValueComponent` function in src/frontend/value-components.jsx:

```
<input
    // ...existing code...
    onClick={(event) => {
        event.stopPropagation()
    }}
/>
```

> ### Exercise 6.8
> - Apply all the preceding code changes, and check that selection works as expected.
> - Verify that editing values on a selected attribute works as before.
> - Verify that adding an AST object is initiated by clicking the corresponding button, and that this works as before.

6.2.2   *Deselecting an attribute*

It's nice that the domain expert now can select an attribute, but what if they selected one that they didn't want to delete? Let's make sure that clicking anywhere outside of an attribute area deselects a selected attribute. We'll use an old-fashioned, non-React DOM event listener to implement that.

Add the following code for a mouse click event listener directly after the definition of the `selection` constant in src/frontend/projection.jsx.

Listing 6.6   An event listener that deselects the current selection

```
                                              Add an event listener for mouse clicks
                                              globally to the whole HTML document.
document.addEventListener("mousedown",   ◁
        action((event) => {
    if (!event.target.classList        ◁                  Inspect the CSS classes
            .contains("selectable")) {                     attached to the DOM element
        selection.selected = undefined   ◁                 to check whether it's marked
    }                                                       as selectable or not.
}))            If it isn't, deselect any currently
              selected object by setting
              selection.selected to undefined.
```

As you'll see in the preceding listing, React names (such as `onClick`) differ from the event type names used by the HTML DOM (`mousedown`). Also, we have to wrap the event listener with MobX's `action` function, because it modifies observable state. When a mouse click happens, the area that's clicked is accessible as `event.target`, which is a DOM element.

The "selectable" CSS class is used solely as a marker so we can distinguish selectable elements from deselectable ones just by looking at the HTML DOM. The CSS class is only used to check whether a mouse click happened on an HTML DOM element that is selectable—if so, that means the HTML element is also deselectable and the selection is wiped. Because "selectable" is only used as a marker, there's no styling defined for it in src/frontend/styling.css.

Let's update how attribute objects are projected to mark them as selectable:

```
case "Data Attribute": return <div                    ┐  Add the CSS class
    className={asClassNameArgument("attribute",        │  "selectable" to the
        "selectable",                            ◁─────┘  outer <div> element.
        ➥ (selection.selected === astObject) && "selected")}
    // ...rest of the existing code...
```

> ### Exercise 6.9
> Apply the preceding code changes, and check that deselection works as expected, with everything else staying the same.

6.2.3 Selecting and deselecting any object

Now that we can select and deselect any attribute object, it shouldn't be too hard to generalize this to making all AST objects selectable and deselectable. Let's do some refactoring to generalize this selection functionality and make the projection of AST objects of any concept selectable.

For objects of concept `Data Attribute`, we manipulated the `className` attribute of its outermost `<div>` element produced by the projection directly, depending on the value of `selection.selected`. Let's replace that with a generic mechanism that *encapsulates* all these details, including how to deselect an object. We're going to implement a new React component called `AstObjectUiWrapper` that performs that encapsulation. We'll put the new component in the src/frontend/support-components.jsx file. As the name implies, its responsibility is to wrap the projection of every AST object to provide additional UI behavior.

Before implementing `<AstObjectUiWrapper>`, we'll move the code from listings 6.4 and 6.6 to the src/frontend/support-components.jsx file.

Listing 6.7   Encapsulating selection/deselection functionality

```
import React from "react"
import { action, observable } from "mobx"
import { observer } from "mobx-react"

const selection = observable({ selected: undefined })

const deselect = () => {                 ◁─┐  Extract the assignment statement that
    selection.selected = undefined         │  deselects a currently selected object.
}
```

```
document.addEventListener("mousedown", action((event) => {
    if (!event.target.classList.contains("selectable")) {
        deselect()                          ⟵┐
    }                                         │
}))                                           │
```

> Replace the assignment statement
> with a call to the deselect function.

We've already provided generic functionality through React components, so let's try that here as well. This means that we want to replace JSX code like this,

```
<div className={asClassNameArgument("attribute", "selectable",
    ➥ (selection.selected === astObject) && "selected")}>
    // ...actual projection code...
</div>
```

with this:

```
<AstObjectUiWrapper className="attribute" astObject={astObject}>
    // ...actual projection code...
</AstObjectUiWrapper>
```

We'll do exactly that. Let's have a first stab at adding an `<AstObjectUiWrapper>` React component function to src/frontend/support-components.jsx:

> Import the asClassNameArgument function near the top
> of the file, as is customary. You can remove the same
> import statement from projection.jsx.

```
import { asClassNameArgument } from "./css-util"   ⟵┐
                                                     │
export const AstObjectUiWrapper =                  ⟵─┤  Define an
    ➥ observer(({ className, astObject }) =>          │  <AstObjectUiWrapper>
    <div                                              │  React component and
        className={asClassNameArgument(className,   ⟵┤  export it.
            ➥ "selectable",                           │
            ➥ (selection.selected === astObject) && "selected")}
        onClick={action((_) => {
            selection.selected = astObject
        })}
    >
        // ...actual projection code...             ⟵┐
    </div>                                            │
)
```

> Produce
> an outer
> <div>
> element.

> Derive the class name of
> the <div> element.

> The actual projection code
> should somehow go here.

The `<AstObjectUiWrapper>` component implemented in the preceding code can be called with two attributes that serve as arguments. The `className` attribute contains whitespace-separated CSS class names. The `astObject` attribute contains an AST object that we want to be able to select or deselect. The CSS class name specified for the `<div>` element is computed using the `asClassNameArgument` by combining the `className` attribute, the "selectable" CSS class, and the "selected" CSS class, provided the AST object is selected. The "selectable" CSS class ensures that the document-level mouse event listener can distinguish selectable DOM elements from other DOM elements.

The component is also an `observer` of observable state. Here, that state consists of both the `selection` object defined before as well as the `astObject` passed in.

We can pass the block of JSX code that makes up the actual projection code by using the special React `children` property. Alter the `AstObjectUiWrapper` function as follows:

Receive an additional React property, children.

```
export const AstObjectUiWrapper = observer(({ className, astObject,
      ⇨ children }) =>
    <div
        // ...specify the className, and onClick attributes as before...
    >
        {children}
    </div>
)
```

Paste the value of children as is into the React DOM output.

To use the `<AstObjectUiWrapper>` component, we have to import it in src/frontend/projection.jsx:

```
import { AddNewButton, AstObjectUiWrapper } from "./support-components"
```

Then we need to change the `Data Attribute` case as follows:

Call the <AstObjectUiWrapper> component instead of producing a <div> directly. The <div> element produced by <AstObjectUiWrapper> is identical to the one produced directly before.

```
case "Data Attribute": return <AstObjectUiWrapper
      ⇨ className="attribute" astObject={astObject}>
    <span className="keyword ws-right">the</span>
    <TextValue editState={editStateFor("name")} placeholderText="<name>" />
    <span className="keyword ws-both">is
        ⇨ {indefiniteArticleFor(settings["type"])}</span>
    // ...rest of the actual projection code for this attribute object...
</AstObjectUiWrapper>
```

Everything inside <AstObjectUiWrapper>...</AstObjectUiWrapper> is passed into the children property.

Exercise 6.10

- Apply the preceding code additions and changes, and test whether they keep attributes selectable and deselectable.
- Change the cases in the `Projection` function for *all* concepts to use `<AstObjectUiWrapper>`. To do that, change any variation of

(continued)

```
case <concept>: return <div className="<CSS class>">
         ...
      </div>
```

to

```
case <concept>: return <AstObjectUiWrapper className="<CSS class>"
   ➥ astObject={astObject}>
         ...
      </AstObjectUiWrapper>
```

Test your changes. Does it work as expected?

After having completed the second item in exercise 6.10, you should find that clicking any non-editable area in the projection now selects the *entire* record type, as shown in figure 6.18.

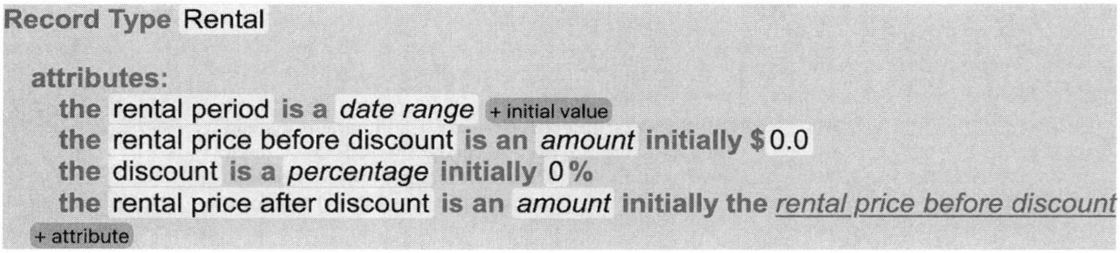

Record Type Rental

attributes:
    the rental period is a *date range* + initial value
    the rental price before discount is an *amount* initially $ 0.0
    the discount is a *percentage* initially 0 %
    the rental price after discount is an *amount* initially the *rental price before discount*
+ attribute

Figure 6.18   The entire `Rental` record type having been selected

The mouse click event on a `<div>` element produced by a call to `<AstObjectUiWrapper>` is propagated to all DOM elements "surrounding" the clicked element. This includes the DOM elements produced by other calls of `<AstObjectUiWrapper>`. Because the event is propagated up the HTML DOM tree, the outermost DOM element is the last to have its mouse click event handler called. In our situation, the outermost DOM element corresponds to the entire record type, which is why the entire record type ends up being selected, instead of any of the other AST objects.

As before with the `<DisplayValue>` and `<AddNewButton>` components, we have to fix this by stopping the propagation of the mouse click event. We'll change the `onClick` event handler on the `<div>` produced by `<AstObjectUiWrapper>` as follows:

```
onClick={action((event) => {
    event.stopPropagation()
```

```
                selection.selected = astObject
    })}
```

> **Exercise 6.11**
> Apply this code change, and verify that things now work as desired.

We can now select an initial value, as shown in figure 6.19.

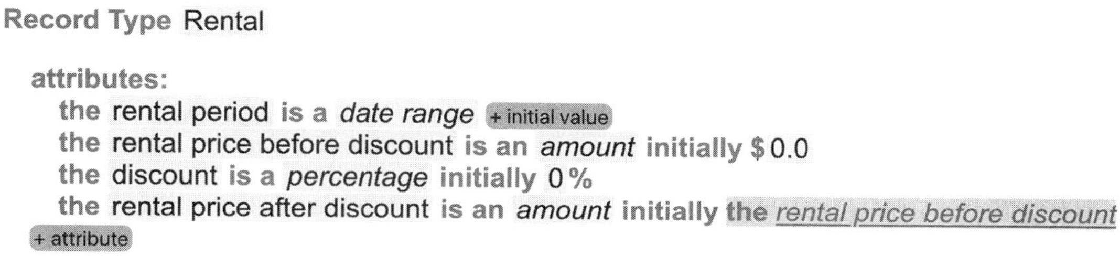

Record Type Rental

attributes:
   the rental period **is a** *date range* `+ initial value`
   the rental price before discount **is an** *amount* **initially** $ 0.0
   the discount **is a** *percentage* **initially** 0 %
   the rental price after discount **is an** *amount* **initially the** *rental price before discount*
`+ attribute`

Figure 6.19 Selecting the attribute reference that's the initial value of the `rental price after discount` attribute

In general, by wrapping the projection code for a specific concept with `<AstObject-UiWrapper astObject={astObject}>...</AstObjectUiWrapper>`, we make any AST object with that concept selectable and deselectable. The domain expert can click anywhere in the area of the projection of a selectable object to select that object. By clicking anywhere outside of that area, that object is deselected, but another object may get selected instead, depending on the exact click point.

6.3 *Deleting objects*

Now that we can select AST objects by clicking the area of their projection, we should be able to implement the deletion of an AST object. The domain expert should trigger deletion through an input action. We could use a button for that again, but I want to trigger on keyboard input instead. Specifically, deletion should be triggered by the Delete key, with the Backspace key as an alternative for keyboard layouts lacking a Delete key.

Using keyboard input to trigger deletion avoids us having to clutter the projection with a deletion button or icon. You could show a visual trigger only on the selected object, but you'd have to take care that parts of the projection didn't "jump" or "twitch" when that trigger is inserted into the visuals after the object is selected.

Let's give the domain expert the option to delete a selected object by pressing either the Backspace or Delete key. We'll implement this first for objects that are the initial value of an attribute, before proceeding to the attributes themselves.

6.3.1   *Deleting initial values*

To remove an initial value from an attribute, the domain expert would first select the initial value. Currently, the initial value can be either an `Attribute Reference` or a `Number`. After having selected such an AST object, the domain expert should be able to press either Backspace or Delete to delete the initial-value object.

How can we detect a Backspace or Delete keypress? More precisely, we want such a keypress to be detected by the `<div>` element corresponding to the currently selected AST object. In React, you need to specify an event handler for `onKeyDown` events *and* a tab index of 0 on that `<div>` element. We'll add the following two attributes to the `<div>` element produced by the `<AstObjectUiWrapper>` component:

```
onKeyDown={action((event) => {
    if (selection.selected === astObject
            && event.key === "Backspace"
            || event.key === "Delete") {
        event.preventDefault()
        // TODO  delete 'astObject'
    }
})}

tabIndex={0}
```

Only trigger a deletion if the AST object we're wrapping is currently selected and either the Backspace or Delete keys are pressed.

Prevent the default browser action for Backspace from happening (going back in history).

We'll figure out how to perform the deletion soon.

Set the tab index of this element to 0. Otherwise, React refuses to capture Backspace or Delete keypresses.

We need to implement the TODO in the preceding code. Figure 6.20 illustrates what happens when `Projection` is called with an attribute AST object passed into the `value` attribute. (We'll ignore the `ancestors` attribute in this figure.)

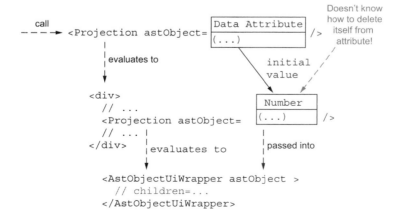

Figure 6.20   Calling `Projection` for an attribute with an initial value

The call to `Projection` with the attribute AST object as the `value` first results in another call to `Projection`, this time with the initial-value AST object as the `value`. That second call results in a call to `<AstObjectUiWrapper>` with the initial-value AST object passed into `astObject`.

The problem is that the initial-value AST object doesn't know how to delete itself. In fact, no AST object knows how to delete itself! This is because the AST object is not aware of all the details of how and where it is contained in the AST. In the case of an initial-value AST object, it would have to know that it's contained by the `initial value` property. It would also have to know whether that property can contain one or more AST objects. If the AST object has "siblings," it would have to know its position among those.

Luckily, any contain*ing* AST object *does* know how to delete any of the AST objects it contains—its contain*ees*, so to speak. An initial-value object is contained by an attribute AST object. Inside the `Data Attribute` case in the `Projection` function, we could simply execute the following statement to delete the initial value:

```
delete settings["initial value"]
```

Using JavaScript's `delete` operator expresses the intent of removing a property from an object just that little bit better than simply setting that property to `undefined`. Let's wrap this statement in a function so that we can pass it around and call it wherever we want:

```
() => {
    delete settings["initial value"]
}
```

We have to call this function from inside a call to `<AstObjectUiWrapper>` because that's where deletion is triggered. That also means we have to be able to pass this function into `AstObjectUiWrapper` as an attribute. Let's alter the `AstObjectUiWrapper` function as follows:

> **Add a deleteAstObject attribute holding an no-argument function.**

```
export const AstObjectUiWrapper = observer(({ className, astObject,
    deleteAstObject, children }) =>
    <div
        // ...specify the className, and onClick attributes as before...
        onKeyDown={action((event) => {
            if (selection.selected === astObject
                ➥ && event.key === "Backspace"
                ➥ || event.key === "Delete") {
                event.preventDefault()
                if (typeof deleteAstObject === "function") {
                    deleteAstObject()
                }
            }
        })}
```

> **Delete the selected AST object by calling deleteAstObject, provided it's really a function (and not, say, undefined).**

As you can see in figure 6.21, we've solved roughly half of our deletion problem. We somehow need to pass the deletion function that's constructed during the projection of the attribute AST object to the call to `<AstObjectUiWrapper>` during the projection of the initial-value AST object. This means that `Projection` should receive both the initial-value AST object and the function to delete that object.

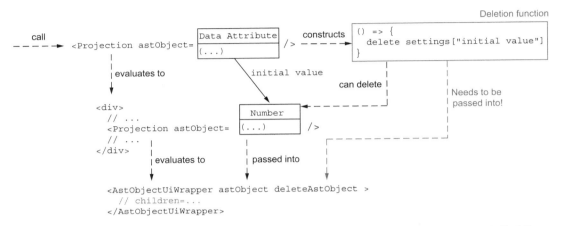

Figure 6.21   Calling `Projection` for an attribute with an initial value, after having solved roughly half of the deletion problem

Let's pass the deletion function as an extra attribute to the `Projection` function by altering the definition of `Projection` as follows:

```
const Projection = observer(({ astObject, ancestors,
    replaceWith }) => {                                    ⟵  Add an optional attribute
  // ...rest of the Projection function's code...             called replaceWith.
})
```

When present, the `replaceWith` attribute holds an no-argument function that should delete `astObject` from the AST.

> **NOTE**   It would be quite logical to call the new attribute `deleteAstObject` instead of `replaceWith`. In this chapter, all functions passed as `replaceWith` arguments do only one thing: delete the corresponding `astObject`. You can read `replaceWith()` calls as "replace with nothing." However, in chapter 12, we'll find situations where we need to replace the `astObject` without deleting it. To avoid having to either introduce another attribute or refactor one called `deleteAstObject`, I chose to use the name `replaceWith`.

To construct and pass our deletion function, we can alter the call to `Projection` in the `Data Attribute` case of `Projection` as follows:

```
<Projection
    astObject{settings["initial value"]}
    ancestors={[ astObject, ...ancestors ]}
    replaceWith={() => {
        delete settings["initial value"]
    }}
/>
```

An initial value is either an `Attribute Reference` or a `Number`. We have to alter the cases for these concepts in the `Projection` function to make any initial value deletable. We can do that by specifying a `deleteAstObject` attribute in every call to `<AstObjectUiWrapper>`. In both cases, these calls look like this:

```
<AstObjectUiWrapper className="inline" astObject={astObject}>
```

Now alter the calls to `<AstObjectUiWrapper>` in the `Attribute Reference` and `Number` cases as follows:

```
<AstObjectUiWrapper className="inline" astObject={astObject}
    deleteAstObject={replaceWith}>
```

Figure 6.22 sums up our solution.

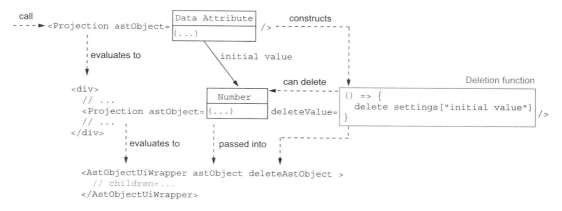

Figure 6.22 Calling `Projection` for an attribute with an initial value, with the full solution to the deletion problem

> ### Exercise 6.12
> - Apply the preceding code changes, and verify that it's now possible to delete the initial values of attributes. It should be possible to delete initial values regardless of their concept.
> - Enable the Escape key to deselect the currently selected object. Hint: Add an `if` statement to the `onKeyDown` event handler on the `<div>` produced by `<AstObjectUiWrapper>`.

6.3.2   Deleting attributes

Now that the domain expert can delete the initial value of an attribute, let's also implement the deletion of an attribute itself. As for an initial value, we have to figure out in which parent AST object we can expect an attribute object. Then we can come up with a suitable deletion function and pass it through the `replaceWith` attribute of `Projection`.

The code we need to alter is in the `Record Type` case in `Projection`:

```
{settings["attributes"].map((attribute, index) =>
    <Projection
        astObject{attribute}
        ancestors={[ astObject, ...ancestors ]}
        key={index}
    />
)}
```

This code calls `Projection` for every attribute of the record type being projected. While iterating over the attributes, the `map` function produces an index for each attribute. We already used this index for the `key` attribute that React insists on getting. We can also use it to delete any attribute by using the `splice` function that's available on any array, such as `settings["attributes"]`. The call `array.splice(n, 1)` removes the element of `array` with index n. The second argument, 1, is called the *delete count*, and it determines that *only* the element with index n is removed.

We'll specify a deletion function by adding a `replaceWith` attribute in the call to `Projection`:

```
replaceWith={() => {
    settings["attributes"].splice(index, 1)        ◁──┐  Remove the current attribute
}}                                                     │  from the array of attributes.
```

We still need to pass this deletion function through to `<AstObjectUiWrapper>`. Alter the `Data Attribute` case in `Projection`:

```
case "Data Attribute": return <AstObjectUiWrapper className="attribute"
    ⇨ astObject={astObject} deleteAstObject={replaceWith}>
```

Exercise 6.13

- Apply the preceding code changes, and test whether you can now delete attributes.
- Can you also still delete initial values? Try to figure out why you can't, and fix that. Hint: You'll have to add the statement `event.stopPropagation()` somewhere.

6.3.3 Deleting any object

Over the last couple of subsections, a pattern has started to become clear. Let's make the code pattern for making the projection of any AST object selectable, deselectable, and deletable explicit, so we can apply it to every concept that we'll be adding to the DSL.

To make the projection of an AST object of a particular concept selectable and deselectable, we wrap the `<AstObjectUiWrapper>` component around the rest of the projection code for that concept. In other words, the case in the `switch` statement inside the `Projection` function for some `<concept>` should look like this:

```
case <concept>: return <AstObjectUiWrapper          ┐  Specify an optional
        [className={<CSS class>}]           ◁────────┘  CSS class.
    astObject={astObject} deleteAstObject={replaceWith}    ◁──────────────┐
>
    // ...rest of the projection code for <concept>...
</AstObjectUiWrapper>                                    Pass the current AST
                                                    object value as well as the
                                                       deletion function for it.
```

Then we figure out what concepts the parents of the AST object can have. In the `case` for each of these parent concepts, implement the required deletion function, and pass it to the `Projection` call for the child object as the `replaceWith` attribute.

For an AST object in a single-valued property, the call to `Projection` looks like this:

```
<Projection
    astObject={settings["<property name>"]}
    ancestors={[ astObject, ...ancestors ]}
    replaceWith={() => {
        delete setting["<property name>"]
    }}
/>
```

For AST objects in a multivalued property, it looks like the following:

```
{settings["<property name>"].map((astObject, index) =>
    <Projection
        astObject={astObject}
        ancestors={[ astObject, ...ancestors ]}
```

```
            replaceWith={() => {
                settings["<property name>"].splice(index, 1)
            }}
            key={index}
        />
    )}
```

In this chapter, you learned how to expand the projection so you can add new objects to the AST, select them, and delete them from the AST. In the next chapter, you'll learn how to implement a backend to the editor frontend, including serializing an AST "to disk" and back again. As part of this, we're going to solve the problem with observable reference relations that we encountered in the last two chapters.

For completeness' sake, the following listings show the source files after applying all the code changes explained in this chapter. They also contain references to some of the exercises that asked you to alter the code yourself. To conserve some space and dead, filleted trees, I'll leave it up to you to gather the additions to src/frontend/styling.css. The src/frontend/index.html file remained unchanged.

As before, I've split up the final code of src/frontend/projection.jsx—this time into four listings.

> ### Listing 6.8   src/frontend/projection.jsx—the outside part

```
import React from "react"
import { observable } from "mobx"
import { observer } from "mobx-react"

import { isAstObject, placeholderAstObject } from "../common/ast"
import { AddNewButton, AstObjectUiWrapper } from "./support-components"
import { DropDownValue, NumberValue, TextValue } from "./value-components"


const indefiniteArticleFor = (nextWord) => "a"
    + ((typeof nextWord === "string"
        && nextWord.toLowerCase().match(/^[aeiou]/)) ? "n" : "")


export const Projection = observer(({ astObject, ancestors,
        replaceWith }) => {
    if (isAstObject(astObject)) {

        const { settings } = astObject
        const editStateFor = (propertyName) => observable({
            value: settings[propertyName],
            inEdit: false,
            setValue: (newValue) => { settings[propertyName] = newValue }
        })

        // (cases are in alphabetical order of concept labels:)
        switch (astObject.concept) {
```

```
                    // ...cases corresponding to concepts...

                    default: return <div className="inline">
                       <em>{"No projection defined for concept: "
                        ➡ + astObject.concept}</em>
                    </div>
            }
        }

    return <em>{"No projection defined for value: " + astObject}</em>
})
```

The cases corresponding to concepts are in listings 6.9, 6.10, and 6.11.

Listing 6.9 src/frontend/projection.jsx—the first inside part

```
case "Attribute Reference": {
    const recordType = ancestors.find(
        ➡ (ancestor) => ancestor.concept === "Record Type")
    const attributes = recordType.settings["attributes"]
    return <AstObjectUiWrapper className="inline"
            ➡ astObject={astObject}
            ➡ deleteAstObject={replaceWith}>
        <span className="keyword ws-right">the</span>
        <DropDownValue
            editState={observable({
                value: settings["attribute"]
                    ➡ && settings["attribute"]
                        ➡ .ref.settings["name"],
                inEdit: false,
                setValue: (newValue) => {
                    settings["attribute"] = {
                        ref: attributes.find(
        ➡ (attribute) => attribute.settings["name"] === newValue)
                    }
                }
            })}
            className="reference"
            options={attributes.map(
                ➡ (attribute) => attribute.settings["name"])}
            actionText="(choose an attribute to reference)"
            placeholderText="<attribute>"
        />
    </AstObjectUiWrapper>
}
```

Listing 6.10 src/frontend/projection.jsx—the second inside part

```
case "Data Attribute": return <AstObjectUiWrapper
        ➡ className="attribute"
        ➡ astObject={astObject}
        ➡ deleteAstObject={replaceWith}>
    <span className="keyword ws-right">the</span>
    <TextValue editState={editStateFor("name")}
        ➡ placeholderText="<name>" />
```

```
        <span className="keyword ws-both">is
           ➡ {indefiniteArticleFor(settings["type"])}</span>
    <DropDownValue
        className="value enum-like ws-right"
        editState={editStateFor("type")}
        options={[ "amount", "date range", "percentage" ]}
        placeholderText="<type>"
    />
    {settings["initial value"]
        ? <div className="inline">
            <span className="keyword ws-right">initially</span>
            {settings["initial value"] === placeholderAstObject
               ? <DropDownValue
                    editState={observable({
                        inEdit: true,
                        setValue: (newValue) => {
                            settings["initial value"] = {
                                concept: newValue,
                                settings: {}
                            }
                        }
                    })}
                    options={[
                        "Attribute Reference",
                        "Number"
                    ]}
                    placeholderText="<initial value>"
                    actionText=
                       ➡ "(choose concept for initial value)"
                 />
               : <Projection
                    astObject={settings["initial value"]}
                    ancestors={[ astObject, ...ancestors ]}
                    replaceWith={() => {
                        delete settings["initial value"]
                    }}
                 />
            }
        </div>
        : <AddNewButton
            ➡ buttonText="+ initial value"
            ➡ actionFunction={() => {
            settings["initial value"] = placeholderAstObject
        }} />
    }
</AstObjectUiWrapper>
```

Exercise 6.6 asks for this refactoring.

Listing 6.11   src/frontend/projection.jsx—the third inside part

```
case "Number": {
    const attribute = ancestors.find(
        ➡ (ancestor) => ancestor.concept === "Data Attribute")
    const type = attribute.settings["type"]
```

```
        return <AstObjectUiWrapper className="inline"
            ➥ astObject={astObject} deleteAstObject={replaceWith}>
            {type === "amount"
                ➥ && <span className="keyword">$</span>}
            <NumberValue editState={editStateFor("value")}
                ➥ placeholderText="<number>" />
            {type === "date range"
                ➥ && <span className="keyword ws-left">
                    ➥ days</span>}
            {type === "percentage"
                ➥ && <span className="keyword">%</span>}
        </AstObjectUiWrapper>
}

case "Record Type": return <AstObjectUiWrapper
        ➥ astObject={astObject}>
    <div>
        <span className="keyword ws-right">Record Type</span>
        <TextValue editState={editStateFor("name")}
            ➥ placeholderText="<name>" />
    </div>
    <div className="section">
        <div><span className="keyword">attributes:</span></div>
        {settings["attributes"].map((attribute, index) =>
            <Projection
                astObject={attribute}
                ancestors={[ astObject, ...ancestors ]}
                replaceWith={() => {
                    // Remove this attribute from the list:
                    settings["attributes"].splice(index, 1)
                }}
                key={index}
            />
        )}
        <AddNewButton
            ➥ buttonText="+ attribute"
            ➥ actionFunction={() => {
            settings["attributes"].push({
                concept: "Data Attribute",
                settings: {}
            })
        }} />
    </div>
</AstObjectUiWrapper>
```

> **Exercise 6.6 asks for this refactoring.**

Because of its length, I've also split up the final code for src/frontend/value-components.jsx into two listings.

Listing 6.12 src/frontend/value-components.jsx—the first part

```
import React from "react"
import { action } from "mobx"
import { observer } from "mobx-react"
```

```
import { asClassNameArgument } from "./css-util"


const isMissing = (value) => value === null || value === undefined

const DisplayValue = ({ editState, className,
    ➡ placeholderText }) =>
    <span
        className={asClassNameArgument(className,
            ➡ isMissing(editState.value) && "value-missing")}
        onClick={action((event) => {
            event.stopPropagation()
            editState.inEdit = true
        })}
    >{isMissing(editState.value) ? placeholderText : editState.value}</span>


const inputValueComponent = ({ inputType, isValid }) =>
    observer(({ editState, placeholderText }) =>
        editState.inEdit
            ? <input
                type={inputType}
                defaultValue={editState.value}
                autoFocus={true}
                onBlur={action((event) => {
                    const newValue = event.target.value
                    if (!isValid || isValid(newValue)) {
                        editState.setValue(newValue)
                    }
                    editState.inEdit = false
                })}
                onKeyUp={action((event) => {
                    if (event.key === "Enter") {
                        const newValue = event.target.value
                        if (!isValid || isValid(newValue)) {
                            editState.setValue(newValue)
                            editState.inEdit = false
                        }
                    }
                    if (event.key === "Escape") {
                        editState.inEdit = false
                    }
                })}
                onClick={(event) => {
                    event.stopPropagation()
                }}
            />
            : <DisplayValue editState={editState}
                ➡ className="value" placeholderText={placeholderText} />
    )


export const TextValue = inputValueComponent({ inputType: "text" })
```

Exercise 6.3 asks you to refactor common code to a **<DisplayValue>** component.

Use the **<DisplayValue>** component.

Listing 6.13 src/frontend/value-components.jsx—the second part

```
const isNumber = (str) => !isNaN(str) && (str.trim().length > 0)
export const NumberValue = inputValueComponent({ inputType: "number",
    isValid: isNumber })

export const DropDownValue = observer((({ editState, className, options,
        placeholderText, actionText }) =>
    editState.inEdit
        ? <select
            autoFocus={true}
            value={editState.value}
            style={{ width: Math.max(
                    ...options.map((option) => option.length),
                    actionText && actionText.length
                ) + "ch"
            }}
            onChange={action((event) => {
                const newValue = event.target.value
                if (newValue !== actionText) {
                    editState.setValue(newValue)
                    editState.inEdit = false
                }
            })}
            onBlur={action((_) => {
                editState.inEdit = false
            })}
            onKeyUp={action((event) => {
                if (event.key === "Escape") {
                    editState.inEdit = false
                }
            })}
            className={className}
        >
            {actionText && <option key={-1} className="action">
                {actionText}</option>}
            {options.map((option, index) =>
                <option key={index}>{option}</option>
            )}
        </select>
        : <DisplayValue editState={editState}        ◁─── Use the
            className={className} placeholderText={placeholderText} />       <DisplayValue>
)                                                                          component.
```

Listing 6.14 src/frontend/support-components.jsx

```
import React from "react"
import { action, observable } from "mobx"
import { observer } from "mobx-react"

import { asClassNameArgument } from "./css-util"

const selection = observable({ selected: undefined })
```

```
const deselect = () => {
    selection.selected = undefined
}

document.addEventListener("mousedown", action((event) => {
    if (!event.target.classList.contains("selectable")) {
        deselect()
    }
}))

export const AstObjectUiWrapper = observer(({ className, astObject,
        deleteAstObject, children }) => {
    return <div
        className={asClassNameArgument(className, "selectable",
            (selection.selected === astObject) && "selected")}
        onClick={action((event) => {
            event.stopPropagation()
            selection.selected = astObject
        })}
        onKeyDown={action((event) => {
            if (selection.selected === astObject
                    && event.key === "Backspace"
                    || event.key === "Delete") {
                event.preventDefault()
                event.stopPropagation()
                if (typeof deleteAstObject === "function") {
                    deleteAstObject()
                }
            }
            if (event.key === "Escape") {
                deselect()
            }
        })}
        tabIndex={0}
    >
        {children}
    </div>
})

export const AddNewButton = ({ buttonText, actionFunction }) =>
    <button
        className="add-new"
        tabIndex={-1}
        onClick={action((event) => {
            event.stopPropagation()
            actionFunction()
        })}
    >{buttonText}</button>
```

The second bullet of exercise 6.13 asks for this fix.

The second bullet of exercise 6.12 asks you to add this event handler.

In this chapter, you learned how to make entire AST objects in the AST selectable and editable. In the next chapter, we're going to see how to retrieve an AST from a back-end and persist it there.

Summary

- In addition to being able to edit a simple setting's value or choose the target of a reference relation, a DSL editor needs to have the following editing capabilities:
  - Create new objects in the AST.
  - Select and deselect AST objects.
  - Delete AST objects after having selected them.
- A *placeholder value* is used to indicate the intention to add a new AST object to the AST. This mechanism is used when the domain expert intends to create a new AST object but has to choose a concept for the new AST object first.
- After creating a new AST object, many or all of its properties won't have received a setting (with a value) yet. The projection has to deal with that lack of value. This is often done by adapting any expression that accesses a setting's value as follows: `settings["<property name>"] && <expression accessing the same property's setting>`.
- The Domain IDE keeps track of whether an AST object is selected, and if so, which one was selected. This is part of the Domain IDE's application state. The Domain IDE also supports deselection.
- To avoid code duplication, a wrapping React component can be used. This wrapping component wraps the projection of an AST object and makes it selectable and deselectable.
- Once an AST object is selected, it can be deleted. The deletion from the AST itself is handled by a function that's passed to the wrapping component.
- The DSL editor needs to take care of DOM events such as mouse clicks and keypresses properly, to avoid such events being propagated in an unwanted way.

7

Implementing persistence and transportation of ASTs

This chapter covers

- Implementing a simple web backend with a REST API to persist an AST
- Serializing an AST to JSON
- Deserializing an AST from its serialized JSON form
- Fixing the reference problem we encountered in chapters 5 and 6

In chapters 4 through 6, you learned how to create a projectional editor that allows domain experts to edit DSL content that's internally represented as an AST. We haven't implemented any *persistence* for that DSL content so far. The AST that our editor works on only exists on the frontend. It's constructed in-memory by code that's part of the bundled frontend code. When the AST is altered, the changes aren't stored.

In this chapter, we're going to implement AST persistence as illustrated in figure 7.1. First, we're going to implement an extremely simple REST web backend, which will store one JSON file on disk. (The implementation will be as simple as possible—maybe even naive.) This might seem limiting, but it will suffice for our

164

purposes, and it will keep things simple. Frontends can GET this JSON file and also PUT a new version of it, which replaces the previous version on disk.

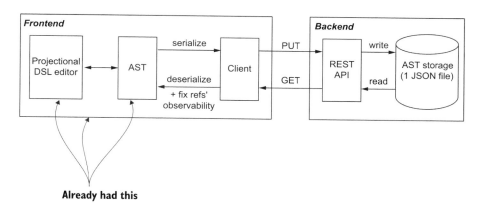

Figure 7.1   Architecture of the frontend and backend for implementing AST persistence

Next, we're going to represent an AST as JSON: this process is called *serialization* (see figure 7.2). For that, we need to deal with reference relations between AST objects. This allows us to store an AST on our backend, and also to transport an AST over HTTP.

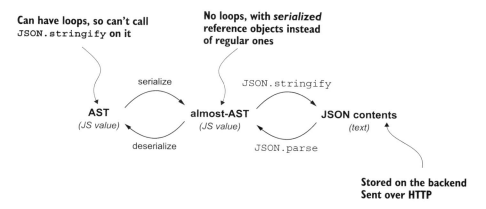

Figure 7.2   What serialization and deserialization do, and how they relate to each other

The reverse process—reconstituting an AST from its serialized form—is called *deserialization*. As with serialization, the tricky bit is taking care of reference relations between AST objects. Deserialization allows us to retrieve an AST from our backend.

With these two capabilities in place, we can extend the frontend with a client that communicates with the backend. We'll have the frontend retrieve the AST from the backend and store or save it when we ask it to.

At various points in chapters 5 and 6, we encountered a problem with reference relations not always behaving as such in the editor. This is a result of making the AST deeply observable and MobX not knowing about reference relations. We'll fix this problem by combining deserialization with making the AST observable. That way, we can tell MobX when a JavaScript object reference corresponds to containment and when it corresponds to a reference.

7.1   *Implementing and using a simple backend*

Let's implement a simple backend that persists one JSON file. To make use of the backend, we'll also integrate a small client into the frontend that we implemented in the previous chapters. Being able to read and write just *one* JSON file might seem ridiculously simplistic, but it's really all we need. We've been dealing with precisely one AST at all times, and that isn't going to change in the rest of this book. We can consider the backend to be part of the "accidental" (or "incidental") complexity of a Domain IDE, so it makes sense to keep it as simple as possible. The added bonus is that we can also keep the client in the frontend simple.

A RESTful API over HTTP is pretty much today's industry standard for the backend of a web app. We'll implement a REST API with just one resource (with the URL /contents), and it will correspond to the one persisted JSON file. This resource will handle only GET and PUT requests. The API will respond to a GET request with the current contents of the persisted JSON file as the response's body. To overwrite the contents of the persisted JSON file, we'll make a PUT request with its body holding the new JSON contents.

We'll put the code for the backend in the path src/backend/. Within that directory, we'll make a data/ directory. That directory is going to contain a contents.json file: the persisted JSON contents file.

First, let's implement storing a JSON file with the path src/backend/data/contents.json. We'll put the code for that in the following two files: src/common/file-utils.js will contain generic functions to deal with (JSON) files, and src/common/storage.js will implement the backend's JSON storage. (Later, we'll use src/common/file-utils.js in another part of the Domain IDE as well.)

Listing 7.1   src/common/file-utils.js—generic functions for JSON files

```
const { readFileSync, writeFileSync } = require("fs")      ◁──  Import functions to read
                                                                 and write files from
                                                                 Node.js's built-in file
                                                                 system module.

const writeString = (path, data) => {      ◁──  Define and export a writeString function
    writeFileSync(path, data)                    that writes the string passed as the second
}                                                data argument to the file with its path
                                                 given by the first path argument.
```

```
module.exports.writeString = writeString

const writeJson = (path, data) => {
    writeString(path, JSON.stringify(data, null, 2))
}
module.exports.writeJson = writeJson

const readJson = (path) =>
    JSON.parse(readFileSync(path,
        { encoding: "utf8" }).toString())
module.exports.readJson = readJson
```

Define and export a writeJson function that writes the JavaScript value passed as the second data argument to the file with the path given by the first path argument.

Define and export a readJson function that reads the file with the path given by the first path argument, assuming it's JSON, and that returns the parsed JavaScript value.

The readFileSync function has no default character encoding. Because the write functions encode everything as UTF-8, we'll configure this function to read files as being encoded in UTF-8 as well.

For information on the file system module `fs`, see https://nodejs.org/api/fs.html. The `writeFileSync` function uses UTF-8 character encoding by default, but we do have to specify that encoding for `readFileSync`.

Listing 7.2   src/backend/storage.js—backend JSON storage

Import the join function from Node.js's built-in path module.

Import the readJson and writeJson functions from listing 7.1.

```
const { join } = require("path")

const { readJson, writeJson } =
    require("../common/file-utils")

const contentsPath =
    join(__dirname, "data", "contents.json")

const readContents = () => readJson(contentsPath)
module.exports.readContents = readContents

const writeContents = (contents) =>
    writeJson(contentsPath, contents)
module.exports.writeContents = writeContents
```

Compute the path for the contents file.

Define and export a readContents function that reads the JSON contents file and returns it as a parsed JavaScript value.

Define and export a writeContents function that writes the given JavaScript value to the JSON contents file.

For information on the module, `path`, see https://nodejs.org/api/path.html. It's good practice to use the functions in this module to avoid problems with platform-dependent path separators (\ on Windows, and / everywhere else). Node.js provides the value `__dirname`, which is always the path of the directory containing the current JavaScript file—in this case, src/backend/. The call to the `join` function then results in a path data/contents.json relative to src/backend/.

Create the src/backend/data/contents.json file, and put the JSON shown in the next listing in it.

Listing 7.3   Initial contents of the src/backend/data/contents.json file

```
{
    "title": "Ceci n'est pas un arbre."
}
```

Either you get the contextual reference to a painting by René Magritte, or you don't.

You probably don't want this file to be tracked by the versioning system. If you're using Git, you can create a .gitignore file in src/backend/data/ with the following as its only contents:

```
/contents.json
```

Now let's implement a REST web backend. We'll use the Express framework (https://expressjs.com/) to code up a simple HTTP server. I've chosen to use Express, instead of another web app/backend framework in the Node.js ecosystem, for a few reasons:

- It's easy to use with minimal configuration.
- It's well known and popular.
- It easily integrates with the Parcel web bundler.
- It's the framework I happen to be most familiar with.

To use Express, we have to add it as a dependency:

```
$ npm install express
```

Now we can implement a simple REST web backend using Express to store and serve one JSON file.

Listing 7.4 Code to start an Express server in src/backend/server.js

Import the readContents function and use it to
read the JSON contents file. Assign the parsed
JavaScript value to the contents variable.

Import the whole
express module,
instead of specific
items inside it.

```
const { readContents } = require("./storage")
let contents = readContents()

const express = require("express")
const server = express()

server.get("/contents", (request, response) => {
    response.json(contents)
})

// TODO  add PUT code

// TODO  add static serving code

const port = 8080
server.listen(port, () => {
    console.log(`Server started on: http://localhost:${port}`)
})
```

Create an Express server—
the express module is also
a constructor function.

We'll replace
these comments
with additional
code later.

Start listening on the
specified port, and report
after it has started.

Configure a handler for a GET request on the /contents
resource. This handler responds with the 200 OK HTTP
status code and passes contents as the response's
body, marked as JSON.

Let's start this server and see whether it works:

```
$ node src/backend/server.js
Server started on: http://localhost:8080/
```

Pointing a browser to http://localhost:8080/contents reproduces listing 7.3, as expected. The only way to stop the server is by pressing Ctrl-C in the command-line interface.

In previous chapters, we had Parcel bundle the frontend code to a dist/ directory and serve the contents of that directory on http://localhost:1234/. We'll have the backend serve the same contents from http://localhost:8080/ by adding the following code to src/backend/server.js. This code sets up serving the contents of the dist/ directory as static content by the Express server. It replaces the `static serving code` comment placeholder in src/backend/server.js.

Listing 7.5 Serving the dist/ directory as static content

```
const { join } = require("path")
server.use(express.static(join(__dirname, "..", "..", "dist")))
```

Serving the frontend as static content avoids the *Cross-Origin Resource Sharing* (CORS) problem. Browsers consider http://localhost:1234/ and http://localhost:8080/ to be different origins, and they block requests between them for security reasons. This means that a frontend served on port 1234 can't communicate with a backend serving requests on port 8080, at least not without serving appropriate CORS headers from the backend to inform the browser that it shouldn't block cross-origin requests coming from the frontend.

> **NOTE** See the Mozilla documentation for more information on CORS: https://developer.mozilla.org/en-US/docs/Web/HTTP/CORS.

For this setup to work, you'll have to run Parcel either once (using `parcel build`), or continuously. To run Parcel continuously, you can execute the following from a separate command line, because running Node.js blocks the terminal:

```
$ npx parcel src/frontend/index.html
```

With this setup, even hot-reloading works correctly.

Exercise 7.1
- Apply the preceding code changes.
  a Populate the src/common/file-utils.js file with the contents of listing 7.1.
  b Populate the src/backend/storage.js file with the contents of listing 7.2.
  c Populate the src/backend/server.js file with the contents of listing 7.4, and replace the `static serving code` comments placeholder with listing 7.5.

(continued)
- Test these changes after restarting the server by pointing your browser to http://localhost:8080/ and http://localhost:8080/contents.
- Check whether the frontend's code is still watched by Parcel and that hot-module replacement still works.

We still have to change the frontend to ask the backend for JSON contents. So far, we've loaded an AST that's constructed in-memory by the following code in src/frontend/index.jsx:

```
import rental from "../ch03/rental-AST"
```

We're going to replace this code with code that relies on the Fetch browser API (https://developer.mozilla.org/en-US/docs/Web/API/Fetch_API). We'll start out by adding the following to src/frontend/index.jsx:

Listing 7.6   Initial code to fetch JSON from the backend

```
const apiUrl = "http://localhost:8080/contents"      ◁       Define a constant for the URL of
                                                             the REST API on the backend.

fetch(apiUrl)                                        ◁       Use the fetch function
    .then((response) => response.json())             ◁       to send a GET request
    .then((json) => {                                ◁       to the REST API.
        // TODO  do something with the fetched JSON
    })                                                       Extract the JSON body
                                                             using the json function on
              The extracted JSON is passed to the next       the response object that's
              .then(...) in the chain, which should do        returned to the Promise
                    something meaningful with it.            object.
```

The `fetch` function used in the preceding listing is asynchronous: it immediately returns a `Promise` object, which sends the request and waits for the backend's response. By calling the `Promise.then` function with a function argument, we can tell the `Promise` object what we want to do with the response when it arrives.

Asynchronous JavaScript

To learn more about this style of asynchronicity using the browser's `Promise` API, you can take a look at the following chapters from books by Manning:

- Chapter 6 of *JavaScript Application Design: A Build First Approach*, by Nicolas G. Bevacqua (Manning, 2015): https://livebook.manning.com/book/javascript-application-design/chapter-6/
- Chapter 30 of *Get Programming with JavaScript Next: New features of ECMAScript 2015, 2016, and beyond*, by J.D. Isaacks (Manning, 2018): https://livebook.manning.com/book/get-programming-with-javascript-next/chapter-30/

Until now, we've held the AST for the `Rental` record type in the `rental` variable, and we've passed that to the `Projection` function as follows:

```
<Projection astObject={observable(rental)} ancestors={[]} />
```

We could modify listing 7.6 to assign the received JSON content to `rental` after parsing it:

```
rental = json
```

However, this doesn't work. The call to `Projection` doesn't react to `rental` changes because `rental` is not observable. To fix that, we'll store the AST in an observable object that initially has a `null`-valued property, `ast`:

```
const state = observable({
    ast: null
})
```

When we receive the JSON content, we can store it in that object:

```
state.ast = json
```

As before, MobX only allows us to change observable state inside *actions*. We can mark the preceding statement as action code by wrapping the entire function argument to the second `then(...)` with MobX's `action` function. Change the code from listing 7.6 as follows:

```
import { action, observable } from "mobx"          ◁─┤ Import MobX's
                                                       action function.
const apiUrl = "http://localhost:8080/contents"

fetch(apiUrl)                                          Wrap the entire
    .then((response) => response.json())               arrow function
    .then(action((json) => {              ◁─────────   argument in action.
        state.ast = json
    }))              ◁─┐ Don't forget the right parenthesis
                       of the action(...) call.
```

Now we have to ensure that any call or invocation of `Projection` is observed. The simplest way to do that is to create a new state-observing component. This one will show a spinner before the AST is loaded and project it afterward.

Listing 7.7 A state-observing React component

```
import { observer } from "mobx-react"          ◁─┤ Import the observer
                                                   function.
const App = observer(({ state }) =>
    state.ast                       ◁─┐ Check whether the value stored
        ? <Projection                  in state.ast is truthy: if it is, it
                                       should be an AST.
```

```
            astObject={state.ast}          ◁──┐   Call Projection with
            ancestors={ [] }                   │   the loaded AST.
        />
        : <div className="spinner"></div>  ◁──┐   React component functions have
)                                              │   to return an HTML DOM element.
```

Here are a few points about the preceding listing:

- MobX reacts to property access of *any* observable object, not only to property access of those objects that are explicitly passed. This means we don't have to pass astContainer explicitly through an attribute, but can directly refer to the variable defined earlier.
- Because state is a deeply observable object, state.ast is automatically deeply observable as well, so we don't have to call observable(...) explicitly.
- If the call to a React component returns undefined or null, React issues an error, and the app crashes. Displaying a spinner avoids this problem and encourages the domain expert to simply wait a bit.

Add the following CSS definitions to src/frontend/styling.css for a nice spinner effect. (This code is adapted from Tobias Ahlin's page at https://tobiasahlin.com/spinkit/.)

Listing 7.8 CSS definitions for an animated spinner

```
div.spinner {
    width: 40px;
    height: 40px;
    margin: 100px auto;
    background-color: #333;
    border-radius: 100%;
    animation: sk-scaleout 1.0s infinite ease-in-out;
}

@keyframes sk-scaleout {
    0% {
        transform: scale(0);
    }
    100% {
        transform: scale(1.0);
        opacity: 0;
    }
}
```

The call to React's render function now looks like the following:

```
createRoot(document.getElementById("root"))
    .render(
        <App state={state} />
    )
```

If we now browse to http://localhost:8080/, we might see the spinner spinning for an instant. Then we'll see the result in figure 7.3. That's because our projection can't deal with the content in listing 7.3, which is not an AST. After all, calling the `isAst-Object` function on the JavaScript value in that listing produces `false`. Our next step should be to produce valid content for src/backend/data/contents.json.

No projection defined for value: [object Object]   **Figure 7.3   Result of trying to project a non-AST**

Let's serialize the example AST for the `Rental` record type to JSON, and store that as the JSON content. We'll do that in a standalone Node.js program in a new file: src/init/jsonify-Rental.js.

Listing 7.9   "JSONifying" the `Rental` example AST

```
const { writeContents } = require("../backend/storage")
const rental = require("../ch03/rental-AST")

writeContents(rental)
```

Run this program as follows:

```
$ node src/init/jsonify-Rental.js
```

If we now run the Node.js program in listing 7.9, we should see the following content in src/backend/data/contents.json.

Listing 7.10   The "JSONified" `Rental` example AST

```
{
  "concept": "Record Type",
  "settings": {
    "name": "Rental",
    "attributes": [
      {
        // ...attribute 1...
      },                                    The second
      {                                 ◁──  attribute
        "concept": "Data Attribute",
        "settings": {
          "name": "rental price before discount",
          "type": "amount",
          "initial value": {
            "concept": "Number",
            "settings": {
              "value": "0.0"
            }
          }
        }
      },
```

```
      {
        // ...attribute 3...
      },
      {
        "concept": "Data Attribute",
        "settings": {
          "name": "rental price after discount",
          "type": "amount",
          "initial value": {
            "concept": "Attribute Reference",
            "settings": {
              "attribute": {
                "ref": {
                  "concept": "Data Attribute",
                  "settings": {
                    "name": "rental price before discount",
                    // ...rest of JSON for attribute 2...
                  }
                }>
              }
            }
          }
        }
      }
    ]
  }
}
```

> JSON.stringify follows the JavaScript object reference to the second attribute that's the value of ref, and it stringifies that whole attribute again.

We can serve this to the frontend, and the frontend will project this happily. That's because the projection doesn't really care whether `settings["attribute"].ref` on an `Attribute Reference` object points to an attribute object that's somewhere else in the AST, or to an entirely new attribute object that's simply defined as "out of place." However, we're projecting an AST that's really not identical to the example AST we were using before. That's because every AST object ends up in the JSON once where it should, but also everywhere it's referenced again. Editing that "wrong" AST likely produces a different AST than intended.

This would become even more apparent if we'd started out with an AST that has relations that "loop around." We say that such an AST has a *cycle*. An AST like this is unlikely and possibly nonsensical. On the other hand, our rules for ASTs from chapter 2 don't forbid it, so we *have* to be able to handle it. Figure 7.4 shows an AST object with a cycle.

Figure 7.4   An AST consisting of one AST object with a loop, or cycle, in the form of a self-reference

We can construct an example of such an AST as follows, using the Node.js REPL:

```
> const astObject = {
    concept: "Foo",
    settings: {
        "self-ref.": {}
    }
}
undefined
> astObject.settings["self-ref."].ref = astObject
<ref *1> {
  concept: 'Foo',
  settings: { 'self-ref.': { ref: [Circular *1] } }
}
```

Create a key-value pair for a self-ref property, and assign an empty object to it.

Fix that empty object to be a proper reference object with { ref: astObject } as the value.

The REPL's response to executing that statement already gives a hint about the circular nature of this AST.

Note that in the preceding code, the value of `astObject` in the Node.js REPL interaction is not yet a valid AST after executing the first statement. The second statement fixes that. It also encodes a *self-reference* from `astObject` to itself. This is also called a *loop*, or cycle of length 1, making the AST *circular*.

When we attempt to use `JSON.stringify`, we get an outright runtime error:

```
> JSON.stringify(astObject, null, 2)
Uncaught TypeError: Converting circular structure to JSON
    --> starting at object with constructor 'Object'
    |      property 'settings' -> object with constructor 'Object'
    |      property 'self-ref.' -> object with constructor 'Object'
    --- property 'ref' closes the circle
    at JSON.stringify (<anonymous>)
```

`JSON.stringify` detects the circularity before losing itself in an infinite recursive loop, throwing an error instead. We need to serialize an AST to JSON in a way that properly deals with reference relations, without an error being thrown. We also need to be able to reconstitute an identical AST from that JSON serialization, including proper reference relations.

Exercise 7.2
- Draw the ORD for the AST serialized shown in listing 7.10. How is it different from the ORD for the actual `Rental` AST?
- Why isn't the `Rental` AST circular, despite the initial value of the fourth attribute pointing back up to the second attribute?
- Some ASTs have more subtle loops that consist of a couple of containment relations, followed by a reference relation back to an ancestor. Create an AST that has a more subtle loop, or cycle. Try to serialize it with `JSON.stringify`. Does it share the same fate as the self-referencing AST in figure 7.4? (Hint: Of course, it does.)

7.2   *Serializing an AST*

You've seen, in the previous section, that serializing an AST to JSON isn't as easy as just calling JSON.stringify. Let's serialize an AST in a way that allows us to turn it into text using JSON.stringify *and* reconstruct that same AST from that text. The core problem we need to solve is how to properly deal with reference relations.

We already know how to recognize reference relations, using the isAstReference function from chapter 3. But a JavaScript object reference points to the target of the reference relation—how can we replace that with "something" that's representable in JSON *and* doesn't cause JSON.stringify to throw an error?

Half of the solution happens to be both simple and standard: *use IDs*! We'll give every AST object a proper, unique ID. Then, serializing an AST boils down to replacing the ref: targetObject key-value pair on any reference object with a refId: targetObject.id key-value pair.

First, we have to decide where to store AST objects' IDs in the in-memory JavaScript representation. The most logical thing would be to use a key-value pair directly on the AST's JavaScript object with id as the key, and some ID value as the value. We'll use a string ID value, but any other type would work, as long as we can produce unique values of that type.

This means that any AST object is going to look like the following, from now on:

```
{
    id: "<unique-ID>",          ◁──┐   The added key-value
    concept: "<concept>",           │   pair for the ID
    settings: {
        // ...
    }
}
```

Next, we're going to *generate* these IDs. We'll use the nanoid JavaScript library. Install its npm package as follows:

```
$ npm install nanoid
```

The newId function in the following listing uses the nanoid library to generate a random ID. The IDs will consist of 10 characters, each of which is either alphanumeric (both lower- and uppercase), an underscore (_), or a hyphen (-).

> **Listing 7.11   Code for a newId function that generates a random ID**

```
const { nanoid } = require("nanoid")
const newId = () => nanoid(10)        ◁──┤   Define a newId function that generates a
                                           random ID consisting of 10 characters.
```

There's no guarantee that the IDs generated by calling the newId function many times are actually unique, which they should be for our purposes. There's a 1% chance of at least one collision in roughly 17 years, provided you generate 1,000 IDs per hour that entire time. I'd say that's good enough for our purposes here. For "real" ASTs, we really should use longer IDs, but for now we'll opt to go easy on our eyeballs.

Just for kicks, let's generate a few IDs on the Node.js REPL:

```
$ node
> const { nanoid } = require("nanoid")
undefined
> const newId = () => nanoid(10)
undefined
> Array(10).fill().map(newId)                ◁─┐  Generate an array of length 10, fill() it
[                                              │  with undefined values, and map each
    'BYTVm4JCcT', 'cbkWqYzIPV',                │  of those using the newId function.
    'HnMKt_pl_y', 'A48XZIz4aC',
    'v_DPkM2aLB', 'OyaVS6dK5S',
    'XCjVpFuCJF', 'LeQhanlICR',
    'YQMXkGPmr1', 'LKlvLNeIcs'
]
```

Because the 10 generated IDs are random, you should see different ID values (but in the same format) when running this code yourself.

Let's recreate the `Rental` example AST, but this time with IDs. To make that a bit less tedious, we'll make use of some *factory functions*. These are functions that help with properly constructing AST objects. The `newAstObject` function constructs a new AST object with the given concept label and settings—which are optionally given—and a generated random ID. The `astReferenceTo` function constructs a reference object, giving the target object. We'll add both to src/common/ast.js. Because these factory functions make use of the `newId` function, we first have to add the contents of listing 7.11 to src/common/ast.js. After we've done that, we can add the following code as well.

> **Listing 7.12 The new `newAstObject` and `astReferenceTo` functions**

Use the newId function to generate a random ID. | **Define and export a newAstObject function that constructs a new AST object.** | **Use JavaScript's shorthand literal notation for key-value pairs to put the given concept label in the object.**

```
   const newAstObject = (concept, settings) => ({     ◁──┐
       id: newId(),
       concept,                                        ◁───
       settings: settings || {}          ◁─┐
   })                                       │    Add the given settings
   module.exports.newAstObject = newAstObject   │    object, or an empty
                                            │    object if settings is falsy.
   const astReferenceTo = (targetAstObject) => ({    ◁─┐
       ref: targetAstObject                            │  Define and export an
   })                                                  │  astReferenceTo function that
   module.exports.astReferenceTo = astReferenceTo      │  constructs an AST reference
                                                        │  object to the target AST object.
```

Because the `newId` function is only used here, it doesn't need to be exported. The `settings` argument to the `newAstObject` function is optional because of the `|| {}` bit. We're going to use that convenience later, in the code of the `<Projection>` function.

Now we can use these functions to construct the example AST. Create a src/init directory to hold code files related to initialization. Then add an example-AST.js file to it with the following contents.

Listing 7.13   Creating the `Rental` example AST with IDs

```
const { newAstObject, astReferenceTo } = require("../common/ast")

const rentalPeriodAttribute = newAstObject("Data Attribute", {
    "name": "rental period",
    "type": "date range"
})

const rentalPriceBeforeDiscountAttribute = newAstObject("Data Attribute", {
    "name": "rental price before discount",
    "type": "amount",
    "initial value": newAstObject("Number", {
        "value": "0.0"
    })
})

const discountAttribute = newAstObject("Data Attribute", {
    "name": "discount",
    "type": "percentage",
    "initial value": newAstObject("Number", {
        "value": "0"
    })
})

const rentalPriceAfterDiscountAttribute = newAstObject("Data Attribute", {
    "name": "rental price after discount",
    "type": "amount",
    "initial value": newAstObject("Attribute Reference", {
        "attribute": astReferenceTo(rentalPriceBeforeDiscountAttribute)
    })
})


const rental = newAstObject("Record Type", {
    "name": "Rental",
    "attributes": [
        rentalPeriodAttribute,
        rentalPriceBeforeDiscountAttribute,
        discountAttribute,
        rentalPriceAfterDiscountAttribute
    ]
})

module.exports = rental
```

This code is a bit shorter than that in listing 3.3, partly because of the use of factory functions and partly because I "inlined" the construction of the AST objects encoding the attributes' initial values.

We can also use the `astReferenceTo` function in existing projection code in src/frontend/projection.jsx, as follows.

Listing 7.14 Code changes to use `astReferenceTo` in projection code

```
import { astReferenceTo, isAstObject,
    placeholderAstObject } from "../common/ast"

// ...in the Data Attribute case in the Projection function...
setValue: (newValue) => {
    settings["attribute"] = astReferenceTo(
        attributes.find((attribute) =>
            attribute.settings["name"] === newValue)
    )
}
```

The plan is now to transform any AST with references into a tree that's almost exactly the same, except that every reference object has been modified. The modification will make use of the IDs. More precisely, a reference object, { ref: *(JavaScript object reference to)* targetObject }, will become { refId: *(a string)* targetObject.id }. Suppose the original AST contained the following:

```
...
    {
        id: "<id1>",
        concept: "<concept1>",
        settings: {
            // ...
        }
    }
...
    {
        id: "<id2>",
        concept: "<concept2>",
        settings: {
            "<ref-property>": {
                "ref": <JavaScript object reference to the AST object
                    with id = id1>
            },
            // ...other settings...
        }
    }
...
```

The modified tree would look like this:

```
...
    {
        id: "<id1>",
        concept: "<concept1>",
        settings: {
```

```
            // ...
        }
    }
    ...
    {
        id: "<id2>",
        concept: "<concept2>",
        settings: {
            "<ref-property>": {
                "refId": "<id1>"
            },
            // ...other settings...
        }
    }
    ...
```

The tree produced by this transformation is not an AST, but it's pretty close: it's an "almost-AST." This tree can't have a cycle, so we can just call JSON.stringify on it to serialize it to JSON.

Let's implement a serialize function in src/common/ast.js that performs this transformation. We'll use the familiar pattern of the depth-first tree traversal (listing 3.9) to implement the transformation.

Listing 7.15 Transforming an AST into a cycle-free "almost-AST"

```
const serialize = (value) => {
    if (isAstObject(value)) {
        const serializedAstObject = {
            id: value.id,
            concept: value.concept,
            settings: {}
        }
        for (const propertyName in value.settings) {
            serializedAstObject.settings[propertyName] =
                ⇒ serialize(value.settings[propertyName])
        }
        return serializedAstObject
    }
    if (isAstReferenceObject(value)) {                    Return a new object instead
        return ({                                         of the reference object.
            refId: isAstObject(value.ref)
                ⇒ ? value.ref.id                          Set refId to targetObject.id
                ⇒ : undefined                             on the new object, or to
        })                                                undefined if the reference
    }                                                     object didn't actually point
    if (Array.isArray(value)) {                           to a target object (yet).
        return value.map(serialize)
    }
    return value
}
module.exports.serialize = serialize
```

When the user saves DSL content that contains a reference for which the target hasn't been selected yet, the corresponding reference object will look like { ref: undefined }. The preceding code deals with that situation by checking explicitly whether value.ref is (a JavaScript object reference to) an actual AST object. If it isn't, evaluating an expression such as value.ref.id would throw an error.

Let's "JSONify" the Rental example AST again, but this time properly, using serialize. We'll do that in a standalone Node.js program in a new file: src/init/install-example-DSL-content.js.

Listing 7.16 Serializing the Rental example AST properly

```
const { writeContents } = require("../backend/storage")      Read in the Rental
const { serialize } = require("../common/ast")               AST as constructed
const rental = require("./example-AST")              ◀────── with IDs.

writeContents(serialize(rental))          ◀──────── Invoke serialize on rental before
                                                    writing it to the JSON contents file.
```

Execute this program from the command line as follows:

```
$ node src/init/install-example-DSL-content.js
```

This overwrites the file src/backend/data/contents.json with contents that we'll describe below. Because of its length, I split this JSON content up into listings 7.17 and 7.18. Listing 7.17 contains the "outer" part of the serialization of the Rental example AST to JSON, focusing on the Rental record type AST object.

Listing 7.17 "Outer" part of the serialization of the Rental AST

```
{
  "id": "rEQR-Q2pER",
  "concept": "Record Type",
  "settings": {
    "name": "Rental",                            The array containing the
    "attributes":                                record type's attributes is
      ...contents of listing 7.18...      ◀───── shown in listing 7.18.
  }
}
```

Listing 7.18 contains the "inner" part of the serialization of the Rental example AST to JSON, consisting of an array with the serializations of the attributes' AST objects. As you can see, every AST object now has an ID, and serialized references use those IDs.

Listing 7.18 "Inner" part of the serialization of the Rental AST

```
[
  {
    "id": "4IU7ekPqF",
    "concept": "Data Attribute",
```

```
      "settings": {
        "name": "rental period",
        "type": "date range"
      }
    },
    {
      "id": "SlLaELvAy0",                    ◄──────   All AST objects—particularly
      "concept": "Data Attribute",                     the AST object for the second
      "settings": {                                    attribute—now have an ID.
        "name": "rental price before discount",
        "type": "amount",
        "initial value": {
          "id": "u1ZXfEd7yn",
          "concept": "Number",
          "settings": {
            "value": "0.0"
          }
        }
      }
    },
    {
      "id": "yeGPC9VqH6",
      "concept": "Data Attribute",
      "settings": {
        "name": "discount",
        "type": "percentage",
        "initial value": {
          "id": "DembP_tUU_",
          "concept": "Number",
          "settings": {
            "value": "0"
          }
        }
      }
    },
    {
      "id": "7Bc1ad_70r",
      "concept": "Data Attribute",
      "settings": {
          "name": "rental price after discount",
          "type": "amount",
          "initial value": {
            "id": "86c8jJ1C3t",
            "concept": "Attribute Reference",
            "settings": {
              "attribute": {
                "refId": "SlLaELvAy0"        ◄──────   A serialized reference object of
              }                                         the form { "refId": "<ID>" },
            }                                           instead of a reference object of
          }                                             the form { ref: <AST object> }.
        }                                               The <ID> here is that of the
      }                                                 second attribute object above.
    }
]
```

NOTE The IDs in the preceding listing are generated randomly, so yours should differ.

After we restart the backend, we notice that the frontend crashes, with an error left on the JavaScript console as shown in figure 7.5.

Figure 7.5   An error occurs after restarting the backend.

This is not surprising, as the backend serves the JSON contents in listing 7.17 (with listing 7.18 nested) verbatim to the frontend, and that JSON is not a proper AST. We'll see in the next section how we can use the `refId` values to reconstitute the value of the `ref` field.

Exercise 7.3
- Explain why the transformed tree is not a proper AST.
- Explain why the transformed tree can't contain a cycle.
- Implement a tree traversal that checks that no `ref` properties have a value (other than `undefined`) in the serialized AST.

7.3   *Deserializing an AST*

Serializing an AST turned out to be pretty easy. What about the reverse process, deserialization? Given an "almost-AST" that was serialized using the `serialize` function from listing 17.5, let's deserialize that JSON to end up with a proper AST. This deserialized AST should be identical to the AST before serialization.

The idea is to look for serialized reference objects in the serialized almost-AST. These are of the form { `refId`: *<some ID>* }. When found, we'll replace that object with an object of the form { `ref`: *<(JavaScript object reference to) AST object with ID equal to <some ID>>* }. The action of replacing the ID of a referenced AST object with an actual reference to that object is called "resolving the reference." We'll have to do this for every serialized reference object.

Sometimes, `<some ID>` was `undefined`. This happens when the user has saved DSL content that contains a reference relation for which the reference target hasn't been selected. That means we have to make sure that we recognize serialized reference objects of the form { `refId: undefined` } as such, and that we deserialize such objects as { `ref: undefined` }.

For reasons that will become clear in the next section, we won't modify the serialized almost-AST—we'll transform it into a completely new, proper AST. We'll use a slight variant of the standard pattern for depth-first tree traversal to implement this transformation. The only difference from the standard traversal is that we have to detect *serialized* reference objects, instead of regular reference objects.

Let's first add a function to the src/common/ast.js file that detects serialized reference objects. It's quite similar to the `isAstReference` function in the same file:

```
const isSerializedAstReference = (value) =>
    isObject(value) && ("refId" in value)
```

With that, we can now start to write a `deserialize` function in the src/common/ast.js file as follows.

Listing 7.19   The initial version of the `deserialize` function

```
const deserialize = (value) => {
    if (isAstObject(value)) {
        const astObject = {
            id: value.id,
            concept: value.concept,
            settings: {}
        }
        for (const propertyName in value.settings) {
            astObject.settings[propertyName] =
                deserialize(value.settings[propertyName])
        }
        return astObject
    }
    if (isSerializedAstReference(value)) {            Call isSerializedAstReference
        return {                                      instead of isAstReference.
            ref: <the AST object with ID = value.refId>        Transform the
        }                                                      serialized reference
    }                                         We still have to   object in value into
    if (Array.isArray(value)) {               somehow look up    a true reference
        return value.map(deserialize)         AST object with an ID  object, and
    }                                         equal to value.refId.  return it.
    return value
}
```

To efficiently look up AST objects based on their ID, we'll create an object that will serve as a lookup table. The key-value pairs in that object will have an ID as a key and the AST object with that ID as the value.

We can adapt the code above as follows.

Listing 7.20   The second iteration of the `deserialize` function

```
const deserialize = (value) => {                    ◁——  Define the deserialize
    const id2AstObject = {}                               function all over again.

                                                    ◁——  Maintain a map holding AST
                                                          objects, indexed by their IDs.
    const deserializeInternal = (value) => {        ◁——
        if (isAstObject(value)) {                         Define a deserializeInternal
            const astObject = {                           function inside the
                id: value.id,                             deserialize function.
                concept: value.concept,
                settings: {}
            }
            for (const propertyName in value.settings) {
                astObject.settings[propertyName] =
                    deserializeInternal(value.settings[propertyName])
            }
            id2AstObject[value.id] = astObject      ◁——  Store the created object in the
            return astObject                              lookup table, under its ID.
        }
        if (isSerializedAstReference(value)) {
            return { ref: id2AstObject[value.refId] }  ◁——
        }                                                   Use the lookup table
        if (Array.isArray(value)) {                         to create the proper
            return value.map(deserializeInternal)           reference object.
        }
        return value
    }

    return deserializeInternal(value)
}
```

The `deserializeInternal` function in listing 7.20 is almost the same as the `deserialize` function defined in listing 7.19, with differences highlighted in bold. The advantage of using an "inner function" of this approach is that `deserializeInternal` can access and modify `id2AstObject`.

The problem with this new version of `deserialize` is that references in an AST can point to objects that are visited by the tree traversal only later. In other words, the `id2AstObject[<some ID>] = astObject` assignment could happen after trying to execute `return { ref: id2AstObject[<some ID>] }`. That would create a reference object with `ref` being `undefined` instead of an AST object, so that the reference is broken.

To avoid that, we'll only start resolving references after the whole tree has been traversed. We'll also keep track of all serialized reference objects we have to "fix" by transforming them into proper reference objects. To do that, we'll store a reference to every serialized reference object in a `referencesToResolve` array. More precisely, the elements in this array will be arrays of the form `[<refId>, <(JavaScript object reference to) reference object (to be)>]`. After we're done traversing through the entire "almost-AST," we go through the `referencesToResolve` array. For every element, we resolve the reference by looking up the target object in the `id2AstObject` object using the `<refId>` value, and assign the target object `<reference object>`.ref.

Listing 7.21 The final iteration of the `deserialize` function

```
const deserialize = (serializedAst) => {
    const id2AstObject = {}
    const referencesToResolve = []                        Maintain an array of
                                                          references to resolve after
                                                          the tree traversal.
    const deserializeInternal = (value) => {
        if (isAstObject(value)) {
            const astObject = {
                id: value.id,
                concept: value.concept,
                settings: {}
            }
            for (const propertyName in value.settings) {
                astObject.settings[propertyName] =
                    deserializeInternal(value.settings[propertyName])
            }
            id2AstObject[value.id] = astObject        Create an empty object that will
            return astObject                          become a reference object after
        }                                             it's been fixed.
        if (isSerializedAstReference(value)) {
            const refObjectToFix = {}                 Store a pair, containing the ID
            referencesToResolve.push(                 of the referenced object and
                [ value.refId, refObjectToFix ])      the reference object, in the
            return refObjectToFix                     referencesToResolve array.
        }
        if (Array.isArray(value)) {
            return value.map(deserializeInternal)     Trigger the tree traversal,
        }                                             and store the result in
        return value                                  deserializedAst.
    }

    const deserializedAst =
        deserializeInternal(serializedAst)            Loop over all pairs of serialized
                                                      reference objects to be fixed,
                                                      and their corresponding
    referencesToResolve.forEach(                      referenced IDs, using the syntax
        ([ refId, refObjectToFix ]) => {              <array>.forEach(...).
        refObjectToFix.ref = id2AstObject[refId]      The syntax ([ refId,
    })                                                refObjectToFix ]) => ... uses
                                                      destructuring to unpack the
    return deserializedAst                            pair of the serialized reference
}                                                     object to be fixed and the
module.exports.deserialize = deserialize              corresponding referenced ID.

                    Export the deserialize function to   Look up the target AST object
                       make it available for code        with ID refId from id2AstObject,
                                 in other files.         and assign it as a JavaScript
                                                         object reference to
                        Return the deserialized AST.     refObjectToFix.ref.
```

The initial value of deserializedAst is not guaranteed to be a real AST. After fixing all serialized reference objects in deserializedAst, it *will* be a proper AST.

Let's write a small, standalone Node.js program in the src/backend/deserialize-contents.js file to deserialize the serialized Rental example AST—which is currently the JSON contents file persisted on the backend—back to an AST.

Listing 7.22 Deserializing the JSON contents file back to an AST

```
const { readContents } = require("./storage")
const { deserialize } = require("../common/ast")

const serializedAst = readContents()
const deserializedAst = deserialize(serializedAst)
require("../ch03/print-pretty")(deserializedAst)
```

Exercise 7.4

- Execute the program in listing 7.22.
- Visually inspect the AST printed on the console, and check that it's indeed identical to the original example AST.
- For bonus points: modify the preceding code to check equality in code.

Let's see how deserialize operates on the serialized Rental example AST in a little more detail. In other words, let's debug it a bit. Here are the contents of the id2AstObject and referencesToResolve variables after calling deserializeInternal on the serialized example AST. We could obtain these values by pretty-printing them right before the last foreach "loop" in listing 7.21:

```
id2AstObject = {            We skip all the key-value pairs in id2AstObject that
  // ...                    are not the source or target of a reference relation.
  "SlLaELvAy0": {
    "id": "SlLaELvAy0",     The key-value pair with
    "concept": "Data Attribute",  the serialization of the
    "settings": {           second attribute object
      "name": "rental price before discount",
      "type": "amount",
      "initial value": {
        "id": "u1ZXfEd7yn",
        "concept": "Number",
        "settings": {
          "value": "0.0"
        }
      }
    }
  },
  // ...                    The serialization of the initial value
  "86c8jJ1C3t": {           of the fourth attribute object
    "id": "86c8jJ1C3t",
    "concept": "Attribute Reference",
```

```
    "settings": {
      "attribute": {
        "refId": "SlLaELvAy0"
      }
    }
  },
  // ...
}
referencesToResolve = [
  [ "SlLaELvAy0", {} ]
]
```

The serialized reference object, with refId equal to the ID of the second attribute object

The same (and only) serialized reference object again, this time as the ID part (which is the first subelement) of an element of referencesToResolve

In this case, we needed only one key-value pair of `id2AstObject`, but that's alright: we had to go over every object in the serialized AST anyway. Building up `id2AstObject` essentially only costs some—and not even that much—memory, which we can free up directly afterward anyway.

Let's modify the frontend's code in src/frontend/index.jsx to properly deserialize the JSON contents retrieved from the backend:

```
// ...near top of file:...
import { deserialize } from "../common/ast"
```

Import the deserialize function.

```
// ...near bottom of file:...
const apiUrl = "http://localhost:8080/contents"

fetch(apiUrl)
    .then((response) => response.json())
    .then(action((json) => {
        state.ast = deserialize(json)
    }))
```

Call deserialize with the parsed JSON contents retrieved from the backend.

Exercise 7.5
- Apply the preceding code changes, and verify that the app is working again.
- Verify that the app still suffers from the problem encountered in chapters 5 and 6. You can (only) do this by changing the name of the one object that's the target of a reference relation.

7.4   *Making an AST observable during deserialization*

In chapters 5 and 6 we noticed a problem with references. When we changed the name of the second attribute, named `rental price before discount`, the projection of the initial value of the fourth attribute, `rental price after discount` *didn't* change. Because that initial value references the second attribute, we expected the projection of that initial value to change as well. We concluded that the reference was not a proper reference at all, as a result of MobX's `observable` function not knowing about reference relations.

Let's fix the problem with observable references. The reason we are only doing that now is that we're going to piggyback on the deserialization process. To do that, we'll create a modified version of the `deserialize` function. This modified version will not only deserialize a serialized AST, but the resulting AST will be observable right away. More importantly, reference relations will be dealt with correctly.

Note that `observable(<thing>)` returns a *deeply observable* version of `<thing>`: all objects and arrays inside it are auto-converted to observable versions as well. In other words, this code fragment

```
observable({
    concept: "Some Thing",
    settings: {
        "property1": 1,
        "property2": {
            concept: "Another Thing",
            settings: {
                "property3": [ "foo", "bar" ]
            }
        }
    }
})
```

achieves the exact same thing as the following code fragment (with differences highlighted in bold):

```
observable({
    concept: "Some Thing",
    settings: observable({
        "property1": 1,
        "property2": observable({
            concept: "Another Thing",
            settings: observable({
                "property3": observable( [ "foo", "bar" ]  )
            })
        })
    })
})
```

The modified version of `deserialize` is going to use this idea: make all implicit conversions of objects to their observable versions explicit. But before we write the modified version of `deserialize`, we have to get a better idea of how to handle reference relations correctly.

Let's go back to the AST in figure 7.4 for that. The idea is that if we can solve the reference problem for this AST, it will likely be solved for any AST with references. This AST can be constructed in-memory as follows.

Listing 7.23 Making a circular AST observable—the wrong way

```
const { observable } = require("mobx")

const astObject = {                    Specify an ID.
    id: "IdOfFooObject",
```

```
        concept: "Foo",
        settings: {
            "self-ref.": {}
        }
    }
}

astObject.settings["self-ref."].ref = astObject

const observableAstObject = observable(astObject)
```

> Try to make the whole AST observable in one go.

When you run this code, you'll find that the last statement errors out with the error "Maximum call stack size exceeded." This is caused by the cycle in this AST: `astObject` `.settings["self-ref."].ref == astObject`. The execution of `observable(astObject)` tries to auto-convert `astObject.settings["self-ref."].ref` at one point. Unfortunately, `observable` doesn't realize it has already created an observable version of the object referenced, which is `astObject`. Instead, `observable` tries to construct a *new* observable version of the target of the reference—a new observable version of `astObject`. While doing so, it encounters `astObject` in `astObject.settings["self-ref."].ref` over and over again. This leads to infinite recursion, which errors out when the stack—which holds information to keep track of the recursion—exceeds its maximum size.

We can solve this problem by relying on MobX to recognize objects that are already observable, and not trying to convert them into a deeply observable object again. This means that we have to be a bit careful about how the `observable` function is called, to prevent infinite recursion from happening.

We can change the previous code to the following (with differences highlighted in bold).

Listing 7.24   Making a circular AST observable—the right way

```
const { observable } = require("mobx")

const observableAstObject = observable({
    id: "IdOfFooObject",
    concept: "Foo",
    settings: {
        "self-ref.": observable({})
    }
})

observableAstObject.settings["self-ref."].ref = observableAstObject
```

> The observable function is called with an object that has nested parts that are already observable.

> This call to observable is evaluated first, returning a deeply observable reference object-to-be.

> Have the reference object point to the correct AST object.

Exercise 7.6
- Run the code in listing 7.23, and verify that it crashes.
- Run the code in listing 7.24, and verify that it doesn't crash. Then add some assertions to the code to check that if something on `observableAstObject`

is changed, that change is reflected in `observableAstObject.settings
["self-ref."].ref`, and vice versa. You can use either of MobX's `observe`
or `spy` functions to react to changes in the observable objects.

- Come up with a hypothetical AST that doesn't have a self-reference but has a
  loop or cycle of length at least 2. Encode this AST, and try to make it observable as a whole. After concluding that this doesn't work, make your AST
  observable, object by object. Pay attention to the order, and create observable
  references in the same way we did for the circular AST in listing 7.24. For bonus
  points, extend your AST to use a multivalued property holding references.

We now have an idea of how to solve our reference problem in general. We can make
an AST observable, with reference relations handled correctly, by creating observable
versions of AST, array, and reference objects explicitly. For an AST object or an array
value, this is simple enough: just wrap it with `observable`.

For any reference object { `ref: <targetAstObject>` } we find as a value of a property of an AST object, `<astObject>`, it's more complicated. When we wrap this object
with `observable`, the following happens:

1 `observable` detects that `<targetAstObject>` isn't observable yet, so it auto-
converts it to an observable version—let's call that version `<observableTarget-
AstObject>`. We might have made an observable version of `<targetAstObject>`
elsewhere, but until we put some infrastructure up, there's no way we can get
hold of that version. Effectively, `<observableTargetAstObject>` is an observable version of a *copy* of `<targetAstObject>`.

2 `observable` creates an observable version of `<observableTargetAstObject>`.

To fix this, we first want to get hold of the observable version of `<targetAstObject>`
that's created when the deserialization process visits that AST object. Let's call that
object `<observableTargetAstObject>` as well. Now, we could produce an observable
reference object as `observable({ ref: <observableTargetAstObject> })`. This observable reference object will recognize that the value assigned to `ref` is already observable
and will not try to convert it to an observable value anymore. It will notify observers of
changes to the value of `ref`, which is what we want to happen.

While creating an observable version of `<astObject>`, how do we get hold of
`<observableTargetAstObject>` *before* we create the observable reference object
`observable({ ref: <observableTargetAstObject> })`? A good, and standard, strategy is to break this problem up into a two-step process:

1 Create an observable version of *every* AST object. While doing that, maintain a
map in such a way that we can look up the observable version of an AST object,
given the original AST object.

 When creating an observable version of an AST object, don't try to create
complete observable versions of reference objects right away. Instead, create

an observable object with the intention to fix it later. Also, keep a record for every such object, including the reference relation's target AST object, `<targetAst-Object>`.

2 Fix every recorded observable object by looking up the observable version of the target AST object in the map maintained, and assigning that as the value of its `ref` property.

If you look closely at this two-step process, it looks remarkably like the deserialization process! Especially, all of the bookkeeping we need for the two-step process is essentially already in place for the deserialization. Let's combine the two and create observable versions of AST objects while we are deserializing them from a serialization. We'll implement this as a new method in src/common/ast.js—see listing 7.25, in which the differences from listing 7.21 are highlighted in bold.

Listing 7.25   Deserializing to an observable AST

```
const { observable } = require("mobx")            Import the observable function in
                                                  src/common/ast.js in a way that's
                                                  compatible with Node.js and Parcel.
const deserializeObservably = (serializedAst) => {
    const id2AstObject = {}
    const referencesToResolve = []                     Whenever the internal function
                                                       deserializeObservablyInternal
    const deserializeInternal = (value) => {           returns an object, that object
        if (isAstObject(value)) {                      will be observable.
            const astObject = observable({             Create an observable
                id: value.id,                          version of the AST
                concept: value.concept,                object in value.
                settings: {}
            })
            for (const propertyName in value.settings) {
                astObject.settings[propertyName] =
                    deserializeInternal(
                        value.settings[propertyName])
            }
            id2AstObject[value.id] = astObject          Create an observable
            return astObject                            empty object that will
        }                                               become a proper
        if (isSerializedAstReference(value)) {          reference object.
            const refObjectToFix = observable({})
            referencesToResolve.push([ value.refId, refObjectToFix ])
            return refObjectToFix                   Return refObjectToFix so
        }                                           the reference object-to-be
        if (Array.isArray(value)) {                 will become part of the
            return observable(                      result AST immediately.
                value.map(deserializeInternal))
        }                                           Create an
        return value                                observable version
    }                                               of the array in value.
```

```
const deserializedAst = deserializeInternal(serializedAst)

referencesToResolve.forEach(
    ➥ ([ refId, refObjectToFix ]) => {
    refObjectToFix.ref = id2AstObject[refId]
})

return deserializedAst
}

module.exports.deserializeObservably =
    ➥ deserializeObservably
```

> **Make the refObjectToFix object a proper reference object by pointing to the looked-up reference's target AST object.**

> **Export the deserializeObservably function to make it available for code in other files.**

As you can see, the difference between the `deserialize` and `deserializeObservably` functions is relatively small. That's the reason that I postponed solving the reference problem until after we discussed how to do deserialization.

Exercise 7.7

Write unit tests for both the `deserialize` and `deserializeObservably` functions to ensure that they work as expected and intended. The largest part of the unit tests should be applicable to both functions, with some extra unit tests to check for correct observability. You could use a JavaScript unit testing framework such as Mocha for this.

Exercise 7.8

The `deserialize` and `deserializeObservably` functions are quite similar, both functionally and code-wise. Refactor these so that they are DRY (Don't Repeat Yourself). Hint: Look at listing 7.25 to see what the actual differences are. Run the unit tests to verify the refactoring is correct.

Now we just have to replace the use of the `deserialize` function in the frontend with `deserializeObservably`. The code that fetches the JSON contents from the backend should be modified as shown in listing 7.26, with the differences highlighted in boldface.

Listing 7.26 Using the `deserializeObservably` function

```
import { deserializeObservably } from "../common/ast"

// ...other code...

fetch(apiUrl)
    .then((response) => response.json())
    .then(action((json) => {
        state.ast = deserializeObservably(json)
    }))
```

> **Import deserializeObservably instead of deserialize.**

> **Call deserializeObservably instead of deserialize.**

Now there's just one more thing to fix: when we create a new AST object through the editor, we should give it an ID, or we can't properly serialize references to it. A new AST object can currently be created in two ways:

- Adding an initial value to an attribute
- Adding an attribute to the record type

Change the code of the `Projection` function to use the `newAstObject` factory function as in the following listing, with the differences highlighted in bold.

Listing 7.27 Changes to the projection to use `newAstObject`

```
import { astReferenceTo, isAstObject, newAstObject,           Import the
    placeholderAstObject } from "../common/ast"                newAstObject
                                                               factory function.
// ...first part of the code of the Projection function,
//      roughly half-way into the Data Attribute case...
{settings["initial value"] === placeholderAstObject
    ? <DropDownValue
        editState={observable({
            inEdit: true,
            setValue: (newValue) => {
                settings["initial value"] =
                    newAstObject(newValue)
            }
        })}                                                    Set the initial
// ...continuation of the code of the Projection function...    value to an AST
                                                               object that's
// ...almost at the end of the Record Type case...             constructed
<AddNewButton buttonText="+ attribute" actionFunction={() => {  using that
    settings["attributes"]                                     factory function.
        .push(newAstObject("Data Attribute"))
}} />
// ...rest of the code of the Projection function...
```

Note that in the code in listing 7.27 the new AST objects are automatically observable because they're contained in a JavaScript `settings` object that was already observable itself.

Exercise 7.9
- Apply the code changes from listings 7.24 and 7.25.
- Verify that the reference problem is solved. You can do that by changing the name of the second attribute, named `rental price before discount`: this change should be reflected in the projection of the initial value of the fourth attribute, `rental price after discount`.

7.5   *Implementing save functionality*

The domain expert can now retrieve a persisted AST from the backend, and project and edit it in the DSL editor on the frontend. After the domain expert has done some editing, they will want to save it as well. Let's provide the domain expert with a Save button to save their work.

We'll start by adding a Save button to the frontend. We do this by changing the App component in src/frontend/index.jsx as follows:

```
const App = observer(({ state }) =>
    state.ast                                    ┌─ Add an extra <div>
        ? <div>                                  │  element around the call to
            <button className="save"        ◄────┘  the Projection function.
                ➥onClick={save}>Save</button> ◄──── Put a button labeled
            <Projection                                "Save" above the
                astObject={state.ast}                  projection.
                ancestors={[]}
            />
        </div>
        : <div className="spinner"></div>
)
```

To style the Save button, we'll copy the definition for the "add-new" CSS class in src/frontend/styling.css, paste it (at the end), and change the color:

```
button.save {
    font-size: 18pt;
    border-radius: 10px;
    border: 0;
    background-color: rgb(236, 52, 52);
    cursor: pointer;
}
```

We now have to define a handler for the mouse click event fired when the domain expert clicks the Save button. We'll again use the Fetch API for that:

```
import { deserializeObservably, serialize } from "../common/ast"

// ...(other code)...              ┌─ Define a function that serves as a handler for any UI
                                   │  event. (Because we don't access the event passed at
const save = (_) => {              │  all, we name the corresponding argument "-.")
    fetch(apiUrl, {         ◄──────┘
        method: "PUT",      ◄──────────────── Call the fetch function, this
        headers: {                            time with a second argument:
            "Content-Type": "application/json"  an object that specifies the JSON
        },                                    body for a PUT request.
        body: JSON.stringify(
            ➥ serialize(state.ast))   ◄────── Import the serialize
    })                                         function.
}
```

The PUT request generated by calling this function is not yet handled by the backend. Let's fix that by adding the following to the server's code in src/backend/server.js, directly after the code for handling a GET on /contents, to replace the PUT comments placeholder from listing 7.4.

Listing 7.28   Server code to handle PUT requests

```
const { readContents, writeContents } =
    require("./storage")                        Import the writeContents
                                                function at the top of this file.
// ...other code...

server.use(express.json({ limit: "1gb" }))      Configure Express to handle
server.put("/contents", (request, response) => {  JSON bodies of PUT requests
    const newContents = request.body            up to 1 GB, rather than the
    writeContents(newContents)                  default of 100 KB.
    contents = newContents
    response.send()
})
```

With that, we have completed the circle.

Exercise 7.10

- Apply the preceding code changes and additions, and test whether the save functionality works. You can do this by changing the DSL content in the app, clicking the Save button, and either reloading the app or inspecting src/backend/data/contents.json.
- Optional: Modify the implementation of the Save button so that the domain expert gets some feedback about whether the save action was successful.

The size of an AST

If your DSL is successful, the ASTs made with it should get larger and larger. You should make sure that your DSL implementation *scales* well enough. You wouldn't want your domain experts to corrupt their ASTs because the backend glitches.

To get to grips with scalability, you should learn about the limits of the technology and frameworks you're using. You should also have automated performance tests for your backend.

You saw in listing 7.28 that we had to fix Express's rather meager default limit of 100 KB for the size of JSON bodies. The JSON serialization of our tiny example DSL already measures about 1.4 KB (pretty-printed), which is around a 1/70th of 100 KB. (I learned about that default limit the hard way.)

In this chapter, you learned how to persist and transport ASTs as JSON. On top of that, you learned how to fix the problem with observable references we encountered in the previous two chapters. In the next chapter, we're going to see how to generate code from ASTs.

Summary

- The Domain IDE's backend can be implemented as a simple web server (using Express) with a REST API.
- The Domain IDE's backend needs to be able to store an AST and to transmit it to the Domain IDE's frontend. The frontend needs to be able to transmit a changed AST to the backend again, so that the backend can store it. For this, the following capabilities need to be implemented:
  - *Serialization* takes an AST and *serializes* it as JSON.
  - *Deserialization* takes the JSON of a serialized AST, and turns it into an AST again.
- The tricky bit of serialization and deserialization is the presence of reference relations. These can introduce loops in the AST, which means we can't just call `JSON.stringify` with the AST's root object. To solve this problem, IDs are added to each AST object as an extra key-value pair, `id: <ID>`.
  - During serialization, any reference object, `{ ref: <target AST object of reference relation> }`, is turned into a *serialized reference object* of the form `{ refId: <ID of the target AST object> }`.
  - During deserialization, any serialized reference object is turned into a reference object again. This process is called *resolving the references*, and it requires us to maintain a map of AST objects indexed by their IDs.
- Because of its reactive architecture, the Domain IDE's frontend—the DSL editor, in particular—requires the AST to be a MobX `observable` value. Once again, it takes a bit of extra work during deserialization to treat reference relations correctly.

8
Generating code from the AST

This chapter covers

- How the build system relates to the Domain IDE and the Runtime
- Why make a reference implementation of the Runtime first
- Implementing a code generator using templates
- Deriving templates iteratively from the reference implementation's code
- Composing templates conveniently, with declarative indentation

In the previous chapters, we started working on a Domain IDE that will allow domain experts to capture their business knowledge in the form of DSL content. I said in chapter 1 that this DSL content should not just be "pretty pictures" or mere documentation, but should be precise enough to build software from (see figure 8.1). In this chapter, we're going to do exactly that: *generate* a Runtime from DSL content written using the Domain IDE.

Our example DSL and its content captures how to compute a rental price based on the data input by business stakeholders. The Runtime for this DSL content

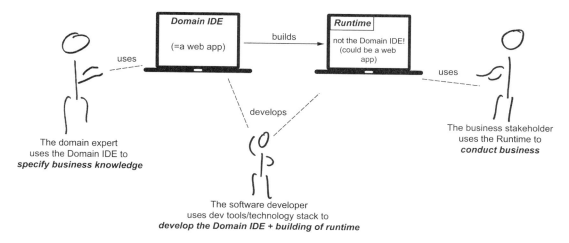

Figure 8.1   Using a DSL-based approach to develop a Runtime using a Domain IDE

could be as simple as a web app that displays a form in which business stakeholders input data about a rental.

Figure 8.2 focuses on the Runtime, and on how its codebase is organized in general.

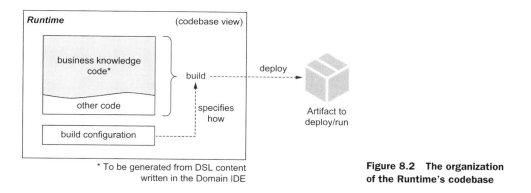

Figure 8.2   The organization of the Runtime's codebase

The Runtime's codebase can be divided into the following parts:

- Code that corresponds directly to business knowledge
- Code that doesn't correspond to business knowledge, but which nevertheless combines seamlessly with it
- A build configuration for combining all the code to build a Runtime artifact, which can then be deployed or run

The first part of the codebase should be generated from DSL content representing that business knowledge—at least as much as possible. It's the job of the domain experts to author that DSL content using the Domain IDE. The second part is all the remaining code that can't be specified using the DSL. It's the job of the software developers to write that code by hand. The third part consists of everything that's needed to build, run, or deploy the Runtime. That's clearly also a job for the software developers.

Figure 8.3 shows what the architecture of the build system should look like. The *code generator* forms the heart of the build system. The business knowledge stored as a serialized AST in the repository is retrieved by the build system and fed into that generator, which generates text from it. This generated text happens to be valid code in the Runtime's programming languages. The build system then triggers the building of the entire Runtime, combining the generated code with the handwritten code, and building it as a deployable artifact. The code generator makes up around 90% of the build system, with "plumbing," like retrieving the AST and triggering the Runtime's build, making up the remainder.

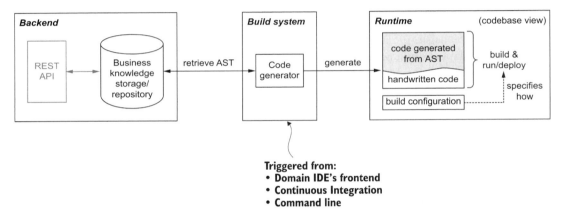

Figure 8.3   The architecture of the build system and Runtime

In this chapter, we'll write a small Runtime that implements some functionality for our usual DSL content: the `Rental` record type. We'll generate part of the code of that Runtime from the example AST by implementing a code generator and running it. We'll implement the code generator in an iterative way that works well for any piece of generated code. In chapter 9, we'll deal with ASTs that break either the code generator or the generated code. In chapters 11 to 14, we'll add new concepts to the example DSL so we can write down expressions and business rules. We'll also extend the code generator for those.

> **NOTE**   It's also possible to create a Runtime that *directly executes* the DSL content, rather than executing code generated from the DSL content. This approach is called *interpretation*.

8.1   Integrating the build system with the software development process

Before we start implementing the build system, let's figure out how we can integrate it with the whole software development process. As you can see in figure 8.3, the build system really only requires two things:

- The serialized AST stored in the business knowledge repository.
- The codebase of the Runtime to put the generated code in, next to the hand-written code and the build configuration.

This gives us a lot of freedom in how the build system can be triggered to do its build work:

- We could put a "Build" button in the Domain IDE that kicks off a build. This puts the domain experts firmly in control over when the build runs.
- A Continuous Integration (CI) system could rebuild the Runtime after every change that's committed to the business knowledge repository.
- We could run the build system manually from the command line.

For the Domain IDE's implementation in this book, I chose the third, CLI-based option for the following reasons:

- We already know how to retrieve the AST representing the business knowledge, by deserializing it from the storage we implemented in chapter 7.
- We can put the Runtime's code next to our other code, and build it from there.
- It keeps the feedback cycle simple, short, and tidy.

For real-life Domain IDEs, this simple approach probably won't be good enough, so you'll have to consider other options such as the ones already mentioned. Ideally, domain experts will be able to build and deploy the Runtime themselves entirely, without ever needing a software developer. A number of low- or no-code platforms have this down pat. In large part, that is what makes these platforms useful and valuable.

Whatever approach you choose, building the Runtime should be an *automatic* process that doesn't need any manual intervention once it's triggered (by either a domain expert or a software developer). After all, the whole idea of adopting a DSL-based approach is to remove as much friction as possible from the process of turning the domain experts' business knowledge into working software. It's also important that the generated code has the same level of quality as the handwritten code, and that it is properly formatted.

8.2   Using a reference implementation

The Runtime is a software system in its own right. It has its own architecture, coding style and conventions, build configuration, versioning system, etc. Generating part of the Runtime's code makes a difference both for the process and economics. It should not make an essential difference in the implementation, on the level of the code itself.

We could start implementing the build system, including the code generator, right away. First, though, we'll have to figure out at least the following things:

- The architecture, coding style and conventions, build configuration, versioning system, etc., of the Runtime
- What part of the Runtime can be generated from the AST, and how

Doing a lot of tricky things at the same time is rarely a good idea. It's better to tackle these items separately, and in this order. That's why it's a best practice to first write a *reference implementation*: essentially, a separate, small software system that serves as a focused example, or template, for the Runtime. It has the following requirements:

- It's a functional software system, separate from the Runtime.
- It follows the architecture chosen for the Runtime, with all the technological layers and aspects fully worked out.
- It conforms to a defined coding style, and to coding conventions.
- It's representative of the type of functionality of the Runtime.

For our purposes of adopting a DSL-based approach, we have an additional requirement:

- The business knowledge part of the reference implementation must be representable as DSL content.

If we can represent the business knowledge part of the reference implementation as DSL content and generate all the business knowledge code from it, it's likely that we can implement the Runtime using the DSL-based approach as well. This is as much a requirement for the DSL and code generator as it is for the reference implementation.

Finally, the reference implementation should be small for two reasons:

- It should be easy to understand. Its code should be easily "grokkable," in little time.
- Building and running or deploying the reference implementation should be quick, so we can efficiently make changes to it and validate them.

Figure 8.4 represents the relation between the Runtime and the reference implementation graphically. Note the relative sizes of the "code to generate" part of the Runtime and the "generatable code" part of the reference implementation.

When it meets all the listed requirements, the reference implementation has a number of uses at the same time:

- It is a reference for how the Runtime should be implemented. This makes sense regardless of whether you use a DSL-based approach or not.
- It serves as a template for the part of the Runtime code that's generated from DSL content. Until we have a code generator, we have to start out creating the reference implementation completely manually. We'll see this in action in this chapter.

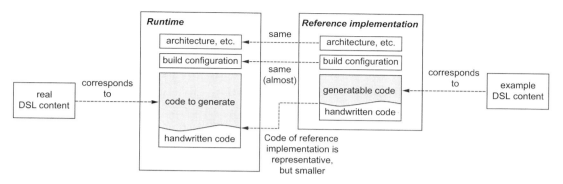

Figure 8.4 The relation between the Runtime and reference implementation

- It is a way to test the DSL, and the code generator for it. We'll see this in action in chapters 10 through 14.
- It is a base for experimentation. You can experiment with the Runtime's architecture, coding style, and conventions, but also with the code generator and the DSL itself. It's easy to add concepts to, or change concepts of, the DSL and see how you can change the code generator accordingly. We'll see this in action in chapters 10 through 14.

The ideal scenario is that you know *up front* that you're going to use a DSL-based approach, but things rarely go the way they theoretically should. It's quite likely that you've already started building the Runtime in the "old-fashioned" way. The result *should* satisfy the first four requirements for a reference implementation: a separate software system, with the same architecture, coding style, and coding conventions as, and functionally similar to, the Runtime. Its code may well be more irregular and quirky than a code generator would, or could, produce, but it should be possible to "regularize" that code. The requirement related to using a DSL—being that the business knowledge part of the reference implementation must be representable as DSL content—is probably not clearly or cleanly met either, not in the least because you might not have a DSL yet.

If you already have a DSL implementation, you might be inclined to skip writing the reference implementation. After all, you could start right away with reverse engineering DSL content from the Runtime implementation, and replacing handwritten code with code generated from that DSL content. In my personal experience, however, it will still pay to invest in creating a reference implementation. Because it's separate from the Runtime, and it's small in size, the feedback cycle on a reference implementation is much shorter. This means that "extracting" a DSL from the Runtime, and implementing a DSL and code generator, can be done much more efficiently.

8.3   *A Runtime for Rental*

Our `Rental` record type in the example DSL content is quite small. It also contains all the concepts of our DSL, even with some variance. Let's implement a Runtime for the `Rental` record type that can also serve as a reference implementation. From there, we can start implementing a code generator.

This Runtime will be a simple React web app displaying a form for one `Rental` record. The form will have four fields, corresponding to the four attributes of the record type (see figure 8.5). It will allow a user to fill out every one of those fields.

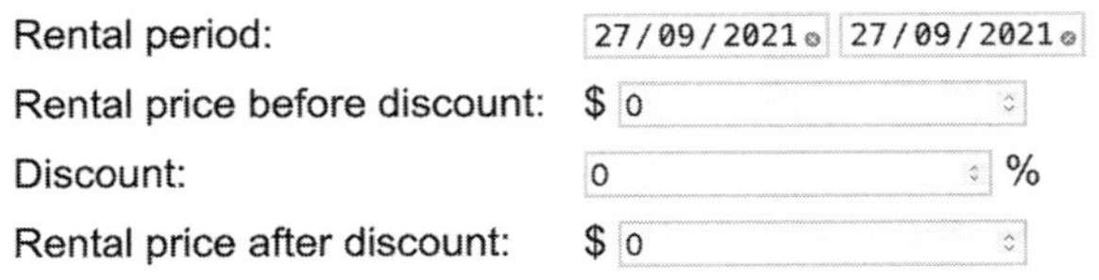

Rental period: `27/09/2021` `27/09/2021`
Rental price before discount: $ `0`
Discount: `0` %
Rental price after discount: $ `0`

Figure 8.5   The example Runtime for the `Rental` record type

We'll put the code of the Runtime's reference implementation in src/runtime. It's going to be a simple React web app quite similar to the Domain IDE's implementation itself. For our own convenience, we'll stick to the Domain IDE's frontend part of the architecture, and its coding style and conventions. I'll go ahead and present the entire code right away. The starting point is again an index.html file.

Listing 8.1   The contents of src/runtime/index.html

```
<!DOCTYPE html>
<html lang="en">

<head>
  <meta charset="UTF-8">
  <title>Rent-A-Car</title>
</head>

<body>
  <div id="root"></div>
  <script type="module" src="index.jsx"></script>
</body>

</html>
```

Next is the index.jsx file that's referenced from index.html.

Listing 8.2   The contents of src/runtime/index.jsx

```
import React from "react"
import { createRoot } from "react-dom/client"
import { makeAutoObservable } from "mobx"
import { observer } from "mobx-react"
```

```
import { FormField, Input } from "./components"
import { DateRange } from "./dates"

require("./styling.css")

class Rental {
    rentalPeriod = new DateRange()
    rentalPriceBeforeDiscount = 0.0
    discount = 0
    rentalPriceAfterDiscount = this.rentalPriceBeforeDiscount
    constructor() {
        makeAutoObservable(this)
    }
}

const RentalForm = observer(({ rental }) => <form>
    <FormField label="Rental period">
        <Input type="date" object={rental.rentalPeriod} fieldName="from" />
        <Input type="date" object={rental.rentalPeriod} fieldName="to" />
    </FormField>
    <FormField label="Rental price before discount">
        $ <Input type="number" object={rental}
            fieldName="rentalPriceBeforeDiscount" />
    </FormField>
    <FormField label="Discount">
        <Input type="number" object={rental} fieldName="discount" /> %
    </FormField>
    <FormField label="Rental price after discount">
        $ <Input type="number" object={rental}
            fieldName="rentalPriceAfterDiscount" />
    </FormField>
</form>)

const rental = new Rental()

createRoot(document.getElementById("root"))
    .render(
        <RentalForm rental={rental} />
    )
```

Import a DateRange class, and instantiate it as the value for the rentalPeriod field.

Define a class called "Rental" corresponding to the Rental record type.

Call the makeAutoObservable MobX function in the class's constructor to make this instance of the class observable—see also section B.4.5.

Define a React component function that shows an editable Rental record, given a rental object.

Create a rental record object by instantiating the Rental class.

Call the Rental record component (as the UI root's only content).

The Rental class in the preceding code has a couple of fields corresponding to the attributes of the Rental record type. Each of these fields holds the current *value* of that attribute, so they must be properly initialized.

The attributes in our example DSL content are specified to have the types amount, date range, or percentage, so we have to map these DSL types to JavaScript types to represent values. Values of DSL types amount and percentage are numeric, so it's logical to represent these as JavaScript Number values (see https://developer.mozilla .org/en-US/docs/Web/JavaScript/Reference/Global_Objects/Number). We'll represent a value of DSL type date range using a DateRange class, which we'll define in src/runtime/dates.js.

Define a DateRange class to represent values of the DSL type "date range."

```
const { makeAutoObservable } = require("mobx")

const leftPad0 = (num, len) => {          ◁──  Define a function that left-pads a given
    let str = "" + num                          number with zeroes to a specified length.
    if (str.length < len) {
        str = "0".repeat(len - str.length) + str
    }
    return str
}                                                    Define and export a
const formatDate = (date) =>              ◁──       function to format a
    `${leftPad0(date.getFullYear(), 4)}               given JavaScript Date.
        -${leftPad0(date.getMonth() + 1, 2)}
        -${leftPad0(date.getDate(), 2)}`
module.exports.formatDate = formatDate

class DateRange {
    _from;
    _to;
    get from() {                          ◁──
        return this._from
    }
    set from(newValue) {                  ◁──
        this._from = newValue                   Define JavaScript
        if (this._to < this._from) {            getter and setter
            this._to = this._from               methods that
        }                                       expose the from
    }                                           and to fields.
    get to() {                            ◁──
        return this._to
    }
    set to(newValue) {                    ◁──
        this._to = newValue
        if (this._from > this._to) {
            this._from = this._to
        }
    }
    toString() {
        return `${formatDate(this._from)}
            - ${formatDate(this._to)}`    ◁──
    }
    constructor(fromStr, toStr) {         ◁──
        makeAutoObservable(this)          ◁──
        const now = new Date()
        this._from = !!fromStr ? new Date(fromStr) : now
        this._to = !!toStr ? new Date(toStr) : now
    }
}
module.exports.DateRange = DateRange
```

Use template literals to generate strings—see section B.1.10 for more details.

Define a constructor method that takes from and to dates as strings. If no value for one or both ends of the date range is given, the current date is used.

Make the whole constructed DateRange instance observable by MobX.

Define the _from and _to fields. (Here we have to insert semicolons—the parser will not understand these class field declarations without them.)

The setter methods of the `from` and `to` fields of the `DateRange` class ensure that you can't create invalid date range values where the `to` comes before the `from`. If you try, you wind up with a `DateRange` instance that has a duration of 0. For more details on JavaScript's `Date` class, see the MDN web docs: https://developer.mozilla.org/en-US/docs/Web/JavaScript/Reference/Global_Objects/Date.

The index.jsx file requires CSS styling to be defined in styling.css. This CSS uses a CSS grid to make the Runtime's UI look acceptable.

Listing 8.4   The contents of src/runtime/styling.css

```css
body {
    font-family: Arial, Helvetica, sans-serif;
    font-size: 24pt;
}

form {
    display: grid;
    grid-gap: 0.5em;
}

div.row {
    display: grid;
    grid-template-columns: 1fr 1fr;
}

label:after {
    content: ":";
    grid-column: 1 / 2;
}

div.field {
    margin-left: 0.5rem;
    grid-column: 2 / 3;
}

input {
    font-size: 18pt;
    border: 3px solid yellow;
    background-color: lightyellow;
}

input[type="date"] {
    margin-right: 0.3em;
}
```

Finally, index.jsx imports two React components from components.jsx.

Listing 8.5   The contents of src/runtime/components.jsx

```jsx
import React from "react"
import { action } from "mobx"
import { observer } from "mobx-react"
```

```
import { formatDate } from "./dates"

export const FormField = observer(({ label, children }) =>
       ➥ <div className="row">
    <label>{label}</label>
    <div className="field">
        {children}
    </div>
</div>)

const convertToType = (newValue, type) => {
    switch (type) {
        case "number": return Number.parseFloat(newValue)
        case "date": return new Date(newValue)
        default: return newValue
    }
}

const convertFromType = (value, type) => {
    switch (type) {
        case "number": return "" + value
        case "date": return formatDate(value)
        default: return value
    }
}

export const Input = observer(({ type, object,
       ➥ fieldName }) => <input
    type={type}
    value={convertFromType(object[fieldName], type)}
    onChange={action((event) => {
        object[fieldName] = convertToType(event.target.value, type)
    })}
/>)
```

Annotations:
- Use the special children React attribute to nest JSX inside a call to this component.
- Define a function to convert a string value to a proper JS Number or Date value, depending on type.
- Define a function to convert a given value corresponding to the given type to a string representation.
- Define a React component that wraps an HTML <input> reactively.

In the `convertToType` function in the preceding code, the `newValue` argument is assumed to be the `event.target.value` string value of an `onChange` event object triggered when an HTML `<input>` element's value is changed. The `type` argument is assumed to equal the `type` attribute of that `<input>` element. The `convertFromType` function is the inverse of the `convertToType` function, so that a string representation of a JavaScript `Number` or `Date` value can be shown as the value of an HTML `<input>` element.

The `Input` React component has three attributes:

- `type` for the `type` attribute of the `<input>` element
- `object` for the JavaScript object the value "lives in" as the value of a key-value pair
- `fieldName` for the key of the key-value pair

Inside this component we use the code fragment `object[fieldName]` both to access the value and to assign a new value to it. The component also takes care of performing appropriate type conversions, using the two conversion functions described.

NOTE Although it's convenient, representing number values using `Number` has drawbacks: this type has limited range and precision, and it doesn't know (or care) about significant trailing zeroes, which might be important for amounts. Because of that, it's not unusual to represent number values at run time as strings. This allows you to more tightly control the precise format of the number values.

We can now build and run this Runtime web app by running Parcel from the command line as follows:

```
$ npx parcel src/runtime/index.html --port 8180 --dist-dir dist-runtime
```

The two extra command-line arguments instruct Parcel to put the web app's bundle in the dist-runtime/ directory instead of the default dist/, and to run the development server on port 8180 instead of the default 1234. That way, we can run the Domain IDE and the Runtime at the same time, without risk of them interfering with each other.

This `npx parcel` command is part of the build configuration for the Runtime. After running it and navigating to http://localhost:8180, you verify that it looks like figure 8.5. If it does, you should save the current state of the code using a versioning system, by checking it in or committing it. This "safe point" can then be used later as a checkpoint to compare the generated code against.

Writing generatable code

Generally, while creating the reference implementation, it's a Good Idea to try and write code that lends itself to being generated. A code generator doesn't have any imagination or creativity of its own, so it will produce extremely similar code for similar instances of concepts. As a result, you should come up with extremely similar solutions for similar problems when writing a reference implementation. It helps to stick as strictly as possible to a coding style and to coding conventions that leave as little "wiggle room" as possible. You should also refrain from using any leftover wiggle room. In other words, thou shalt not be "creative" or "original."

It also helps to write the business knowledge present in the reference implementation as DSL content as early as possible. That way, you can try to think like a code generator while writing the reference implementation.

8.4 Implementing a code generator using templates

As you can see from listing 8.2, the src/runtime/index.jsx file contains a lot of details that look like data in the example AST. That file is also the *only* file with details from the AST, which means that we can't generate code for the other files in src/runtime/: components.jsx, index.html, or styling.css. There's simply no information in the AST that could describe the contents of those files.

Figure 8.6 explains what a code generator is. In essence, it's a function that turns an AST into a piece of text, which happens to be code in some programming language. We define a *template function* as any function that takes input data and returns a string. A shorter name for such a function is *template*. The data passed into the template is (a piece of) an AST, data derived from it, and, optionally, some other arguments.

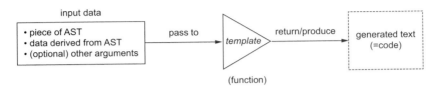

Figure 8.6   Code generation using a template (function)

Let's set up a place for a template function that turns the Rental example AST into the contents of src/runtime/index.jsx. Create a src/generator/ directory, and a generate.js file in it. First, we read in the AST, the same way we did in listing 7.22. Then, we use the `generatedIndexJsx` function exported from src/generator/index-Jsx-template.js.

Listing 8.6   Contents of src/generator/generate.js

```
const { join } = require("path")

const { deserialize } = require("../common/ast")
const { writeString } = require("../common/file-utils")          Import the
const { readContents } = require("../backend/storage")           generatedIndexJsx
const { generatedIndexJsx } =                          ◀─────    function.
    ➥ require("./indexJsx-template")

const indexJsxPath = join(__dirname, "..", "runtime", "index.jsx")

const serializedAst = readContents()                             Deserialize the AST
const deserializedAst = deserialize(serializedAst)      ◀───     from the JSON content
writeString(indexJsxPath,                                        that's read in.
    ➥ generatedIndexJsx(deserializedAst))      ◀───────┐
                                                        │
            Call the generatedIndexJsx function, and write
                    the returned string value to disk.
```

Create a src/generator/indexJsx-template.js file to export a `generatedIndexJsx` template function from. This template function simply produces the contents of src/runtime/index.jsx by copying in those contents verbatim. For the moment, it doesn't access the AST at all, but that will change in section 8.4.1.

Listing 8.7   First version of src/generator/indexJsx-template.js

Define a function that takes an AST representing a record type and produces the contents of src/runtime/index.jsx as a string value.

Quote the entire contents of src/runtime/index.jsx verbatim inside a template literal delimited by backticks (`` ` ``). Because we're using multiline strings, the quoted code can't be indented in the normal way, or that indentation would end up in the generated code.

```
const indexJsx = (recordType) => {
    return `import React from "react"
import { createRoot } from "react-dom/client"
import { makeAutoObservable } from "mobx"
import { observer } from "mobx-react"

import { FormField, Input } from "./components"
import { DateRange } from "./dates"
// ...rest of the contents of src/runtime/index.jsx...
createRoot(document.getElementById("root"))
    .render(
        <RentalForm rental={rental} />
    )
`
}
```

Close the quote with a second backtick.

```
module.exports.generatedIndexJsx = indexJsx
```

Export the indexJsx function under the name generatedIndexJsx. This export will change later on, which is why we don't export indexJsx directly under that name.

Refer to section B.1.11 for more information about template literals. As you can see in listing 8.7, template literals support *multiline strings*. Because template literals are delimited by backticks, it's not necessary to escape the delimiters for regular literals as \' or \". That's convenient because generated code tends to contain plenty of regular string literals but rarely template literals.

We can now run this on the command line:

```
$ node src/generator/generate.js
```

The src/runtime/index.jsx file shouldn't change (apart from its "Last modified" time-stamp), because we copied its contents verbatim in the code generator. Your versioning system should agree on that. If it doesn't, you could ask the versioning system what the difference from listing 8.2 is. This setup might seem useless, but it lets us check whether we're doing the right thing: no change to src/runtime/index.jsx means "generator working fine!"

8.4.1   Iterating from reference source to template

In this subsection, you'll learn how to gradually replace parts of the textual contents of the template literal inside the `indexJsx` function with suitable embedded expressions that access the AST. In general, this iterative process—which is visualized in figure 8.7—starts with a template that's just the textual contents of the generatable code from the reference implementation. It ends with a template that's fully parameterized in the AST that represents the example DSL content corresponding to the reference implementation (see figure 8.4). Every iteration, this process takes these steps:

1 Find literal text that's parameterizable with some detail in the AST.
2 Replace that literal text with parameterized template code.
3 Run the code generator, and check whether the generated code is the same (possibly up to irrelevant details such as whitespace) as the original code.

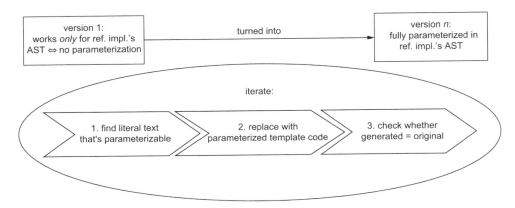

Figure 8.7   The iterative process to turn an unparameterized template into a parameterized one

Right now, the `indexJsx` function returns code as text that's effectively independent of the AST going in. That's because the `indexJsx` function doesn't look at the AST that's passed into the `recordType` argument at all. In other words: it's not *parameterized* in the AST. If the AST changes, that will not be reflected at all in src/runtime/index.jsx.

We're going to iteratively parameterize the template literal in `indexJsx` using embedded expressions. Once again, when calling `indexJsx` with the example AST, src/runtime/index.jsx shouldn't change.

Generating code in watch mode

To make the feedback cycle while iterating tighter, you can use something called "watch mode" to rerun the code generator every time the src/generator/generate.js file changes. Three common possibilities for engaging a watch mode are listed below. These all continuously monitor the code generator's entry point src/generator/generate.js, as well as any file that it relies on—in particular, src/generator/indexJsx-template.js. Every time any of those files change, src/generator/generate.js gets rerun, and the monitoring continues until the user disengages watch mode by pressing Ctrl-C:

- Node.js has a built-in watch mode, which can be triggered as follows:

```
$ node --watch src/generator/generate.js
```

- Many operating systems, including Linux (natively), macOS, and Windows (both via Homebrew), have a built-in `watch` command-line utility, which can be used as follows:

```
$ watch node src/generator/generate.js
```

- You can install the `nodemon` (which is short for `node-demon`) utility with the following command:

```
$ npm install nodemon --save-dev
```

- You can then run the generator in watch mode as follows:

```
$ npx nodemon src/generator/generate.js
```

In listing 8.7, we'll now find literal text that we can relate to the example AST, and replace it with an embedded expression that accesses the AST and evaluates to the same text. The occurrences of Rental and rental are probably the most obvious. Consider the following piece of code from listing 8.2.

> **Listing 8.8 The `Rental` class definition in src/runtime/index.jsx**

```
class Rental {
    rentalPeriod = new DateRange()
    rentalPriceBeforeDiscount = 0.0
    discount = 0
    rentalPriceAfterDiscount = this.rentalPriceBeforeDiscount
    constructor() {
        makeAutoObservable(this)
    }
}
```

The one occurrence of Rental—as the name of the class—is highlighted in bold in the preceding code. The text "Rental" occurs as the value Rental of the setting of the name property of the AST's root object of concept Record Type (see figure 8.8).

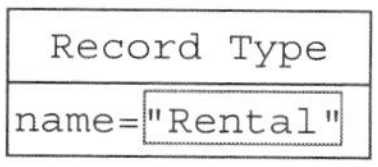

```
┌─────────────────────┐
│ Record Type         │
├─────────────────────┤
│ name=│"Rental"│     │
└─────────────────────┘
```

Figure 8.8   The AST object encoding the `Rental` record type

It's very likely that the occurrence of `Rental` in listing 8.8 is derived from the record type's name. Let's define a constant at the top of `indexJsx` to derive and hold the text "Rental" from the example record type's name. Change the existing code as in listing 8.9 (with the difference highlighted in bold).

Listing 8.9   Code change to the `indexJsx` function

```
const indexJsx = (recordType) => {
    const ucName = recordType.settings["name"]     ⟵    Define a constant named
    // ...rest of the code...                              ucName, and initialize it to the
                                                           name of the given record type.
```

The name `ucName` for the constant in the preceding code is short for "uppercased name," and is meant to convey that the constant's value is a string that starts with an uppercase character. Right now, we can only *assume* that's the case, but we'll ensure it later on.

Let's parameterize the occurrence of `Rental` in listing 8.8, using the embedded expression `${ucName}`. To do that, we'll alter the template literal inside the `indexJsx` function from listing 8.7 as follows:

```
class ${ucName} {
    rentalPeriod = new DateRange()
    rentalPriceBeforeDiscount = 0.0
    discount = 0
    rentalPriceAfterDiscount = this.rentalPriceBeforeDiscount
    constructor() {
        makeAutoObservable(this)
    }
}
```

We could also replace all other occurrences of `Rental`, but I prefer to work from top to bottom and do as much as possible "locally" before moving on to the next part of the code to generate.

Let's turn our attention to the following line of code in src/runtime/index.jsx:

```
rentalPeriod = new DateRange()
```

This is an assignment that initializes a field on the `Rental` class. The obvious source for this line of code is the first attribute, shown in figure 8.9.

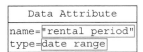

Figure 8.9   The AST object encoding the first attribute

Apparently, three facts are going into the preceding line of code:

- The key of the key-value pair *almost* equals the setting of the `name` property on the `Data Attribute` object: "rental period" versus `rentalPeriod`.

- This attribute doesn't specify an initial value.
- This attribute does specify that it is of type "date range."

Let's tackle the almost-matching names first. A human-readable name like "rental period" is not necessarily a valid JavaScript identifier. Typically, a name has to be turned into a valid JavaScript identifier—otherwise, the generated code won't always parse, in which case it won't run, either. One popular way of doing that is by *camel-casing* that string. In this case, "rental period" is turned into its camel-cased version `rentalPeriod`. This works as long as the string you're camel-casing is not something weird, like only whitespace or something that doesn't start with a letter, an underscore (_), or a dollar sign ($).

Let's define a function for camel-casing strings in a new src/generator/template-utils.js file as follows:

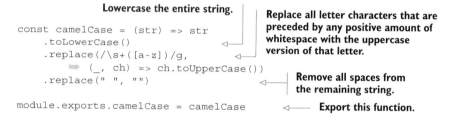

Lowercase the entire string.

```
const camelCase = (str) => str
  .toLowerCase()
  .replace(/\s+([a-z])/g,
  ⇒  (_, ch) => ch.toUpperCase())
  .replace(" ", "")

module.exports.camelCase = camelCase
```

Replace all letter characters that are preceded by any positive amount of whitespace with the uppercase version of that letter.

Remove all spaces from the remaining string.

◁───── **Export this function.**

Exercise 8.1

Write a unit test for the `camelCase` function. Hint: Section B.1.11 of appendix B explains how you could do that.

Exercise 8.2

In hindsight, using the record type's name directly in listing 8.9 seems unwise: there's no guarantee it's a valid JavaScript identifier, nor that it starts with an uppercase character.

- Fix that by adding the following function to src/generator/template-utils.js:

    Define a function that returns the string with its first character converted to uppercase.

    ```
    const withFirstUpper = (str) =>   ◁─┘
    ⇒  str.charAt(0).toUpperCase() + str.substring(1)
    module.exports.withFirstUpper = withFirstUpper
    ```
    Export it.

- Also write a unit test for this function.
- Change `indexJsx` so that `name` is computed first as the camel-cased version of the record type's name, and then `Name` as `withFirstUpper(name)`.

Let's use the `camelCase` function.

Listing 8.10 Using the `camelCase` function on named AST objects

```
const { camelCase } = require("./template-utils")        ⟵─── Import the
                                                               camelCase function.
const ccNameOf = (namedObject) =>                       ⟵
    ➥ camelCase(namedObject.settings["name"])
```

Define a ccNameOf function that returns the camel-cased name of any AST object that has a "name" property.

We have to map the value of the `name` property of an AST object to a valid JavaScript identifier several times, so it makes sense to implement some convenience in the form of the `ccNameOf` function for that.

If we only had to produce the line of code for the `rental period` attribute, the following template code inside `indexJsx` would do that.

Listing 8.11 Iteration 1: Parameterizing the field's name

```
const attribute =                                   ⟵
    ➥ recordType.settings["attributes"][1 - 1]
`${ccNameOf(attribute)} =                            ⟵
    ➥ new DateRange()`
```

Hold the first attribute's AST object in an attribute constant. We'll iterate over all attributes later, but now we're focusing only on the first one.

Produce the line of code for the "rental period" attribute as a template literal.

The literal text `new DateRange()` seems to be a result of the attribute having the "date range" type but no initial value. Let's expand listing 8.11 to take that into account:

Listing 8.12 Iteration 2: Parameterizing the field's type

Define a function that returns a default initialization expression for the given type. This is a template function because it returns a string.

If the type equals "date range," return "new DateRange()."

In all other cases, return a JavaScript comment that indicates that the generator doesn't handle a certain type.

```
const defaultInitExpressionForType = (type) => {
    switch (type) {
        case "date range": return `new DateRange()`    ⟵
        default: return `/* [GENERATION PROBLEM]        ⟵
                     ➥ type "${type}" isn't handled
                     ➥ in defaultInitExpressionForType */`
    }
}

const attribute = recordType.settings["attributes"][1 - 1]
const initialValue =                                    ⟵
    ➥ attribute.settings["initial value"]
`${ccNameOf(attribute)} = ${                            ⟵
    initialValue                                         ⟵
```

Store the attribute's initial value (or undefined if it hasn't got one) in a constant.

Check whether the attribute specifies an initial value.

Replace the object literal "new DateRange()" with an embedded expression.

```
      ? `/* [GENERATION PROBLEM] initial value
          ➥ not handled */`
      : defaultInitExpressionForType(
          ➥ attribute.settings["type"])
}`
```

If it does, produce a JavaScript comment that indicates that this template code doesn't handle initial values.

If the attribute only specifies a type, call the defaultInitExpressionForType function with that type.

Note that you can nest template literals inside embedded expressions in template literals—to arbitrary depth, even. You can see this in action in the `true` branch of the ternary expression in the last statement of the preceding code.

Using code comments to flag unhandled input

When you implement a code generator, your template will almost always be in a state where it doesn't handle everything you could throw at it. It's a Good Idea to write template code in such a way that it can detect that it has encountered a situation it doesn't handle yet, and can alert you, but doesn't stop generating. A simple alert method is to produce a code comment identifying a [GENERATION PROBLEM], containing a hint as to what piece of template code doesn't handle what bit of the AST.

The resulting generated code will most likely not be syntactically correct, but that's OK: the code generator isn't complete, so it would be strange if the generated code were to parse despite that. Even if the generated code parses correctly, it's still unlikely it will run without blowing up in some way. In any case, you should search the generated code for occurrences of the alert string, such as [GENERATION PROBLEM].

Let's generate code for all attributes, rather than just for the first one. (After that, we can try to generate code for their initial values.) Let's refactor the code in listing 8.12 into a separate template function.

Listing 8.13   Iteration 3: Extracting the initialization to a function

```
const defaultInitExpressionForType = (type) => {
    switch (type) {
        case "date range": return `new DateRange()`
        default: return `/* [GENERATION PROBLEM] type "${type}"
                    ➥ isn't handled in defaultInitExpressionForType */`
    }
}

const initializationFor = (attribute) => {
    const { settings } = attribute
    const initialValue = settings["initial value"]
    return `${ccNameOf(attribute)} = ${
        initialValue
            ? `/* [GENERATION PROBLEM] initial value not handled */`
            : defaultInitExpressionForType(settings["type"])
    }`
}
```

Now we can replace this code,

```
rentalPeriod = new DateRange()
rentalPriceBeforeDiscount = 0.0
discount = 0
rentalPriceAfterDiscount = this.rentalPriceBeforeDiscount
```

with the following code, which iterates over all attributes and calls `initializationFor` for each of them:

```
${recordType.settings["attributes"].map(initializationFor)}
```

This produces the following generated code:

```
rentalPeriod = new DateRange(),
    rentalPriceBeforeDiscount = /* [GENERATION PROBLEM] initial value
        not handled */,
    discount = /* [GENERATION PROBLEM] initial value not handled */,
    rentalPriceAfterDiscount = /* [GENERATION PROBLEM] initial value
        not handled */
```

You'll notice three problems with this:

- We get hints, tagged with `[GENERATION PROBLEM]`, that initial values are not handled, but we already knew that.
- The initialization statements generated for the attributes are separated by commas instead of newlines. This is because the embedded expression evaluates to an array of strings, which is then coerced to a string by calling `.join(",")` on it. (The default value for the optional argument of the `join` function defined on arrays is `","`.)
- Even if those initialization statements had been separated by newlines, the only indentation is that which happens to be in front of the first statement.

We can fix the second problem by *joining with newlines*: we append `.join("\n")` to the embedded expression. We can fix the third problem by putting in the proper indentation explicitly. The whole embedded expression then looks like this:

```
${recordType.settings["attributes"].map((attribute) =>
    `    ${initializationFor(attribute)}`).join("\n")}
```

This embedded expression should be on a line of its own, so that the newline following it ensures that the code generated for the last attribute is followed by a newline. The expression should also not be indented, so the first attribute doesn't receive an extra level of indentation. The generated code now looks like this (indented at level 1):

```
rentalPeriod = new DateRange()
rentalPriceBeforeDiscount = /* [GENERATION PROBLEM] initial value
    not handled */
```

```
discount = /* [GENERATION PROBLEM] initial value not handled */
rentalPriceAfterDiscount = /* [GENERATION PROBLEM] initial value
    not handled */
```

To properly generate this part of the code, we should handle the initial value as well. Let's start by focusing on the initialization expression for the second attribute: 0.0. That code fragment seems to be derivable from the details highlighted on the AST object that's the initial value of the second attribute (see figure 8.10).

Figure 8.10   An AST object encoding the number value 0.0

Add the following template function before the initializationFor function:

```
const expressionFor = (astObject) => {          ◁——  Define a function that
    const { settings } = astObject                     takes an AST object.
    switch (astObject.concept) {
        case "Number": return `${settings["value"]}`       ◁— Look at the
        default: return `/* [GENERATION PROBLEM] value   ◁—  concept label on
            of concept "${astObject.concept}"                 the initial value's
            isn't handled in expressionFor */`                AST object. For
    }                                                         now, we'll only
}                                          Generate a helpful hint for other    handle the
                                           concepts that aren't handled (yet).  Number case.
```

I've given this function the pretty generic name expressionFor, because experience tells me that we'll likely want to reuse it in the future.

We still need to call this function. To do that, change the ternary expression in initializationFor in listing 8.13 as follows:

```
isAstObject(initialValue)           ◁——  Check that initialValue is a proper AST
    ? expressionFor(initialValue)         object—and, in particular, not undefined—
    : defaultInitExpressionForType(settings["type"])   using the isAstObject function.
```

For this code to work, we have to import the isAstObject function from src/common/ast.js.

The code generated for attributes 2 through 4 now looks like this:

```
rentalPriceBeforeDiscount = 0.0
discount = 0
rentalPriceAfterDiscount = /* [GENERATION PROBLEM] value
    of concept "Attribute Reference" isn't handled in expressionFor */
```

The generation already works for the (initial value of the) third attribute, so now we only need to handle the Attribute Reference case for the initial value of the fourth attribute. Figure 8.11 highlights the details we'll need to generate the initialization expression for `rentalPriceBeforeDiscount`.

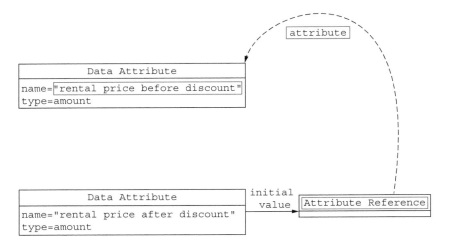

Figure 8.11   Part of the example AST with an `Attribute Reference`

Adding the following `case` to the `switch` statement in the `expressionFor` function in src/generator/indexJsx-template.js will do that:

```
case "Attribute Reference": {
    const targetAttribute = settings["attribute"].ref
    return `this.${ccNameOf(targetAttribute)}`
}
```

Navigate to the referenced attribute.

Compute the initialization expression, taking care that the reference attribute's name is turned into a camel-cased JavaScript identifier.

> ### Exercise 8.3
> Apply the preceding code changes one by one, and check after every change whether the code generator runs and works as expected. Hint: Refer to the "Generating code in watch mode" sidebar at the start of this subsection.

We have now parameterized part of the `indexJsx` template function in terms of an input AST. There's plenty of verbatim code, though. Before we finish the generator, we're going to improve how we compose template functions, especially when iterating over arrays.

8.4.2   *Composing template functions*

So far we've generated code for every attribute using the following embedded expression:

```
${recordType.settings["attributes"].map((attribute) =>
  `        ${initializationFor(attribute)}`).join("\n")}
```

In general, the pattern would be as follows:

```
${<some array>.map((<item>) =>
  `        ${<sub template function>(<item>, ...)}`).join("\n")}
```

Nesting template functions like this is awkward to decipher/unpack even in this simple case. When combining or *composing* template functions that are even more deeply nested, producing valid and properly formatted code with correct indentation becomes more and more difficult. Templates should produce correctly formatted code, because the generated code should conform to the same coding style and conventions as the rest of the code of the Runtime, or of the reference implementation. Let's devise a way to compose template functions so that we don't have to insert indentation, and to join with newlines, explicitly.

Previously, we defined a template function to be a function that returns a string. We're going to redefine a template function to be any function that returns a value that's composed entirely of strings and arrays. The arrays are allowed to be nested arbitrarily deeply, and the strings can be single- or multiline. As an example, this is allowed:

```
[
    "foo (as string)",
    [
        [
            "bar"
        ],
        []
    ],
    `        multi-
line string (as template literal)`
]
```

Let's call any such value a "nested string." This type definition also includes any regular string, without any nesting.

The idea behind a freely defined data structure like a nested string is that it's flexible, but it's also easy to produce *and* process. That frees us up from having to make sure that every template function returns one string, using string concatenation and joining with newlines. Instead, a template function can produce a nested string of any shape. Basically, array creation takes over the roles of both string concatenation and joining with newlines. We just have to turn the outermost nested string produced by the code generator into an actual string so we can write it to a destination. We'll see in section 8.4.3 how this approach also helps with indenting.

With this changed definition of template functions, we can rewrite the `indexJsx` function in src/generator/indexJsx-template.js as follows (with differences highlighted in bold):

Store the record type's attributes in a separate constant, using object destructuring, to make later code more readable.

Use the ccNameOf function to turn the record type's name into a JavaScript identifier.

```
const indexJsx = (recordType) => {
    const name = ccNameOf(recordType)
    const ucName = withFirstUpper(name)
    const { attributes } = recordType.settings
```

Uppercase name and assign it to ucName to ensure the assumption we made in listing 8.9.

```
    return [
        `import React from "react"
import { createRoot } from "react-dom/client"
import { makeAutoObservable } from "mobx"
import { observer } from "mobx-react"

import { FormField, Input } from "./components"
import { DateRange } from "./dates"

require("./styling.css")

class ${ucName} {`,
        attributes.map((attribute) =>
            `    ${initializationFor(attribute)}`),
        `constructor() {
        makeAutoObservable(this)
    }
}

// ...rest of the code...

createRoot(document.getElementById("root"))
    .render(
        <RentalForm rental={rental} />
    )
`
    ]
}
```

Return an array instead of a string, and divide the template literal in the previous version of the indexJsx function into three parts. These parts turn into the members of the array returned.

This line closes the template literal making up the first part.

Call the initializationFor subtemplate function for every attribute, but without joining with newlines. This produces an array of strings: the second part of the divided template literal contents.

Produce the remaining, third part of the divided template literal contents.

Close the array of the nested string after the last template literal.

The `indexJsx` function now produces an array that has the following shape: `[ string, [ strings… ], string ]`. To write the result of a call to `indexJsx` to file, we need to turn it into a string again. Add the following code to src/generator/template-utils.js for that.

Listing 8.14   The `asString` function in src/generator/template-utils.js

Define a withNewlineEnsured helper function
(that's not exported) that adds a newline to a
string when it doesn't already end in one.

Check whether the given nestedString
value is a single string or an array of
nested strings.

```
const withNewlineEnsured = (str) => str
    + (str.endsWith("\n") ? "" : "\n")
const asString = (nestedString) =>
    Array.isArray(nestedString)
    ? nestedString.flat(Infinity)
        .map(withNewlineEnsured)
        .join("")
    : withNewlineEnsured(nestedString)

module.exports.asString = asString
```

If nestedString is an array, flatten it
using <array>.flat(Infinity)—more
on that shortly.

Ensure that each of those strings ends in
a newline, adding one where necessary,
by mapping withNewlineEnsured over
the flat array.

Concatenate the strings in the
array (without newlines or
commas) using .join("").

Export the
asString function.

If nestedString is a single string,
ensure it ends in a newline.

Flattening arrays

The JavaScript built-in `flat` function "flattens" an array by moving members of sub-arrays up. In other words, it removes nesting. As an example, `[ 1, [ 2 ], [] ].flat()` evaluates to `[ 1, 2 ]`. (Note that empty subarrays have no members, so these basically disappear.)

The `flat` function takes an optional argument: the *depth* to which an array should be flattened. This argument has a default value of 1. For example, `[ [1, [2] ] ].flat()` evaluates to `[ 1, [2] ]`, while `[ [1, [2] ] ].flat(2)` evaluates to `[ 1, 2 ]`. Passing `Infinity` for the argument ensures that an array is flattened *completely*, with no nested arrays remaining. This is exactly what we need to work with nested strings, which can be nested to arbitrary depths.

Now we have to change src/generator/indexJsx-template.js as follows (with the differences highlighted in bold):

```
const { asString, camelCase, withFirstUpper } = require("./template-utils")

// ...rest of the previous code...

module.exports.generatedIndexJsx = (ast) =>
    asString(indexJsx(ast))
```

Make sure we return a
regular string instead
of a nested one.

Exercise 8.4

Apply the code changes, and check that code generation works as before.

> **Exercise 8.5**
>
> Write a unit test for the `asString` function. That will help with most of the exercises in the next subsection.

8.4.3 *Indenting declaratively*

We've made composing template functions more convenient by allowing them to return a nested string rather than a single string. Let's step up our game even more and improve how we indent pieces of code. Right now, we still indent code returned by `initializationFor` explicitly:

```
${attributes.map((attribute) => `     ${initializationFor(attribute)}`)}
```

To improve on this, we could make an `indent` function that indents all strings of an array (one level), like this:

```
${indent(attributes.map(initializationFor))}
```

This is also better because the reference to the `indent` function is at the spot in the template literal where indentation should happen. As you'll see later, it's convenient to be able to indent more levels at the same time.

We could also have `indent` take an indentation level as an argument, so its use would look like `${indent(1, attributes...)}$`. I prefer an approach using a *higher-order function*: have `indent(<n>)` return a *function* that, when called with a nested string as an argument, indents every string in that value. The preceding code fragment could then be changed to this:

```
${indent(1)(attributes.map(initializationFor))}
```

Let's implement this `indent` function in src/generator/template-utils. Don't forget to import it in src/generator/indexJsx-template.js. The implementation of the `indent` function looks a lot like that of the `asString` function in listing 8.14.

Listing 8.15   The `indent` function in src/generator/template-utils.js

Precompute the string to prefix as indentation.

Define a local function to prefix a string with the requested indentation. This function assumes that the string passed is one line (with or without newlines).

```
const indent = (indentLevel) => {
    const indentationPrefix =
        "    ".repeat(indentLevel)
    const indentLine = (str) => indentationPrefix + str
    return (nestedString) =>
        Array.isArray(nestedString)
        ? nestedString.flat(Infinity).map(indentLine)
        : indentLine(nestedString)
}

module.exports.indent = indent
```

Return a function that indents all strings inside the nested string passed with the requested level.

Export the indent function.

Exercise 8.6

- Apply the preceding code additions to src/generator/template-utils.js, and changes to src/generator/indexJsx-template.js, and check that code generation works as before.
- Write unit tests for the `indent` function. That will help with the following exercises.
- It would be useful if the `asString` and `indent` functions were to skip over falsy values. For example, `asString([ undefined, indent(1)([ "before", null, "after"])])` could evaluate to `" before\n after\n"`.

  That way, we could conditionally add pieces of code by producing a falsy value instead of a proper nested string. This trick is analogous to using the shortcut AND operator `&&` in JSX code: `<some condition> && [ "some code" ]`.

  Modify the `asString` and `indent` functions accordingly. Make sure to expand the unit tests for these functions as well.
- Change the `indentLine` function inside the `indent` function so that it only adds the `indentationPrefix` if the string passed is non-empty. You can define empty either as "has length 0" or as "only contains whitespace (including newlines)."
- The `indentLine` function inside the `indent` function assumes that it's passed a string that's one line, either with or without newlines. Change the code so that it first splits the string passed on newlines before it injects the `indentationPrefix` for each line.
- Optional: The `asString` and `indent` functions in src/generator/template-utils.js look rather similar. Try to refactor and DRY them. Hint: Create a higher-order `mapNestedString` function that returns a function taking a nested string. The `mapNestedString` function should take two mapping functions as arguments, one for each of the possible outcomes of `Array.isArray(...)`, and apply these mapping functions to a nested string.

8.4.4 Finishing the code generator

We're not done iterating over the template yet, because `indexJsx` still contains text taken or derived literally from the example AST. Let's parameterize the part of the template that generates code for `<RentalForm>`.

Exercise 8.7

Parameterize the following literal piece of code in the latter part of `indexJsx`:

```
const RentalForm = observer(({ rental }) => <form>
    <FormField label="Rental period">
        <Input type="date" object={rental.rentalPeriod} fieldName="from" />
        <Input type="date" object={rental.rentalPeriod} fieldName="to" />
    </FormField>
```

(continued)
```
    <FormField label="Rental price before discount">
        $ <Input type="number" object={rental}
            ➥ fieldName="rentalPriceBeforeDiscount" />
    </FormField>
    <FormField label="Discount">
        <Input type="number" object={rental} fieldName="discount" /> %
    </FormField>
    <FormField label="Rental price after discount">
        $ <Input type="number" object={rental}
            ➥ fieldName="rentalPriceAfterDiscount" />
    </FormField>
</form>)

const rental = new Rental()

createRoot(document.getElementById("root"))
    .render(
        <RentalForm rental={rental} />
    )
```

Hint: Use helper template functions.

You can find my preferred solution to this exercise in the following three listings, which together contain the complete, final contents of src/generator/indexJsx-template.js, with the remaining part parameterized, and code changes for that highlighted in bold.

Listing 8.16   Part 1 (of 3) of the final `indexJsx` template

```
const { isAstObject } = require("../common/ast")
const { asString, camelCase, indent, withFirstUpper } =
    ➥ require("./template-utils")

const ccNameOf = (namedObject) =>
    ➥ camelCase(namedObject.settings["name"])

const expressionFor = (astObject) => {
    const { settings } = astObject
    switch (astObject.concept) {
        case "Attribute Reference": {
            const targetAttribute = settings["attribute"].ref
            return `this.${ccNameOf(targetAttribute)}`
        }
        case "Number": return `${settings["value"]}`
        default: return `/* [GENERATION PROBLEM] value
                    ➥ of concept "${astObject.concept}"
                    ➥ isn't handled in expressionFor */`
    }
}
```

```
const defaultInitExpressionForType = (type) => {
    switch (type) {
        case "date range": return `new DateRange()`
        default: return `/* [GENERATION PROBLEM] type "${type}"
                     isn't handled in defaultInitExpressionForType */`
    }
}

const initializationFor = (attribute) => {
    const { settings } = attribute
    const initialValue = settings["initial value"]
    return `${ccNameOf(attribute)} = ${
        isAstObject(initialValue)
            ? expressionFor(initialValue)
            : defaultInitExpressionForType(settings["type"])
    }`
}

const formFieldInput = (type, objectExpr, fieldName) =>
    `<Input type="${type}" object={${objectExpr}}
        fieldName="${fieldName}" />`
```

The formFieldInputs function returns either a string or a tuple of the shape [string, string]: the children in the call to <FormField> for the given attribute.

This case of the switch statement returns a tuple of two strings. All other cases return just a string. Because we're using nested strings, that's not a problem for the calling formField function.

```
const formFieldInputs = (objectExpr, attribute) => {    ◀
    const { settings } = attribute
    const { type } = settings
    const fieldName = ccNameOf(attribute)
    switch (type) {
        case "amount": return
            "$ " + formFieldInput("number", objectExpr, fieldName)
        case "date range": return [ "from", "to" ].map(    ◀
            (subFieldName) => formFieldInput(
                        "date",
                        `${objectExpr}.${fieldName}`,
                        subFieldName
                    )
        )
        case "percentage": return
            formFieldInput("number", objectExpr, fieldName) + " %"
        default: return `// [GENERATION PROBLEM] type "${type}"
                     isn't handled in formFieldInputs`
    }
}

const formField = (objectExpr, attribute) => [
    `<FormField label="${withFirstUpper(attribute.settings["name"])}">`,
    indent(1)(formFieldInputs(objectExpr, attribute)),
    `</FormField>`
]
```

```
const indexJsx = (recordType) => {
    const name = camelCase(recordType.settings["name"])
    const ucName = withFirstUpper(name)
    const { attributes } = recordType.settings

    return [
        `import React from "react"
import { createRoot } from "react-dom/client"
import { makeAutoObservable } from "mobx"
import { observer } from "mobx-react"
import { FormField, Input } from "./components"

require("./styling.css")

class ${ucName} {`,
        indent(1)(
            attributes.map(initializationFor)
        ),
        `
        constructor() {
        makeAutoObservable(this)
    }
}

const ${ucName}Form = observer(({ ${name} }) => <form>`,
        indent(1)(
            attributes.map(
                (attribute) => formField(name, attribute)
            )
        ),
        `</form>)

const ${name} = new ${ucName}**()
```

```
createRoot(document.getElementById("root"))
    .render(
        <${ucName}Form ${name}={${name}} />
    )
`
    ]
}

module.exports.generatedIndexJsx = (ast) => asString(indexJsx(ast))
```

For completeness' sake, here's also the final version of src/generator/template-utils.js.

```
const camelCase = (str) => str
    .toLowerCase()
    .replace(/\s+([a-z])/g, (_, ch) => ch.toUpperCase())
    .replace(" ", "")
module.exports.camelCase = camelCase
```

```
const withFirstUpper = (str) =>
    ⟹  str.charAt(0).toUpperCase() + str.substring(1)
module.exports.withFirstUpper = withFirstUpper

const withNewlineEnsured = (str) => str + (str.endsWith("\n") ? "" : "\n")
const asString = (nestedString) => Array.isArray(nestedString)
    ? nestedString.flat(Infinity)
        .map(withNewlineEnsured)
        .join("")
    : withNewlineEnsured(nestedString)
module.exports.asString = asString

const indent = (indentLevel) => {
    const indentationPrefix = "   ".repeat(indentLevel)
    const indentLine = (str) => indentationPrefix + str
    return (nestedString) => Array.isArray(nestedString)
        ? nestedString.flat(Infinity).map(indentLine)
        : indentLine(nestedString)
}
module.exports.indent = indent
```

Note that src/generator/generate.js hasn't been altered since listing 8.6.

Our template started out looking completely like code in the Runtime's programming language (listing 8.7), and it ended up looking mostly like JavaScript with some literal pieces of code here and there (listings 8.16 and 8.17). In my experience, it's more important that templates be good pieces of code in their own right than that they look like text with expression-shaped holes. That means that templates should be maintainable, properly engineered and modularized, and sufficiently documented. It's very difficult to check whether a template produces valid code just by looking at the template's code. It's better to always check the generated code as an integral part of all the code, using the conventional code quality techniques that you should use anyway.

NOTE Any detail in the AST usually corresponds to multiple—often many—details in the generated code. I like to call this the *fan-out effect*, because details have the tendency to "fan out."

Exercise 8.8

- Can you find details in the AST for which *no* code has been generated? Hint: There are three.
- Do you think it's suspicious that there's no code directly related to these details?

NOTE One of the boons of generating code instead of writing it by hand is that we're not as bogged down writing the tedious part of the code. This tedious part is also referred to as *boilerplate* or *accidental complexity* (both of which you'll find defined in Wikipedia), although I like the term *incidental* *complexity* much better myself. Boilerplate is formed by the pieces of code that are required for technical reasons but are essentially repetitive, and contribute only little functionally.

> ## Exercise 8.9
> What part of the reference implementation would you consider to be boilerplate?

> ## Exercise 8.10
> Either of the following two tasks are enough to attach the generator to the backend, so you only have to implement one of them:
>
> - Make an alternative version of listing 8.6 that fetches the AST from the REST API of a running backend, instead of loading it from storage. Hint: Use Node.js's HTTP module for that.
> - Extend the REST API of the backend with an endpoint that calls the code generator and returns the source for src/runtime/index.jsx.

8.4.5   *Alternative approaches for writing templates*

We were able to use regular JavaScript to write templates, thanks to ES2015 template literals. That also allowed us to continue using our development environment without changes. In your situation, however, things might be different, so I should mention a number of alternative approaches for writing templates:

- You can use a template framework, like Mustache, Handlebars, Velocity, String-Template, etc. Table 8.1 lists the pros and cons of using these as opposed to using the template literals built into JavaScript (ES2015)—possibly augmented with the declarative approach.
- Using a code formatter like Prettier to automatically reformat generated code. That may save you from having to take care of indentation and such in the template code, but it does add a dependency and an extra build step. Configuring the autoformatting to conform to your coding styling and conventions might not be trivial either.
- Using an AST-to-AST transformation. Instead of producing plain text that "happens" to be valid code in some programming language, you transform the AST for the DSL content into an AST that coincides with parsed generated code. I'll mention this approach briefly again in section 15.4.2, but for space reasons it's outside of the scope of this book.

In this chapter, you learned how to generate code from an AST. In the next chapter, you're going to learn how to *validate* an AST, to prevent that generated code from breaking.

Table 8.1 Pros and cons of using template literals versus template frameworks

	ES 2015 template literals	Other template framework
Pro	■ Works out of the box. ■ Uses standard JavaScript, so you can use all of JavaScript's language features to properly engineer a code generator.	■ May have a facility to help you with properly indenting the generated code. (Often, though, that facility depends on the availability of proper IDE support in the form of a plugin.)
Con	■ All code formatting has to be done explicitly.	■ It's an extra dependency. ■ Comes with its own syntax and peculiarities, which you'll have to learn and understand. ■ Your IDE of choice might not support a plugin for that framework that provides syntax checking and highlighting, content assist, etc. ■ It may force you to precompute derived data, such as camel-cased names, separate from the actual template.

Using LLMs to generate code

Another alternative approach that surfaced relatively recently is to use Large Language Models (LLMs), like ChatGPT. You could use an LLM in two ways:

- Ask the LLM to produce a template given some example DSL content (which has to be in some textual syntax) and a description of its desired semantics.
- Generate a series of descriptions of desired semantics from actual DSL content, and ask the LLM to produce code implementing those semantics.

At the time of writing (April 2024), neither approach has really been investigated to sufficient depth. Nevertheless, this direction is certainly interesting.

The first method above could initially speed up the development of a code generator, but you should still be wary of the LLM's answers. At best, you should regard these as a half-product, which should be validated (by providing sufficient automated test coverage), refactored for maximum readability and maintainability, and documented. The second method essentially functions as a black box (or as a "can of hired offshore developers," or "an infinite number of monkeys with typewriters"...), over which you have little to no control. It could produce working code, but you'd also have to validate, refactor, and document that code. Because generated code is much larger than template code (because of the fan-out effect alluded to previously, before exercise 8.7), that just means more work.

Summary

- The *build system* is the part of the Domain IDE that turns DSL content into runnable or running software: the Runtime. At its heart, a *code generator* takes the persisted AST and generates the business knowledge part of the Runtime.

- The Runtime's codebase can be divided into the following parts:
  - Code that corresponds directly to business knowledge that can be specified in the form of DSL content authored by the domain experts.
  - Other code that doesn't correspond to business knowledge, but which combines seamlessly with it.
  - A build configuration for combining all the code, to build a Runtime artifact, which can then be deployed or run.
- The build system can be *triggered* in many ways, among which is running a CLI command.
- It's important to implement a *reference implementation* for the Runtime manually, before starting to implement a code generator. This reference implementation provides a good starting point for implementing the build system. In particular, the code generator part of the build system can be implemented by gradually parameterizing the code to be generated with information coming from an AST. (This is very similar to the iterative approach to implementing the projection shown in chapter 4.)
- JavaScript ES2015 *template literals* with embedded expressions can be used to conveniently implement *template functions*: JavaScript functions that generate code from (pieces of) an AST.
- *Nested strings* are a mechanism for conveniently *composing* template functions. Nested strings allow declarative indentation and make template functions more readable and maintainable, while at the same time generating code with proper formatting—especially indentation.
- Alternatively, a code formatter could be used to turn code without indentation into properly formatted code.

Preventing things from blowing up

This chapter covers

- Determining the various ways the build system and Runtime can fail
- Adding constraints to the DSL so that domain experts are warned about "faulty" DSL content that can cause failures
- Strengthening the generator so it can deal with some failures

In chapter 8, we implemented a code generator to generate code from an AST representing DSL content. (This DSL content would be written using the Domain IDE.) That generator, and the generated code, worked for the AST of the example DSL content, and it would probably also work for a lot of other DSL content. However, some ASTs could cause the generator to produce *code* that can't be built, or code that crashes or runs incorrectly. The generator itself can even crash on a particular AST—for example, when the generator expects some property to have a setting, but it doesn't.

Figure 9.1 divides the process of building a Runtime from DSL content into several stages and indicates how they might fail.

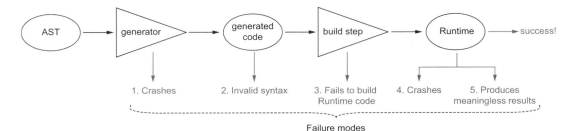

Figure 9.1 Building the Runtime from DSL content, divided into several separate stages with their failure modes

Table 9.1 explains these stages and their associated failure and success modes in a little more detail.

Table 9.1 Stages in building the Runtime from DSL content with their failure modes and success criteria

Stage #	Failure	Success
1	The generator crashes because of an invalid AST.	The generator runs to completion, but may contain syntactically invalid or flagged code.
2	The generated code is syntactically invalid.	The generated code is syntactically valid.
3	The Runtime's code, combining generated and handwritten code, produces build errors.	The Runtime's code builds to completion.
4	Running the Runtime throws an error, or it crashes.	The Runtime runs without throwing an error or crashing in some other way.
5	The Runtime produces nonsensical or meaningless results.	The Runtime runs correctly.

In this chapter, we're going to see how to deal with these failure modes. Phrased positively: we're going to find out how we can avoid ending up in a situation where things blow up in the first place. Sometimes we'll do that by adapting, or "strengthening," the generator so that any "explosion" that does happen, cuses much less damage. Most of the time, we'll impose constraints on the AST representing the DSL content.

A *constraint* is a condition that must be satisfied throughout the entire AST, *or else*! Whenever and wherever a constraint condition is not satisfied, that's a *violation* of that constraint. Each violation is reported to the domain experts as an *issue* via a helpful message, which helps them repair the problem. This is analogous to programming languages, where a compiler can report errors (which prevent code from compiling) or warnings (which don't). We'll implement a *constraints checker* that computes constraint violations in the AST as *issues* (errors or warnings). We'll then report these constraint violations where they occur through the reactive projection in the Domain IDE, so that we provide the domain experts with immediate feedback. Figure 9.2 illustrates that approach.

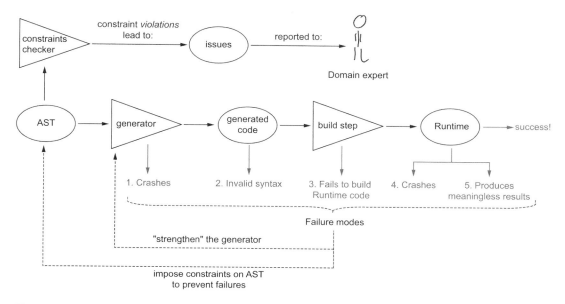

Figure 9.2   How to mitigate failure modes when building the Runtime

We're not going to be able to prevent failures altogether. We'll try to make sure that domain experts know when to prevent a failure they can fix, and how to do that. Beyond that, it's up to the software developers to diagnose failures that (might) occur. They'll have to decide whether to impose additional constraints, and/or strengthen the generator to ward off failure modes 2–5 in figure 9.2.

9.1 Preventing failures by adding constraints

Let's discover as many faulty situations as we can, before the domain experts run into them. We can do this by looping over this simple four-step plan:

1 Create an AST that we suspect might cause an explosion of sorts.
2 Hide behind a blast shield, and feed the AST to the generator and the build step.
3 Figure out what went wrong after the smoke clears.
4 Decide how to prevent this particular explosion from happening or from causing damage.

We'll create the AST through the DSL editor, save it to the AST persistent storage, and trigger the generator. After the generator has run, we'll check how it ran and inspect the code generated (if any). If the code is OK, we'll try to build the Runtime with the generated code. Our build step doesn't really check anything beyond syntactic validity, so the generated code will virtually always build, even if it's plainly wrong. For that reason, running the Runtime is the ultimate test.

If anything goes wrong during these steps, we'll investigate the problem to determine its root cause and then decide how we can best fix it. Starting from the perspective of the domain experts, by creating an AST using the Domain IDE, allows us to gain a good insight into how we can help them prevent mistakes. It also prepares us for when a domain expert creates an AST that causes a failure, despite our best efforts to prevent that from happening. In that situation, the domain expert would file a bug with the software developers. To make that bug reproducible, the domain expert should be able to share their particular AST with the software developers.

The main mechanism for fixing a faulty situation is implementing a constraint. The following principle should hold: *if the Domain IDE doesn't report issues on the DSL content, the generator should run to completion, the build step should be able to build the Runtime, and the Runtime should run without crashing or producing meaningless results.* It's a tall order to live up to, and you won't always be able to. The domain experts will do their best to keep you honest on this, though.

Vice versa, *if issues are reported on the DSL content, then the generator, the build step, or the built Runtime can't be expected to work fully correctly.* You can hold the domain experts to this "inverse" principle: if they wrote DSL content that has issues, they shouldn't be surprised when things blow up.

ASTs that violate constraints are said to be *invalid* (or "inconsistent"). A recurring question among DSL engineers is whether you should allow invalid ASTs to exist outside of the DSL editor. In my experience, you should do so for various reasons:

- Any AST is invalid *most of the time* because the domain expert is editing the DSL content. Not being able to save an invalid AST means that the domain expert always has to complete the DSL content enough to make it valid. That doesn't mean it makes complete sense at that point, just that the DSL content *looks* complete, though it might not be.
- You can share an invalid AST to try and fix it.
- The Domain IDE is software, so it probably has bugs. Anything from the DSL editor to the serialized AST storage on the backend might contain a bug that corrupts the AST, making it invalid through no fault of the domain experts. Ideally, domain experts should be able to fix corruption through the DSL editor. If that's not possible, they can ask one of the software developers to fix it on the JSON level.
- In chapter 10, we'll talk about versioning a DSL. An AST that's valid in the current version of the DSL implementation could be (considered to be) invalid in the new version. This means you need to implement an *AST migration* that turns any AST for the current version of the DSL implementation into an AST that's suitable for the new version.

  It can happen that an AST migration turns an AST that's valid in the current version into an AST that's invalid in the new version. (Sometimes the opposite happens: the AST migration may "fix" the AST.) This is most likely due to a bug in the AST migration. Sometimes there's a fundamental incompatibility between the two versions, such as a property or even a concept that's removed after it's been properly deprecated.

You will probably need to add code to the Domain IDE and generator implementations to deal with invalid ASTs without throwing errors or crashing in some other way. As far as I'm concerned, this code bloat is justified. Not only does it leave your domain experts stranded less often, it also forces you to think about possible failure modes and corner cases. The only effect you need to watch out for is obscuring actual problems in the AST, or separating the root cause of the failure too much from where it first manifests itself.

9.2   A template case: Dealing with an attribute without a name

In this section, we'll deal with one kind of faulty DSL content: attributes without a name. We'll deploy the techniques we develop throughout the rest of this chapter, and the book. Our handling of this kind of faulty DSL content will serve as a template of sorts: the design choices and implementation strategies we encounter here will carry over to every kind of failure.

Let's add an attribute to the `Rental` record type in our example DSL content, without filling out its name or specifying its type. We do that by just clicking the "+ attribute" button. The result is shown in figure 9.3.

Figure 9.3   An attribute with an empty name and unspecified type, created by clicking the "+ attribute" button

We'll see that this situation produces a failure, and therefore violates the principle from section 9.1. We're going to fix that by finding, formulating, and implementing a suitable constraint. As we do so, we'll set up essential infrastructure and also strengthen the generator.

We can save the DSL content that includes the nameless attribute from figure 9.3, and trigger the generator from the command line. That throws the following error:

```
.toLowerCase()
 ^
```

```
TypeError: Cannot read property 'toLowerCase' of undefined
```

According to the stack trace that's printed out by Node.js, the error is thrown from the second line of the `camelCase` function in the src/generator/template-utils.js file:

```
const camelCase = (str) => str
    .toLowerCase()          ⟵    The code fails on this line, with an error
                                 indicating that str is undefined.
```

```
        .replace(/\s+([a-z])/g, (_, ch) => ch.toUpperCase())
...
```

Let's see how `camelCase` comes to be called with the value `undefined` as its argument. Inspecting the stack trace reveals that this happens inside the `initializationFor` function:

```
const initializationFor = (attribute) => {
    const { settings } = attribute
    const initialValue = settings["initial value"]
    return `${ccNameOf(attribute)} = ${
        isAstObject(initialValue)
            ? expressionFor(initialValue)
            : defaultInitExpressionForType(settings["type"])
    }`
}
```

> **An error is thrown from this line, and specifically from the italicized expression.**

Because we know that `attribute` is an AST object, we can conclude that `settings["name"]` (which is accessed by the `ccNameOf` function) must be `undefined`.

We can inspect the src/backend/data/contents.json file to find the AST object representing the added attribute:

```
{
  "id": "G3HR-vHXL",
  "concept": "Data Attribute",
  "settings": {}
}
```

> **This is a randomly generated ID, so yours is very likely to differ.**

Indeed, `settings["name"]` has the value `undefined`.

9.2.1   *Constraint strategies*

We can deal with this problem using a handful of strategies. I've labeled these descriptively, so we can refer back to them:

- *ImposeConstraints*—We can clearly signal to the domain expert that they need to fill out the name. The `<TextValue>` component in src/frontend/value-components.jsx already does this to some extent, by styling the placeholder text with a reddish color. We could do better by also presenting the domain expert with an explicit error saying something like "An attribute must have a name." This constitutes our first constraint.

- *HandleFaultyContent*—We can adapt the generator so it doesn't crash when `camelCase` is called with a non-string argument. The simplest way to do this would be to check whether `str` is a string, return its camel-cased version when it is, and return some suitable camel-cased string when it isn't.

  Alternatively, we could adapt the generator to skip over attributes that have problems, such as a missing name or type. That would also prevent the failure we analyzed previously from happening.

- *PreventPersistence*—We could prevent the domain expert from being able to save DSL content that has missing properties. That also would also prevent running the generator with DSL content that makes it crash.

Applying any combination of these strategies would be an improvement, but the last two strategies come with some tradeoffs that we'll discuss.

In the case of the HandleFaultyContent approach, what would be a sensible value to return from `camelCase` for a non-string argument? We could, in the spirit of "defensive programming," return a value that makes the code syntactically valid: in this case, a valid JavaScript identifier string would do. Honoring the name of the function, the identifier should be camel-cased.

The problem with this strategy is that we can't choose a sensible name for the attribute on behalf of the domain expert. We'd also be purposely separating the root cause of the fault—an `undefined` value—from the point in time where it has a clear consequence. Even if the generator runs to completion, and the generated code is syntactically valid overall, the Runtime produced might still not run. We just made it harder for the domain expert to understand why the generator or Runtime isn't working properly. If we chose this strategy, we would also have to present the domain expert with an explicit issue, which means implementing the ImposeConstraints strategy.

The best we can seem to do here, in addition to using the ImposeConstraints strategy, is to prevent the generator from crashing, and return some camel-cased string that will act as a *flag* inside the generated code: `__generationProblemDueToNonString-ArgumentToCamelCase` is long, but it works. (The `__` prefix, consisting of two underscores, is meant to distinguish it from more regular JavaScript identifiers.) When the software developers find this identifier in the generated source, they use some deductive reasoning to trace the flagged code back to the missing value for the `name` property. They can then check whether the ImposeConstraints strategy has been implemented properly and explain to the domain expert how they can fix the DSL content themselves.

Instead of, or in addition to, generating flagged code, we could also *log* the problem while running the generator. If we do that, we have to ensure the log item provides some kind of reference into either the contents of the AST or the generated code. Without that, it'd be very hard for the software developers to investigate the problem and act on it.

The alternative, of skipping over faulty content, seems quite benign to the domain expert, but it can only work if none of the nameless attributes are referenced from somewhere else. What code could you generate for that reference? The answer to this question has to be good enough that the generator runs to completion and produces buildable and runnable code. If that can't be done, there's no point in choosing this strategy.

Using the PreventPersistence strategy to prevent the domain expert from saving an AST "with holes" means they have to choose between losing work or filling those holes anyway they can, *if* they can. I wouldn't begrudge them for refusing to work with such software. This "solution" also prevents them from sharing a faulty AST with the software development team when filing a bug.

A more benign version of this PreventPersistence strategy is to prevent the generator and build step from running on ASTs for which issues have been reported, thanks to repeated application of the ImposeConstraints strategy. But, in that case, applying the HandleFaultyContent strategy is usually preferable, even if it means that generation and building would still fail.

Which strategies you apply, and how, is a *design choice*. This choice should primarily serve the DSL's usability for domain experts. The amount of work that a particular choice inflicts on the software developers is of lesser concern.

In this case, we'll implement the ImposeConstraints strategy. In addition, we'll implement the HandleFaultyContent strategy to avoid the generator failing outright because of such a simple problem. We'll do that by generating flags in the code that alert the software developers to the problem, rather than ignoring, or skipping over, the nameless attribute, in case there are references to it. We won't implement either version of the PreventPersistence strategy, because it's unfair to the domain expert and would require us to implement more logic in the Domain IDE's UI.

The constraint resulting from the ImposeConstraints strategy is as follows: any `Data Attribute` must have a string as the value of the setting for its `name` property. Any `Data Attribute` that has a non-string as `name` should signal the domain experts with a message saying "An attribute must have a name." A violation of this constraint happens in a specific context, and the issue for that violation should be shown in its context: in our case, that's the nameless attribute.

9.2.2 *Implementing the constraints checker*

Let's write a constraints-checker function that, given any AST object, computes all constraint violations that occur in the context of that AST object and returns those as an array. To keep things simple, we'll equate an issue to its issue message—a string. Create a constraints.js file in the src/language directory. This directory will contain everything that's language-specific and that will be used in the frontend and the code generator. The constraints.js file will contain the constraints checker in the form of the `issuesFor` function. The initial version will implement the constraint that an attribute must have a string as `name`. Put the following code in it.

Listing 9.1 The initial implementation of the constraints checker

Define a function that returns an array of strings for the given AST object: its issues.

Define a function that determines whether a given value is a non-empty string. A string consisting of only whitespace is considered to be empty.

```
const isNonEmptyString = (value) =>
    typeof value === "string" && value.trim().length > 0

const issuesFor = (astObject) => {
    const issues = []
```

Declare a constant for the list of all issues to be returned at the end of the function.

```
const { settings } = astObject

switch (astObject.concept) {
    case "Data Attribute": {
        if (!isNonEmptyString(settings["name"])) {
            issues.push(
                "An attribute must have a name")
        }
        break
    }
    // ...cases for other concepts to be added...
}

return issues
}
module.exports.issuesFor = issuesFor
```

Destructure settings from the AST object, for convenience.

Switch on the concept label of the given AST object.

For a Data Attribute object, check whether the setting for name is a non-empty string.

If it isn't, add a meaningful message to the list of issues.

Break out of the switch statement.

We'll add cases for other concept labels later on. Don't provide a default case, because some concepts might genuinely have no constraints defined on them.

NOTE   A constraint is a condition that must be satisfied. That's why I like to implement constraints using the pattern `if (!<condition>) { issues.push (<violation message>) }`, even if that sometimes makes it look like a double negation that could be refactored out.

We can now compute the issues by calling `issuesFor(astObject)`. We can do that anywhere, but a good place for it is inside the `Projection` function in src/front-end/projection.jsx. That way, the issue information stays close to its context, and the computation is reactive.

How should we show the issues' messages? The placeholder styling of `<TextValue>` already provides a decent visual marker in the form of a reddish text "<name>". Since the context of the issue is the whole attribute, we could simply show a tooltip with the issue's message when hovering anywhere over the attribute's screen area. Alternatively, and because tooltips are problematic on mobile devices, we could additionally provide a small icon that shows the issues' messages when clicked.

We'll also provide the domain experts with another visual marker that a particular attribute has a problem. That marker should encourage them to hover over the attribute to see the issues' messages.

Add a call to the `issuesFor` function before the `switch` statement in the `Projection` function in src/frontend/projection.jsx:

```
const issues = issuesFor(astObject)
```

(We have to import the `issuesFor` function from src/language/constraints.js as well.) Change the projection of a `Data Attribute` (in the corresponding `case` in the `Projection` function in src/frontend/projection.jsx) as follows:

Wrap the existing projection code in a <div> element. Use the title attribute of the HTML element to show all issues' messages on separate lines.

When there is at least one issue, show a visual marker in front of the attribute: a red "⚠".

```
case "Data Attribute": {
    return <div title={issues.join("\n")}>
        {issues.length > 0
            && <span className="issue-marker">⚠</span>}
        <AstObjectUiWrapper className="attribute"
            ↪astObject={astObject} deleteAstObject={replaceWith}>
            // ...the rest of the existing code...
        </AstObjectUiWrapper>
    </div>
}
```

Project the AST object as before.

We also need to add the following definition to src/frontend/styling.css:

```
span.issue-marker {
    color: red;
    float: left;
}
```

These changes produce the result shown in figure 9.4.

Figure 9.4   An attribute with an empty name showing an issue marker, and the issue message in a tooltip

What makes a good issue message?

An issue's message should be both meaningful and helpful to (at least) *the domain experts*. That means

- It should clearly describe what constraint was violated.
- Ideally, it also describes how to fix the problem.
- Too short is worse than too long.

Exercise 9.1

Apply the preceding code changes, and verify that the Domain IDE reports an issue on a newly created attribute. Also verify that the computation and reporting of issues really is reactive.

As promised before, we'll also implement the HandleFaultyContent strategy. To do that, change the `camelCase` function in src/generator/template-utils.js as follows:

Check whether the str argument is actually a string.

Use a ternary operator with the "then" branch containing the original code.

```
const camelCase = (str) => typeof str === "string"
    ? str
        .toLowerCase()
        .replace(/\s+([a-z])/g, (_, ch) => ch.toUpperCase())
        .replace(" ", "")
    : "__generationProblem DueToNonStringArgumentToCamelCase"
```

In the "else" branch, produce a camel-cased string, "__generationProblemDueToNonStringArgumentToCamelCase", that acts as a flag for the underlying problem, as well as being a valid and camel-cased JavaScript identifier.

When we now run the generator, it throws an error again:

```
const withFirstUpper = (str) =>
    str.charAt(0).toUpperCase() + str.substring(1)
        ^

TypeError: Cannot read property 'charAt' of undefined
```

We conclude that the `withFirstUpper` function in src/generator/template-utils.js suffers from the same problem that `camelCase` did: it can't cope with its argument being `undefined`. Let's fix that function as follows:

Check whether the str argument is actually a string.

If it is a string, do as before.

```
const withFirstUpper = (str) => typeof str === "string"
    ? str.charAt(0).toUpperCase() + str.substring(1)
    : "GenerationProblem DueToNonStringArgumentToWithFirstUpper"
```

If str isn't a string, return the string GenerationProblemDueToNonStringArgumentToWithFirstUpper to flag the underlying problem, while still starting with an uppercase character.

Note that the JavaScript expressions `""`.`charAt(0)` and `"a"`.`substring(1)` both evaluate to an empty string, without throwing an error. This means that the `then` branch even works correctly on empty strings, or ones of length 1.

Exercise 9.2

Apply the preceding code changes, and verify that the generator runs to completion on an incomplete AST, without crashing. Also check the generated code in /index.jsx

Exercise 9.3

It would be useful to know whether you're running the generator on DSL content that has issues. Extend src/generator/generate.js to find and print *all* issues on *any* AST object in the persisted DSL content. (Use `console.log(…)` to print from a Node.js program.) Hint: Implement this as a depth-first tree traversal.

Would you find and print all issues before or after running the generator? Why?

Exercise 9.4

- Can you find attribute names that don't produce valid JavaScript code, despite our efforts?
- Can you think of ways to fix that?
- Is adding constraints a good solution for all situations?
- Is changing the generator, and the generated code, always a good solution?

This exercise is intentionally open ended. It should encourage you to be aware of corner cases, and of how to handle them in a way that also makes sense for the domain experts.

Exercise 9.5

The name of a record type should be a non-empty string as well.

- Implement this constraint. You will have to add code in the `Record Type` case in the `Projection` function in src/frontend/projection.jsx to do that.
- You should now notice some code duplication across the `Projection` function. Refactor that duplicate code out to the `<AstObjectUiWrapper>` component in src/frontend/support-components.jsx. (You can put the `title` attribute on the outer `<div>` element returned from that component.) That component should gain an extra `issues` attribute in the process. All calls to that component should gain a corresponding `issues` argument.

9.3   *Dealing with all attribute-related faults*

In this section, we'll deal with all attribute-related faults that might still occur. We'll rely on the infrastructure and framework we established in the previous section, and we'll expand on it by adding several techniques for detecting faults up front and strengthening the generator.

So far, we've only seen one constraint that checks for a certain property having no settings. We're going to look at other kinds of constraints as well.

9.3.1 An attribute without a type

With the changes we've made so far, the generator now runs fine. However, the generated code in src/runtime/index.jsx contains extra, flagged code:

```
__generationProblemDueToNonStringArgumentToCamelCase =
    ⇢ /* [GENERATION PROBLEM] type "undefined"
    ⇢ isn't handled in defaultInitExpressionForType */
...
<FormField label="GenerationProblemDueToNonStringArgumentToWithFirstUpper">
    // [GENERATION PROBLEM] type "undefined"
        ⇢ isn't handled in formFieldInputs
</FormField>
```

The code flags resulting from the new attribute lacking a name are highlighted. The other code flags of the form `// [GENERATION] PROBLEM <explanation>` are a consequence of adding the attribute, but not of it lacking a name.

> **Exercise 9.6**
> Verify that code flags of the form `// [GENERATION] PROBLEM <explanation>` are caused by the new attribute lacking a type. Choose some name for the new attribute, and run the generator again. Verify that the flags that correlate to the attribute lacking a name are gone, but the other ones are still there

Let's give the added attribute a name but leave its type empty, so that the appropriately styled "<type>" placeholder text is shown. Running the generator after saving the AST produces the following extra, flagged code:

Returned from the default case of the switch statement in the defaultInitExpressionForType function in src/generator/indexJsx-template.js

```
foo = /* [GENERATION PROBLEM] type "undefined"
    ⇢ isn't handled in defaultInitExpressionForType */    ◁
...
<FormField label="Foo">
    // [GENERATION PROBLEM] type "undefined"       ◁
        ⇢ isn't handled in formFieldInputs
</FormField>
```

Returned from the default case of the switch statement in the formFieldInputs function in the same file

It's clear that the template code doesn't like the attribute's type being undefined. Let's implement a constraint that an attribute's type must be specified. Change src/language/constraints.js as follows.

Listing 9.2 The second iteration of the constraints checker

```
const isNonEmptyString = (value) =>
    ⇢ typeof value === "string" && value.trim().length > 0
```

```
const issuesFor = (astObject) => {
    const issues = []
    const { settings } = astObject

    switch (astObject.concept) {

        case "Data Attribute": {
            if (!isNonEmptyString(settings["name"])) {
                issues.push("An attribute must have a name")
            }
            if (settings["type"] === undefined) {
                issues.push("An attribute must have a type")
            }
            break
        }

    }
    return issues
}
module.exports.issuesFor = issuesFor
```

Add an if statement that implements the constraint on the attribute's type.

That has the result shown in figure 9.5.

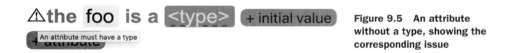

Figure 9.5   An attribute without a type, showing the corresponding issue

Even before we added the constraint, the generator ran to completion, so we don't have to change anything else, such as trying to apply the HandleFaultyContent strategy. If you add another new attribute, you'll now get two issues, as shown in figure 9.6.

Figure 9.6   An attribute without a name or type, showing both corresponding issues

There's one more thing to note, though. For an attribute with type amount, but without an initial value, the following code is generated:

```
foo = /* [GENERATION PROBLEM] type "amount"
    ➡ isn't handled in defaultInitExpressionForType */
```

A similar thing would have happened for an attribute with type percentage, but without an initial value. Should we add another constraint, producing an issue when an attribute has no initial value, and its type is anything other than `date range`? We could, but this failure is really a matter of template code being incomplete: the `defaultInitExpressionForType` function only handles the `date range` type. There's no intrinsic reason why we shouldn't handle other types.

The reference implementation and the AST corresponding to it don't cover this situation yet. Doing exercise 9.7 changes that.

Exercise 9.7

Complete the `defaultInitExpressionForType` function:

1. Add cases for the `amount` and `percentage` types. You'll have to come up with sensible default values yourself.
2. Test the generator by adding attributes with these types.
3. Test the generated Runtime as well.

9.3.2   *An attribute with an initial value "with holes"*

We changed the generator so that it handles any values for an attribute's name and type that we can give using the editor. As soon as we start adding initial values, however, we'll discover new potential failures. Some of these involve navigating over a reference. Others are of the "… didn't expect *that* here!" kind that we saw in section 9.3.1. We can fix these by adding appropriate constraints.

Exercise 9.8

1. Look at the `expressionFor` function, and try to think of when that code could throw an error. Assume that the AST follows the rules for ASTs represented as JavaScript, but doesn't necessarily conform to the shape expected by the DSL's implementation. You should find *four* such situations. Spoiler alert! The next callout lists those.
2. Add DSL content to include the four situations identified in the first point.
3. Run the generator, and see what happens. What constraints could we add to prevent that?
4. Apply the ImposeConstraints strategy to all situations. Is it useful to try and apply the HandleFaultyContent strategy to all situations? Try to do so at least for situations 1–3.
5. Did you have to add code in src/projection.jsx to apply the ImposeConstraints strategy to all situations? If that code has duplication, refactor it out to a separate React component.

(Before the end of this chapter, you'll see my implementation of this exercise as part of all the code changes.)

Situations that make the expressionFor function throw an error

These are the situations to find in item 1 of exercise 9.8:

1   The `value` argument passed to `expressionFor` is not an AST object.
2   The `attribute` of an `Attribute Reference` is unspecified.
3   The `value` of a `Number` is unspecified. Note that `<NumberValue>` prevents it from being anything other than `undefined` or a proper number (represented as a string).
4   The initial value is the placeholder AST object from src/common/ast.js.

All of these make the `expressionFor` function throw an error.

9.3.3   *Related attributes with unequal types*

Let's turn our attention to attributes that refer to an actual attribute through their initial value.

References are a powerful thing: they allow you to tie together two locations in the DSL content, so that the reference's source effectively reuses the knowledge captured by the referenced target. To make this reuse safe, you typically have to add a lot of constraints. That's a lot of work, but each constraint brings immediate value: it's one more thing the domain experts can get wrong, but that they'll receive immediate feedback about when they do so. Whenever a constraint involves navigating over a reference, it's also one more thing the domain experts don't have to specify redundantly in two distinct places. That not only saves them work, but it also makes the DSL content, and knowledge capturing, less brittle.

Consider the DSL content in figure 9.7.

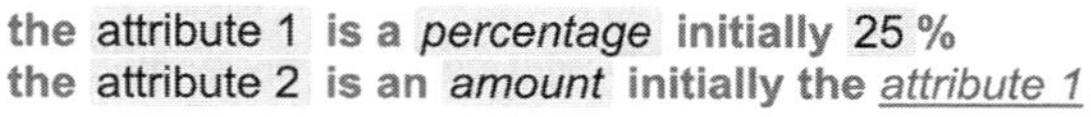

the attribute 1 is a *percentage* initially 25 %
the attribute 2 is an *amount* initially the *attribute 1*

Figure 9.7   Two attributes with non-matching types

This DSL content suggests that the initial value of "attribute 2" should get assigned the value 25%, which is the initial value of "attribute 1." Although percentages and amounts are both numeric, this clearly shouldn't make sense. (That the concept `Number` serves both these types doesn't change that.)

The code generated from this DSL content looks OK, and it builds and runs without a hitch. The corresponding addition to the Runtime looks just as nonsensical, as you can see in figure 9.8.

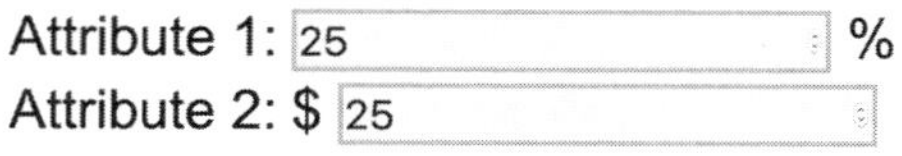

Attribute 1: 25   %
Attribute 2: $ 25

Figure 9.8   Two input fields in the Runtime corresponding to the attributes with non-matching types

The generated code represents *any* number value as a JavaScript `Number`, regardless of whether it's meant to represent an amount or a percentage. This means the Runtime's code builds and runs, despite the result not making total sense. Let's rectify this situation by adding an appropriate constraint. Given an `Attribute Reference`, this constraint should check whether the following two types are equal:

- The type of the attribute that this attribute reference refers to—let's call the referred attribute the "*other* attribute."
- The type of the attribute that contains this attribute reference—let's call the containing attribute "*this* attribute."

Such a constraint is appropriately known as a *type checking constraint*. Let's implement this constraint in the `Attribute Reference` case in the `issuesFor` function in src/language/constraints.js. I'll assume you've already added the following code for part 4 of exercise 9.8:

```
case "Attribute Reference": {
    if (settings["attribute"] === undefined) {
        issues.push("The attribute to reference is not yet specified")
    } // else { ... }
    break
}
```

Apply the ImposeConstraints strategy to situation 2 from exercise 9.8.

We're going to add an "else" branch below. When this branch is executed, the reference will be specified.

We can compute the type of the "other" attribute as the expression `astObject.settings["attribute"].ref.settings["type"]`. The second type resides on the "this" attribute, which is the parent of the attribute reference in the AST. Within `issuesFor`, we don't have access to that parent AST object. To get hold of it, we'll pass a second argument to the `issuesFor` function: an array containing the ancestors of `astObject` in reverse order, so that the parent AST object of the current AST object is that array's first element. This is the same trick we employed for the `<Projection>` function in section 5.4, so we could traverse *up* the AST to get hold of the information we needed:

```
const issuesFor = (astObject, ancestors) => {
    ...
```

We also have to change the call to this function from inside the `Projection` function in src/frontend/projection.jsx:

```
const issues = issuesFor(astObject, ancestors)
```

Now we can compute the "this" attribute as follows:

```
const thisAttribute = ancestors[0]
```

We completely rely on the `Attribute Reference` being contained directly by the `Data Attribute`. If the DSL is expanded, and an attribute reference might be contained by something other than the `initial value` property of an attribute, this assumption doesn't hold anymore. When that happens, we need to revisit this code. For now, it's good enough.

We can now compute the types of the "this" and "other" attributes as follows:

```
const { type: thisType } = thisAttribute.settings
const { type: otherType } = settings["attribute"].ref.settings
```

This code uses the renaming functionality of the destructuring assignment. The first statement is equivalent to

```
const thisType = thisAttribute.settings["type"]
```

The advantage of this construct is that we can destructure and rename multiple members at the same time. Let's use that to also compute the "other" attribute's name and type, so we can use these in the issue's message string:

```
const { type: otherType, name: otherName } =
    ➡ settings["attribute"].ref.settings
```

Now we can compare the types and produce an issue when they're not equal:

```
if (thisType !== undefined && thisType !== otherType) {
    issues.push(
`The types of this attribute and the attribute named '${otherName}'
        ➡ must match,
    but they are: '${thisType}', resp., '${otherType}'`
    )
}
```

For this constraint, it only makes sense to compare the types after the type of the "this" attribute has been specified. When domain experts specify a new attribute, they might want to start by specifying its initial value as an attribute reference before they specify its type. It would be annoying if, after choosing the target attribute, they were left with *two* issues: first, that the attribute's type should be specified, and second, that the types of the "this" and "other" attributes are not equal. The latter issue would even bluntly state `'undefined'` for the "this" type.

After adding the preceding constraint, the DSL content now reports an issue, as shown in figure 9.9.

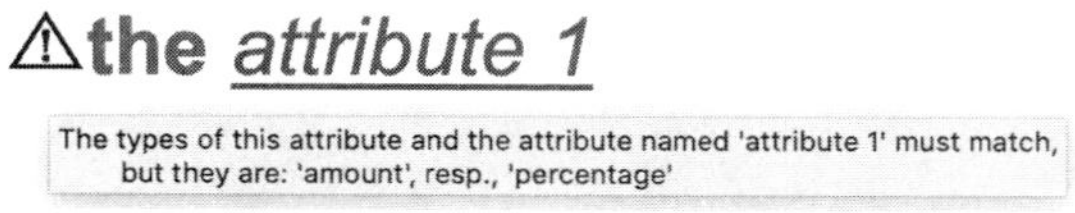

⚠**the** *attribute 1*

The types of this attribute and the attribute named 'attribute 1' must match, but they are: 'amount', resp., 'percentage'

Figure 9.9 The issue shown for the initial value of "attribute 2"

9.3.4 Sorting attributes according to dependency order

The attributes of a record type have an explicit order: the order in which they appear. This order mainly determines in which order the fields in the Runtime's UI appear, but it doesn't really have any meaning other than that.

Consider the DSL content shown in figure 9.10.

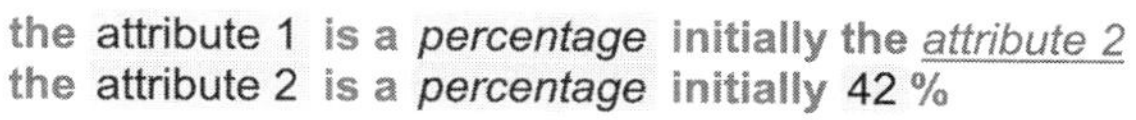

the attribute 1 is a *percentage* initially the *attribute 2*
the attribute 2 is a *percentage* initially 42 %

Figure 9.10   Two attributes that have initial values that are "out of order"

Because order only influences the presentation, it should not matter that these attributes appear "out of order." After running the generator, and building and running the Runtime, the attributes will look like figure 9.11.

Attribute 1: [   ] %
Attribute 2: [42   ] %

Figure 9.11   Part of the Runtime's UI corresponding to the two attributes that have initial values that are "out of order"

What did we expect here? I would say that "attribute 1" should have an initial value of 42%, the same one as "attribute 1," because order shouldn't matter. Instead, "attribute 1" doesn't seem to have an initial value at all. Let's look at the code generated from the DSL content in figure 9.10, which ends up as two fields of the `Rental` class's definition in src/runtime/index.jsx.

Listing 9.3   The code generated for the first two "attribute" fields

```
class Rental {
    // ...initializing assignments for other attributes...
    attribute1 = this.attribute2
    attribute2 = 42
    constructor() {
        makeAutoObservable(this)
    }
}
```

This explains what we see in the Runtime. The field `attribute1` is first initialized to `this.attribute2`. But at that time, `attribute2` has not been initialized yet, so it has the value `undefined`, and `attribute1` is set to `undefined` (which happens to be the value it already had). Only then is `attribute2` initialized to `42`. So, after instantiating an object of the `Rental` class, its `attribute2` field will hold the value `42` as intended, but its `attribute1` field will still be `undefined`. That's not what we intended when we specified the initial value of `attribute 1` to equal that of `attribute 2`. The initialization of the field corresponding to `attribute 1` is *dependent* on the initialization of the field corresponding to `attribute 2`.

How do we fix this situation? We could implement a constraint that prevents an attribute from having an initial value that references another attribute that's only defined later. That would mean two things:

- Domain experts would have to move attributes around to find an order that doesn't trigger this constraint. We haven't implemented any functionality in the DSL editor to move attributes around. The only way to change the order is by duplicating attributes at the end, and deleting the duplicate ones. Besides that, it can be tricky to find an order that actually works like this, especially with many attributes.

- The order in which fields appear in the Runtime's UI is the same as the order of the attributes in the record type. The only way the domain experts can control the order of the fields in the Runtime UI is through the order of the attributes. Imposing a constraint on these attributes robs the domain experts of that control.

I think adding a constraint that restricts order is unfair to the domain experts, for these reasons. In this situation, fixing the generator (instead of adding a constraint) is my preference. Because this situation doesn't represent a fault in the AST, this fix doesn't correspond to any of the strategies.

It seems easy to improve the generated code: swapping the two lines of code in listing 9.3 that initialize the `attribute1` and `attribute2` fields is enough. But how could we know that we had to swap these? More generally, how can we compute an order that works for the attributes of any record type? Luckily, there's an algorithm for that, known as *topological sorting*. You might have encountered this algorithm before, but I'll explain and implement it from scratch here anyway.

To discuss this, we're going to use a simple shorthand notation that emphasizes the reference relations that express dependency and strips away unnecessary details. Suppose that an attribute denoted as a_1 has an initial value that's an attribute reference to an attribute denoted as a_2. This means that the initialization for attribute a_1 depends on the initialization of attribute a_2. We represent that dependency with the following notation: $a_1 \rightarrow a_2$. In this shorthand notation, the arrow goes from the *dependent*, a_1, to the *dependency*, a_2. For brevity, we notate an attribute by its index number in its record type's definition, starting from 1, instead of $a_{something}$. The attributes of the `Rental` record type, as well as their relations, are then represented using this shorthand notation in figure 9.12.

The idea is that attributes make up *chains* through attribute references, which are attributes' initial values. A *chain* is defined as a sequence of attributes where every attribute, except the last one, has the next attribute in the sequence as a dependency. We represent a chain in shorthand notation as $a_1 \rightarrow a_2 \rightarrow ... \rightarrow a_{n-1} \rightarrow a_n$. This notation uses n attributes a_1, a_2, ..., a_{n-1}, a_n. For every i equal to 1, 2, ..., $n - 1$, attribute a_i is dependent on a_{i+1}: $a_i \rightarrow a_{i+1}$.

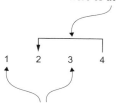

The initial value of attribute 4 refers to attribute 2.

Attributes 1 and 3 are not involved in any reference relation between attributes.

Figure 9.12   The attributes of the `Rental` record type, in shorthand notation

Figure 9.12 contains no less than *five* chains:

- One chain of length 2: 4 → 2. This chain says that we should generate the initialization statements for these attributes in this order: first 2, then 4. We can't extend this chain to either side: 2 doesn't depend on any other attribute, and no attribute depends on 4. We say that this chain is *complete*.
- Two chains both of length 1: 1 and 3. These chains are complete as well: neither attribute depends on any other attribute, and no other attribute depends on them.
- Two *incomplete* chains, also of length 1, one consisting of *only* attribute 2, and one of *only* attribute 4. Both attributes are also members of a longer chain: 4 → 2. Our definition of a chain doesn't demand that they're complete. It will turn out later that it's useful to consider incomplete chains.

We say that an ordered list of attributes a_1, a_2, ..., a_{n-1}, a_n is in *dependency order* when none of these attributes depend on another attribute that's closer to the beginning of the list. Mathematically speaking, there's no a_i in that list that's dependent on an a_j with $j < i$. The goal of the topological sorting algorithm is to put attributes in dependency order. If we can sort a list of attributes into dependency order, we can generate the initialization assignments for these attributes in that order.

If $a_1 \to a_2 \to \ldots a_{(n-1)} \to a_n$ is a chain of attributes, then the list a_n, $a_{(n-1)}$, ..., a_2, a_1 is in dependency order. In other words, the dependency order of a chain is in reverse order, going against the arrows. A list that's in dependency order doesn't have to be the reverse of a chain, though. You can make a list in dependency order from a chain, but not vice versa.

The attributes in figure 9.12 are already in dependency order. In figure 9.10, attribute 1 depends on attribute 2. In shorthand notation, 1 → 2. We already determined that, because of this dependency, we should switch these attributes around when generating initialization assignments, as we did in listing 9.3. That order matches the dependency order of this chain of two attributes: 2, 1.

Let's rearrange the list of *all* attributes of any record type into a list where the attributes are in dependency order. We can do that with the topological sorting algorithm, which can be expressed in pseudocode as follows:

1 Maintain a list of attributes, in dependency order, that's initially empty.
2 For every attribute, do the following:
   a Determine the chain starting at that attribute, stopping before we reach the end, when we encounter an attribute that's already in the dependency order list.
   b Add the (potentially incomplete) chain in reverse order to the dependency order list.

Step 2 can nicely be implemented using recursion, as we'll see in listings 9.5 and 9.8.

Exercise 9.9
Execute the topological sorting algorithm on paper for the following situations:

1   1   2 ← 3 ← 4

2   1 → 2 → 3 → 4

3   1 ← 2   3 ← 4

4   1 → 2   3 ← 4

The answers you should have gotten are

1 1 2 3 4
2 4 3 2 1
3 1 2 3 4
4 2 1 3 4

Exercise 9.10
Any attribute can have only one outgoing arrow, but what about incoming arrows?

Exercise 9.11
Verify that the topological sorting algorithm does what we need it to do. In particular, verify that

- The dependency order list is always in dependency order.
- All attributes end up in the dependency order list.

Exercise 9.12

- Do attributes have a *unique* dependency order?
- For figure 9.12, is the list 2, 3, 1, 4 in dependency order?
- How can you change a list that is in dependency order into another one that's still in dependency order?
- What dependency order does the topological sorting algorithm choose?

Exercise 9.13

Hard bonus question: How would you adapt the topological sorting algorithm if an attribute could have more than one outgoing arrow?

To implement this algorithm for real, we'll first implement a `referencedAttributes-InValueOf` helper function that, given an attribute, tries to "follow the arrow":

- If the given attribute depends on another attribute (through its initial value), then return that other attribute, the target of the reference relation, in an array of length 1.
- If not, return "nothing" in the form of an empty array.

This function is called `referencedAttributesInValueOf`, with plural "attributes," because it returns an array of attributes (possibly empty). There are two reasons for doing that:

- I don't want to exclude the possibility that we pass AST objects to `referenced-AttributesInValueOf` that reference more than one attribute.
- An array is a neat data structure for clearly, and conveniently, distinguishing between "something(s)" and "nothing."

We know we can't extend a chain any farther to the right when this function returns `[]`. Create a new src/language/queries.js file to hold language-specific query functions that can be used in the frontend, the generator, and other language-specific functions such as the constraints computation. Add the following code to this file.

Listing 9.4 The `referencedAttributesInValueOf` function

Import the isAstObject and
isAstReference functions.

```
const { isAstObject, isAstReference } =
    require("../common/ast")

const referencedAttributesInValueOf = (attribute) => {
    const initialValue = attribute.settings["initial value"]
    if (isAstObject(initialValue)
            && initialValue.concept === "Attribute Reference") {
```

Check whether an initial
value is specified, and
that it's an Attribute
Reference.

```
        const refObject =
    ➡ initialValue.settings["attribute"]          ◁──┐ Obtain the
        return isAstReference(refObject)                │ reference object
            ? [ refObject.ref ]                         │ from the setting.
            : []
    }
    return []          ◁──┐ Return an empty array
}                         │ in all other situations.
module.exports.referencedAttributesInValueOf = referencedAttributesInValueOf
```

**If it's really an AST reference, return the referenced object in
a single-item array, and an empty array if it's not.**

In the preceding code, we perform the extra `isAstReference(refObject)` check on
an `Attribute Reference` AST object because it's possible that, after it's created, the
domain expert didn't specify the attribute to reference yet. The generator shouldn't
fail as a result of assuming that the domain expert already specified the attribute to
reference. In that situation, the setting's value is either `undefined` or it doesn't reference an actual AST object—in both cases, `isAstReference(refObject)` returns
`false`.

We can now translate the topological sorting algorithm from pseudocode to a
JavaScript function using the `referencedAttributesInValueOf` helper function. Create a new src/common/dependency-utils.js file to hold functions that deal with
dependency orders and such. Add the following code to it.

Listing 9.5   The initial version of the `dependencyOrderOf` function

**Define a function to visit chained attributes, which will recursively call itself and
not return anything. Its first argument is the attribute to visit, and the second
argument is an array of the part of the chain before the current one.**

```
const { referencedAttributesInValueOf } = require("../language/queries")

const dependencyOrderOf = (attributes) => {          ┐ Declare an array variable to hold a list
    const ordered = []                       ◁───────┘ of attributes in dependency order.

    const visit = (current, chain) => {                   ┐ We've visited this attribute before,
        if (ordered.indexOf(current) > -1) {     ◁────────┤ so we don't have to visit it, or the
            return                                        ┘ attributes it references, anymore.
        }
        const extendedChain = [ ...chain, current ]   ◁──┐ Extend the
        referencedAttributesInValueOf(current).forEach(  │ current chain to
            (dependency) =>                              │ the right with the
                ➡ visit(dependency, extendedChain)  ◁───┤ current attribute.
        )
        ordered.push(current)          ◁──┐
    }
```

**Push the current attribute onto the end of the
ordered array after visiting the next attributes in
the chain. That ensures the ordered array is
always in dependency order.**

**Visit each attribute
referenced by the
current attribute by
calling visit with that
referenced attribute,
and the extended chain
as arguments.**

```
    attributes.forEach(
        (attribute) => visit(attribute, [])
    )

    return ordered
}
module.exports.dependencyOrderOf = dependencyOrderOf
```

◁── **Make sure you visit all attributes, each one starting a new chain, which may turn out to be partial.**

We can use this function in src/generator/indexJsx-template.js. First, we'll import it (at the top of the file):

```
const { dependencyOrderOf } = require("../common/dependency-utils")
```

Then we change these lines

```
indent(1)(
    attributes
        .map(initializationFor)
),
```

to call `dependencyOrderOf` on the list of attributes before generating the initialization assignments:

```
indent(1)(
    dependencyOrderOf(attributes)
        .map(initializationFor)
),
```

Exercise 9.14
- Apply all of the preceding code changes in this subsection.
- Recreate the situations in exercise 9.9 as DSL content.
- Verify for all of them that the generated code performs the initialization assignments in the right order.

Exercise 9.15
- What happens when the last attribute in a chain doesn't specify an initial value?
- Would you consider this worthy of a constraint? If so, how is this situation different from an attribute without an initial value on which no other attributes depend?

9.3.5 *Detecting cycles of attributes*

Earlier, in section 9.3.4, we used topological sorting to rearrange the attributes of a record type according to the implicit order imposed by the relation "this assignment relies on that assignment having been executed before." As the `dependencyOrderOf` function stands now, that doesn't always work. Consider the DSL content shown in figure 9.13.

the attribute 1 is an *amount* initially the *attribute 3*
the attribute 2 is an *amount* initially the *attribute 1*
the attribute 3 is an *amount* initially the *attribute 2*   **Figure 9.13   A chain of attributes**
the attribute 4 is an *amount* initially the *attribute 3*   **that contains a cycle**

In shorthand notation, this boils down to what's shown in figure 9.14.

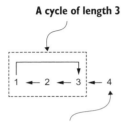

Attribute 4 is not part of the   Figure 9.14   A chain of attributes that
cycle, but it is part of the chain.   contains a cycle, in shorthand notation

If we try to generate code for this DSL content, the call to `dependencyOrderOf` enters an infinite loop trying to follow this chain. That's because this chain is *cyclic* (it *contains a cycle*). Following this chain just loops forever over attributes 3, 2, and 1, in that order. (The chain starts at attribute 4, but that attribute is itself not part of the cycle.) Eventually, the generator runs out of memory because the `chain` list keeps growing, after which Node.js exits with a fatal error.

It doesn't seem likely that such a cycle is intentional. We're going to add a constraint to warn domain experts about cycles in their DSL content. We could also apply the HandleFaultyContent strategy by picking any attribute in the cycle and initializing it with some default, breaking the cycle that way. Because we are already applying the ImposeConstraints strategy, and we'd have to choose a default value for the HandleFaultyContent strategy, I've opted not to apply that in this situation.

To implement the constraint, we'll add a `cycleWith` function to src/common/dependency-utils.js. This function returns an array with the cycle that the given attribute is part of, or an empty array if that attribute isn't part of any cycle.

Listing 9.6 The `cycleWith` function that can detect a cycle

If the call to visit returns a non-empty array, we found a cycle. We then return that array, immediately breaking out of the for loop.

Define a function to visit chained attributes.

If we already visited this attribute in the current chain, it must be part of a cycle.

In that case, return an array of all attributes in this chain, with the current one tacked on to the end, meaning it appears twice in the returned array.

```
const cycleWith = (attribute) => {

    const visit = (current, chain) => {
        if (chain.indexOf(current) > -1) {
            return [ ...chain, current ]
        }
        const extendedChain = [ ...chain, current ]
        for (const dependency of referencedAttributesInValueOf(current)) {
            const recursion =
                visit(dependency, extendedChain)
            if (recursion.length > 0) {
                return recursion
            }
        }
        return []
    }

    const result = visit(attribute, [])
    return result.length > 0
        && result[result.length - 1] === attribute
            ? result
            : []
}
module.exports.cycleWith = cycleWith
```

Recursively visit all attributes referenced by the current one, with the chain extended to the right with the current attribute.

If we haven't found a cycle after visiting all referenced attributes, return an empty array.

Visit the given attribute, start a chain from it, and try to find a cycle.

Check whether the given attribute is the last item in any cycle found.

The first argument of the `visit` function is the attribute to visit, and the second argument is an array of the part of the chain before the current one. Each call to `visit` returns an array of attributes in a cyclic chain, or an empty array.

If the `visit` function detects a cycle, it returns an array with the given attribute—the value of the `attribute` argument—appearing twice: once at the end, and once before. The double appearance is used to determine whether we actually encountered a cycle starting at the given attribute. We're only interested in the given attribute if it's part of a cycle, not if it starts a chain that eventually cycles but doesn't actually contain it. If the given attribute is part of the cycle, the `cycleWith` function returns an array with that cycle. In all other cases, it returns an empty array.

Add the following helper function to src/language/queries.js.

Listing 9.7 The code of the `quotedNamesOf` function

Define a function to extract the value of the setting of the name property on a given AST object.

Define a function to wrap a string in single quotes.

Define a function that composes the nameOf and quote functions.

```
const nameOf = (astObject) =>
    astObject.settings["name"]
const quote = (str) => `'${str}'`
const quotedNamesOf = (astObjects) =>
```

```
    ➥ astObjects.map(nameOf).map(quote)
module.exports.quotedNamesOf = quotedNamesOf
```

The `quotedNamesOf` function in the preceding code maps an array of AST objects to an array of their single-quoted names, assuming they all have a setting for `name`. Change the code at the top of src/language/constraints.js as follows (differences highlighted in bold):

```
const { cycleWith, dependencyOrderOf } =
    ➥ require("../common/dependency-utils")
const { quotedNamesOf, referencedAttributesInValueOf } =
    ➥ require("./queries")
```

Add the following code to the `Data Attribute` case in the `issuesFor` function in the same file:

```
const cycle = cycleWith(astObject)        ⟵─┐  Call cycleWith with the
if (cycle.length > 0) {                        current attribute AST
    issues.push(                               object as the argument.
`This attribute is part of a cycle through attribute references
        ➥ in attributes' initial values:                       ⟵─┐
    ${quotedNamesOf(cycle).join(" -> ")} -> [go back to first]...`
    )
}                        Produce a nice message for the issue that
                         clearly states the cycle's members.
```

Adding this constraint makes our cyclic DSL content look like figure 9.15.

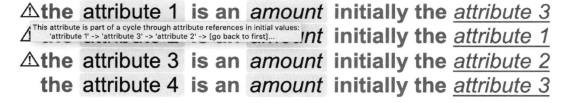

Figure 9.15   An issue is shown for attribute 1, which is part of a cycle of attributes.

We also have to change the `dependencyOrderOf` function to deal with cycles of attributes. With that function as it is in listing 9.5, a cycle of attributes would cause the `visit` function to recurse infinitely over that cycle. To prevent that, we keep checking that the chain doesn't circle back to an attribute that's already in it. If it does, we break off the entire algorithm by immediately returning `false`. If it never does, we return `true`.

Modify the code of the `dependencyOrderOf` function in the src/common/dependency-utils.js file as follows to achieve that (differences highlighted in bold).

Listing 9.8   The final version of the `dependencyOrderOf` function

```
const dependencyOrderOf = (attributes) => {
    const ordered = []

    const visit = (current, chain) => {                    ◁ The visit function now returns
        if (ordered.indexOf(current) > -1) {                 true when it detects a cycle,
            return false                                      and false if there's none.
        }
        if (chain.indexOf(current) > -1) {     ◁  If we already visited this
            return true                            attribute in the current chain,
        }                                          it must be part of a cycle.
        const extendedChain = [ ...chain, current ]
        const hasCycle = referencedAttributesInValueOf(current)
            ➡ .some(
                (reffedAttrib) => visit(reffedAttrib, extendedChain)
            )
        ordered.push(current)            │ Return whether a cycle was detected, but
        return hasCycle        ◁────────┤ only after the current attribute has been
    }                                    │ pushed onto the end of the ordered array.

    const hasCycle = attributes.some(        ◁  Make sure to visit all
        (attribute) => visit(attribute, [])      attributes, unless a cycle
    )                                            is found along the way.

    return hasCycle ? false : ordered
}
```

As soon as we detect a cycle, we can stop calling visit: that's why
.forEach has been changed to .some. Instead of immediately returning
the result of the call to .some, we save it as a constant.

Note that an equivalent expression for the return statement would be `!hasCycle && ordered`.

The `dependencyOrderOf` function returns a `false` value if it encounters a cycle: we have to handle that return value explicitly. Modify the line that calls `dependency-OrderOf` as follows:

```
indent(1)(
    (dependencyOrderOf(attributes) || attributes)
        .map(initializationFor)
),
```

The expression in bold evaluates to the dependency order of `attributes`, or to the original `attributes` array if `dependencyOrderOf` indicated there's a cycle in `attributes` by returning `false`. Whenever there's a cycle, the generated code doesn't make sense, but that's OK: the domain experts are warned about the cycle, and the generator doesn't crash.

This solution also correctly deals with *self-reference*, which is clearly nonsensical, as shown in figure 9.16. This has the shorthand notation shown in figure 9.17.

⚠the attribute 1 **is an** *amount* **initially the** *attribute 1*

> This attribute is part of a cycle through attribute references in initial values:
> 'attribute 1' -> [go back to first]...

Figure 9.16   An attribute that references itself

Figure 9.17   A chain that consists of one attribute with a self-reference

---

Exercise 9.16
- Apply all the code changes from listings 9.6 and 9.8.
- Recreate the DSL content shown in figures 9.13 and 9.16, and check that running the generator produces the expected result for both.
- Do you think it would be useful to *prevent* a domain expert from creating a cyclic chain of attributes altogether? Is there an element of the UI that you could change to do that? Think about whether it would be clear to the domain expert why they couldn't choose some attribute from the dropdown list. Also think about how you would decide what options to show, and which not to.

9.3.6   *Attributes with too similar names*

We have explored the potential problems with attributes referencing each other (or themselves) for long enough. Let's turn our attention back to the attributes' names, but this time comparing them to each other. Consider the DSL content in figure 9.18.

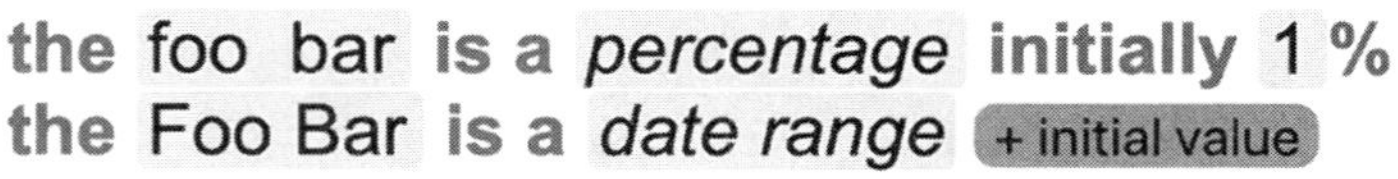

the foo bar **is a** *percentage* **initially 1 %**
the Foo Bar **is a** *date range* + initial value

Figure 9.18   Two attributes that have similar names

The names of these two attributes are quite similar: `foo bar` (with two spaces) versus `Foo Bar`. Let's see how the generator fares with this input. The following code inside the record object constructor function is generated for these attributes:

```
fooBar = 1
fooBar = new DateRange()
```

The field `fooBar` is assigned a value twice—with incompatible types, even! This is clearly wrong, even if none of the generator, build step, or Runtime protest. The name of a field of the `Rental` class is computed as the camel-cased version of the attribute's name, with the first character made lowercase. That computation yields `fooBar` for both of these attributes' names.

The generated code corresponding to these attributes in the `RentalForm` React component function is equally suspect. It doesn't make running the Runtime fail, but it does produce the nonsensical UI shown in figure 9.19.

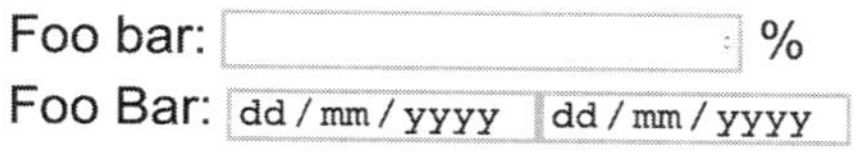

Foo bar: `[           ] : %`
Foo Bar: `[dd / mm / yyyy] [dd / mm / yyyy]`

Figure 9.19   Two form fields in the Runtime's UI that have similar names but different apparent types

We could apply either the ImposeConstraints or HandleFaultyContent strategy here. As usual, applying the ImposeConstraints strategy is easiest, and it makes sense for the domain experts as well: names that are too similar can cause an awful lot of confusion. Let's do that. Add the following code to the `Data Attribute` case in the `issuesFor` function in src/language/constraints.js:

Obtain all attributes of the record type that contains the current attribute: ancestors[0].settings["attributes"]. That array contains the current attribute.

Precompute camel-casing the name of the attribute in astObject that we're currently looking at.

```
const thisCamelCasedName =
    camelCase(astObject.settings["name"])
const similarlyNamed =
    ancestors[0].settings["attributes"].filter((attribute) =>
    attribute !== astObject
        && camelCase(attribute.settings["name"])
            === thisCamelCasedName
)
if (similarlyNamed.length > 0) {
    issues.push(
    `This attribute's name is too similar to the following
        other attributes' names:
            ${quotedNamesOf(similarlyNamed).join(", ")}`
    )
}
```

Exclude the current attribute.

If such attributes exist, then issue a message.

Keep the attributes whose names camel-case to the precomputed thisCamelCasedName.

Explicitly report the names of the similarly named attributes so that the domain experts can find them and decide which names to change.

You'll also have to import the `camelCase` function from src/generator/template-utils.js in the src/language/constraints.js file.

The name similarity is now reported as shown in figure 9.20. This kind of constraint is often called a *uniqueness* (or sometimes a *unicity*) constraint.

Because our example DSL is far from complete, we can expect to implement a lot more constraints in the remainder of this book. In particular, we can expect to implement a lot more constraints that check whether some property has been set, and whether it has been set validly. You can make that a bit more convenient by performing some DRY in exercise 9.17.

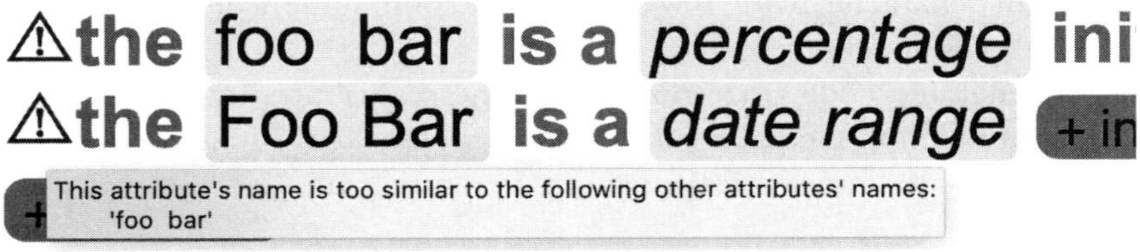

⚠the foo bar is a *percentage* ini
⚠the Foo Bar is a *date range* + in

+ This attribute's name is too similar to the following other attributes' names:
'foo bar'

Figure 9.20   Two attributes that have similar names, with an issue for the second one showing

Exercise 9.17

Add the code that's shown in bold in the following listing to the `issuesFor` function:

```
const issuesFor = (astObject, ancestors) => {
    const issues = []
    const { settings } = astObject

    const issueIfEmpty = (propertyName, message) => {
        if (!isNonEmptyString(settings[propertyName])) {
            issues.push(message)
        }
    }
    const issueIfUndefined = (propertyName, message) => {
        if (settings[propertyName] === undefined) {
            issues.push(message)
        }
    }

    // ...rest of the code...
```

Using these convenience functions, in code such as this,

```
if (!isNonEmptyString(settings["name"])) {
    issues.push("An attribute must have a name")
}
```

can be written more succinctly as follows:

```
issueIfEmpty("name", "An attribute must have a name")
```

Similarly, the following code,

```
if (settings["type"] === undefined) {
    issues.push("An attribute must have a type")
}
```

can be written like this:

```
issueIfUndefined("type", "An attribute must have a type")
```

> Use these `issueIfEmpty` and `issueIfUndefined` functions to make the code in src/language/constraints.js shorter and more readable. Hint: You should end up using both functions twice. Also, not every occurrence of `issues.push(...)` can be rewritten.

Listings 9.9 through 9.11 show the src/language/constraints.js file in its entirety, after all the modifications. Because of its length, I split it up into three listings, in the usual way: first the "outside" part of the code and then two "inner" parts consisting of `cases` of the `switch` statement corresponding to concepts.

Listing 9.9 "Outer" part of src/language/constraints.js

```
const { isAstReference, placeholderAstObject } = require("../common/ast")
const { cycleWith } = require("../common/dependency-utils")
const { quotedNamesOf, referencedAttributesInValueOf } =
    require("./queries")
const { camelCase } = require("../generator/template-utils")

const isNonEmptyString = (value) =>
    typeof value === "string" && value.trim().length > 0

const issuesFor = (astObject, ancestors) => {
    const issues = []
    const { settings } = astObject

    const issueIfEmpty = (propertyName, message) => {
        if (!isNonEmptyString(settings[propertyName])) {
            issues.push(message)
        }
    }
    const issueIfUndefined = (propertyName, message) => {
        if (settings[propertyName] === undefined) {
            issues.push(message)
        }
    }

    switch (astObject.concept) {          ◄──  Cases in the switch statement
                                               are in alphabetical order of
                                               concept labels.
        // ...cases corresponding to concepts...   ◄── The cases corresponding to
                                                       concepts are in listings 9.10
                                                       and 9.11.
    }                          ◄──
    return issues                  There is no default case: some concepts
}                                  might genuinely have no constraints
module.exports.issuesFor = issuesFor   defined on them.
```

Listing 9.10 First "inner" part of src/language/constraints.js

```
case "Attribute Reference": {
    if (!isAstReference(settings["attribute"])) {
```

**Handle situation 2
of exercise 9.8.**

```
        issues.push(                ←──┘
            ⇒ "The attribute to reference is not yet specified")
    } else {                                                        ←──  Handle the
        const thisAttribute = ancestors[0]                               situation of
        const { type: thisType } = thisAttribute.settings               section 9.3.3.
        const { type: otherType, name: otherName } =
            ⇒ settings["attribute"].ref.settings
        if (thisType !== undefined && thisType !== otherType) {
            issues.push(
    ⇒ `The types of this attribute and the attribute named '${otherName}'
            ⇒ must match,
            ⇒ but they are: '${thisType}', resp., '${otherType}'`
            )
        }
    }
    break
}
case "Data Attribute": {
    issueIfEmpty("name",
        ⇒ "An attribute must have a name")
    issueIfUndefined("type",
        ⇒ "An attribute must have a type")
    if (settings["initial value"] === placeholderAstObject) {
        issues.push(
    ⇒ "The initial value of this attribute is not yet defined")
    }
    const cycle = cycleWith(astObject)
    if (cycle.length > 0) {
        issues.push(
        `This attribute is part of a cycle through attribute references in
            ⇒ attributes' initial values:
            ${quotedNamesOf(cycle).join(" -> ")} -> [go back to first]...`
        )
    }
    const thisCamelCasedName =
        ⇒ camelCase(astObject.settings["name"])
    const similarlyNamed = ancestors[0].settings["attributes"]
        .filter((attribute) =>
            attribute !== astObject
    ⇒ && camelCase(attribute.settings["name"]) === thisCamelCasedName
        )
    if (similarlyNamed.length > 0) {
        issues.push(
    ⇒ `This attribute's name is too similar
        ⇒ to the following other attributes' names:
        ⇒     ${quotedNamesOf(similarlyNamed).join(", ")}`
        )
    }
    break
}
```

**Handle the situation
of section 9.2, after
exercise 9.17.**

**Handle the situation
of section 9.3.1, after
exercise 9.17.**

**Handle
situation 4 of
exercise 9.8.**

**Handle the situation
of section 9.3.5.**

**Handle the situation
of section 9.3.6.**

Listing 9.11 Second "inner" part src/language/constraints.js

```
case "Number": {
    issueIfUndefined("value",
        "The number's value must be defined")
    break
}

case "Record Type": {
    issueIfEmpty("name",
        "A record type must have a name")
    break
}
```

Handle situation 3 of exercise 9.8, after exercise 9.17.

Handle the situation of exercise 9.5, after exercise 9.17.

We changed the following existing source files (differences highlighted in bold).

Listing 9.12 The changed content in src/generator/template-utils.js

```
const camelCase = (str) => typeof str === "string"
    ? str
        .toLowerCase()
        .replace(/\s+([a-z])/g, (_, ch) => ch.toUpperCase())
        .replace(" ", "")
    : "__generationProblemDueToNonStringArgumentToCamelCase"
module.exports.camelCase = camelCase

const withFirstUpper = (str) => typeof str === "string"
    ? str.charAt(0).toUpperCase() + str.substring(1)
    : "GenerationProblemDueToNonStringArgumentToWithFirstUpper"
module.exports.withFirstUpper = withFirstUpper
```

Apply the HandleFaultyContent strategy to the situation of section 9.2.

Listing 9.13 Changed content in src/generator/indexJsx-template.js

Apply the HandleFaultyContent strategy to situation 1 of exercise 9.8.

```
const { isAstObject, isAstReference } = require("../common/ast")
const { asString, camelCase, indent, withFirstUpper } =
    require("./template-utils")
const { dependencyOrderOf } = require("../common/dependency-utils")

const expressionFor = (astObject) => {
    if (!isAstObject(astObject)) {
        return `/* [GENERATION PROBLEM] value "${astObject}"
            isn't handled in expressionFor */`
    }
    const { settings } = astObject
    switch (astObject.concept) {
        case "Attribute Reference": {
            const targetAttribute = isAstReference(settings["attribute"])
                && settings["attribute"].ref
            return targetAttribute
                ? `this.${camelCase(targetAttribute.settings["name"])}`
```

Apply the HandleFaultyContent strategy to situation 2 of exercise 9.8.

```
            ➥  : `/* [GENERATION PROBLEM] attribute reference
                     ➥ is undefined */`
        }
        case "Number": {                                    ◄──┐  Apply the HandleFaultyContent
            const numberValue = settings["value"]              │  strategy to situation 3 of
            return numberValue === undefined                      exercise 9.8.
        ➥? `/* [GENERATION PROBLEM] number's value is undefined */`
        ➥: `${numberValue}`
        }
        default: return `/* [GENERATION PROBLEM] value
                      ➥ of concept "${astObject.concept}"
                      ➥ isn't handled in expressionFor */`
    }
}

const defaultInitExpressionForType = (type) => {
  switch (type) {
      case "amount": return `0.0`               ◄──┐
      case "date range": return `new DateRange()`   │  Complete for all types,
      case "percentage": return `0`              ◄──┘  as per exercise 9.7.
      default: return `/* [GENERATION PROBLEM] type "${type}"
                   ➥ isn't handled in defaultInitExpressionForType */`
  }
}

...
const indexJsx = (recordType) => {
  ...
      indent(1)(
          (dependencyOrderOf(attributes) || attributes)
              .map(initializationFor)
      ),                                    ◄──  Fix the situations of
  ...                                            sections 9.3.4 and 9.3.5.
```

Optionally, an issue could also have a *severity* such as "error," "warning," or something else. A constraint usually produces issues with severity "error." All of the constraints we implemented in this chapter arguably have severity "error," so I didn't bother with a severity.

Constraints can also be used to make it easy to conform to conventions on the DSL content. Violating such a constraint tends to make some*one* blow up, rather than some*thing*—usually the resident software architect. Such "soft" constraints usually produce issues with a severity below "error," such as "warning."

Exercise 9.18
- Change the implementation of the constraints checker so that issues are objects of the form { message: "<*message*>", severity: "<*severity*>" } instead of just strings with the issues' messages. Change the styling of issues to look different for severity "warning."

- Change the constraint warning about cycles of attributes to have severity "warning."
- Think about how you would add an optional property name to the issue object. How would you report issues on their property name (if they specify one), instead of on the whole AST object? Change one of the constraints so that its issues are reported on a specific property.

In this chapter, you learned how to protect domain experts against mistakes by implementing numerous constraints that report helpful issues. You also learned how, and when, to strengthen template code so it fails softly. We're going to use this mechanism in the coming chapters. In chapter 13, we'll implement a type system that makes adding type checking constraints a lot more efficient. In chapter 15, we'll add more constraints for business rules.

Summary

- Building the Runtime from DSL content happens in several stages, each of which can be considered to succeed or fail.
- A constraint is a condition that must be satisfied throughout the entire AST. A violation of a constraint happens in the context of some DSL content and must be reported to the domain experts as an *issue* with a helpful message, which will help them repair the problem. Some constraints only look at the value of individual settings. The more valuable constraints are typically those that look at different parts of the AST by navigating over reference relations, because they effectively safeguard the consistency of the DSL content.
  - *Unspecified content constraints* check for properties having no settings, or settings with a placeholder value.
  - *Type checking constraints* check whether the types of related DSL content match.
  - *Uniqueness constraints* complain when things that are sufficiently alike (or that "live" next to each other) have names that are too similar, or even equal.
- Every failure in the generator, build step, or Runtime that's directly caused by the contents of an AST is solvable by applying a suitable combination of the following strategies. Which strategies to apply, and how, is a design choice based on tradeoffs.
  - *ImposeConstraints*—Prevent the failure from happening by adding one or more constraints to the Domain IDE. Violations of those constraints are issues that are reported to the domain experts, explaining what problem they have to fix and where. This strategy should almost always be applied as a first measure and possibly in combination with the next strategy.
  - *HandleFaultyContent*—Strengthen the generator so it doesn't crash, especially not on parts of ASTs for which issues have already been reported as a result

of applying the ImposeConstraints strategy. This doesn't ultimately *prevent* failure, but it mitigates the consequences of faulty DSL content and should get you to success stage 1. The generated code doesn't have to make sense, or even have to be syntactically valid, so success stage 2 is not necessarily reached. It usually should contain *flags* that indicate to the software developers what issue caused the incorrect code. The build step will still not be able to build the Runtime, but that's OK: an issue should be reported to the domain expert.

– *PreventPersistence*—Prevent the generator and build step from running on ASTs with issues. The domain expert should be able to persist such ASTs so they can share it with the software developers, so this strategy should be used as a last measure only. Instead, apply the HandleFaultyContent strategy.

▪ *Topological sort* is an algorithm that can be used to do the following:

– Arrange attributes in *dependency order*, to generate initialization assignments in a valid working order.

– Detect *cycles* in chains of attributes that are built up by following attribute references that are attributes' initial values.

Managing change

This chapter covers

- Managing change of the DSL content
- Identifying what kind of change we can expect when using a DSL-based approach for software development
- Changing and versioning the DSL itself

Ceaseless change is the only constant thing in nature.

—John Candee Dean, *Popular Astronomy*, vol. 19, no. 1 (January 1911)

A large part of the attraction of adopting a DSL-based approach for software development is being able to handle change in a better, more efficient way. The DSL-based approach actually *embraces* change by facilitating more team members to actively contribute changes, which tends to have a relatively big effect.

In this chapter, we're going to see how to deal with change, having adopted a DSL-based approach. Two distinct things can change in a DSL-based approach:

- Domain experts change the *DSL content* by working on it using the Domain IDE.
- The software developers change aspects of the *DSL itself* due to requests from domain experts.

Figure 10.1 showcases both kinds of change. We'll discuss these two kinds of change in much more detail and see what impact we can expect from those changes.

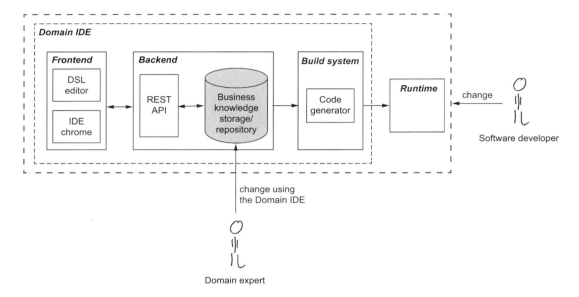

Figure 10.1   The high-level architecture of the DSL-based approach, and the two sources of change

This chapter will be relatively theoretical and quite light on code and exercises. We won't extend the functionality of the Domain IDE or the implementation of our example DSL. We will use the knowledge we gain here in subsequent chapters to evolve our example DSL.

10.1   *Managing DSL content change*

One of the sources of change is the DSL content changing. This is a Good Thing: it means that the domain experts are using the Domain IDE. The goal is that they grow the DSL content so that it contains enough of the knowledge in the business domain to drive the software development. In this section, we'll discuss how domain experts could manage changing the DSL content.

Before we look at this from the viewpoint of the domain experts, however, let's look at how people who use IDEs all the time manage changes in their IDEs' content: software developers. Software developers typically work together, or *collaborate*, on a codebase using some agreed-on workflow. Ideally that workflow is supported by features of the tools they're using, such as

- Being able to *share* code (and changes to it) with each other
- Being able to *work concurrently* on (different parts of) the code

- Being able to put DSL content under *version control*, as part of release management or for auditing and regulatory compliance

For code, this usually means putting the code in a distributed version control system (DVCS). Git is probably the most used, if not the most popular, DVCS. Figure 10.2 constitutes my visual summary of the well-known Gitflow workflow methodology.

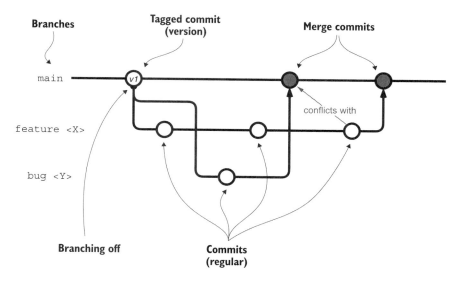

Figure 10.2   **The main concepts of a DVCS, and a typical interaction**

A DVCS typically relies on concepts such as

- *Commit*—A representation of the state of the code at a certain point in time. A commit has its own identity—for example, each commit in Git has a SHA hash, which is a string containing 40 hexadecimals.
- *Branch*—A named sequence of commits that represents an independent work package focusing on a bug, feature, etc. It's customary to name the mainline `main` and then name feature and bug-fixing branches something like `feature <X>` or `bug <Y>`.
- *Tag*—A string that's associated with a particular commit. This is used to tag specific commits with *versions*.

A DVCS such as Git enables distributed and asynchronous workflows, such as ones where contributors

- *Branch* off of a mainline version
- Record and share their changes to the code through a sequence of *commits* on a branch

- Have completed work reviewed by fellow developers
- *Merge* those changes into the mainline again

Managing change through sequences of commits is somewhat crude: a sequence of commits can accrue a lot of changes relative to a mainline version. Merging that accrued change back again can be challenging when the mainline itself has changed in the meanwhile. This can lead to *merge conflicts* when the DVCS can't figure out on its own how to consolidate concurrent changes to a piece of code. Merge conflicts require a developer to resolve the conflicts manually—this is often referred to as "merge hell."

Alternatively, there's *real-time collaborative editing*. For a couple of years, platforms that support real-time collaborative editing have been on the rise, with Google Docs having become pervasively popular. The essence of real-time collaborative editing is that multiple collaborators are editing the same, shared content using multiple devices at the same time.

A common way of implementing this is to use a client-server architecture. When one collaborator edits the content, that change is sent immediately to a central server. This server then broadcasts that change to all collaborators, after which their content is updated with the change, synchronizing the content across all devices. These changes tend to be small: typically a couple of keystrokes, with the occasional large-scale change due to copying, cutting, pasting, shuffling, or deleting.

Unfortunately, network latency can lead to a situation where collaborators have made changes locally before having received other collaborators' potentially conflicting changes. Before broadcasting a change received from one collaborator to all other collaborators, the server therefore determines whether a change conflicts with the current content. If it does, the conflicting change isn't broadcast to all collaborators and is rolled back on the content of the collaborator having made it. Because changes tend to be small, rolling back a change doesn't cause much work loss, and it's easy to redo the change against the synchronized content. This strategy basically resolves conflicts by letting the change that's received by the server first "win."

An even better strategy is to use a *conflict-free replicated data type* (CRDT) to record changes in a way that prevents conflict. That strategy even makes it possible to use peer-to-peer communication between collaborators instead of a client-server architecture.

Multiple IDEs have latched on to this idea and have started offering functionality to collaborate on code, supporting collaborative editing on files in a shared codebase. For example, Visual Studio Code offers Live Share functionality via a plugin, while Codeshare (https://codeshare.io/) is an online collaborative editor.

Domain experts will want to collaborate on the DSL content and organize that collaboration, just as developers do. Because of that, they need collaborative functionality in their Domain IDE, either real-time (synchronous), through a DVCS (asynchronous), or both. Domain experts might not follow the same workflow as developers do, which means that their collaborative functionality likely needs to be different as well. So far, we've been building a Domain IDE that doesn't support any collaborative functionality. The Domain IDE's backend persists just one AST at any time, without any version control or regard for previous versions. The backend serves the frontend to any number of domain experts, but as soon as one of them clicks the Save button, their version of the DSL content overrules everything else.

We're not going to fix that shortcoming in this book by actually implementing collaboration functionality. That would constitute a lot of work on both the frontend and backend of the Domain IDE—work that, in itself, has very little to do with DSLs. Instead, let's look at what's special about DSL content changing, and at how we can use that to facilitate the implementation of collaboration functionality.

DSL content is represented in a very specific form: as an AST that follows a specific set of rules about what each AST object and it settlings look like. We could serialize an AST as JSON text and put that text under the management of a DVCS. Unfortunately, there's no guarantee that the DVCS understands how to merge changes to JSON text so that the merged text is valid JSON again. There's even less guarantee that the DVCS is able to maintain the rules for a serialized AST, which are the same as for a deserialized AST, except for references.

Instead of hoping that we can make a DVCS understand our rules for a serialized AST, we can take control over how we record changes. Changes made while editing projectionally tend to be clearly identifiable and local. Here's a list of all the *delta types*—the types of AST changes (∂s):

- A value of a simple setting of a particular AST object is changed (see chapter 5).
- An AST object is created or deleted (see chapter 6).
- The location of an AST object contained by a multivalued setting is changed, such as through drag and drop.

I like to call such changes *deltas*, and because I'm a recovering mathematician, I tend to abbreviate "delta" as "∂." These ∂s are direct results of a UI action. That means it should be relatively easy to record them as they happen. Recording ∂s as they happen as a direct result of UI actions means that you could also do the following:

- You could broadcast changes to the backend in small increments, in the form of an individual ∂ or a sequence of ∂s. This has several advantages:
  - Reduction of network and server load
  - Autosaving reduces the chances of domain experts losing work because of forgetting to save, or because of a failure.
- You could implement *undo/redo functionality*, as well as real-time collaborative editing. This requires that you can do the following with a ∂:
  - Revert it or roll it back.
  - Determine whether it conflicts with an earlier one.

  To be able to do that, you need to record additional information in each ∂. (This should turn ∂s into a CRDT.)

These ideas put you in a decent position to design, architect, and implement collaboration functionality in the Domain IDE.

Exercise 10.1
- Identify all actions in our DSL editor that change the AST. What delta type (from the list of delta types) does each correspond to?
- Add logging statements to the DSL editor's code that logs any ∂ when it happens.

Use a statement like this,

```
console.dir(<∂ object>)
```

or this,

```
console.log(JSON.stringify(<∂ object>, null, 2))
```

to print a plain JavaScript object <∂ *object*> describing the ∂ to the JavaScript console. Make sure that <∂ *object*> contains enough information to implement the requirements that every ∂ can be reverted/rolled back, and that it's possible to detect conflicts among ∂s.

A <∂ *object*> for a ∂ that changes the name of an attribute could look like this:

```
{
    "changeType": "valueUpdate",
    "objectID": "<ID>",
    "propertyName": "name",
    "newValue": "bar",
    "oldValue": "foo"
}
```

How would you combine this logging with performing the actual change?

10.2   *Categorizing and charting coupling*

In the previous section, we discussed how we could support the domain experts in changing the DSL content. In this section, we're going to determine how changing the DSL itself impacts the other parts of the DSL-based approach. In turn, that's going to tell us how we can best change and evolve the DSL.

   Consider figure 10.3, which shows all the moving parts in a DSL-based approach. These parts are all *software components*. As such, they are prone to *coupling*, which means that they are interdependent to a lesser or greater degree. Coupling *resists* change because you have to change coupled components in sync, which leads to more effort and more complexity. Coupling is undesirable, but also unavoidable. We're going to chart the coupling between these components and the key aspects of a DSL. This will help us determine how a change to one component propagates to other components.

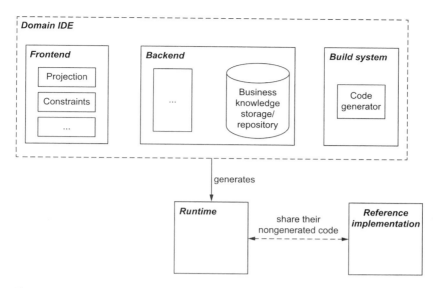

Figure 10.3   The software components in a DSL-based approach (some internal parts are identified separately)

Most components implement one or more aspects of the DSL. This means we can say that these components are effectively coupled to the DSL itself. Let's determine, for every component, how and to what extent they're coupled to the DSL. First, we're going to reduce our problem a bit and identify the three kinds of code in each component.

In figure 10.4, and the subsequent diagrams in this chapter, the coupling of pairs of components is expressed through arrows. A coupling arrow's direction is an indication of cause and effect: it goes from the "causing" component to the "affected" component. The coupled component that *has to* change when the component at the other end of the arrow is changed is the "effect" component. In contrast, a change in the "effect" component doesn't necessitate a change in the "cause" component. The thickness of the coupling arrows is an indication of the strength of the coupling.

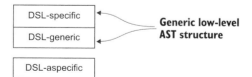

Figure 10.4   Categorizing code into three kinds, and illustrating their coupling (with arrows) to the generic low-level AST structure

Let's go over all the boxes, which correspond to the code categories:

- *DSL-specific*—Such code is strongly coupled to any or all of the key aspects of the DSL. It usually also relies on DSL-generic code to function.
- *DSL-generic*—Such code provides (part of) a framework for DSL implementation, but it's not coupled to the specifics of the key aspects of the DSL itself. An example would be the React component functions used by the DSL's projection.
- *DSL-aspecific (meaning neither DSL-specific nor DSL-generic)*—Such code is "stuff" you need in a working software component but that has nothing to do with DSLs. DSL-aspecific code usually consists mainly of boilerplate (discussed in chapter 8).

This categorization allows us to concentrate on the DSL-specific parts of components when figuring out how a change to the DSL changes the implementation. This division is also useful for coming up with a good test strategy for a DSL implementation.

Both DSL-specific and DSL-generic code are typically strongly coupled to the generic low-level structure of ASTs, as described in chapters 2 and 3. This generic low-level structure boils down to representing AST objects and reference relations as plain JavaScript objects of a prescribed form:

- AST object—`{ "id": "<an ID>", "concept": "<concept label>", "settings": { ... } }`
- Reference relation—`{ "ref": "<target AST object>" }`

This generic low-level structure is captured by the functions in the src/common/ast.js source file, which is DSL-generic because of that. It's not surprising that this file is imported in various components and by various parts of them.

Let's use figure 10.5 to go over the components and explicitly identify which parts of their code are DSL-specific, -generic, and -aspecific.

The Domain IDE's frontend can be divided up as follows:

- *DSL-specific*—The implementation of the projection, the constraints checker, the queries it uses, and some of the styling (as CSS).
- *DSL-generic*—A framework for implementing a DSL editor, in the form of JSX files implementing reusable React components, including some of the styling. This framework is not coupled to the ASTs' generic low-level structure, nor to anything DSL-specific: all interaction with the AST is performed through values and functions passed by the projection function (which is already coupled to the generic low-level AST structure) to the reusable React components.
- *DSL-aspecific*—The HTML and JSX entry points of the web app, and some of the styling. This part essentially implements the IDE's chrome.

The Domain IDE's backend implements persistence for just one piece of JSON. This JSON should be a serialized AST representing the DSL content. There's nothing in the backend's code to enforce that, though. We can verify that claim by checking that the backend code doesn't use src/common/ast.js at all. So the backend's code is entirely DSL-aspecific.

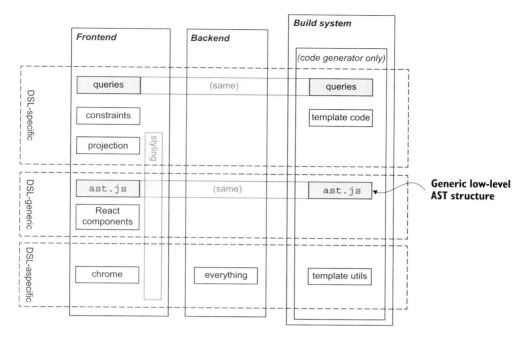

Figure 10.5   Categorizing the code in each component of the Domain IDE

The code generator part of the Domain IDE's build system can be divided up as follows:

- *DSL-specific*—The template code (in src/generator/indexJsx-template.js) implements the meaning aspect of the DSL, while the query functions it relies on are strongly coupled to the DSL's structure aspect. (It can be helpful to rerun the constraints' computation prior to generation, but I chose not to represent that in figure 10.5.)
- *DSL-generic*—The src/common/ast.js file, which is also used by the frontend, and which provides functions dealing with the generic low-level AST structure.
- *DSL-aspecific*—A collection of convenience functions to help with writing templates and dealing with dependencies.

The code in the src/language directory is completely, and intentionally, DSL-specific. It houses the constraints checker and query functions that other DSL-specific code relies on. As such, it's naturally used by both the frontend and the code generator.

Exercise 10.2

- Determine, for every source file of the Domain IDE, whether it's DSL-specific, -generic, or -aspecific. Include the files of the code generator, but exclude any file that's not really part of the Domain IDE, such as files containing unit tests.
- Do all files fall into exactly one category?

The Runtime and its reference implementation consist of code in one of the following categories:

- *Code generated from DSL content*—For the reference implementation, code is generated from its own "special" DSL content. The AST that represents that special DSL content is stored in serialized form somewhere alongside the reference implementation, but not in the Domain IDE's backend.
- *Handwritten code that generated code might rely on*—This code is shared among the Runtime and its reference implementation.
- *Other handwritten code*—This code is likely also shared among the Runtime and its reference implementation.

This categorization is visualized in figure 10.6.

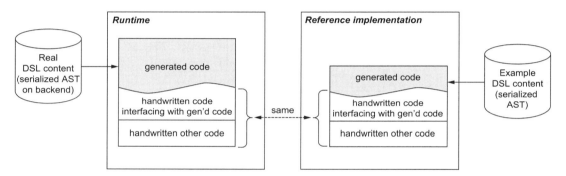

Figure 10.6 The relations between the code parts of the Runtime and its reference implementation, and the coupling between other components

Generated code is strongly coupled to the DSL *content* it's generated from. It's also strongly coupled to the code generator, because it's generated from it. The handwritten code that generated code might rely on is weakly coupled to the code generator: it's not generated by it, but it has to interface, or interact, with code that is generated by it. Interacting means either calling, or being called by, generated code. The other handwritten code in the third point is completely DSL-aspecific.

We can expect the code of DSL-specific components to change whenever the DSL changes in any of its aspects. Let's determine how, and to what extent, a component's code changes under a DSL change. In other words, let's determine for every key aspect of the DSL to which components it's coupled. To be affected, the key aspect *must* be coupled to a DSL-specific part of a component, so we only have to search in the DSL-specific code we already identified.

Exercise 10.3

Identify what code in the files in src/runtime/ corresponds to the three code categories: code generated from DSL content, handwritten code that generated code might rely on, and other handwritten code. Some files will contain more than one category of code: divide such files into labeled regions of the same category. Hint: Have a look at the template code in src/generator/indexJsx-template.js (especially the `indexJsx` function) to divide the code in src/runtime/index.jsx.

In the interest of drawing tidy diagrams, we'll first chart the coupling between the DSL's key aspects. To do that, we'll reduce figure 1.18 to figure 10.7 by only showing the key aspects and their relations through coupling arrows.

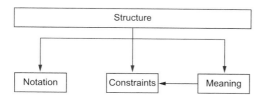

Figure 10.7   The key aspects of a DSL and their coupling

All of a DSL's key aspects are strongly coupled to the DSL's structure. As you saw in chapter 9, many of the constraints of a DSL are a direct result of the meaning aspect. This is because the meaning aspect is implemented by the code generator, and the validity and correctness of generated code depends on those constraints. All the coupling in figure 10.7 is one-way, which makes life a bit easier. Now we can draw the chart in figure 10.8, showing the coupling between the key aspects and the DSL-specific code of the Domain IDE.

One last coupling we have to take into account is DSL content that's coupled to the DSL's structure, even if it's not code. Technically, this couples DSL content that's stored as serialized ASTs to the DSL's structure. We have two pieces of DSL content: real DSL content for the Runtime and the example DSL content for the reference implementation. The real DSL content is persisted on the backend, while the example DSL content is stored somewhere along the reference implementation's code.

When we combine all of the information we've gathered so far, we can draw figure 10.9, which shows all the coupling. (Because the Domain IDE's backend only has DSL-aspecific code, I left it out of this diagram for clarity.)

We'll use this figure in the next section to reason about what kinds of changes can be made to separate components, and how these changes propagate to all other components.

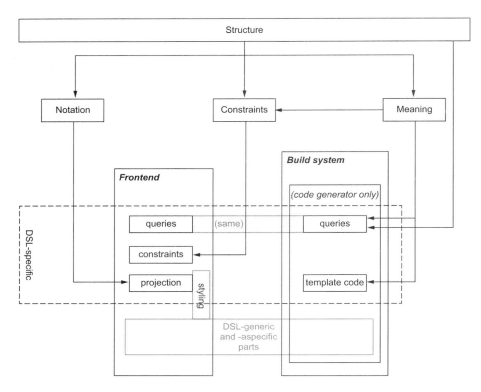

Figure 10.8   Categorizing the DSL-specific code in each component of the Domain IDE

10.3   *Changing the DSL*

In this section, we'll explore what changes we can make to the DSL and how we can manage them.

10.3.1   *Versioning the Domain IDE*

Software systems tend to change in discrete steps, in the form of commits, some of which are tagged explicitly as versions. The same is true for the Domain IDE, which is, after all, "just software" as well. We can equate the version of the DSL to the version of the Domain IDE that implements that DSL's version. DSL content and the AST representing it tend to be compatible with a particular version, or a limited set of versions, of the Domain IDE. You should know which exact version of the Domain IDE has been used to persist the DSL content—in our case, as a serialized AST in JSON format in src/backend/data/contents.json. Each version is identified by a specific version ID, which is typically represented as a string.

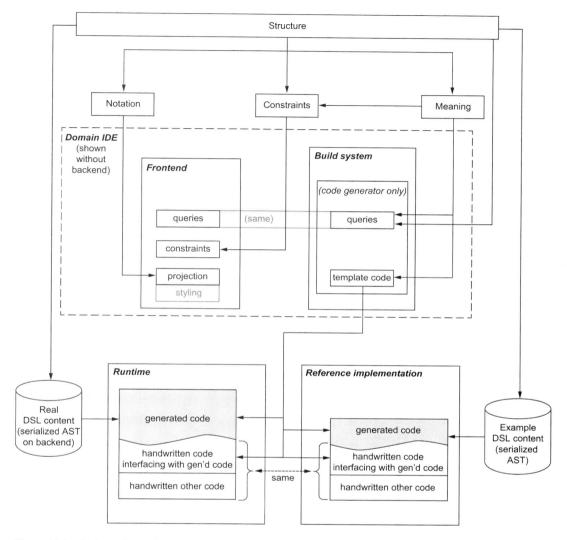

Figure 10.9 A chart of coupling between the DSL's key aspects and the DSL-specific parts of components

To be able to do anything with a persisted AST, we have to *load* it. Loading of DSL content can happen at the following points:

- In the *backend*, when the AST that's stored in serialized form as JSON content is read from disk and deserialized
- In the *frontend*, after the AST has been transmitted by the backend in serialized form
- In the *code generator*, after the AST has been retrieved from the backend's storage, and a build has been triggered

Every time you load DSL content in the form of an AST, you should compare the version ID associated with the AST with that of the currently running version of the Domain IDE, in order to determine how to proceed:

- If the DSL content's version ID matches that of the Domain IDE, proceed to project the DSL content as before.
- If the DSL content's version ID corresponds to a newer version of the Domain IDE, you're apparently running an outdated version of the Domain IDE. That outdated version of the Domain IDE should refuse to load this DSL content.
- If the DSL content's version ID corresponds to an older version of the Domain IDE, you might need to update the AST using an *AST migration*, which I'll explain in section 10.3.2.

You should perform all these version checks and corresponding actions (where required) to avoid DSL content getting corrupted by a mismatch of versions. All this means we can load DSL content that's made with an older version of the IDE into a newer version of the IDE. The other way around doesn't work: you can't load DSL content made with a newer version of the IDE into an older version of the IDE.

> **Exercise 10.4**
> - Persist a version ID next to the persisted, serialized AST. You can choose any kind of version ID, but something like "v1," "v2," etc., is good enough for now.
> - Have the REST API return the persisted version ID as a header, and check it in the frontend. Report an error on the console if there is a mismatch.
> - You could try to put the version ID somewhere in the AST itself, for example, as a key-value pair `"version ID": "v1"` on the AST's root object (not on its `settings` object). What do you run into when doing that? What other problems might you encounter when doing that?

10.3.2 *Changing the DSL's structure*

In figure 10.9, it's clear that essentially everything is strongly coupled to the DSL's structure. Because of that, we should first sum up all the ways we can change a DSL's structure. These are all the types of changes we need to express *any* change to a DSL's structure:

- *Add a new property to an existing concept* when we need to capture more details directly with an existing concept.
- *Add a new concept* when we need to capture an entirely new type of data.
- *Change the type of an existing property* to something that's incompatible with the old type.
- *Remove an existing property, or even an existing concept* when it's no longer useful, or when it's undesirable to continue supporting it. We should only remove a property or concept after we've properly *deprecated* it—more on that in section 10.3.3.

- *Rename an existing property or concept* when we discover a better name for it, and we can improve the code of the DSL's implementation. This is a simple rename *refactoring*.
- *Change a set of concepts and (some of) their properties in lockstep* when we discover a way to represent certain constructs involving multiple properties, or AST objects, in a better way. This is a nontrivial refactoring that transforms data in the AST and moves it around but doesn't lose it.

The first two of these types of changes *widen* the structure: after such a change, more ASTs conform to the DSL's widened structure. Because of that, these changes don't require any modification to existing ASTs to conform to the DSL's changed structure.

The remaining types of changes are not widening, but *modifying*. Any existing AST needs to be modified to conform to the DSL's new structure. An *AST migration* is an algorithm that performs that modification, turning an AST that conforms to the DSL's *pre*-change structure into an AST that conforms to the DSL's *post*-change structure. Unsurprisingly, this algorithm is often a depth-first tree traversal.

As an example of such a migration, let's change the name of the `initial value` property of the `Data Attribute` concept to `value`, and change that concept's label to `Attribute`. We're going to use this migration in the next chapter. Create a src/init/ migrations.js file, and populate it with the following code.

Listing 10.1   The implementation of an AST migration

```
const { isAstObject } = require("../common/ast")

const modifyDataAttribute = (value) => {
    if (isAstObject(value)) {
        const { settings } = value
        for (const propertyName in settings) {
            modifyDataAttribute(settings[propertyName])
        }
        if (value.concept === "Data Attribute") {
            value.concept = "Attribute"
             settings["value"] =
                ⟹ settings["initial value"]
            delete settings["initial value"]
        }
    }
    if (Array.isArray(value)) {
        value.forEach(modifyDataAttribute)
    }
}
module.exports.modifyDataAttribute = modifyDataAttribute
```

Change the concept label, dropping "Data."

Move the value of the "initial value" property to the "value" property, reassigning and deleting the original key-value pair.

You can now migrate the AST with this call:

```
modifyDataAttribute(ast)
```

Exercise 10.5

The AST migration in listing 10.1 *modifies* the existing AST. That's often undesirable. Write a second function, called `migrateDataAttribute`, that implements this migration so that it returns a modified copy of the AST.

An AST migration typically has a "from" and a "to" version ID. The migration can be run on an AST whose associated version ID matches the "from" version ID. Afterward, the AST conforms to the structure of the "to" version ID. Before running the AST migration, you should check whether the DSL content has a version ID that matches the "from" version ID. After running the AST migration, the version ID of the DSL content should be updated to the "to" version ID.

> **TIP**   In theory, a migration could work for multiple (or a *range* of) "from" version IDs. Typically, such a migration tries to do too much at once, which makes it difficult to get it working correctly on every AST. Try to keep changes to the DSL structure small, so the corresponding migrations are simple as well.

Once you start changing the DSL's structure, that change propagates to all components that are, directly or indirectly, coupled to the structure. Judging from figure 10.9, that's the DSL-specific parts of almost *all* components. This is evidenced by the preceding migration: every occurrence of the string `"Data Attribute"` (used as a concept label) in code for the projection, constraints computation, and code generation should be replaced by `"Attribute"`. Likewise, every occurrence of the string `"initial value"` (used as a property name) in the same code should be replaced by `"value"`.

Exercise 10.6

- Perform the AST migration in listing 10.1 on the example AST. You can choose where in the code you would like to do that.
- Replace the `Data Attribute` concept label with `Attribute` in all code.
- Do likewise for the `initial value` property name, replacing it with `value`, including in textual occurrences such as placeholder, button, and issue texts.
- After having done these replacements, check whether everything works as before.

10.3.3 *Deprecating concepts and properties*

You can't just remove a concept from a DSL's structure if the DSL content contains instances of that concept. Likewise, you can't remove a property if the DSL content contains settings for that property. Domain experts have used that feature (concept or property) to express some domain knowledge. Simply removing it without fair warning would destroy that knowledge and leave it up to the domain experts to reconstitute it somehow.

Let's explicitly deprecate a property or concept of the DSL before technically removing it. There are two main facets of deprecation:

- *Warn* the domain experts about the impending removal of a feature.
- *Offer a migration path* to the domain experts.

We already have a good mechanism in place to cater to both aspects: we can add a constraint that reports an issue for every use of the deprecated feature. The issue's message should explain the following about the feature:

- *That* it's deprecated.
- *Why* it's deprecated.
- *When* it will no longer be supported and ultimately removed.
- *How* to rephrase domain knowledge that uses the deprecated feature in terms of DSL constructs that are supported and undeprecated. Ideally, a migration path is performed through an AST migration, but that's not always possible.

You should give the domain experts ample time and opportunity to respond to these issues. It's a good idea to plan ahead and start the deprecation at least a couple of released versions before actually removing the feature. You can ramp up the intensity of the issues by initially giving them severity level "warning" before moving to level "error."

Technically, removing a feature requires you to do two things:

- Remove any remaining usage from any DSL content: instances of a concept, or settings of a property. Provided you have properly deprecated the feature according to the preceding guidelines, you can now assume that any remaining uses can be scrubbed with impunity. This action should be performed by an AST migration that should also unset references to instances of the concept being removed.
- Remove all traces of the deprecated feature from the DSL implementation itself. Cleaning up by deletion tends to simplify code quite a bit, which is a desirable side effect. The DVCS holding the Domain IDE's code will remember if you become nostalgic.

10.3.4 Changing a DSL key aspect other than structure

We saw in section 10.3.2 how impactful changes to a DSL's structure can be. The other aspects of a DSL can change without being forced to by the DSL's structure. We need to discuss what those changes can be, how they propagate to the DSL's implementation, and what impact they can have.

Let's go over the DSL's key aspects other than the structure, and what happens when it's changed without changing the structure itself. As before, we'll use figure 10.9 to judge the impact.

Changes to the *notation* only impact the Domain IDE's frontend. Changes usually only impact the DSL-specific parts of the frontend: the projection and its styling. Occasionally, they also impact the DSL-generic parts, such as the framework of reusable React components.

Modifying or deleting existing *constraints*, or adding new ones, changes the notion of what a valid AST is. This has no impact other than how many issues are reported to the domain experts. Code-wise, such changes are reflected in src/language/constraints.js.

The following commonly occurring two changes look like structure changes, but they're actually changes to the constraints aspect:

- *Widen the type of an existing property* when we need to capture a wider range of details through that property. This is done by loosening an existing constraint that reported an error when a value of a type that was previously not allowed was encountered in a setting of that property.
- *The type of an existing property is narrowed* when we discover we need to constrain the DSL content so that the generator doesn't produce wrong code (or fails itself). This is done by adding a new constraint or sharpening an existing one. In either case, an error should be reported when a value of a type that's no longer allowed after the narrowing is encountered in a setting of that property.

The most interesting aspect to change besides structure is that of *meaning*. A change to the meaning propagates to several things coupled to the meaning aspect:

- The *code generator*—almost certainly the template code, but sometimes the helper functions as well.
- The handwritten code that's part of the Runtime and its reference implementation, and which interfaces with generated code. When the generated code changes, the handwritten code it interfaces with often has to change as well. Sometimes, this handwritten code changes independently of the code generator and generated code, though.
- The *constraints*—most constraints exist to prevent failure in either the code generator or the generated code. Changing the meaning by changing the code generator often leads to changes in the constraints aspect as well.

We can conclude that changing a DSL's structure has a lot of impact, but that changing any other aspect has relatively little.

In this chapter, you learned how the various moving parts in a DSL-based approach for software development can evolve. In the next chapters, you'll see this in action when we make changes to the example DSL, some of which are breaking changes.

Summary

- Change in a DSL-based approach can essentially mean two things:
  - The DSL content changes.
  - The DSL itself changes.
- Change of the DSL content must be managed such that it supports the domain experts' workflow. This requires collaborative functionality in the Domain IDE. Two (possibly complementary) styles of such functionality can be identified: synchronous (real-time collaborative editing) and asynchronous (distributed

version control system, or DVCS). Projectional editing can help deal with changes to the DSL content by expressing those as small *deltas* (∂s) on the AST.

- The various moving parts in a DSL-based approach to software development are coupled in varying degrees to each other, and to the DSL's key aspects. The software components of the Domain IDE can be divided into the following categories:
  - *DSL-specific*—Everything that implements a part of a key aspect for a particular DSL
  - *DSL-generic*—Everything that can be used for multiple DSLs, such as the generic low-level AST structure and UI frameworks
  - *DSL-aspecific*—Everything else (boilerplate)

  The DSL-specific code parts of the components and the DSL's key aspects are coupled in a specific, predictable way. Figure 10.9 shows all coupling between (both code and non-code parts of the) components, and to the DSL's key aspects.

- The Domain IDE needs to be *versioned*, and DSL content needs to be annotated with a *version ID* so that the Domain IDE can check whether it can handle the DSL content correctly. This check should happen whenever DSL content is loaded. An appropriate migration action should be performed if the versions don't match.

- Almost everything that's DSL-specific is coupled to the DSL's structure. Any change to the DSL's structure can be described in terms of (one or more of) the following types of changes:
  - Add a new property to an existing concept.
  - Add a new concept.
  - Change the type of an existing property.
  - Remove an existing property, or even an existing concept.
  - Rename an existing property or concept.
  - Change a set of concepts and (some of) their properties in lockstep.

  Some of these types of changes are widening, but most are modifying. Changing the DSL's structure aspect has a lot of impact.

- Changes that modify the structure require an *AST migration* to be performed: an algorithm transforms an AST conforming to the *pre*-change structure into an AST conforming to the *post*-change structure. An AST migration has a set of "from" version IDs (pre-change) and a "to" version ID (post-change). Before running an AST migration, it should be check whether the version ID of the (AST representing the) DSL content is in the set of "from" version IDs.

- Concepts and properties of concepts can't be removed just like that: you need to *deprecate* features before you remove them, so domain experts can deal correctly with business knowledge relying on deprecated features.

- Changing a key aspect of a DSL other than its structure has relatively little impact, because the coupling of such an aspect to the DSL implementation is quite straightforward and simple.

Implementing expressions: Binary operations

11

This chapter covers

- Why, how, and what expressions are useful for
- Why binary operations are especially useful
- How to represent expressions with binary operations as ASTs
- How to implement binary operations across all key aspects of a DSL

If you look at our example DSL content, you'll notice that the attributes of the Rental record type should be related more intricately than they currently are. The value of rental price after discount should be calculated from the values of rental price before discount and discount—see figure 11.1.

Unfortunately, we can't *express* such relations yet: the DSL doesn't have any concept with the appropriate notation and the corresponding meaning. Leaving it up to the user of the generated web app to set the rental price after discount to a value governed by the preceding arithmetical relation is unfair.

In this chapter, we're going to add expressions to the DSL to remedy that. An *expression* is a piece of DSL content whose meaning aspect consists of it evaluating to a value. We can stick that value in other expressions to get another value, and so on, and so on. Expressions can be anything, ranging from constant values, to references to "things" holding values, to arithmetical computations such as the one in figure 11.1. The only rule is that they evaluate to a value. Arithmetical formulas—of the sort you learned in school and that you also see in figure 11.1—form a well-known class of expressions.

Figure 11.1   The relation between the *values* of the four attributes of the `Rental` record type

In a DSL-based approach for software development, expressions are typically used to express detailed *business logic*. The two most important kinds of business logic are

- Calculating values from other values (possibly coming from input data). A subcase is specifying a condition that evaluates to a `true` or a `false` value.
- Specifying an outcome based on conditions and calculations.

We're going to allow the domain experts to write an expression that specifies arithmetical relations between the values of attributes. The generated web app will calculate the value of `rental price after discount` from the values of `rental price before discount` and `discount`, without the user being able to set its value themselves. It turns out that we only need to add *one* new concept, the `Binary Operation`, to our example DSL for that. This concept covers a lot of ground on its own: many expressions have a "skeleton" consisting of binary operations.

Most of the work in this chapter revolves around the `Binary Operation` concept. The remainder of the work will go into "promoting" two existing DSL concepts to *expression concepts*. An *expression concept* is a concept whose instances can be used in an expression. The meaning aspect of those instances is that they evaluate to a value. Expression concepts take a fairly special place among all concepts of a DSL, and we'll see why in section 11.5.

In chapter 12, we'll improve the projection of binary operations to take their *order of operations* into account. In chapter 13, we'll formulate and implement constraints on expressions. In chapter 14, we'll use expressions to specify business rules.

11.1 Representing expressions as DSL content

In this section, we're going to represent the arithmetical relation in figure 11.1 as DSL content. That includes turning that DSL content into an AST and making the necessary changes to the DSL's structure. To see what we need to add to the example DSL so that the domain experts can write the expression in figure 11.1 using the Domain IDE, we break down that expression's notation in figure 11.2.

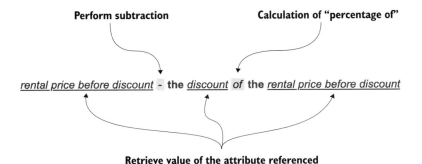

Figure 11.2   The expression for calculating the value of rental price after discount **from the values of** discount **and** rental price before discount

The most obvious new piece of notation we can see is the "*of*" in "discount of the rental price before discount." This part of the notation will be a *subexpression* of the entire expression. Its meaning is to calculate the discount percentage value *of* the rental price before discount amount value. For example, "20% *of* $60" evaluates to "$12."

To express an "*of*" calculation as DSL content, we need to add a new concept to the DSL's structure. We could call this new concept Percentage Of, or something else that's tied to percentages, but I'd rather pick something more generic. Binary Operation is a good choice for a few reasons:

- The name conveys that it performs an *operation*.
- It takes *two* (hence "binary") values as input to operate on: the *operands*.
- It's a term already well known in computer science.

An instance of this new concept will contain three pieces of data:

- An *operator*: in this case "*of*"
- A *left operand*: "something" that evaluates to the value of the discount attribute
- A *right operand*: "something" that evaluates to the value of the rental price before discount attribute

The notation of a Binary Operation looks like this: *<projection of left operand><operator><projection of right operand>*. This structure and notation should work for a wide range of operations.

Operator placement

Most operators are shown between their operands, such as "1 / 2." This is also why `Binary Operation` has properties "*left* operand" and "*right* operand." This placement is called *infix notation*: the operator is affixed *in* between its operands. We say such an operator is an *infix operator*.

Two other standard "*<placement>*fix" notations exist besides the infix one:

- *Prefix* operators are notated *in front* ("pre") of their operand(s):

  <operator><operand 1><operand 2> ... <last operand>

  Common examples of prefix operators from programming languages are logical (`! false`) and arithmetical (`- 42`) negation.

- *Postfix* operators are notated *after* ("post") their operand(s):

  <operand 1><operand 2> ... <last operand><operator>

Common examples of postfix operators from programming languages are the post increment/decrement operations `i++` and `j--`.

Infix operators are always binary, but any operator can have pre- or postfix notation. Most operators we encounter on a daily basis are binary infix operators, but some programming languages are famously different in this respect: Lisp favors prefix operators, while Forth prefers postfix operators.

In principle, pre- and postfix operators can have arbitrary numbers of operands. That's because their syntax doesn't limit them to one left and one right operand—the operator just has to be the first or last element of the syntax, respectively. It's rare for them to have more than two operands, though. Operations with more than two operands are often represented using a *function invocation operator* with (a reference to) the function to be invoked as the first argument, and the operation's own operands as the remaining arguments.

For projectional DSLs, operator placement is only a notational concern: the AST doesn't care where the projection shows the operator value. It's good to be aware of the prefix, infix, and postfix terms though.

To represent the entire "*of*" operation, we have to have "something" that evaluates to the value of a referenced attribute. We already seem to have a suitable concept for that: `Attribute Reference`. Before, we used an instance of that concept to specify that the initial value of the `rental price after discount` attribute should be set to the value of the `rental price before discount` attribute. We can turn `Attribute Reference` into an expression concept by specifying how its instances must be evaluated. Let's specify that an instance of `Attribute Reference` evaluates to the value held by the referenced attribute at the time of evaluation. This specification is compatible with the previous meaning of `Attribute Reference`.

Let's draw an AST representing the subexpression "*discount of rental price before discount*" as an ORD—see figure 11.3. From now on, we'll call an AST an *expression AST* if it represents only an expression. In figure 11.3, only the three upper AST objects make up an expression AST. The AST objects of the Data Attribute concept are referenced from that expression AST but are not contained by it. Instead, they are contained by the AST representing the entire DSL content.

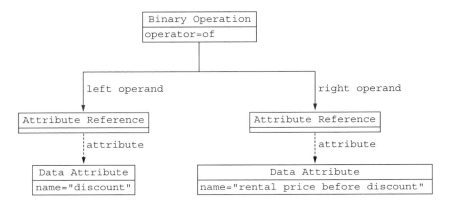

Figure 11.3   An ORD of the AST representing the subexpression "*discount of rental price before discount*," including the attributes involved

The next new piece of notation to handle is the subtraction indicated with "–". To represent the subtraction, we can use an instance of Binary Operation as well. The Binary Operation concept is generic enough to also express subtraction. The representing instance has the following data:

- "–" as the operator.
- A reference to the rental price before discount attribute as the left operand
- The subexpression "*discount of rental price before discount*," represented as an AST in figure 11.3, as the right operand.

  This pertains to all the new AST objects in figure 11.3, but not the preexisting ones, which are only reference targets anyway. The apparent root of these AST objects is the one representing the "*of*" operation: this will become contained by a new binary operation (that's going to represent the "–" operation), through its "right operand" property.

Combining both binary operations produces the expression AST shown in figure 11.4, which then fully captures figure 11.2. The binary operations in figure 11.4 form a sort of "skeleton," with the other objects being analogous to the "meat." Binary operations

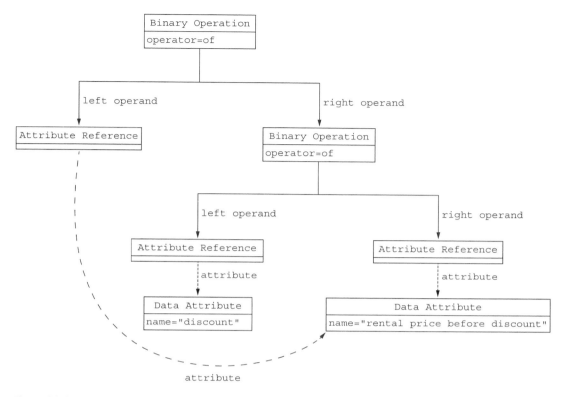

Figure 11.4 An ORD of the AST representing the entire expression in figure 11.2, including the attributes that are only referenced

allow us to "grow" an AST from subexpressions at an exponential rate, because each binary operation has two subexpressions as operands. This makes the `Binary Operation` essentially the most important and most powerful expression concept, which is why we treat it before other expression concepts.

Earlier, we also identified `Attribute Reference` as an expression concept. Our DSL contains one more concept that's really an expression concept: `Number` already represents a specific value, so it naturally evaluates to that same value.

11.1.1 Changing the structure

Now that we know how we can represent figure 11.1 as an expression, we need to adapt and extend the DSL's implementation accordingly. Where should we put the attribute's value expression?

We could give `Data Attribute` a new "computed value" property to store the expression. But an attribute should have either a "computed value" *or* an "initial value"—having both at the same time doesn't make sense. That means we could just as well rename "initial value" to "value." We could then use that property to store either the initial value or an expression for the computed value.

Let's change the DSL's structure accordingly, taking care to still distinguish between the value being an initial or a computed value. Before, an attribute in the DSL content corresponded to a field in the Runtime that holds a data value. Now that an attribute can specify a computed value as well, it seems inappropriate to label such an attribute as a `Data Attribute`, so let's drop the "Data" part from the concept label.

This change to the DSL's structure also changes the meaning aspect of the concept that we're renaming from `Data Attribute` to `Attribute`. Each attribute in the DSL content corresponds to a field in the Runtime. Before the change, an attribute *<a>* referencing another attribute *<t>* meant the following in the Runtime: initialize the field for *<a>* with the value that the field for *<t>* has been initialized with. After the change, we can no longer distinguish an attribute reference that's an initial value from an attribute reference that's a computed value just by looking at the expression itself, because an `Attribute Reference` is itself an expression.

Instead of determining the kind of value automatically, we're going to adapt the DSL so the kind of value is chosen explicitly. We're going to add a `value kind` property to the `Attribute` concept for that. This property will either have the value `initially` (which is a sensible default) or `computed as`.

Relabeling the `Data Attribute` concept to `Attribute`, and renaming its property `initial value` to `value` would already have been achieved by performing the AST migration in listing 10.1. Let's extend that AST migration—which is implemented by the `modifyDataAttribute` function in src/init/migrations.js—to set an appropriate value for `value kind` as well. This is as simple as adding one line to the code, which is highlighted in listing 11.1.

Listing 11.1   The addition to the AST migration to set `value kind`

```
// ...other existing code...
if (value.concept === "Data Attribute") {
    value.concept = "Attribute"
    settings["value"] = settings["initial value"]
    delete settings["initial value"]
    settings["value kind"] = "initially"          ◁—
}
// ...other existing code...
```

Set the value of "value kind" to "initially" because that's the only value kind we could have seen before this migration.

Exercise 11.1
Determine what type of change (from the list at the beginning of section 10.3.2) adding the `value kind` property corresponds to.

Exercise 11.2

1 Apply the code change from listing 11.1 to src/init/migrations.js.
2 Run the migration on DSL content having version label `v1`. You can do this by running the following on the command line:

> Reset storage to the standard example DSL content, corresponding to version **v1**.

```
$ node src/init/install-example-DSL-content.js   ◁
$ node src/init/migrations.js            ◁
```

> Run the migration again, which now also modifies settings of the (initial) value property.

3 Check whether the AST migration has had the desired effect, such as by looking at src/backend/data/contents.json: attributes should have the concept label `Attribute` (instead of `Data Attribute`), they should have a property `value` instead of `initial value`, and `initially` should be `true` when a `value` is specified.
4 Propagate the name changes (concept label `Data Attribute` → `Attribute`, and property name `initial value` → `value`) throughout the codebase.
5 Test the Domain IDE to verify that everything still works as before.

Note that instead of changing an existing migration and running it on DSL content having version label `v1`, you could implement a second AST migration. This second AST migration just sets the `value kind` property of all attributes to `initially` and updates the version label from `v2` to `v3`. Implement this migration and run it after having run the original AST migration from chapter 10. This is conceptually a cleaner way of achieving the same result, but requires implementing another AST migration.

TIP   We could have chosen to make a Boolean-valued property instead of the enumeration-typed `value kind` property. In my experience, it's usually better not to restrict yourself to a two-value range (`true`/`false`) for a property's values. Even if you think you'll never need more than two values, you've pretty much painted yourself into a corner once it does happen.

11.2 Changing the projection

Before we extend the projection for `Binary Operation`, let's adapt the existing projection to take the `value kind` property into account. We're going to have to let the domain expert choose between an attribute having an `initially` or a `computed as` value. We can use the `<DropDownValue>` component to implement that. In the `case` for `Attribute` in src/frontend/projection.jsx, replace this code,

```
<span className="keyword ws-right">initially</span>
```

with the code in the following listing.

Listing 11.2   Choosing between the two value kinds

```
<DropDownValue
    className="value keyword ws-right"
    editState={editStateFor("value kind")}
    options={[ "initially", "computed as" ]}
/>
```

When creating a new attribute value, the value of `value kind` initially is unset, so `undefined`. The preceding code implies that `undefined` is not a valid value. We can fix that by explicitly setting `value kind` when the domain expert adds a value to an attribute using the "+ value" button. To do so, add the line that's highlighted in listing 11.3 to the `case` code for `Attribute`. (Note that we replaced all occurrences of "initial value" with "value" as part of exercise 10.6, including in the button text "+ initial value".)

Listing 11.3   Initializing the value of `value kind`

```
// (...other code in the Attribute case...)
: <AddNewButton buttonText="+ value" actionFunction={() => {
    settings["value"] = placeholderAstObject
    settings["value kind"] = "initially"
}} />
```

Exercise 11.3

1 Apply the code changes from listings 11.2 and 11.3.
2 Test the Domain IDE to verify that everything still works as intended.
3 Change the `rental period after discount` attribute (as it is now) to have a computed value, using the Domain IDE.
4 Consider the scenario where you, using the Domain IDE, add a value to an attribute, and then remove that value again. What's the value of the `value kind` property then? Is that a problem?

Setting the value of an attribute to `computed as` doesn't affect the generated code yet. We'll combine adapting the code generator for that with extending the code generator for binary operations in section 11.4.

Figure 11.5 showcases—as an "animation"—the steps a domain expert performs to turn the `rental price after discount` attribute into one with a computed value.

We're now going to adapt the Domain IDE to allow the domain experts to construct a binary operation as a value of an attribute. Specifically, we want to replace the reference to the `rental price before discount` attribute, which is the current value of the `rental price after discount` attribute, with an instance of `Binary Operation`. Currently, a domain expert can instantiate either an `Attribute Reference` or a `Number` as the value of an `Attribute`. This is implemented inside the projection for the rental price after discount is an *amount* initially the <u>rental price before discount</u>   **1. Select initial value**

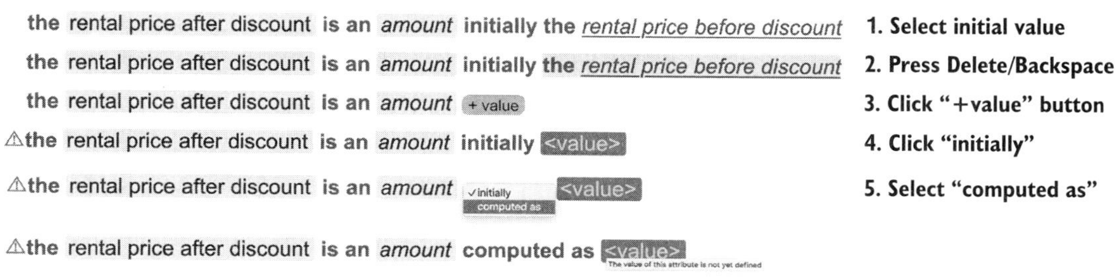

the rental price after discount is an *amount* initially the <u>rental price before discount</u>   **2. Press Delete/Backspace**

the rental price after discount is an *amount* `+ value`   **3. Click "+value" button**

⚠the rental price after discount is an *amount* initially `<value>`   **4. Click "initially"**

⚠the rental price after discount is an *amount* `✓ initially`   `<value>`   **5. Select "computed as"**
                                              `computed as`

⚠the rental price after discount is an *amount* computed as `<value>`
                                              The value of this attribute is not yet defined

Figure 11.5   Making the fourth attribute have a computed value

`Attribute` using a `<DropDownValue>` component function, which we pass the array
`[ "Attribute Reference", "Number" ]`. Adding the string `"Binary Operation"` to this
array allows a domain expert to start creating the expression in figure 11.2.

> **Exercise 11.4**
> In src/frontend/projection.jsx, in the `case` for `Attribute`, add the string `"Binary`
> `Operation"` to the array passed as the value for the `options` attribute to the call to
> the `<DropDownValue>` component function.

With the preceding code change performed, we can try to create the expression in figure 11.2 in the Domain IDE. Figure 11.6 shows an animation of the steps a domain
expert would perform to start doing that.

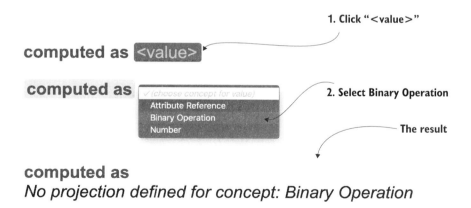

Figure 11.6   An "animation" of the steps to create the arithmetical expression in figure 11.2

Figure 11.7 shows that we have to extend the projection to handle a `Binary Operation`.

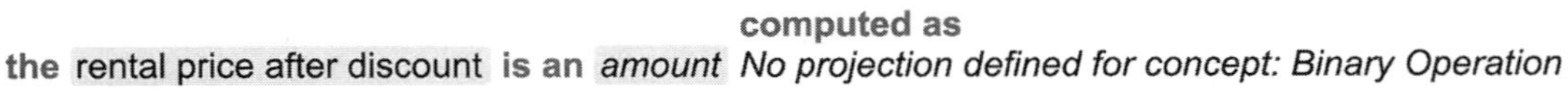

computed as

the rental price after discount is an *amount* *No projection defined for concept: Binary Operation*

Figure 11.7   A screenshot of the fourth attribute after instantiating a `Binary Operation`

We could implement the projection of `Binary Operation` (in the corresponding case in src/frontend/projection.jsx) as follows. (We'll modify this implementation later on.)

Listing 11.4   Initial implementation of projecting a `Binary Operation`

```
case "Binary Operation": {
    return <AstObjectUiWrapper
            className="inline"
            astObject={astObject}
            deleteAstObject={replaceWith}
            issues={issues}
        >
        <Projection                                          ◁── Project the left
            astObject={settings["left operand"]}                  operand.
            ancestors={[ astObject, ...ancestors ]}
            replaceWith={() => {
                delete settings["left operand"]
            }}
        />
        <DropDownValue                                       ◁── Show the operator as a
            className="value enum-like ws-both"                  selectable value. For now,
            editState={editStateFor("operator")}                 only make the operators
            options={[ "of", "-" ]}                              that we need for figure 11.2
            placeholderText="<operator>"                         available: "of" and
        />                                                       arithmetical minus ("-").
        <Projection                                          ◁── Project the
            astObject={settings["right operand"]}                right operand.
            ancestors={[ astObject, ...ancestors ]}
            replaceWith={() => {
                delete settings["right operand"]
            }}
        />
    </AstObjectUiWrapper>
}
```

The problem with this code is that directly after instantiating the `Binary Operation`, the values of the settings for the `left operand` and `right operand` properties are `undefined`. That means both calls to the `<Projection>` function in the preceding code will just produce the text "No projection defined for value: undefined" where you expect the left and right operands. Even worse, this text doesn't function as a placeholder that allows you to instantiate an operand.

Luckily, we already solved this problem for adding a value to an attribute. Let's refactor the code that solves this problem for an attribute out of the `Attribute` case of the `<Projection>` function into a separate `projectionExpressionFor` function that's added to src/frontend/projection.jsx. This function will project the AST object that's the value of a designated property of a given AST object. The function assumes that that value is either an instance of an expression concept, or `undefined`, or the AST object placeholder value defined in src/common/ast.js. If the value is not an AST object, the function produces a UI that can instantiate a new AST object that is an instance of an expression concept. Add the new `projectionExpressionFor` function in listing 11.5 to the src/frontend/projection.jsx file before the `Projection` function, so we can use it in the `case` for any concept.

Listing 11.5 The added `projectionExpressionFor` function

```
const projectionExpressionFor = (astObject, ancestors, propertyName) => {
    const { settings } = astObject
    const value = settings[propertyName]
    return (value === undefined ||
            value === placeholderAstObject)          ◁─── Check for undefined
        ? <DropDownValue                                   and the AST object
            editState={observable({                        placeholder value.
                setValue: (newValue) => {
                    settings[propertyName] =
                        newAstObject(newValue)
                }
            })}
            options={[                              The expression concepts we've identified
                "Attribute Reference",             (so far) are Attribute Reference, Binary
                "Binary Operation",        ◁────── Operation, and Number.
                "Number"
            ]}                                         Generate placeholder
            placeholderText={`<${propertyName}>`}      and action texts specific
            actionText={`(choose concept for ${propertyName})`}  ◁── for the property's name.
        />
        : <Projection
            astObject={value}
            ancestors={[ astObject, ...ancestors ]}
            replaceWith={() => {                 Pass a function that deletes
                delete settings[propertyName]  ◁── the designated property from
            }}                                   astObject to the replaceWith
        />                                       attribute of <Projection>.
}
```

As you can see from the size of this function, it does a lot of work. This means that the more often we use this function by calling it, the more functionality we implement in the Domain IDE. Let's use the `projectionExpressionFor` function in the code of the `case` for `Attribute`, replacing a lot of the earlier code in the src/frontend/projection.jsx file—see listing 11.6, which has the differences highlighted in bold.

Listing 11.6 Using `projectionExpressionFor` for `Attribute`

```
{settings["value"]
    ? <div className="inline">
        <DropDownValue
```

```
            className="value keyword ws-right"
            editState={editStateFor("value kind")}
            options={[ "initially", "computed as" ]}
        />
        {projectionExpressionFor(astObject, ancestors, "value")}
    </div>
    : <AddNewButton buttonText="+ value" actionFunction={() => {
        settings["value"] = placeholderAstObject
        settings["value kind"] = "initially"
    }} />
}
```

> ### Exercise 11.5
> - Add the code in listing 11.5, and apply the code change from listing 11.6 to src/frontend/projections.jsx.
> - Check whether the Domain IDE works as expected.

Now let's use the `projectionExpressionFor` function to implement the projection for any instance of `Binary Operation`. Listing 11.7 shows the working implementation of the projection for `Binary Operation` (in src/frontend/projection.jsx) after replacing part of the code in listing 11.4 with calls to `projectionExpressionFor`. (The differences from listing 11.4 are highlighted in bold.)

Listing 11.7   The working projection of `Binary Operation`

```
case "Binary Operation": {
    return <AstObjectUiWrapper
        className="inline"
        astObject={astObject}
        deleteAstObject={replaceWith}
        issues={issues}
    >
        {projectionExpressionFor(astObject, ancestors, "left operand")}
        <DropDownValue
            className="value enum-like ws-both"
            editState={editStateFor("operator")}
            options={[ "of", "-" ]}
            placeholderText="<operator>"
        />
        {projectionExpressionFor(astObject, ancestors, "right operand")}
    </AstObjectUiWrapper>
}
```

Not only is this code quite a bit shorter than that in listing 11.4, but it also handles unset left and right operands. The projection of the fourth attribute now looks like figure 11.8.

the rental price after discount is an *amount* computed as `<left operand>` `<operator>` `<right operand>`

Figure 11.8 **A screenshot of the `rental price after discount` attribute after implementing the projection for `Binary Operation`, before inputting the expression**

Exercise 11.6

- Add the code from listing 11.7 to the `switch` statement in the projection function.
- Check whether the editor works by recreating the expression in figure 11.2 as the value of the fourth `rental price after discount` attribute. It should look like this:

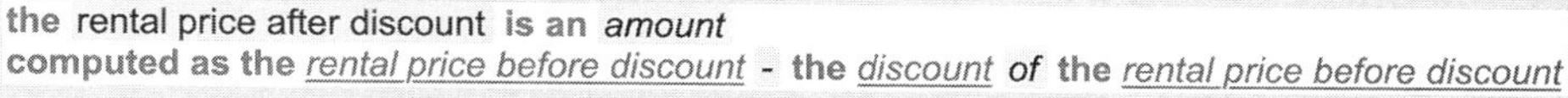

the rental price after discount is an *amount*
computed as the *rental price before discount* - the *discount* of the *rental price before discount*

- Was the editing experience sufficiently intuitive? Do you see any way to improve this?

Every case in the `Projection` function in src/frontend/projection.jsx calls `<AstObject-UiWrapper>`, and almost every call looks the same.

Listing 11.8 Generic call to `<AstObjectUiWrapper>`

```
(return) <AstObjectUiWrapper
    className="<CSS class name>"
    astObject={astObject}
    deleteAstObject={replaceWith}
    issues={issues}
>
    // ...code that implements the actual projection...
</AstObjectUiWrapper>
```

Exercise 11.7 asks you to DRY this by defining a React component—see listing 11.9. This React component will be defined *inside* the `Projection` function so that most of the information it needs is already conveniently in scope.

Listing 11.9 The `UiWrapped` React component

```
const UiWrapped = ({ className, children }) => <AstObjectUiWrapper
    className={className}
    astObject={astObject}
    deleteAstObject={replaceWith}
    issues={issues}
>
    {children}
</AstObjectUiWrapper>
```

Exercise 11.7

- Add the code fragment in listing 11.9 just before the `switch` statement in the `Projection` function.
- Replace all calls to `<AstObjectUiWrapper>` with a corresponding call:

```
<UiWrapped className={<CSS class name>}>
    // ...code that implements the actual projection...
</UiWrapped>
```

- Reason why you can use `<UiWrapped>` for the one `case` that didn't follow the pattern of listing 11.8.
- Test whether the UI works as before.

11.3   *Changing the runtime*

Now that we can write the expression in figure 11.2, we should implement its meaning. That means we have to extend and adapt the code generator so that it generates the appropriate code in the Runtime. Before we actually start changing the code generator, let's first figure out what we need it to generate.

The record type in the DSL content corresponds to a class in the generated Runtime in the src/runtime/index.jsx file, and to a form in the UI. Each attribute in the DSL content corresponds to a property in the `Rental` class corresponding to the record type, and to a form field in the UI. We respecified the `rental price after discount` attribute as having a computed value. That means two things for what's generated from the `rental price after discount` attribute:

- The `rentalPriceAfterDiscount` property should have a read-only computed value. That also means that it should not be initialized to any value, nor should it be settable to an arbitrary value.
- The form field for `rental price after discount` should not be an input field, but a read-only display field that upholds the relation in figure 11.1. As soon as the user changes the value of any of the `rental price before discount` or `discount` fields, the value shown for `rental price after discount` should be updated as well. In other words, the value of `rental price after discount` should *react* to changes of the `rental price before discount` and `discount` fields.

We can define a computed property on a class using *JavaScript getters*. If you aren't familiar with JavaScript getters, see section B.4.5. A getter for the `rentalPriceAfter-Discount` property in the src/runtime/index.jsx file is shown in listing 11.10. This getter implements the computation of the value of the `rentalPriceAfterDiscount` attribute in the `Rental` class.

Listing 11.10 Using a JavaScript getter for computed values

```
class Rental {
    // ...
    get rentalPriceAfterDiscount() {
        return <an expression that computes the value>
    }
    // ...
}
```

Define a computed **rentalPriceAfterDiscount** property through a getter with this syntax: **get <property name>() { ... }.**

Return a value computed as a JavaScript expression. This expression can reference the other fields in an object of this class as this.**rentalPriceAfterDiscount**.

With this definition, we can obtain the computed value of a `rental` object of this class as `rental.rentalPriceAfterDiscount`, or as `this.rentalPriceAfterDiscount` when executing code inside the object itself.

We still have to figure out what the code of the computation of the value should look like, so for now we return a bogus value of the JavaScript `Number` type to conveniently represent an amount. In listing 11.11, we implement a computed property for the field corresponding to the `rental price after discount` attribute, in the src/runtime/index.jsx file—changes to existing code are highlighted in bold.

Listing 11.11 Adding a getter for rental price after discount

```
class Rental {
    rentalPeriod = new DateRange()
    rentalPriceBeforeDiscount = 0.0
    discount = 0
    get rentalPriceAfterDiscount() {
        return 1.23
    }
    constructor() {
        makeAutoObservable(this)
    }
}
```

For now, return the numeric placeholder value 1.23 without computing the proper value according to the formula from the beginning of this chapter.

Now we need to update the UI code in src/runtime/index.jsx to display the computed value instead of an input field. To do that, we replace the call to `<InputField ... fieldName="rentalPriceAfterDiscount" />` with a JSX expression that obtains the value of `rental price after discount`. We'll also let this JSX expression format the value obtained in a way that's suitable for an amount (in dollars): we use the function call `Number.toFixed(2)` to round the number to, and show it with, two decimal digits. Listing 11.12 shows the code changes required in the src/runtime/index.jsx file to turn the form field corresponding to the `rental price after discount` attribute into a computed value (with changes to existing code highlighted in bold).

Listing 11.12 Turning a form field into a computed value

```
<FormField label="Rental price after discount">
    $ {rental.rentalPriceAfterDiscount.toFixed(2)}
</FormField>
```

Now we need to actually compute the value of `rental price after discount` in the getter of `rentalPriceAfterDiscount` with a suitable JavaScript expression, conforming to figure 11.1. Let's look at the AST representation of figure 11.2 in figure 11.4, working our way up from the leaves to its root. (As before, the attribute objects are only referenced, so they're not actually leaves of this AST.)

We first have to obtain the values of the `rental price before discount` and `discount` attributes referenced by the two `Attribute Reference` objects in figure 11.4. In code inside the functions in this class, we can obtain the values of these attributes as `this.rentalPriceBeforeDiscount` and `this.discount`, respectively. These values already have a suitable JavaScript runtime type to calculate with: `Number`.

Next, let's look at how we can turn the expression "*discount of rental price before discount*" in the DSL content into a JavaScript expression. The type of the `discount` attribute is `percentage`. To calculate <y>% of <x>, we multiply <x> with <y> multiplied by 0.01. So "*discount of rental price before discount*" turns into the following:

```
this.discount * 0.01 * this.rentalPriceBeforeDiscount
```

Finally, we can implement the arithmetical minus operation as well. Listing 11.13 shows the expression in figure 11.2 as a JavaScript expression to be evaluated inside an object of the `Rental` class.

> **Listing 11.13 The expression in figure 11.2 as JavaScript**

```
this.rentalPriceBeforeDiscount -
    ⟼ this.discount * 0.01 * this.rentalPriceBeforeDiscount
```

NOTE There's a subtlety here: *x - y * z* means the same as *x - (y * z)*, because the multiplication operator * has higher *precedence* than the subtraction operator -. This is true for arithmetic in general, as for JavaScript specifically. By extension, *x - a * b * c* means the same as *x - (a * b * c)*. So in the case of listing 11.13, we don't *need* to add parentheses (but we could choose to do so for clarity). We'll come back to this topic in the next chapter.

Now put the code in listing 11.13 into the `rentalPriceAfterDiscount` getter, so it looks like the following listing.

> **Listing 11.14 The completed implementation of `rentalPriceAfterDiscount` with `rentalPriceAfterDiscount`**

```
get rentalPriceAfterDiscount() {
    return this.rentalPriceBeforeDiscount -
        ⟼ this.discount * 0.01 * this.rentalPriceBeforeDiscount
}
```

> **Exercise 11.8**
> - Apply the code changes in listings 11.12 and 11.14 in the Runtime's code in src/runtime/index.jsx.
> - Test whether the Runtime now works as intended.
> - Make sure you can somehow revert, or roll back, to the changed version of src/runtime/index.jsx. That way you can check whether your changes to the code generator produce the desired generated code.

11.4   Changing the code generator

Now let's change the code generator so that it generates the changed runtime code for the DSL content with `rental price after discount` as a computed value. First, we'll add an `isComputedFromExpression` convenience function to src/language/queries.js that returns `true` precisely when the given attribute has a value that's computed.

Listing 11.15   Determining whether an attribute has a computed value

```
const isComputedFromExpression = (attribute) => {
    const { settings } = attribute
    return settings["value"] && settings["value kind"] === "computed as"
}
module.exports.isComputedFromExpression = isComputedFromExpression
```

Before the notion of an attribute with a computed value existed, the `initialization-For` template function in src/generator/indexJsx-template.js always generated correct code for an attribute. That's no longer the case, so we have to fix that: instead of calling `initializationFor` directly from the `indexJsx` template function, we're going to call a new template function, `classField`. That function generates a getter for attributes with computed values and an initializer statement otherwise. We'll add that function to src/generator/indexJsx-template.js, as shown in the following listing.

Listing 11.16   The `classField` template function

```
const classField = (attribute) => {
    const { settings } = attribute
    const value = settings["value"]
    const fieldName = camelCase(settings["name"])
    if (isComputedFromExpression(attribute)) {
        return [
            `get ${fieldName}() {`,
            `    return ${expressionFor(value)}`,
            `}`
        ]
    }
    return initializationFor(attribute)
}
```

Handle a computed value. This uses the isComputedFromExpression query function, which we'll have to import from src/language/queries.js.

Use an array of template literals to generate the code for the getter—one array item for each line separately.

Handle an initial (possibly default) value, as we did before.

Next, we can change the part of the `indexJsx` template function (in src/generator/indexJsx-template.js) generating the class definition for a `Record Type`. Instead of calling `initializationFor`, we call `classField`, as shown in the following listing with the change highlighted in bold.

Listing 11.17 Using `classField` in the template code in `indexJsx`

```
class ${Name} {`,
        indent(1)(
            (dependencyOrderOf(attributes, referencedAttributesInValueOf)
                ⟿ || attributes).map(classField)
        ),
        `    constructor() {
        makeAutoObservable(this)
    }
}
```

The `expressionFor` function doesn't handle `Binary Operation` yet, so this leads to the following code being generated inside the `Rental` class, instead of the desired code from listing 11.14:

```
get rentalPriceAfterDiscount() {
    return /* [GENERATION PROBLEM] value of concept 'Binary Operation'
        ⟿ isn't handled in expressionFor */
}
```

Let's fix that by adding a `case` for `Binary Operation` in the `switch` statement in the `expressionFor` function in src/generator/indexJsx-template.js.

Listing 11.18 The case for `Binary Operation` in `expressionFor`

```
case "Binary Operation": {
    const { operator } = settings
    return `${expressionFor(settings["left operand"])}
        ⟿ ${operator === "of" ? "* 0.01 *" : operator}
        ⟿ ${expressionFor(settings["right operand"])}`
}
```

The code in listing 11.18 recurses into the left and right operands of the `Binary Operation`. The value of the operator property is either `of` or an already valid JavaScript operator, such as `-`. For the `of` case, we multiply both operands with each other and with `0.01` to take the left operand being a percentage into account.

There's one more thing to fix: before the introduction of binary operations, an attribute's value was either an `Attribute Reference` or something else (such as a number) that couldn't reference an attribute. As a result, it was pretty straightforward to compute which attribute (if any) was referenced, as implemented by the `referenced-AttributesInValueOf` function in src/language/queries.js. Now that we've expanded our example DSL with the `Binary Operation` concept, an attribute's computed value is an expression that can reference *any* number of other attributes, because we can make expression ASTs arbitrarily large using binary operations. The value expression in figure 11.4 already references two distinct attributes, through a total of three `Attribute References`.

We'll adapt the `referencedAttributesInValueOf` function to also handle binary operations. Because we only need to know which attributes are referenced, but not how many times or in what order, we're also going to make every referenced attribute appear just once in that array.

Is it necessary to adapt the `referencedAttributesInValueOf` function every time we add an expression concept? Or can we do this in a smarter, more generic way? We certainly can, by observing that only instances of `Attribute Reference` influence the result of calling `referencedAttributesInValueOf`. So if we first gather those instances, we can filter out the unique attributes referenced by those instances to produce the desired result.

To that end, we'll first introduce a new generic `allInstancesOf` function in src/common/ast.js that finds all instances of a given concept in the tree hanging off of a given AST object. Like many of our functions, it's a DFTT. Because it's generic (and not in any way specific to the structure of our example DSL), we'll put it in the ast.js file.

Listing 11.19   The `allInstancesOf` function in src/common/ast.js

```
const allInstancesOf = (concept, astObject) => {
    const instances = []

    const visit = (value) => {                    Define an inner function
        if (isAstObject(value)) {                 that performs a DFTT.
            if (value.concept === concept) {      If we're visiting an AST object
                instances.push(value)             with the specified concept,
            }                                     add it to the result to return.
            const { settings } = value
            for (const propertyName in settings) {   Recurse into the
                visit(settings[propertyName])         settings' values.
            }
        }
        if (Array.isArray(value)) {               If a setting's value was an array,
            return value.forEach(visit)           visit each array member separately.
        }
    }                           Don't do anything for other values—especially not for AST
                                reference objects, or we might trigger infinite recursion.

    visit(astObject)            Kick off the DFTT by visiting the given astObject,
                                which might be of the specified concept.

    return instances            Return all instances found.
}
module.exports.allInstancesOf = allInstancesOf
```

We'll now add the following `referencedAttributesIn` function to src/language/queries.js.

Listing 11.20 The `referencedAttributesIn` function

Find all Attribute References using the allInstancesOf function from src/common/ast.js. Make sure you import the allInstancesOf function as well.

The JavaScript expression [...new Set(<collection>)] produces an array of the unique objects within <collection>.

```
const referencedAttributesIn = (astObject) => [ ...new Set(
    allInstancesOf("Attribute Reference", astObject)
        .map((attributeReference) =>
            attributeReference.settings["attribute"])
        .filter(isAstReference)
        .map((refObject) => refObject.ref)
) ]
module.exports.referencedAttributesIn = referencedAttributesIn
```

Follow those references.

Filter out the ones that are actually AST references.

Gather the values of their "property" settings.

Even though we don't need the referencedAttributesIn function outside the queries.js file right now, chances are that we will later, so export it right away.

Finally, we can reimplement `referencedAttributesInValueOf` in src/language/queries.js. The reworked version of that function in listing 11.21 computes which attributes are referenced by any `Attribute Reference` occurring anywhere in the value expression of the given attribute.

Listing 11.21 The reworked version of `referencedAttributesInValueOf`

```
const referencedAttributesInValueOf = (attribute) =>
    referencedAttributesIn(attribute.settings["value"])
```

Exercise 11.9
- Apply the code changes in listings 11.13 through 11.19.
- Test whether the code generator works as intended and doesn't change src/runtime/index.jsx inadvertently.

Introducing the `Binary Operation` concept took quite a bit of work: we had to change and extend the structure, the projection, and the code generator (which corresponds to the meaning aspect). The return on investment is considerable, though: binary operations occur frequently and are the fundamental building blocks for expressions. The code changes we performed paved the way for a much wider range of binary operators than just "*of*" and "–": we can expect that it will take much less effort to add other operators to the palette. They also made our code less ad hoc and more generic in various places, such as in `referencedAttributesInValueOf`. This will help with introducing other expression concepts.

Exercise 11.10

We didn't explicitly adapt the constraints aspect of our DSL for the introduction of binary operations.

- Think about how we changed the constraints aspect *implicitly* by changing the `referencedAttributesInValueOf` function.
- Implement explicit constraints that correspond to properties of a `Binary Operation` not having a value. To this end, introduce another convenience function inside the `issuesFor` function in src/language/constraints.js, after the `issueIfEmpty` and `issueIfUndefined` ones:

```
const issueIfNotAstObject = (propertyName, message) => {
    const value = settings[propertyName]
    if (!isAstObject(value)) {            ◀─── Import the isAstObject function from
        issues.push(message)                   src/common/ast.js at the top of the
    }                                          src/language/constraints.js file.
}
```

Use this new function to report an issue if the left or right operand happens to be the placeholder AST object.

11.5   Postscript: Expressions in general

So far, we've constructed expressions with only three expression concepts: `Attribute Reference`, `Binary Operation`, and `Number`. It's rare that a DSL has so few expression concepts. In the next chapter, we're going to add one more expression concept.

Here, though, we'll first talk about expressions and their concepts more generally than we've done so far. This will establish a framework that should help you recognize expressions where and when they occur. It should also help you appreciate why expressions are so useful to have in your DSLs.

11.5.1   Characterizing expressions by arity

The *arity* of an expression concept is how many subexpressions (or *operands*) can be contained by an AST object of that concept. An expression (concept) is said to have arity *n*, or is called *n*-ary, when it contains at most (and almost always *exactly*) *n* subexpressions. Not all properties of an expression concept have subexpressions as values: these don't count toward the arity. Let's consider the three expression concepts we know and go over their properties—see table 11.1.

Typically, the arity is small: 0, 1, 2, and 3 occur most often. These arities have specific names, which are shown in table 11.2, along with one "exotic" case. The table also provides some JavaScript expressions as examples.

Table 11.1   Expression concepts and their properties

Concept	Arity (properties containing subexpressions)	Other properties
Attribute Reference	0	"attribute" (a reference to an Attribute)
Binary Operation	2 ("left operand", "right operand")	"operator" (a value from a small, fixed set of strings)
Number	0	"value" (a string that represents a number value)

Table 11.2   Arities that occur most often, together with their specific names and JavaScript expressions as examples

n	Specific arity name	Examples from JavaScript
0	Nullary	Any literal data value, such as a string ("…"), a number (123), or a Boolean (true, false)
		Any references to an AST object (usually not of an expression concept)
1	Unary	Logical: ! false, arithmetical negation: - 42
		(Grouping) parentheses: (*<sub expr>*)
		Increment and decrement, both as prefix and postfix : ++i, j--
2	Binary	Arithmetical operations, such as multiplication (*), division (/), etc.
		Logical operations, such as (&&) and (||)
		Comparison operations, such as <, ≤, =, ≠, ≥, >
		String concatenation, often notated as + as well
3	Ternary	if-then-else (*<guard>* ? *<then>* : *<else>*)
Variable	Variadic	Function call/invocation f(*<arg1>*, *<arg2>*, ..., *<last arg>*)
		Array-constructing literal [*<item 0>*, *<item 1>*, ..., *<last item>*]

11.5.2 *Compositionality and expressiveness*

The arity is the main characteristic of expressions: the existence of expression concepts of arity greater than 0 implies that expressions exhibit *compositionality*. Compositionality is the principle that smaller, simpler "things" can be combined with other "things" to form larger, more complex "things." The meaning of any "thing" is determined by its constituent "things" and the way they're composed together. The evaluation of an expression demonstrates this principle: the value returned by the evaluation of a subexpression can replace that subexpression without changing the evaluation result of the whole expression. We're going to revisit this phenomenon in chapter 12 when we discuss the order of operations for binary operations.

Expressions are, well, *expressive* because of compositionality: by being able to compose arbitrary subexpressions, arbitrary large ASTs (in the sense of the number of AST objects in them) can be constructed. The binary operation we introduced in this chapter already allows the domain expert to create binary trees of arbitrary size. This means that expressions can capture arbitrary amounts of detail. Typically, a small number of expression concepts suffice to achieve this expressiveness, so you can achieve much within a limited amount of implementation code.

A LEGO metaphor

LEGO blocks are a useful and fun metaphor for expressions. There's a limited "base" set of single blocks. Some of these occur frequently, and some of these occur rarely. Blocks can be combined by stacking them according to precise "rules." Some blocks only make sense when combined with certain other blocks. Using a sufficient supply of base blocks, we can build an endless variety of buildings, contraptions, etc. (The LEGO analogy also works on another level: expressions can be quite painful, especially when implementing them.)

Here's a "fantastic tree" to showcase that metaphor:

Construction by Nadine Boersma, photograph by Meinte Boersma. Both are published under CC-BY-3.0 and constructed from LEGO DUPLO blocks, as well as some auxiliary non-block elements.

Expressions compose well because they produce a value. They're also supposed to not do anything else—this is called being *free of side effects*. Lots of concepts in software languages do something that produces a value, which means that such concepts can be seen as expression concepts. (Functional programming languages take that idea even further: functions are *themselves* values, which can be composed through expressions.)

This is also generally true for DSLs: the more expression concepts a DSL has, the more possibilities the domain experts will have to express their domain knowledge and business logic. With a well-designed DSL and a well-engineered implementation of it, it shouldn't take much effort to add an expression concept. For our example DSL, now that we have "promoted" existing concepts to the rank of expression concept and made their implementation sufficiently generic, we only have to add the concept's label to the list of options for the `<DropDownValue>` in the `projectionExpressionFor` function.

11.5.3 *Characterizing expressions by operator*

Many, if not most, expression concepts mean to perform some *operation* on their contained subexpression(s). Literal values form the obvious—but not necessarily only—exceptions. Which operation is performed is usually governed by exactly one operator. Our `Binary Operation` concept has an aptly named `operator` property, which determines what arithmetical JavaScript expression is generated.

Without loss of generality, we can say that an expression concept has *at most one* operator attached to it: if an expression concept were to contain more than one operator, then it's likely that we could refactor that concept into more expression concepts in such a way that each of these has at most one operator attached to them. That makes it fair to say that its (single) operator is a characteristic of any expression concept having one.

Exercise 11.11

1 Look at table 11.1, and determine which examples of expressions (concepts) have an operator attached to them.

2 List these operators, together with information such as

   a How is the operator notated (prefix/infix/postfix, or something else)?

   b How many operands does the operator have?

   c What are the types of the operands?

   d What type does the result of the operation have?

3 Extend this list with the *"of"* operator we used in figure 11.2.

4 Try to extend this list with examples of operators we haven't seen so far. Feel free to borrow from

   a The (screenshots of the) Domain IDE as presented in chapters 1 and 15

   b Other tools, such as spreadsheet programs

   c Existing software languages, such as programming languages (JavaScript)

5 What percentage of the operators in this list is binary?

In this chapter, you learned how to extend a DSL with an expression concept for binary operations. You also learned what expressions can be used for, and why and how they're useful. In the next chapter, we're going to see how to take their *order of operations* into account when implementing expressions in a projectional DSL.

Summary

- An *expression* is a piece of DSL content that is meant to evaluate to a value. Any expression is built from instances of *expression concepts*. Expressions are typically used to describe detailed business logic that performs calculations or makes decisions.

- Many, if not most, expression concepts mean to perform some *operation* on their contained subexpression(s), governed by an *operator*. All operations can be assumed to have exactly one operator, without loss of generality.

  A `Binary Operation` is an expression concept that combines two subexpressions, its *left* and *right operand*, with a *binary operator*. Examples of binary operators are arithmetical (`*`, `/`, `+`, `-`, etc.), logical (`&&`, `||`), and comparison (`<`, `≤`, `=`, `≠`, `≥`, `>`). This kind of operation is very common.

- During the evolution of a DSL, already existing concepts may be "promoted" to expression concepts. This usually necessitates making changes to all of the DSL's key aspects. The return on investment of this effort is that the DSL immediately becomes considerably more expressive.

- Many DSLs have a `Binary Operation` expression concept to capture binary operations.

- The *arity* of an expression concept is how many subexpressions (or *operands*) can be contained by an AST object of that concept. Arity is the main characteristic of expression concepts because concepts of arity greater than 0 can be used recursively to build expressions whose ASTs contain any number of AST objects. Another way of saying the same thing is that expressions *compose*. This lends expressions their expressiveness. Most software languages (including DSLs) only need a small number of expression concepts to achieve that.

Implementing expressions:
Order of operations

This chapter covers

- What "order of operations" means for expressions
- How and why the evaluation of an expression should shape the AST representing it
- How to take the order of operations into account in a projectional DSL
- How to use side-transforms to improve the editing experience for domain experts

The notion of expressions should be very familiar: when you learned arithmetic and algebra in school, that was expressed in terms of expressions. You can't do anything "science-y" or any engineering without writing down formulas and doing math—all of this relies heavily on expressions. Almost any statement in a programming language has one or more expressions at its heart. This means that expressions are essentially everywhere, even if they're not always explicitly identified as such.

This ubiquity comes at a price: almost everyone has a lot of intuition, assumptions, and expectations around expressions. We've become accustomed to writing them down as strings of symbols such as +, -, 42, x, etc. We do that when using paper, when using tools such as spreadsheet programs, and certainly when writing code. This linear, textual structure, which can be navigated with a cursor, also shapes the editing experience: expressions are typically created and edited as text, using a keyboard. To convert this text into an AST that can be processed further, it has to be *parsed*—I'll explain that a bit more in section 15.1.

A projectional DSL, on the other hand, starts with an AST and projects that AST as DSL content in a projectional editor. The domain expert then edits the AST directly using this projectional editor. Even if a projectional editor makes expressions look textual, it will not necessarily "think" of them that way. This presents us with a challenge: the process of editing expressions—whose representation as DSL content is inherently tree-like—should not be too different from editing expressions as text. Familiar-*looking* DSL content should also *behave* familiarly during editing. This is especially important for expressions, which are needed to capture the most complex parts of the domain knowledge.

This chapter aims at emulating, or mimicking, part of the editing experience of expressions that we're accustomed to when implementing a projectional DSL. To that end, we'll also study binary operators in more depth.

12.1   *Evaluating and building expression ASTs*

Essentially everyone has been taught about arithmetical operators from an early age onwards. Addition comes right after counting, followed naturally by subtraction, multiplication, division, etc. In school, we also learn about something called the "*order of operations*" in the form of the mnemonic "PEMDAS" (*P*arentheses, *E*xponents, *M*ulti-plication/*D*ivision, *A*ddition/*S*ubtraction) or one of its variants. The order of operations is a specification of how an expression should be evaluated in terms of its subexpressions. It has that name because a large part of such a specification usually revolves around the order in which subexpressions should be evaluated based on the operators of operations.

To evaluate an expression, you look at its subexpressions, figure out what these evaluate to, and then combine them appropriately to yield an evaluation result of the desired type. For arithmetical expressions, that result is probably a number value. To evaluate a subexpression, you look at *its* subexpressions, and so on. This process only stops when a subexpression doesn't have subexpressions itself, and it is of a type you expect an evaluation result to have. When a subexpression has been evaluated, you can replace that subexpression with the evaluation result and carry on as if that evaluation result was always there instead of the subexpression it was evaluated from. (That principle is known as *referential integrity*.) This process is essentially recursive.

Let's see how arithmetical expressions are to be evaluated according to the PEMDAS rule. The PEMDAS rule breaks down into "subrules" that I'll refer to as R1 and R2.

- *R1*—Evaluate what's inside parentheses (or rather, a matched pair of parentheses) first, as a subexpression, following R1 and then R2. (This is the *P* in the PEMDAS rule.) Replace the parentheses and their contents with the evaluation result, which is always a number value.

- *R2*—If no parentheses are present (anymore), evaluate *all* exponentiation operations first, then *all* multiplication and division operations, and finally *all* addition and subtraction operations, in that order. (This is the *EMDAS* part of the rule.) Each time an operation is evaluated, replace the subexpression formed by that operation with the number which is the evaluation result.

(We haven't actually introduced exponentiation and division yet, but that doesn't change the explanation.)

The order of operations imposed by the PEMDAS rule makes the expression 1 + 2 * 3 evaluate to 7, rather than 9. If we wanted the result to equal 9, then we should have written (1 + 2) * 3.

Let's play the evaluation of 1 + 2 * 3 according to the PEMDAS rule back in "slow motion"—see figure 12.1.

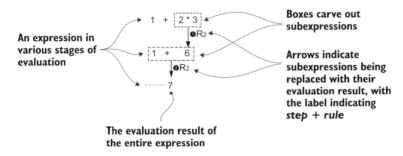

Figure 12.1   Evaluation of 1 + 2 * 3 according to the PEMDAS rule

This evaluation process has two steps:

1 Apply R2 to the operation 2 * 3 to yield 6.
2 Apply R2 to the operation 1 + 6 to yield 7.

R2 says that the various operators are subject to a strict ordering:

- Exponentiation
- Multiplication and division
- Addition and subtraction

This ordering of operators is called the *operator precedence* or sometimes also *operator priority*. The items in this list consist of groups of operators with the same precedence, in descending order of precedence. Operations should be evaluated according to this order: first all operations with operators in the first group, then all operations with operators in the second group, etc. The operators in one group have the same precedence: we'll come back to in which order such operations should be evaluated in section 12.3.

Notation of example expressions: Placeholders for subexpressions and whitespace

I tend to use integers 1, 2, ... in examples of expressions. These are intended as placeholders for subexpressions.

I assume that such subexpressions don't interfere with the interpretation of the expression as a whole. As an example, in the expression "1 + 2 * 3," it would be OK to replace "3" with the subexpression "the number of Stooges/Tenors/Blind Mice." It wouldn't be OK to replace "3" with an expression such as "4 + 5" because "1 + 2 * 4 + 5" really means something different than "1 + 2 * 3," precisely because of the order of operations we're wrapping our heads around.

When writing down example expressions as plain text, I add whitespace around their constituent operands and operators. This is for clarity only: that whitespace doesn't correspond to anything in the AST, and the projection is assumed to show an appropriate amount of whitespace.

Let's build an AST for the expression 1 + 2 * 3. Instead of using the PEMDAS rule to *evaluate* an expression, we'll use it to *build* an AST for that expression. This should make it easier to generate code that evaluates that expression at run time from its AST. The shape and structure of the AST already matches the evaluation, so the code generator doesn't have to gather information from various parts of the expression and stitch that information together. This is especially true if the generated code is in a language that happens to exhibit the same, or a similar, order of operations.

Because the ORD for an expression AST tends to be somewhat unwieldy, we'll first establish a "shorthand" notation for diagrams of expression ASTs. This shorthand notation will essentially be a stylized variant of the ORD notation that works for expression concepts. It will help with describing the AST-building process in the remainder of this chapter.

Figure 12.2 shows and explains the shorthand notation of a single AST object. The AST object is drawn as a simple, square box, instead of as a two-compartment box. The AST object's concept label, as well as its simple settings, are left off. Instead, the interior of the simplified box encodes that same information.

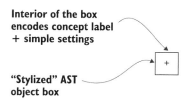

Interior of the box
encodes concept label
+ simple settings

"Stylized" AST
object box

Figure 12.2   Explanation of the shorthand notation for a single AST object

A slightly larger example expression AST is notated in figure 12.3, explaining how the label and simple settings for the various expression concepts are encoded in the interior of an AST object box:

- `Attribute Reference`—An outgoing arrow, without specifying the target attribute
- `Binary Operation`—The operator
- `Number`—The value

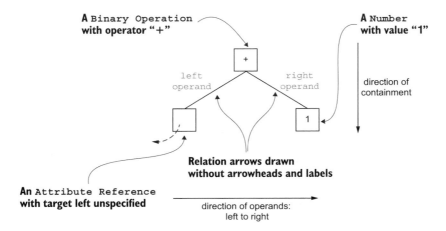

Figure 12.3   **Explanation of the shorthand notation for an example expression AST**

The relation arrows are drawn without arrowheads: the direction of containment is always from top to bottom. From now on, the relation labels (which are still shown in figure 12.3, but opaquely) will also be left off: the relation for "left operand" is always drawn left of the one for "right operand."

The expression AST in figure 11.4 is indeed more compact in shorthand notation, as you can see in figure 12.4.

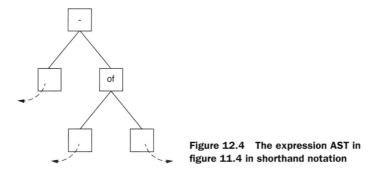

Figure 12.4   The expression AST in figure 11.4 in shorthand notation

Now we can build an AST—using shorthand notation—for the expression 1 + 2 * 3, following its evaluation according to the PEMDAS rule in figure 12.1—we effectively redraw figure 12.1 as figure 12.5.

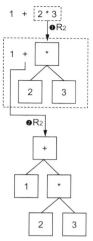

Figure 12.5 Building an AST for the expression 1 + 2 * 3

This building process has two steps:

1 Represent the * operation as a `Binary Operation` with `operator` set to `*`, left operand containing the number 2 box, and right operand containing the number 3 box. This corresponds to applying R2 to the operation 2 * 3.

2 Represent the + operation as a `Binary Operation` with `operator` +, the left operand as the number 1 box, and the right operand as the box from step 1. This corresponds to applying R2 to the operation 1 + 6, where 6 is obtained as the result of evaluating the operation 2 * 3.

The PEMDAS rule doesn't say anything about how to evaluate numbers, because it's obvious what to do: a number evaluates to itself. For building an AST, however, we need to be explicit about them: we turn each number we encounter into its own, separate `Number` instance, with that number as the setting for its `value` property.

Let's try the same with an example with parentheses: the expression $1 + 2 * (3 + 4)$. This means we have to apply R1 as well. We haven't got a concept to represent parentheses yet, so I'll leave that as an exercise for you.

Exercise 12.1

Implement the expression concept `Parentheses` across the DSL's key aspects:

- *Structure*—A `Parentheses` AST object has a single setting for `sub` containing a subexpression.
- *Notation*—It should be notated as (*<projection of its "sub" expression>*).
- *Meaning*—It should generate JavaScript code of the following form: (*<Java-Script expression generated from the "sub" expression>*).
- *Constraints*—The value of `sub` should be set (not `undefined`).

We also need a shorthand notation for parentheses. Figure 12.6 shows this for an AST object representing a pair of parentheses. The box for that object has as its interior the text "(…)", and a line leaves the box vertically for the sub relation, connecting with another AST object.

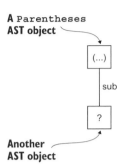

A Parentheses AST object

Another AST object

Figure 12.6   Explanation of the shorthand notation for a Parentheses AST object

We first evaluate the expression 1 + 2 * (3 + 4) according to the PEMDAS rule in figure 12.7.

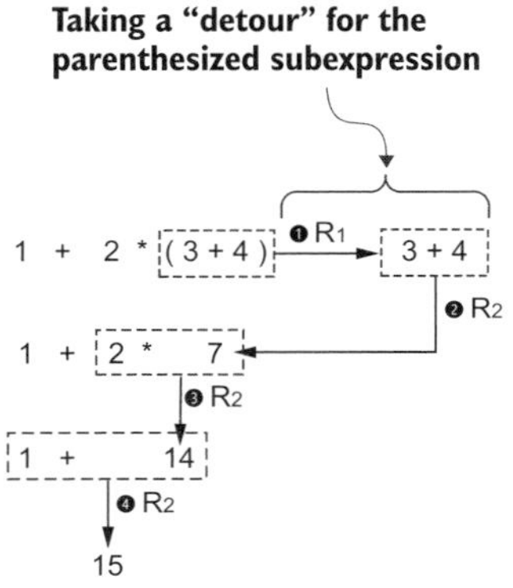

Taking a "detour" for the parenthesized subexpression

1 + 2 * (3 + 4) ❶ R₁ → 3 + 4
                         ❷ R₂
1 + 2 *   7
           ❸ R₂
1 +   14
❹ R₂
15

Figure 12.7   Evaluation of 1 + 2 * (3 + 4)

The first step in this evaluation applies R1 to the (3 + 4) part of the expression. That forces us to apply R2 on the operation 3 + 4 *first*, even though the + operator has *lower* precedence than the * operator, which also occurs in the expression.

Figure 12.8 performs the AST-building process for 1 + 2 * (3 + 4) according to figure 12.7.

The steps in this building process are as follows:

1 Represent the parentheses as a Parentheses AST object with its sub property containing the object from the *next* step.

2 Represent the + operation involving 3 and 4, containing this Binary Operation object in the one from the *previous* step in its sub.

3   Represent the * operation.

4   Represent the + operation with 1 as the left operand.

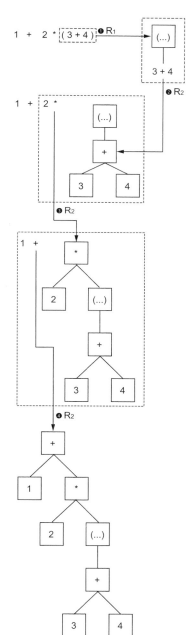

Figure 12.8   Building an AST for the expression 1 + 2 * (3 + 4)

Figure 12.8 is rather large, so we won't build complete ASTs in this explicit way. Instead, we'll just draw up the final AST built from the rules of evaluation.

Exercise 12.2
- Make a list of every operator for binary operations you know, extended with the "*of*" operator from our example DSL. Order these operators according to descending precedence, grouping operators of equal precedence together.
- Optional: Add the operators with a clear equivalent in JavaScript to the implementation of the example DSL.

Let's recap the AST-building process for an expression based on how that expression gets evaluated according to the order of operations (illustrated in figure 12.9):

- Represent every number as a separate `Number` object.
- Represent every reference to an attribute as an `Attribute Reference` object.
- Represent every matched pair of parentheses as a `Parentheses` object. Build the AST for the subexpression inside that pair, and contain the AST for that subexpression in the `sub` property of the `Parentheses` object.
- After all parentheses have been processed, represent every operation as a `Binary Operation` object. Do that in the order prescribed by the order of operations. For arithmetical expressions, that's the EMDAS part of the PEMDAS rule: first, represent *all* operations with an operator of the highest precedence, then *all* operations with an operator of the next-highest precedence, until all operations have been represented.

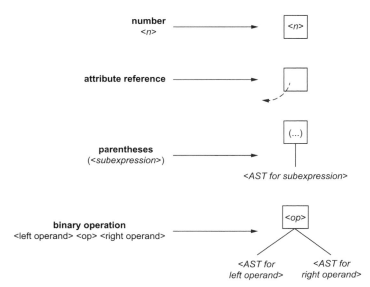

Figure 12.9   The AST-building process recapped using shorthand notation

12.2 Adapting the projection for operator precedence

The previous section may seem to bear no direct relevance to projectional DSLs. In a projectional DSL, the notation of an expression is the result of projecting its AST, not the other way around. The order of operations is effectively entirely bypassed. However, domain experts will expect arithmetical expressions to behave the way they're accustomed to, which means according to operator precedence. If they see the expression 1 * 2 + 3, it should correspond to the AST in figure 12.10.

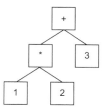

Figure 12.10 The AST representing the expression 1 * 2 + 3 with the usual operator precedence

Now consider the AST in figure 12.11. This AST represents the expression we have to write down textually as 1 * (2 + 3). We need to add the "extra" parentheses to indicate how operator precedence is effectively "overridden" or "sidestepped" by the AST. Such parentheses are effectively "show-only": they're not represented in the AST.

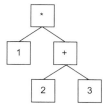

Figure 12.11 The AST representing the expression 1 * (2 + 3)

With the projection as it's implemented now, both of these ASTs would look exactly the same, as shown in figure 12.12.

1 * 2 + 3

Figure 12.12 A screenshot of the projections of figures 12.10 and 12.11—currently identical

Exercise 12.3

1 Input the two expressions that correspond to figures 12.10 and 12.11.
2 You'll find that the Domain IDE will show *all* instances of `Number` with a "$" prefix for attributes of type "amount" and a "%" postfix for attributes of type "percentage." Do you think this kind of visual clutter is desirable?
3 Change the projection so that these pre- or postfixes are only shown when the `Number` is directly contained by the `value` property (regardless of the attribute being computed). In all other cases, it shouldn't show anything extra.

That the projections of two different expressions that evaluate to different values look identical is confusing: that difference can't be seen in the Domain IDE! Because of that, it would be unfair to ask the domain experts to explicitly put in parentheses themselves. They can only guess that a difference exists at all by

- Selecting individual operations in the Domain IDE to discover the grouping—this is cumbersome, because you have to keep performing manual actions.
- Seeing an unexpected result when running generated code—this is too late, indirect, and circumstantial to be of any use.

The AST-building process represents operations with operators of higher precedence *before* it represents operators of lower precedence. This means that (as long as no parentheses are involved) boxes representing operators appear in *ascending* order of precedence in the expression AST. Figure 12.10 follows that rule, but figure 12.11 doesn't. That means figure 12.10 can be the result of the AST-building process, but figure 12.11 can't be.

We could alter figure 12.11 to follow the rules by inserting an extra Parentheses object that effectively wraps the subexpression 2 + 3 in parentheses, as shown in figure 12.13.

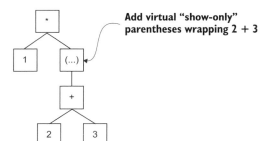

Add virtual "show-only" parentheses wrapping 2 + 3

Figure 12.13   The AST representing the expression 1 * (2 + 3), "fixed" by wrapping 2 + 3 in parentheses

Inserting the parentheses into the expression AST like this means that the subexpression 2 + 3 was going to be processed before any other part of the whole expression, because of R1. Let's automatically insert virtual "show-only" parentheses into the projection of an expression AST that has nested binary operations like in figure 12.11 so that the notated expression matches the AST, taking operator precedence into account. This approach doesn't really improve the editing experience, but at least it avoids having domain experts not be able to see that they've created an expression that's different from what they intended. We're not going to alter the actual expression AST: we're only going to change the projection so that it shows virtual parentheses where needed.

The criterion to wrap a binary operation that's nested as an operand of another binary operation in virtual parentheses can be expressed nicely in diagram form, shown in figure 12.14. In this diagram, the * and + operators serve as stand-ins for two operators, one of which (*) has higher precedence than the other (+).

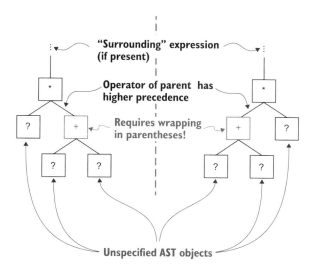

Figure 12.14   The criterion to decide whether a binary operation needs to be wrapped in parentheses because of order of operations in combination with operator precedence

Exercise 12.4

- Convince yourself that the criterion from figure 12.14 is correct.
- Redraw figure 12.14, but swap the * and + operators. Verify that such expression ASTs don't require virtual "show-only" parentheses. Conclude that the criterion from figure 12.14 is complete in the sense that it describes all situations where the binary operators have unequal precedence.
- You could show virtual parentheses around *every* binary operation. What would be the pros and cons of this?

To implement the criterion from figure 12.14, create a src/language/operators.js file. This file will contain functions that help deal with (binary infix) operators.

To conveniently compare operators with each other in terms of their precedence, we're going to assign an integer value to each precedence group. We implement a precedenceOfOperator function in src/language/operators.js that computes that integer for a given operator.

Listing 12.1   The `precedenceOfOperator` function

```
const operatorsPerPrecedence =
    [ [ "-", "+" ], [ "/", "*", "of" ] ]
const precedenceOfOperator = (operator) =>
    operatorsPerPrecedence.findIndex((opGroup) =>
        opGroup.indexOf(operator) > -1)
```

Define a constant array that contains the precedence groups as arrays, in ascending order of precedence.

Define a function that looks up the index (which is an integer value) of the precedence group the given operator is contained in.

Now we can use the `precedenceOfOperator` function to implement a `requiresParentheses` function in src/language/operators.js that determines whether the criterion from figure 12.14 applies to a given subexpression AST.

Listing 12.2   The `precedenceOfOperator` function

Define a function that takes an expression (which is assumed to be a binary operation) and its parent.

Check whether the parent exists, is an AST object, and is a binary operation. If not, return false right away.

```
const { isAstObject } = require("../common/ast")

const requiresParentheses = (expr, parent) => {
    if (!(isAstObject(parent)
            && parent.concept === "Binary Operation")) {
        return false
    }
    const precExpr =
        precedenceOfOperator(expr.settings["operator"])
    const precParent =
        precedenceOfOperator(parent.settings["operator"])
    return precParent > precExpr
}
module.exports.requiresParentheses = requiresParentheses
```

Compute the precedences of the operators of the expression itself, as well as its parent, as a number.

Compare these precedences, and return true/false according to the criterion from figure 12.14.

Now we alter the projection of `Binary Operation` to use the `requiresParentheses` function. Listing 12.3 shows the corresponding code changes (highlighted in bold) in src/frontend/projection.jsx to show the virtual parentheses when required.

Listing 12.3   Adapting the projection for "show-only" parentheses

Import the requiresParentheses function from src/language/operators.js, somewhere at the top of the src/frontend/projection.jsx file.

In the case for Binary Operation, use the requiresParentheses function to determine whether parentheses are required around the current binary operation.

```
import { requiresParentheses } from
    "../language/operators"

// ...other existing code...

case "Binary Operation": {
    const hasVirtualParentheses =
        requiresParentheses(astObject, ancestors[0])
    return <UiWrapped className="inline">
        {hasVirtualParentheses &&
            <span className="keyword">(</span>}
        {projectionExpressionFor(astObject, ancestors, "left operand")}
        <DropDownValue ...rest of the existing code.. />
        {projectionExpressionFor(astObject, ancestors, "right operand")}
        {hasVirtualParentheses
            && <span className="keyword">)</span>}
    </UiWrapped>
}
```

Do the same for the right parenthesis.

Project a left parenthesis depending on the value of the hasVirtualParentheses constant, using the {<condition> && <DOM element>} JSX trick.

Precedence impacts not only the projection but also the code generator. JavaScript obeys the PEMDAS rule as well, so we have to wrap parentheses around subexpressions in exactly the same way. Listing 12.4 shows the corresponding code changes (highlighted in bold) in src/generator/indexJsx-template.js.

Listing 12.4   Adapting the code generator for "show-only" parentheses

Compute the JavaScript expression without virtual parentheses.

Change the expressionFor function to also take a reversed array of ancestors of the current value.

```
// ...pre-existing import statements...
const { requiresParentheses } = require("../language/operators")

const expressionFor = (astObject, ancestors) => {
    // in the switch statement inside the "expressionFor" function:
    case "Binary Operation": {
        const { operator } = settings
        const nextAncestors = [ astObject, ...ancestors ]
        const withoutParentheses =
            `${expressionFor(settings["left operand"], nextAncestors)}
            ${operator === "of" ? "* 0.01 *" : operator}
            ${expressionFor(settings["right operand"], nextAncestors)}`
        return requiresParentheses(astObject, ancestors[0])
            ? `(${withoutParentheses})`
            : withoutParentheses
    }
    // ...
}
```

Return that JavaScript expression wrapped in parentheses when required.

We also have to alter every nonrecursive call to `expressionFor` so a reversed array of ancestors is passed in as the second argument. This amounts to two calls, in both of which the empty array value `[]` is appropriate.

Exercise 12.5

- Apply the code changes in listings 12.1 through 12.4.
- Alter every nonrecursive call to `expressionFor` to pass an empty array value `[]` as the second argument. Hint: There are two such calls.
- Test whether the Domain IDE, including the code generator, functions as expected.

This adaption of the projection protects the domain experts from inputting expressions in a way that would violate the order of operations for binary infix operators.

12.3   Adapting the projection for associativity

We've covered mixing binary (infix) operations with operators of *unequal* precedence. Let's now look at mixing binary operations with operators of *equal* precedence. We haven't specified an order of operations for those yet, and the PEMDAS rule also doesn't say anything about it.

To show that it's important to choose an order, try to evaluate the following expression: $3 - 2 - 1$. Evaluating the first minus operator first yields a different result than evaluating the second minus operator first: $(3 - 2) - 1 = 0$, but $3 - (2 - 1) = 2$. From that, we see that we really have to make a choice and make that choice a fixed part of the order of operations.

The standard choice for the MDAS part of the arithmetical operations is to evaluate them from *left to right*. We call binary (infix) operators that should be evaluated from left to right *left-associative* operators. When $<op_1>$ and $<op_2>$ are left-associative operators having equal precedence (or even being the same operator), the expression $x_1<op_1>x_2<op_2>x_3$ is evaluated as $(x_1<op_1>x_2)\ <op_2>x_3$. We have to apply this rule repeatedly for longer expressions: $x_1<op_1>x_2<op_2>x_3<op_3>x_4 = (x_1<op_1>x_2<op_2>x_3)\ <op_3>x_4 = ((x_1<op_1>x_2)\ <op_2>x_3)\ <op_3>x_4$, etc., as long as all $<op_i>$ are left-associative and have the same precedence.

We said earlier that the AST-building process should follow the order of operations of evaluation, so the corresponding expression ASTs should look like figure 12.15. This AST seems to "favor growing to the left" in the sense that it's built up in a left-down direction. This is true for any AST built from an expression with binary operations with left-associative operators of equal precedence.

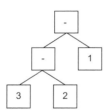

**Figure 12.15   The AST representing the expression 3 – 2 – 1,
taking the order of operations for the left-associative – operator
into account**

> **Exercise 12.6**
>
> Notate the ASTs for the expressions $1 + 2 + 3$, $1 + 2 + 3 + 4$, and $1 + 2 + 3 + 4 + 5$ in shorthand. Verify that these all favor growing to the left.

Some operators are *right-associative*: an expression with such operators evaluates from *right to left*. When $<op_1>$ and $<op_2>$ are *right-associative* operators of equal precedence (or even being the same operator), the expression $x_1<op_1>x_2<op_2>x_3$ is evaluated as $x_1<op_1>\ (x_2<op_2>x_3)$. We also have to apply this rule repeatedly for longer expressions: $x_1<op_1>x_2<op_2>x_3<op_3>x_4 = x_1<op_1>\ (x_2<op_2>x_3<op_3>x_4) = x_1<op_1>\ (x_2<op_2>\ (x_3<op_3>x_4))$, etc., as long as all $<op_i>$ are right-associative and have the same precedence.

Exponentiation, which can be notated using the caret (^), is the usual example of a right-associative operator, because it's also addressed by the PEMDAS rule. For example,   2   ^   3   ^   4   =   2   ^   (3   ^   4)   =   2   ^   81,   which   evaluates   to 2,417,851,639,229,258,349,412,352, and not to (2 ^ 3) ^ 4 = 8 ^ 4 = 4,096, which is "slightly" smaller. The AST for 2 ^ 3 ^ 4 should look like figure 12.16.

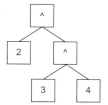

Figure 12.16   The AST representing the expression 2 ^ 3 ^ 4, taking the order of operations for the right-associative ^ operator into account

Associativity gives the same type of problem that we tackled earlier for operator precedence. Consider the expression AST in figure 12.17. This AST doesn't favor growing to the left, so it can't have been built from the expression 1 + 2 − 3.

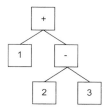

Figure 12.17   The AST representing the expression 1 + 2 − 3, going against the order of operations imposed by + being left-associative

We can "fix" this mismatch by wrapping the subexpression 2 − 3 in parentheses, as in figure 12.18.

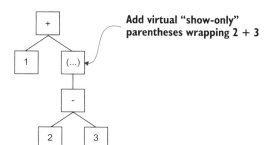

Add virtual "show-only" parentheses wrapping 2 + 3

Figure 12.18   The AST representing the expression 1 + (2 − 3), "fixed" by wrapping the subexpression 2 − 3 in parentheses

As in figure 12.14, we should wrap a binary operation that's the right operand of a binary operation with an operator of equal precedence in parentheses. This criterion is explained in figure 12.19. In this figure, the + and − operators serve as stand-ins for two operators—possibly even the same operator—of equal precedence.

It's relatively easy to extend the `requiresParentheses` function in src/language/ operators.js for this by altering the expression in its `return` statement. Listing 12.15

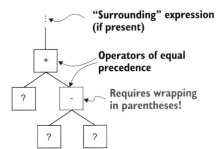

"Surrounding" expression
(if present)

Operators of equal
precedence

Requires wrapping
in parentheses!

**Figure 12.19   The criterion for deciding whether
a binary operation needs to be wrapped in
parentheses because of the order of operations
in combination with associativity**

shows the corresponding code changes (highlighted in bold) to the `requires-Parentheses` function in src/language/operators.js to also implement the criterion from figure 12.19 for left-associative operators.

Listing 12.5   Adapting the `requiresParentheses` for equal precedences

```
return precParent > precExpr || (precExpr === precParent &&
    expr === parent.settings["right operand"])
```

Exercise 12.7
- Apply the code change from listing 12.5.
- Check whether the Domain IDE functions as expected after creating DSL content with expressions like the ones in figures 12.15 and 12.17.

Exercise 12.8
- Implement the exponentiation operator ^.

    Note that the JavaScript operator ^ doesn't perform exponentiation, but the ** one does. You have to perform an explicit mapping here, which you might want to do in a separate method that's refactored out from the `expression-For` function in src/generator/indexJsx-template.js.
- Derive a criterion similar to the one in figure 12.19, and implement it in the `requiresParentheses` function.
- Test whether the Domain IDE works correctly after creating DSL content with an expression like the one in figure 12.16.

Exercise 12.9
Consider two binary infix operators, $<op_1>$ and $<op_2>$, of equal precedence but with $<op_1>$ left-associative and $<op_2>$ right-associative.

1 How would you go about evaluating an expression as $x_1<op_1>x_2<op_2>x_3$? Which order would make sense to you?

2 Can you think of any such operators?

3 Would it make sense to have such operators at all?

12.4 *Using side-transforms to improve editing*

In the previous two sections, we explored what an order of operations is. We also saw how the order of operations can lead to a mismatch with how ASTs for expressions in a projectional DSL are projected and edited, and how they are understood by domain experts. We prevented confusion by adapting the projection to show virtual parentheses where necessary, to comply with the order of operations.

Even with the virtual parentheses fix in place, creating expressions is still quite different from what we're accustomed to doing when typing them in character by character. Let's type in the expression 1 + 2 as you would in a text-based tool like a spreadsheet program and figure out what the corresponding expression ASTs would be—see figure 12.20.

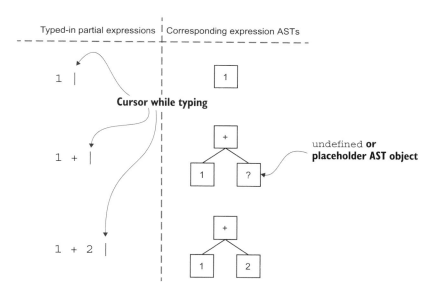

Figure 12.20   Typing in the expression 1 + 2 character by character, with the corresponding expression ASTs

Figure 12.21 shows an animation of the steps a domain expert would perform to create the same expression in the editor of our example DSL.

Comparing figures 12.20 and 12.21, it's clear that typing in 1 + 2 character by character is more convenient than creating the same expression in a projectional editor.

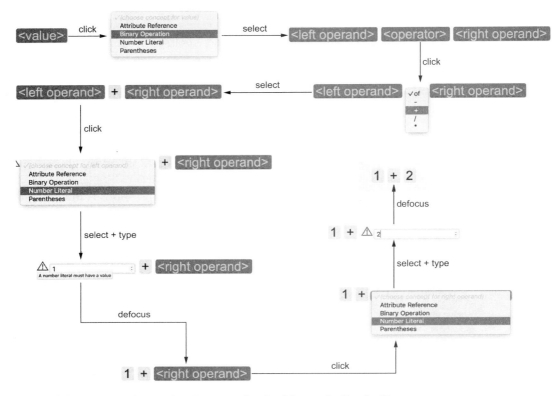

Figure 12.21   All steps for creating the expression 1 + 2 in a projectional editor

This is not just because typing is a more familiar input method: creating the expression 1 + 2 in a projectional editor requires 12 manual actions instead of 3. Even more importantly, it requires planning ahead: the domain expert *has* to start with creating a binary operation. Starting with creating a Number object with the value 1 has them stuck after just one step.

What the domain experts need is a way to turn "1" into something that can be turned into "1 + 2." Figure 12.22 shows the solution we're going to be using.

Figure 12.22   Turning the expression "1" into a binary operation

Now the domain expert can click the "operator" area and select the "+" operator from the drop-down menu. We're going to implement a *side-transform* as the "do something" in figure 12.22.

A side-transform is a transformation of the AST that replaces a particular AST object in it with a `Binary Operation` AST object that has that particular AST object as either its `left` or `right` operand. Figure 12.23 explains the *right-transform* graphically. The name "*right*-transform" indicates that it allows the domain expert to extend an existing AST "to the right" by inserting a binary operation into it. That means that the existing AST object ends up being the left operand of the binary operation that replaces it, with the right operand being unset.

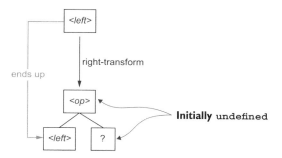

Figure 12.23   Right-transforming an existing AST for the expression *<left>* into an AST representing "*<left><op>* ?"

In our case, *<left>* equals "1" and *<op>* is going to equal "+" (after the domain expert has selected that option from the drop-down menu). The first two steps in figure 12.20 are examples of right-transforms.

Let's implement this right-transform so that we can perform it when the domain expert asks to. The AST object indicated with *<left>* in figure 12.23 is generally not the root of the AST, but rather a part of it. Figure 12.24 shows the situation including the parent of the AST object being right-transformed.

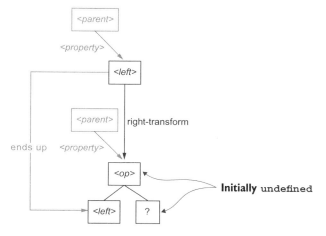

Figure 12.24   Right-transforming an AST, also showing the parent

To replace the *<left>* AST object with the value of the setting for *<property>* on *<parent>*, we should be able to use the `replaceWith` function that's passed to the `Projection` function. Listing 12.6 shows the code fragment that performs the right-transform from figure 12.24. This fragment should be embedded somewhere in the `Projection` function in src/frontend/projection.jsx, and executed from there.

Listing 12.6   Performing the right-transform from figure 12.24

```
replaceWith(
    newAstObject("Binary Operation",
       ⇨ { "left operand": <left> })
)
```
⟵ Use the newAstObject factory function from src/common/ast.js to instantiate a new Binary Operation AST object, leaving both "operator" and "right operand" undefined.

Every `replaceWith` function that's been passed to the `Projection` function so far can do only one thing: replace an AST object with *nothing*, which is the same as deleting that AST object. The code in listing 12.6 expects `replaceWith` to perform a function befitting its name. Listing 12.7 adds two higher-order functions, which construct proper `replaceWith` functions, to src/common/ast.js.

Listing 12.7   Constructing proper `replaceWith` functions

Define a function that replaces the value of a single-valued property, identified through the propertyName argument of the AST object passed as the astObject argument.

Return an arrow function that receives the new value to be assigned to astObject.settings[propertyName].

```
const replaceSingleValue =                ⟵
       ⇨ (astObject, propertyName) => {
    const { settings } = astObject
    return (newValue) => {                ⟵
        if (newValue === undefined) {     ⟵
            delete settings[propertyName]  ⟵
        } else {
            settings[propertyName] = newValue  ⟵
        }
    }
}
module.exports.replaceSingleValue = replaceSingleValue

const replaceInMultipleValue =
       ⇨ (astObject, propertyName, index) => {   ⟵
    const arrayValue = astObject.settings[propertyName]
    return (newValue) => {
        if (newValue === undefined) {
            arrayValue.splice(index, 1)
        } else {
            arrayValue.splice(index, 1, newValue)
        }
    }
}
module.exports.replaceInMultipleValue = replaceInMultipleValue
```

Check whether the new value equals undefined.

If it does, delete whatever is held by astObject.settings[propertyName].

If it doesn't, assign newValue to astObject.settings[propertyName].

Define a function that replaces the index-th value of a multivalued property, identified through the propertyName argument, of the AST object passed as the astObject argument. (As always, indices are 0-based, so index 0 refers to the first/head item of the indicated property.)

Now we can do some code replacements in src/frontend/projection.jsx. In the `projectionExpressionFor` function, we'll replace the bold part of this code,

```
replaceWith={() => {
    delete settings[propertyName]
}}
```

with the bold part of this:

```
replaceWith={replaceSingleValue(astObject, propertyName)}
```

In the `Projection` function, we'll replace

```
replaceWith={() => {
    settings["attributes"].splice(index, 1)
}}
```

the same way, with

```
replaceWith={replaceInMultipleValue(astObject, "attributes", index)}
```

Finally, we have to import the `replaceWith` functions from listing 12.7 in src/frontend/projection.jsx, with the added imports highlighted in bold:

```
import { /* ...existing imports... */,
    replaceInMultipleValue, replaceSingleValue }
        ➡ from "../common/ast"
```

> ### Exercise 12.10
> Apply the preceding code changes: listing 12.7 in src/common/ast.js, and the two code replacements and adding of imports in src/frontend/projection.jsx. Test whether the Domain IDE works as before.

To trigger the code in listing 12.6, we have to provide a *call to action* in the projection. A call to action can be as simple as a clickable icon. To not litter the projection, we'll only show a call to action icon when hovering over the projection of an expression on which a side-transform can be performed. For this right-transform, I've chosen the right arrow (→) as the icon, encoded as the HTML entity "`&rarr;`". For now, we'll only put a call to action on `Number` objects, so we can mimic typing `1 + 2`. Later on, we'll generalize that so it's easy to switch on both right- and left-transforms for any concept.

Let's add a clickable icon to the projection for `Number`. Listing 12.8 shows the code changes (highlighted in bold) to the `Projection` function in src/frontend/projection.jsx that add a right-transform and corresponding call to action to the projection for `Number`.

Listing 12.8   Adding a right-transform to the projection of `Number`

```
case "Number": {
    const type = ancestors[0].concept === "Attribute"
        ⮕ ? ancestors[0].settings["type"] : undefined
    return <UiWrapped className="inline">
        <div className="side-transformable">
            // ...other pre-existing code...
            <span className="side-transform"
                ⮕ onClick={action(() => {
                replaceWith(newAstObject("Binary Operation",
                    ⮕ { "left operand": astObject }))
            })}>&rarr;</span>
        </div>
    </UiWrapped>
}
```

Wrap the visible contents of the projection in a <div> with CSS class side-transformable.

Perform the right-transform from before.

Make a <span> element with a side-transform CSS class (which we'll define shortly), and an onClick event handler that triggers the right-transform.

We now need to add a little bit of CSS to src/frontend/styling.css to hide and show calls to action for side-transforms.

Listing 12.9   CSS styles for calls to action for side-transforms

```
.side-transform {
    display: none;
}

.side-transformable:hover > .side-transform {
    display: inline-block;
}
```

Define a style to hide elements with calls to action for side-transforms.

Define another style to show these elements when hovering over a container element that has the side-transformable CSS class.

After adding the code from listings 12.8 and 12.9, the domain expert will be able to perform the actions shown in figure 12.25 in the Domain IDE.

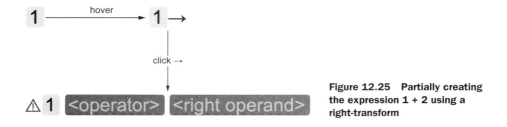

Figure 12.25   Partially creating the expression 1 + 2 using a right-transform

Exercise 12.11

Apply the code changes from listings 12.8 and 12.9, and check whether domain experts can now do right-transforms.

So far, we've only added a right-transform and a corresponding call to action for Num-ber objects. It makes sense to do the same for other subexpressions, such as attribute references and parentheses. Let's generalize the code from listing 12.8 first, so we can use it on the projection of any concept. We already have a place for such generalizations: the `<AstObjectUiWrapper>` component, which wraps the projection of every AST object.

Listing 12.10 shows how to change the `<AstObjectUiWrapper>` component in src/frontend/support-components.jsx to add right-transformability generically.

Listing 12.10   Adding right-transformability generically

> Add an optional rightTransform attribute whose value is either falsy or an argumentless function that performs the right-transform when called like this: rightTransform().

```
export const AstObjectUiWrapper = observer((({ className, astObject,
      deleteAstObject, issues, children,
      rightTransform }) => {                          ◁
   return <div
      className={asClassNameArgument(className,
            "selectable",
            (selection.selected === astObject) && "selected",
            rightTransform && "side-transformable"      ◁
      )}
      // ...existing code...
   >
      {hasIssues && <span className="issue-marker">⚠</span>}
      {children}
      {rightTransform && <span              ▷
            className="side-transform"
            onClick={action(rightTransform)}>&rarr;</span>}
   </div>
})
```

Show a call to action for a right-transform, which triggers the rightTransform function argument.

Tag the outer `<div>` element with the side-transformable CSS class if the rightTransform argument is truthy.

We still have to pass an appropriate `rightTransform` function to `<AstObjectUiWrap-per>` whenever we're projecting an AST object that should be right-transformable. We wrapped all calls to `<AstObjectUiWrapper>` in the "local" `<UiWrapped>` component in the `Projection` function in src/frontend/projection.jsx. Listing 12.11 shows how to adapt (with changes highlighted in bold) the `<UiWrapped>` component for switchable right-transformability.

Listing 12.11   Adapting for switchable right-transformability

```
const UiWrapped = ({ className, children,
      sideTransformable }) => <AstObjectUiWrapper       ◁
   className={className}
   astObject={astObject}
   deleteAstObject={replaceWith}
```

Add a sideTransformable attribute whose truthiness triggers the wrapped astObject AST object to be right-transformable, and later on to be side-transformable.

```
    issues={issues}
    rightTransform={sideTransformable && (() => {
        replaceWith(newAstObject("Binary Operation",
            { "left operand": astObject }))
    })}
>
    {children}
</AstObjectUiWrapper>
```

If sideTransformable contains a falsy value, that value is passed in as the rightTransform argument, preventing anything from happening. If sideTransformable is truthy, the right-transforming code from before is passed in, wrapped in a no-args arrow function.

We'll now replace the additions in listing 12.8 to the projection for `Number` with a simple flag in the form of the Boolean `sideTransformable` attribute. Listing 12.12 shows the corresponding code change (highlighted in bold) to the `Projection` function in src/frontend/projection.jsx.

Listing 12.12   Using the `sideTransformable` attribute

```
case "Number": {
    const type = ancestors[0].concept === "Attribute"
        ? ancestors[0].settings["type"] : undefined
    return <UiWrapped className="inline"
            sideTransformable>
        // ...other pre-existing code...
    </UiWrapped>
}
```

The preexisting code here should be without the additions from listing 12.8, so without the <div> and <span> elements added in that listing.

A useful feature of HTML syntax, which also works for JSX, is that specifying an element's attribute without explicit value assignment gives that attribute the value true. That means this line actually means <UiWrapped ... sideTransformable={true}>.

The other expression concepts for which it makes sense to have side-transforms are `Attribute Reference` and `Parentheses`. It doesn't make much sense to add side-transforms to `Binary Operation` in the same way that we can't interpret a typed-in expression like `1 + +` without additional information.

Exercise 12.12

1 Apply the code changes from listings 12.10 through 12.12.
2 Add right-transforms to the projection for `Attribute Reference` and `Parentheses` by tagging their calls to `<AstObjectUiWrapper>` with `sideTransformable`.
3 Check whether the Domain IDE works as before with added right-transform functionality.

Now that we've added right-transforms for all expression concepts where that makes sense, how about adding *left-transforms*? Exercise 12.13 guides you in doing exactly that.

Exercise 12.13

A *left-transform* looks like this:

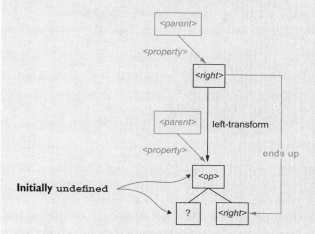

Much like the right-transform, the name "*left*-transform" indicates that it allows the domain expert to extend an existing AST "to the left" by inserting a binary operation into it.

1. Write the code to perform a left-transform as we did in listing 12.6 for the right-transform.
2. Extend the `<AstObjectUiWrapper>` component as follows:
   a. Add another attribute, called `leftTransform`, to its signature. As for `rightTransform`, the value of `leftTransform` should either be falsy or an argumentless function that performs the right-transform.
   b. Use the value of `leftTransform` to conditionally project a call to action in the form of the left-arrow (←), encoded as the HTML entity "`&larr;`", to the left of the wrapped projection.
   c. Tag the outer `<div>` element with the `side-transformable` CSS class when either `leftTransform` or `rightTransform` is truthy.
3. Extend the definition of `<UiWrapped>` with a suitable value for the `left-Transform` attribute.

Triggering side-transforms from the keyboard

Using side-transforms, we're slowly approaching the standard quality of the textual editing experience for expressions, but we're not there yet. One disadvantage of the current implementation is that we have to switch between the keyboard and the pointing device (mouse, trackpad, etc.) to click the call to action and back again.

We could use the keyboard more than we do now if we had a *cursor* like in figure 12.20. Typing a + could trigger an appropriate side-transform, but to determine which side-transform to apply to what AST object, we'd need a cursor-like mechanism.

(continued)

It's entirely possible to augment the projection with keyboard-oriented functionality like that. Unfortunately, I have to leave that out for space reasons, which is doubly unfortunate since no resources I'm aware of treat this to any depth.

Exercise 12.14

1 Play around with creating and editing expressions.
2 What is comfortable about that experience?
3 What aspects could benefit still from some improvement?

In this chapter, you learned what an order of operations is and how it impacts the implementation of expressions in a projectional DSL. We partially remedied that impact by adding virtual "show-only" parentheses to the projection and code generator, and by adding left and right side-transforms, and their corresponding calls to action, to the projection. In the next chapter, we're going to implement a *type system* to assign a *type* to any expression, and we'll formulate and add type-related constraints for expressions. In chapter 14, we'll use the techniques from this and the previous chapter to extend the DSL with the concept of a *business rule*, which relies heavily on the use of expressions.

Summary

- Any expression is evaluated essentially recursively, with the evaluation result of a subexpression replacing that subexpression.
- The order of operations is a specification of how an expression should be evaluated in terms of its subexpressions, a large part of which revolves around the order in which the subexpressions should be evaluated, based on the operators of operations. A well-known example is the PEMDAS rule for evaluating arithmetical expressions.
- The *precedence* or *priority* of operators is an ordering of operators. Operations should be evaluated in descending order of precedence of their operators.
- Expression ASTs can be notated using a shorthand notation that only shows the essential bits of expression ASTs. This shorthand notation helps us think and talk more efficiently about expression ASTs.
- The AST of an expression should be shaped by the order of operations for evaluating that expression. This helps make the (editing) behavior of the projectional DSL match the corresponding linear, textual experience and match pre-existing knowledge, assumptions, and intuition. It also makes it easier to generate code that evaluates that expression at run time from its AST.

- It's possible to construct expression ASTs in the Domain IDE that end up being projected in a way that doesn't match the order of operations, and is even identical to the projection of a different AST. In particular, this can happen when binary operations are nested within one another. The resulting confusion can be prevented by wrapping specific operations in virtual "show-only" parentheses. This solution requires formulating criteria for when this wrapping is necessary and adapting the projection accordingly.

- In expressions written as $x_1<op_1>x_2<op_2>x_3$, the determination of the order of operations divides into two cases, depending on how the precedences of $<op_1>$ and $<op_2>$ compare to each other:
  - *Unequal*—The operation with the operator of higher precedence is evaluated first.
  - *Equal*—If $<op_1>$ and $<op_2>$ are *left-associative*, then $x_1<op_1>x_2$ evaluates first. If $<op_1>$ and $<op_2>$ are *right-associative*, then $x_2<op_2>x_3$ evaluates first.

- A *side-transform* is a transformation of the AST that *transforms* one particular operand *side* (left or right) of a binary operation AST object somewhere in an AST. A *left-transform* is a side-transform that extends the AST to the left, and a *right-transform* does the same but to the right. Side-transforms are useful for mimicking (to some extent) typing an expression in character by character. It reduces the number of actions a domain expert has to perform, and, more importantly, the domain expert doesn't have to plan out the entire creation and editing of an expression.

Implementing a type system

13

This chapter covers

- Computing a type for any expression
- Representing types as objects
- Implementing type checking constraints by comparing computed types

Our example DSL lets domain experts specify each attribute as having a type of `amount`, `date range`, or `percentage`. An attribute's type describes the values that the attribute can hold, and what meaning those values have. (You can think of a type as a set of values—often a very big set.) Attributes that have either `amount` or `percentage` as their type hold numbers, but a value of "$3.0" is different from "3.0%" or even "300%." Attributes of type `date range` can hold a completely different range of values, such as "July 25, 2021 until August 7, 2021." Ultimately, an attribute's type determines what Runtime code is generated for that attribute.

In chapter 9, we added a type checking constraint to make sure that attributes that were dependent on each other through an initial value had matching types. That makes sense when just looking at the DSL content, but it's also crucial to prevent incorrect or faulty behavior of the Runtime.

NOTE For our purposes, we'll say that two types *match* when they are equal. We'll briefly talk about *type compatibility* as well, in the "Beyond type equality" sidebar in section 13.3.

In the chapters 11 and 12, we added expressions, but we didn't get around to implementing type checking constraints for expression concepts. That means that the Domain IDE doesn't report any issues on the expression shown in figure 13.1.

10 % *of* the *rental period* + $ 3.0

Figure 13.1 An expression that doesn't make sense due to the types of its subexpressions

It's already hard to find a sensible meaning for a fraction of a date range, and even if we did, it would probably make even less sense to add the resulting value to a dollar amount. In this chapter, we're going to prevent that sort of nonsense by implementing a *type system* for our example DSL. A type system does the following:

- It represents ranges of domain-specific values as *types*.
- It computes the types of expressions (and possibly of other DSL content that can be considered to have, or even be, a type).
- It implements type checking constraints by comparing computed types, and it reports violations of those as *type errors* with messages that help the domain experts fix the problem.

The *type of an expression* is the type of the result of the evaluation of that expression for any combination of data accessed in the expression. Being able to compute the type of any expression allows us to implement type checking constraints. In particular, if an attribute defines an expression as its value, the type of that expression should match the attribute's type as well. An example is `rental price after discount`, which specifies an expression (shown later, in figure 13.3) as its value, but also an `amount` type.

The goal of a type system is to add *type safety* to your DSL by allowing you to implement type checking constraints. When done right, a type system allows you to do that without suffering from a combinatorial explosion when you introduce new types, new (binary) operators, or new expression concepts. Figure 13.2 introduces the type system as a new component within the constraints aspect of the Domain IDE's architecture and highlights its role and its relations to other components.

Typically, a DSL's generator uses the type system to generate correct, or even optimized, code. A good example is when you generate code for a statically typed target language such as Java. Such code typically specifies explicit types for values, fields, variables, etc. The DSL's type system helps by computing types for those, which can then be mapped to types in the target language.

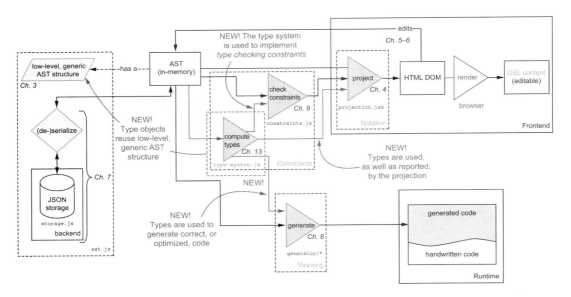

Figure 13.2   The Domain IDE's architecture, highlighting and annotating the new type system component and its relations to other components

It turns out that the code generator for our example DSL doesn't need computed types to generate correct JavaScript code. It relies on the AST not having any type errors, but it doesn't call the type system itself.

13.1   Computing types of expressions

In this section, we're going to explore what we mean when we say "the type of an expression" and how we can compute that type. We'll take the value expression of the `rental price after discount` attribute as an example (figure 13.3).

the *rental price before discount* **- the** *discount* **of the** *rental price before discount*

Figure 13.3   The rental price expression

When evaluated, this expression should produce a value of type `amount`—after all, that's what was specified as the type of the attribute. To check the attribute's specified type, and the type of any evaluation of the expression match, let's compute the type of that expression.

We're going to compute a type for this expression by considering how we'd evaluate it according to the PEMDAS rule—or more generally, the order of operations. We'll use a diagram that starts with the entire expression from figure 13.3, and instead of gradually replacing subexpressions with the results of their evaluations, we'll replace them with the *types* of their evaluations, as shown in figure 13.4.

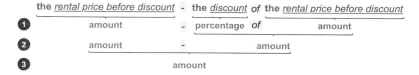

Figure 13.4 **The type computation of the rental price expression, in terms of the notation**

These are the steps in this evaluation process:

1 The type of an `Attribute Reference` is the specified type of the attribute it references. Evaluating an attribute reference results in a value of the specified type of the referenced attribute. In this case, the two attribute references to `rental price before discount` both have type `amount`, and the reference to `discount` has type `percentage`.

2 The "*of*" operator has higher precedence than the "−" operator, so we evaluate that first. Taking a percentage of an amount produces an amount, so the type of the "*of*" operation is `amount`.

3 The "−" operator with two amounts as operands again produces an amount, so the type of the entire expression is `amount`.

In practice, we're not going to perform type computations on notated DSL content. Instead, we're going to run the type computation directly on expression ASTs. Let's redo the type computation using an AST for the expression in figure 13.3, shown in shorthand notation in figure 13.5.

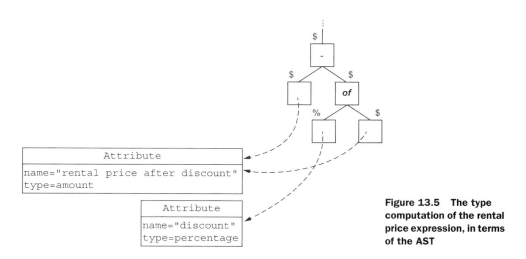

Figure 13.5 **The type computation of the rental price expression, in terms of the AST**

As when evaluating any expression AST, we can start at the leaves of the tree and work our way up. Once we've computed a type for an AST object corresponding to a subexpression, we simply put the computed type on top of the AST object's box. To save space, I've used "$" as shorthand for the amount type and "%" for percentage.

This computation looks suspiciously like a recursive function on an AST. Let's implement a recursive typeOf function that computes the type of an expression given as an AST object. Listing 13.1 shows the first iteration of the type system's implementation. Put the following code in a new src/language/type-system.js file that will contain the entire type system.

Listing 13.1   The first iteration of the type system's implementation

Define a separate function for computing the type of an attribute. We'll use this function later more often.

```
const typeOfAttribute = (attribute) =>
    attribute.settings["type"]

const typeOf = (astObject) => {
    const { settings } = astObject
    switch (astObject.concept) {
        case "Attribute": return typeOfAttribute(
            astObject)
        case "Attribute Reference": return typeOf(
            settings["attribute"].ref)
        // ...cases for other expression concepts
            (and a default case) to follow...
    }
}
module.exports.typeOf = typeOf
```

Even though Attribute is not an expression concept, it's obvious that we can compute its type as the value of its "type" property.

The type of an attribute reference is the type of the referenced attribute.

The type computation for a binary operation is more intricate. We have to consider all combinations of the three types for the left and the right operand, across the two operators "−" and "*of.*" That makes for a total of 18 combinations, only 2 of which correspond to the two binary operations in figure 13.5.

Exercise 13.1
Try to complete the following two tables.

typeOf(↓ - →)	amount	date range	percentage
amount	amount		
date range			
percentage			

typeOf (↓ *of* →)	amount	date range	percentage
amount			
date range			
percentage	amount		x

Each cell corresponds to the type of the evaluation result of a binary operation "*<left operand> <op> <right operand>.*" Try to figure out the correct type (among the three known types) for every empty cell, or conclude that there isn't one (indicated by the x symbol).

You'll learn from exercise 13.1 that very few of these combinations make complete sense. The "*of*" operation in figure 13.1 is an example of a subexpression for which the evaluation result doesn't have an obviously correct type, as we discussed in the introduction to this chapter. In section 13.2 we'll implement type checking constraints to report appropriate errors on any combination that doesn't make complete sense.

What can we do when there's no obviously correct type for an expression? There are two ways that typeOf can be called:

- *During the execution of a type checking constraint*—The constraint relies on an answer from the type system to decide whether to report an error, and if so, with what message.
- *Recursively by itself*—The type computation of some expression relies on the types computed for its subexpressions.

We can't just abort a type computation by throwing an Error, or do something else that causes it to crash altogether. Because of this, the type computation of any expression should try to return a *"best-effort" type* if the expression doesn't make sense. Typically, a best-effort type is the type that would be computed for the expression after some minimal modification to (the types of) one or more subexpressions. Often, we can come up with such a best-effort type if we effectively ignore (the type of) one of the subexpressions. When typeOf returns a best-effort type for an expression, at least one type checking constraint should report an appropriate error on that expression. Type computation and type checking constraints are essentially two sides of the same coin.

As an example, it's quite reasonable that typeOf always returns amount for any expression "*<left operand> of <amount-typed right operand>.*" Likewise, it makes sense that "*<percentage-typed left operand> - <right operand>*" always produces a percentage. In both cases, we'd still want to produce a type error.

Exercise 13.2

- Copy the tables from (your execution of) exercise 13.1, and consider all occurrences of the x symbol:
  - If a best-effort type exists for that cell, replace the x symbol with that type, and mark it with a ! symbol. (The ! symbol means we should report an appropriate error for operations with that type combination. We're going to figure out what error to report later.)
  - Otherwise, leave the x symbol in.

NOTE In theory, we could give some meaning to subtracting values of type date range from each other, or to taking a percentage of a date range value. In practice, such a meaning is likely going to be quite confusing (or even "magical") for the domain experts. In my experience, it's better to avoid stretching the meaning of operators in that way. Instead, you could think of introducing a new kind of expression (either as a special-purpose operator, or as a separate expression concept) with its own specialized notation.

Whenever no best-effort type exists, typeOf still should return *some* value, as discussed previously. To that end, we'll introduce a new, very special type: the "*untype.*" This type is and isn't a type at the same time. We're going to return it from typeOf to let callers of typeOf know that no sensible type could be computed for the given expression. Similar to the three existing types, we're going to represent this "untype" in our code with the string "untype".

Figure 13.6 sums up the behavior of the typeOf function.

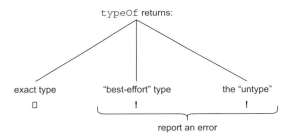

Figure 13.6 The categories of types returned by typeOf, and their consequences

Introducing a new type also means that typeOf will have to handle it correctly. We're going to do that over the course of the next exercises, and in listing 13.2.

WARNING Best-effort types and the untype have a tendency to "bubble up" from subexpressions to their ancestors. That also means that errors would be reported on many of the ancestors of that subexpression, obscuring the location of the root problem in the process. To avoid that, type computations should always try to produce a correct or best-effort type, even when a subexpression is untyped.

Exercise 13.3

- Copy the tables from exercise 13.2, and expand them to include "untype" as a possible type of the left operand, right operand, or both.
- Replace all remaining occurrences of the x symbol with "untype" and the ! symbol.
- Complete the remaining cells as before, with either
  - An obviously correct type
  - A best-effort type or "untype," both marked with the ! symbol.

Exercise 13.4

Reformulate the type tables from exercise 13.3 as logical conditions in terms of the types of the left and right operands. Abbreviate those types as *<left type>* and *<right type>*. Use any notation that you're comfortable with, such as (pseudo-)code or mathematical notation.

We can now implement the conditions we came up with as answers to exercise 13.4. Listing 13.2 shows the type system's implementation after updating it for the "untype" and expanding the `typeOf` function for binary operations.

Listing 13.2   The second iteration of the type system's implementation

Represent the "untype" as a string.

Define and export a function that determines whether the given type is numeric.

```
const { isAstObject, isAstReference } = require("../common/ast")

const isNumberType = (type) =>
    type === "amount" || type === "percentage")
module.exports.isNumberType = isNumberType

const untype = "untype"
module.exports.untype = untype

const typeOfBinaryOperation = (operator,
        leftType, rightType) => {
    switch (operator) {
        case "-": {
            if (isNumberType(leftType)) {
                return leftType
            }
            if (leftType === untype
                    && isNumberType(rightType)) {
                return rightType
            }
            return untype
        }
}
```

Implement the type computation separately for binary operations. That helps with code readability and testability.

If <left type> (= type of the <left operand>) is numeric, return <left type>.

If <left type> = "untype" and <right type> (= type of the <right operand>) is numeric, return <right type>.

Otherwise, return "untype."

Return
"untype" in all
other cases.

```
        case "of": return rightType === "amount"
            ⮕ ? rightType
            ⮕ : untype
        default: return untype
      }
    }
```

If <right type> =
"amount", then
"amount", otherwise,
"untype."

```
    const typeOfAttribute = (attribute) =>
        attribute.settings["type"]
```

```
    const typeOf = (astObject) => {
        if (!isAstObject(astObject)) {
            return untype
        }
```

If a non-AST object (such as undefined
or the placeholder object) is passed
in, return "untype."

```
        const { settings } = astObject
        switch (astObject.concept) {
            case "Attribute": return typeOfAttribute(astObject)
            case "Attribute Reference": return
```

Check whether the
reference is valid.

If it isn't,
return
"untype."

```
                ⮕ isAstReference(settings["attribute"])
                ? typeOfAttribute(
                    ⮕ settings["attribute"].ref)
                : untype
```

If the reference is valid,
return the type of the
referenced attribute.

```
            case "Binary Operation": {
                const leftType =
                    ⮕ typeOf(settings["left operand"])
                const rightType = typeOf(settings["right operand"])
                return typeOfBinaryOperation(
                    ⮕ settings["operator"], leftType, rightType)
            }
            case "Parentheses": return typeOf(settings["sub"])
            // ...cases for the other expression concepts to follow...
            default: return untype
        }
    }
    module.exports.typeOf = typeOf
```

Return "untype" in
all other cases.

Call the type computation
implemented specifically
for binary operations.

Compute the types of the
left and right operands.

Exercise 13.5
- Create a new src/language/type-system.js file, and populate it with the code from listing 13.2. This file will contain the entire type system.
- Write unit tests to assert that the results of the `typeOfBinaryOperation` function match the tables from exercise 13.3.

We haven't handled the expression concepts `Number` and `Parentheses` so far. For `Parentheses`, it's obvious that its type is the type of its value for the "sub" property. Listing 13.3 shows how to implement this by adding a `case` for `Parentheses` to the `switch` statement in the `typeOf` function in src/language/type-system.js.

Listing 13.3 Computing the type of a parenthesized expression

```
case "Parentheses": return typeOf(settings["sub"])
```

We decided in chapter 4 to determine whether a `Number` object represented an amount or a percentage by looking at the attribute that the number was the value of. That means we have to figure out which attribute contains that number. We can do that the same way we did earlier for functions similar to the `typeOf` function: by passing in, as the second argument of `typeOf`, an array of the AST objects of the ancestors (in reverse order) of the first argument of `typeOf`. That allows us to look up and inspect objects elsewhere in the AST—not even necessarily inside the expression AST itself.

Listing 13.4 shows the corresponding code changes (highlighted in bold) to the `typeOf` function in src/language/type-system.js. Specifically, it adds passing in ancestors and using them to compute the type of `Number` objects.

Listing 13.4 Type computation for `Number` objects using ancestors

```
const typeOf = (astObject, ancestors) => {
    if (!isAstObject(astObject)) {
        return untype
    }
    const { settings } = astObject
    const nextAncestors =
        [ astObject, ...ancestors ]
    switch (astObject.concept) {
        case "Attribute": return typeOfAttribute(astObject)
        case "Attribute Reference": return
            isAstReference(settings["attribute"])
                ? typeOfAttribute(settings["attribute"].ref)
                : untype
        case "Binary Operation": {
            const leftType =
                typeOf(settings, nextAncestors)
            const rightType =
                typeOf(settings, nextAncestors)
            return
                typeOfBinaryOperation(settings["operator"], leftType, rightType)
        }
        case "Number": {
            if (ancestors.length === 0) {
                return untype
            }
            const parent = ancestors[0]
            if (parent.concept === "Attribute") {
                return typeOfAttribute(parent)
            }
```

Annotations:

Precompute the ancestors array for any child of astObject. (points to `const nextAncestors = [ astObject, ...ancestors ]`)

Without ancestors, there's not enough information to infer a type, so return "untype" instead. (points to `return untype`)

If the number is directly contained by a parent Attribute, that attribute's type determines the number's type. (points to `if (parent.concept === "Attribute")` block)

```
        return untype
    }
    case "Parentheses": return typeOf(settings, ancestors)
    default: return untype
  }
}
```
}

Return "untype" in all other situations.

> **NOTE** Computing the type of something from its context (and not just from subexpressions) is called *type inference*. In listing 13.4, we implemented a very simple example of type inference: computing the type of a number value *directly* contained by an attribute. Type inference can be made much smarter than that, such as by using the Hindley-Milner type inference algorithm (explained in Wikipedia: https://mng.bz/Ddvn). Unfortunately, that's outside the scope of this book.

We can now use the `typeOf` function in the `<Projection>` function to determine the projection of a number. Listing 13.5 shows the corresponding code changes (highlighted in bold) to src/frontend/projection.jsx to use the `typeOf` function in the projection of `Number` objects.

Listing 13.5   Using the `typeOf` function to project `Number` objects

```
import { typeOf } from "../language/type-system"

// ...other code...

    case "Number": {
        const type = typeOf(astObject, ancestors)
        // ...other pre-existing code...
```

Import the typeOf function.

Inside the switch statement in the <Projection> function ...

... use the typeOf function instead of directly inspecting the parent.

Before this change, `type` was computed explicitly by inspecting the first element of the `ancestors` array. This computation also assumed the AST to have a certain, very specific shape. It's now replaced with a generic call to the type system that doesn't make that assumption.

This code change is minimal, but it moves the type logic out of the projection code, where it doesn't belong. This also makes it possible to expand that type logic so it can deal with a wider range of DSL content.

Exercise 13.6
- Apply the code additions and changes from listings 13.3 through 13.5.
- Check whether the Domain IDE's editor still works and projects `Number` objects correctly. You might need to create new attributes for this. These should have expressions as their "computed as" values that use "–" and "*of*" operators with numbers as operands.

Exercise 13.7

Expand the projection to compute the type for all expression concepts, and show it as a simple tooltip (hover text) using the `title` attribute on an appropriate, enclosing `<div>` element.

Hint: You'll probably want to change the `<AstObjectUiWrapper>` component, adding an optional attribute `type` that passes a type to be shown. Then you can add a Boolean attribute to the `<UiWrapped>` component to trigger type computation.

13.2   Implementing type checking constraints

In the previous section, we computed types of expressions. In this section, we're going to implement type checking constraints. Violations of these alert domain experts to expressions that don't make sense type-wise. The error reported for such a violation should give a meaningful message as to why that is, so they can fix the problem.

In chapter 9, we implemented one type checking constraint on the `attribute` property of an `Attribute Reference` object. The implementation of that check assumes that the attribute reference is directly contained by an attribute as the value of that attribute—see figure 13.7. It then compares the type of that containing attribute with the type of the target attribute. Whenever these types aren't equal, we report the violation on the containing attribute with the text, "The types of this attribute and the attribute named '*<other attribute>*' must match, but they are: '*<type of this attribute>*', resp., '*<type of other attribute>*'". The error message helpfully reports the computed types of the containing and the target attribute.

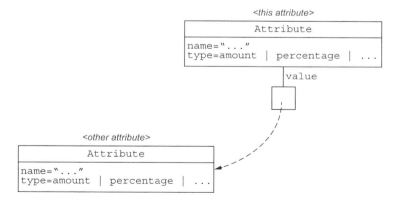

Figure 13.7   The assumption underlying the implementation of the existing type checking constraint on `Attribute Reference`

This is not optimal for two reasons:

- This constraint's implementation only works for `Attribute Reference`, not for any of the other expression concepts that could be the value of an attribute.
- The assumption about the shape of the AST is wrong most of the time. It's already wrong for any of the attribute references occurring in the computed value of the `rental price after discount` attribute.

Let's use the `typeOf` function to implement a type checking constraint on the `value` of an `Attribute` that's correct *and* works for all values, not just for values that happen to be attribute references. To do so, we'll change the code in src/language/constraints.js as follows:

1 Add the following importing statement to the file somewhere where it makes sense: `const { typeOf } = require("./type-system")`.
2 Remove the `else` branch in the `case` for `Attribute Reference` inside the big `switch` statement in the `issuesFor` function in the same file. This `else` branch assumed that any attribute reference is always directly contained by an attribute.
3 Add the `if` statement in listing 13.6 to the `case` for `Attribute` in the same `switch` statement in the `typeOf` function.

Exercise 13.8
- Make the code changes to src/language/constraints.js described in the previous list.
- Check whether this constraint works, such as through testing by hand.

Listing 13.6 Type checking the `value` of an `Attribute`

Use the typeOf function to compute the attribute's declared type, even though settings["type"] works as well.

Compute the type of the attribute's value, passing in an updated array of ancestors.

Perform a string comparison to check whether the types are equal.

```
case "Attribute": {
    // ...code that checks existing constraints...
    if (isAstObject(settings["value"])) {
        const typeOfAttribute =
            typeOf(astObject, ancestors)
        const typeOfValue =
            typeOf(settings["value"], [ astObject, ...ancestors ])
        if (typeOfAttribute !== typeOfValue) {
            issues.push(
`The types of this attribute and its value must match,
    but they are: '${typeOfAttribute}', resp., '${typeOfValue}'`)
        }
    }
}
```

If they aren't equal, produce a meaningful error message.

Changing the src/language/constraints.js file according to the preceding description (and exercise 13.8) implements a type checking constraint that works for all attributes having values, not just for an attribute reference that happens to be directly contained by an attribute.

Finally, let's implement a type checking constraint on `Binary Operation` so that we're covering all concepts that we consider to have a type. Add the following `type-IssuesForBinaryOperator` function to the src/language/constraints.js file. This function implements type checking constraints specifically for `Binary Operation`.

Listing 13.7 Type checking constraints on `Binary Operation`

```
const { isNumberType, typeOf } = require("./type-system")

const typeIssuesForBinaryOperator = (binaryOperation,
    ➥ ancestors) => {
    const issues = []
    const { settings } = binaryOperation
    const nextAncestors =
    ➥ [ binaryOperation, ...ancestors ]
    const leftType =
    ➥ typeOf(settings["left operand"], nextAncestors)
    const rightType = typeOf(settings["right operand"], nextAncestors)
    switch (settings["operator"]) {
        case "-": {
            if (!isNumberType(leftType)) {
                issues.push(`The left operand of this '-' operator has
                ➥ type '${leftType}', but must have a number type
                ➥ ('amount', or 'percentage')`)
            }
            if (!isNumberType(rightType)) {
                issues.push(`The right operand of this '-' operator has
                ➥ type '${rightType}', but must have a number type
                ➥ ('amount', or 'percentage')`)
            }
            if (leftType !== rightType) {
                issues.push(`The types of both operands of this '-'
                ➥ operator differ
                ➥ (left '${leftType}' vs. '${rightType}' right),
                ➥ but must be the same`)
            }
            break
        }
        case "of": {
            if (leftType !== "percentage") {
                issues.push(`The left operand of this 'of' operator has
                ➥ type '${leftType}', but must have type 'percentage'`)
            }
            if (rightType !== "amount") {
                issues.push(`The right operand of this 'of' operator has
                ➥ type '${rightType}', but must have type 'amount'`)
            }
            break
        }
        default: {
            console.warn(`no type constraints checking implemented for
```

Define a function specifically for the type checking constraints of a binary operation.

Precompute the ancestors array for any child of binaryOperation.

Compute the types of the left and right operands.

Check that both the left and right operands of a "-" operator are numeric.

Check for the only valid combination of types for an "of" operator: <percentage> of <amount>.

Produce a warning on the console to alert about unhandled operators.

```
         ⮩ binary operation with operator '${settings["operator"]}'`)
      }
   }
   return issues
}
```

Now we can use the `typeIssuesForBinaryOperator` function in the `case` for `Binary Operation` in the `switch` statement in the `issuesFor` function in src/language/constraints.js. The following listing shows the corresponding code change, highlighted in bold.

Listing 13.8   Using the `typeIssuesForBinaryOperator` function

```
case "Binary Operation": {
   // ...code that implements the existing
      ⮩ unspecified content constraints...
   issues.push(...typeIssuesForBinaryOperator(astObject, ancestors))
   break
}
```

Exercise 13.9
- Perform the code changes in listings 13.7 and 13.8.
- Check whether the type checking constraints added for binary operations work as expected.

Implementing type checking constraints takes some effort, but that's not surprising given the amount of detail we saw in the tables in exercise 13.3. Even then, the type computation does a lot of the heavy lifting on its own.

13.3   *Representing types as objects*

Until now we have represented types as strings, which seemed to work OK for our small example DSL. When your DSL grows, this approach can become cumbersome. You need to make sure that string representations of types don't clash with each other. It might also become convenient and useful to group the types and subject them to a hierarchy. You even could *parameterize* types, similar to Java generic types or the `varchar(<n>)` from SQL—but be aware: that would introduce a lot of complexity! With types represented as strings, you'll probably soon be doing lots of horrible string manipulation to work with types.

Luckily, this problem has a simple solution: represent types as *structured data* instead of strings. We're already quite familiar with a specific format for structured data: the low-level format for AST objects used throughout this book. Let's reuse that format to represent any type as a *type object* instead of as a string.

NOTE   Language engineers often use the term "type literal" for what I call "type object" here. Regardless of the precise term, the idea is the same: a machine-processable representation of a specific type.

The values of the `amount` and `percentage` types are both numbers, but they are different types nevertheless. Let's use objects of a new concept label `Number Type` to represent these types. To distinguish between `amount` and `percentage` types, we'll give the `Number Type` concept a property called `unit`. For that property, the value "$" will correspond to the `amount` type, and "%" will correspond to `percentage`. (The notation uses these units as well: "$" as prefix and "%" as postfix.)

The values of the `date range` type are quite different: these are pairs (*<from>*, *<to>*) of dates, with *<from>* predating *<to>*. Let's introduce an `Interval Type` concept label to represent this type. We'll also use a `unit` property to express that *<from>* and *<to>* are dates that are accurate up to a day.

We can now map the four existing types to type objects, as shown in table 13.1

Table 13.1 The type objects for built-in types

Type name	ID	Concept label	Settings
amount	numberType_amount	Number Type	`{ "unit": "$" }`
date range	numberType_dateRange	Interval Type	`{ "unit": "day" }`
percentage	numberType_percentage	Number Type	`{ "unit": "%" }`
untype	untype_untype	Untype	`{}`

We'll interpret type objects as follows:

- The concept label differentiates type "classes" (such as "numbers" versus "intervals") from each other.
- The settings capture specific properties of a type (such as the unit).

These objects look a lot like regular AST objects, but there are some differences:

- A type object is not necessarily contained by an AST. It typically exists independently as a "vehicle" for type information.
- Instead of autogenerating a random ID for each type object, we set the ID to a value of our own choosing. That allows us to use this ID as the type object's identity—provided we don't touch the settings, of course. We'll use an ID of the form *<camel-cased concept label>_<camel-cased type name>*. An ID of that form always differs from an autogenerated, random ID.

The code in listing 13.9 defines the type objects for built-in types. It has to be added to the top of src/language/type-system.js.

Listing 13.9 Defining type objects for built-in types

```
const { camelCase } = require("../generator/template-utils")

const typeObject = (name, concept, settings) => ({
    id: camelCase(concept) + "_" + camelCase(name),
    concept,
```

Define a factory function for type objects. The first argument is the type's name.

Generate a stable ID from the type's concept label and name.

Define the concept label as a constant string.

The third settings argument of this function is optional: if it's falsy, replace it with an empty object: {}.

```
        settings: settings || {}     ◁
    })
```

Define a factory function specifically for the number type objects.

```
    const numberTypeConceptLabel = "Number Type"
    const numberType = (name, unit) =>                    ◁
        ⟼ typeObject(name, numberTypeConceptLabel, { unit })
    const isNumberType = (typeObject) =>                  ◁
        ⟼ typeObject.concept === numberTypeConceptLabel
    module.exports.isNumberType = isNumberType

    const untypeName = "Untype"
    const untype = typeObject(untypeName, untypeName)     ◁
    module.exports.untype = untype

    const builtInTypes = {
        "amount": numberType("amount", "$"),
        "date range":
            ⟼ typeObject("date range", "Interval Type", { unit: "day" }),
        "percentage": numberType("percentage", "%"),
        [untypeName]: untype                              ◁
    }
    module.exports.builtInTypes = builtInTypes
```

Redefine the function that determines whether the given type object is numeric.

Redefine the "untype" as a type object.

This JavaScript object literal syntax evaluates the expression between square brackets, [<expression>], and uses it as the key of this key-value pair. In this case, it produces the key-value pair "untype": untype.

Construct a map from the names of built-in types to their corresponding type objects. In particular, we can map the value of the setting for "type" on an attribute as builtInTypes[attribute.settings["type"]].

The constant `builtInTypes` map effectively serves as a *standard library* of built-in types.

Replacing the "stringy" representation of types with type objects breaks some existing code: we'll have to change src/language/type-system.js and src/language/constraints.js to take the object nature of types into account. First of all, we'll replace all occurrences of `"amount"`, `"date range"`, and `"percentage"` as type representations with a lookup, `builtInTypes[<type as string>]`. Second, when we represented types as strings, we could check whether they matched by comparing them as strings. To fix that, we'll add a comparison function for type objects to src/language/type-system.js—see the next listing. The `areEqual` function checks whether two given type objects are equal, meaning that the types match.

Listing 13.10   The `areEqual` function checks equality of type objects

```
const areEqual = (actual, expected) =>
    ⟼ actual.id === expected.id
module.exports.areEqual = areEqual
```

Types are now represented as objects that look like AST objects. In particular, their identity is completely determined by their ID. That means it's enough to just compare the IDs to check equality. We're not going to rely on JavaScript's object equality to compare type objects, because it's not reliable when using MobX and web bundlers.

> ## Beyond type equality: Type compatibility
>
> Our notion of "matching types" here is quite simplistic: two types are considered to match, or be *compatible*, precisely when they're equal.
>
> In practice, *type compatibility* is often defined through *assignability*. A type *<T>* is *assignable* to a type *<U>* precisely when any value of type *<T>* can be assigned as a value of type *<U>*. This gives type compatibility a *direction*: if *<T>* is assignable to *<U>*, it's not necessarily true that *<U>* is also assignable to *<T>*.
>
> Assignability is a more general mechanism than the following notions:
>
> - *Inheritance/generalization*—A type *<T>* can be declared to be a *subtype* of a *supertype<U>*. Alternatively, we can say that *<T>* *inherits* from *<U>*, or that *<U>* is a *generalization* of *<T>*.
> - *Type coercion*—A type coercion from a type *<T>* to a type *<U>* is a transformation that coerces a value *<t>* of type *<T>* to a value *<u>* of type *<U>* in an "appropriate" way. This transformation is automatically applied to a *<T>*-typed value whenever a value of type *<U>* is expected.
>
> In both these cases, we can say "*<T>* is assignable to *<U>*."

After adding the `areEqual` function, we modify the existing code in src/language/type-system.js to use it. The following listing shows the corresponding code changes, highlighted in bold.

Listing 13.11   Using the `areEqual` function with type objects

```
const typeOfBinaryOperation = (operator, leftType, rightType) => {
    switch (operator) {
        case "-": {
            if (isNumberType(leftType)) {
                return leftType
            }
            if (areEqual(leftType, untype) && isNumberType(rightType)) {
                return rightType
            }
            return untype
        }
        case "of": return areEqual(rightType,
            builtInTypes["amount"])
                ? rightType
                : untype
        default: return untype
    }
}

const typeOfAttribute = (attribute) =>
    builtInTypes[attribute.settings] || untype
```

Look up the type object for the type with name "amount" in the builtInTypes map.

The type object indexed by the attribute's declared type, or the "untype" if there's no corresponding built-in type.

The lookup `builtInTypes[…]` happening in the `typeOfAttribute` function in listing 13.11 can produce `undefined` either because the attribute didn't declare a type yet, or because it declares one without a corresponding built-in type object. In those cases, we return the "untype" instead.

Before, we also used the string representing a type as a textual representation for display purposes. In the message reporting a violation of a type checking constraint to the domain experts, we just quoted those type strings. Now that types are represented by objects, the same approach would produce an unhelpful `[object Object]` for every type. Listing 13.12 implements a `typeAsText` function in src/language/type-system.js that renders a textual representation of a given type object.

Listing 13.12   Rendering a textual representation of a type object

```
const typeAsText = (typeObject) => {              ◁─┐   Define a function that renders a textual
    const { settings } = typeObject                     representation of a given type object.
    switch (typeObject.concept) {                       If that type object is not familiar, it
        case "Interval Type": {                         returns a best-effort representation.
            switch (settings["unit"]) {
                case "day": return "date range"                      ◁──────
                default: return
              ➡     `Interval Type(unit='${settings["unit"]}')`
            }                                             Return a textual representation
        }                                                quoting the unit as a fallback
        case numberTypeConceptLabel: {                        for unhandled units.
            switch (settings["unit"]) {
                case "$": return "amount"               Return a sensible fallback (just
                case "%": return "percentage"           as in the case for Interval Type).
                default: return                     ◁─┘
              ➡     `Number Type(unit='${settings["unit"]}')`
            }
        }
        case untypeName: return untypeName
        default: return                                                ◁──────
          ➡     `type object(concept='${typeObject.concept}', ???)`
    }
}                                                    Return a textual representation that gives
}                                                    some partial information about the given
module.exports.typeAsText = typeAsText               type object. We don't print the settings
                                                     object in case it has a cyclic reference.
```

Now we can propagate using type objects to the constraints implementation in src/language/constraints.js. We replace all occurrences of `'${<type>}'` in template literals with `'${typeAsText(<type object>)}'`, wrapping the `typeAsText` function (imported from src/language/type-system.js) around the type object. We also use the `areEqual` function to check type equality. Listing 13.13 shows the corresponding code changes, highlighted in bold. As you can see, the code changes to the constraints implementation are quite minimal.

Listing 13.13   Propagating using type objects to constraints checking

Import the new type functions.

```
const { areEqual, builtInTypes,
    isNumberType, typeAsText, typeOf } =
    require("./type-system")
```

This code block resides in the
Attribute case inside the switch
statement in the issuesFor function.

```
    if (isAstObject(settings["value"])) {
        const typeOfAttribute =
            typeOf(astObject, ancestors)
        const typeOfValue =
            typeOf(settings["value"], [ astObject, ...ancestors ])
        if (!areEqual(typeOfAttribute, typeOfValue)) {
            issues.push(
`The types of this attribute and its value must match,
    but they are: '${typeAsText(typeOfAttribute)}',
    resp., '${typeAsText(typeOfValue)}'`)
        }
    }
    // ...
```

Use typeOf to compute the
attribute's declared type, as
well as the type of its value.

Use the areEqual
function to
compare those
two types.

Wrap type objects with typeAsText(\<type object\>)
before displaying them to the domain expert.

```
const typeIssuesForBinaryOperator = (binaryOperation, ancestors) => {
    // ...other code...
    switch (settings["operator"]) {
        case "-": {
            if (!isNumberType(leftType)) {
                issues.push(`The left operand of this '-' operator has type
    '${typeAsText(leftType)}', but must have a number type
    ('amount', or 'percentage')`)
            }
            if (!isNumberType(rightType)) {
                issues.push(`The right operand of this '-' operator has type
    '${typeAsText(rightType)}', but must have a number type
    ('amount', or 'percentage')`)
            }
            if (!areEqual(leftType, rightType)) {
                issues.push(`The types of both operands of this '-' operator
    differ (left '${typeAsText(leftType)}' vs.
    '${typeAsText(rightType)}' right),
    but must be the same`)
            }
            break
        }
        case "of": {
            if (!areEqual(leftType, builtInTypes["percentage"])) {
                issues.push(
                    `The left operand of this 'of' operator has type
                        '${typeAsText(leftType)}',
                        but must have type 'percentage'`)
            }
            if (!areEqual(rightType, builtInTypes["amount"])) {
                issues.push(
```

```
                        `The right operand of this 'of' operator has type
                    ⇒   '${typeAsText(rightType)}',
                    ⇒   but must have type 'amount'`)
                }
                break
            }
            // ...
        }
    }
}
```

Finally, we also have to change the projection code for Number: the next listing shows the corresponding code changes (highlighted in bold) in src/frontend/projection.jsx.

Listing 13.14 Using type objects in the projection of a Number

```
import { areEqual, builtInTypes, typeOf } from "../language/type-system"

// ...in the switch statement in the <Projection> function:...
    case "Number": {
        const type = typeOf(value, ancestors)
        return <UiWrapped className="inline" sideTransformable showType>
            {areEqual(type, builtInTypes["amount"])
            ⇒   && <span className="keyword">$</span>}
            <NumberValue editState={editStateFor("value")}
                ⇒   placeholderText="<number>" />
            {areEqual(type, builtInTypes["date range"])
            ⇒   && <span className="keyword whitespace-left">days</span>}
            {areEqual(type, builtInTypes["percentage"])
            ⇒   && <span className="keyword">%</span>}
        </UiWrapped>
    }
```

Finally, we have to change the code you implemented for exercise 13.7, wrapping typeAsText(…) around any computed type.

Exercise 13.10
- Perform all code changes from listings 13.9 through 13.14.
- Wrap every quotation of a (computed) type with a call in typeAsText(…). (Also, make sure you import typeAsText from src/language/type-system.js.) This affects the src/language/constraints.js file and the <AstObjectUi-Wrapper> component, provided you completed exercise 13.7.
- Check whether everything still works as expected.

NOTE Often, AST objects make perfect sense as type objects. In our example DSL, any record type can itself be seen as a type, as already implied by the name. Reusing the AST object format would allow us to conveniently use the record type directly as a type object.

Exercise 13.11

Experiment with promoting record types to types by regarding the record type AST object as a type object. Make sure you can undo all the changes during this experiment, as we don't want that to actually use that.

- Extend the `typeOf` function so it works on any record type. Calling `typeOf` with a record type value should return that record type, which is then "promoted" to a type object.
- Also adapt the `typeAsText` function and the constraints checking implementation.

Exercise 13.12

Instead of the expression in figure 13.3, we could have used the expression "(100% – the discount) of the rental price before discount":

(100 % - the *discount*) *of* the *rental price before discount*

- Replace the value of the `rental price after discount` attribute with that expression.
- What aspect of this doesn't work? Do you see a way of improving that aspect, preferably using the type system?

Exercise 13.13

We put some effort into checking that the type of an attribute's value matches its defined type. Think about how you can turn this around and *infer* the attribute's type from its value (when it has one).

What changes would you have to make to the DSL implementation? What would become simpler, and what more complicated (for both the domain experts and the language engineer)?

Hint: This is a very open-ended exercise. Its main purpose is to get you thinking about the DSL's design, and whether/how type inference could improve that.

Exercise 13.14

So far, we've only implemented the type computation for the "–" and "*of*" operations. We haven't yet taken care of the "+", "*", "/", and "^" operators we added in the previous two chapters. Do that now, following these steps:

1 Make a combination table for the operator, as in exercise 13.3. As before, it's OK to use the "untype" where necessary.

(continued)

2 Reformulate that table as a logical condition in terms of *<left type>* and *<right type>*, as in exercise 13.4.

3 Implement that logical condition in code.

Note: These steps form a useful pattern for implementing the type computation for binary operators.

What did you run into when performing these steps for the "^" operator? How did you solve them? Did you have to add a type to the system? Hint: If you want, you can forget about the "^" operator for now.

In this chapter, you learned how to implement a simple type system that can compute the types of expressions. With that, we were able to implement the type checking constraints that were still missing for binary operations, with relatively little code. We then changed our code to represent types as objects with the low-level structure of AST objects.

In chapter 14, we're going to extend the type system again when we add a couple of binary operators that we need for formulating business rules.

Summary

- A DSL uses a *type system* to help domain experts write down expressions that can be meaningfully evaluated without causing a failure in the Runtime. This is known as *type safety*.

    The *type system* is a component of the constraints aspect of a DSL that

    – Represents ranges of domain-specific values as *types*

    – Computes the types of expressions (and possibly other DSL content that can be considered to have, or even be, a type)

    – Implements type checking constraints by comparing computed types, and reports violations of those with messages that help the domain experts fix the problem

- *Type computation* is the process of computing the type that the evaluation result of an expression would have, represented as a type in the type system. The type computation of an expression typically computes the types of all its subexpressions and combines it with additional data, such as an operator or a reference. If it's not possible to compute an obviously correct type, the type computation should produce a sensible *best-effort* type. This prevents type mismatches from propagating throughout the entire expression, potentially obscuring the problem's root cause. When no best-effort type exists, the type computation should return a special "untype," which means "we couldn't compute any sensible type for this expression."

- *Type inference* is the idea of computing a type of an AST object from its surrounding context, instead of only from the data in the AST object itself or any of its children or descendants. Typically you need an AST object's ancestors to do type inference.

- *Type checking constraints* check, for every expression, whether their combination of (computed types of) subexpressions and other data make sense. As with type computations, these constraints typically compute the types of all (direct) subexpressions.

- *Type objects* are objects that represent types as structured data using the low-level structure of AST objects. That's more flexible, and more future-proof, than representing types as strings.

14 Implementing business rules

This chapter covers

- Evolving our example DSL for writing business rules
- Implementing business rules
- Generating code for running business rules

Our example DSL allows us to define a (single) record type in a type-safe way, and to generate a Runtime UI from that. That's useful but not very valuable yet. It's especially weird that the user of the UI is able to set the discount themselves. The discount should be computed by the Runtime based on logic defined by the business.

In chapter 1, I promised that we'd be building a DSL with which domain experts could write down business logic. Figure 14.1 shows an example of some business logic defined as a *business rule*. (This figure is a screenshot of a part of the Domain IDE that we'll have built by the end of this chapter.)

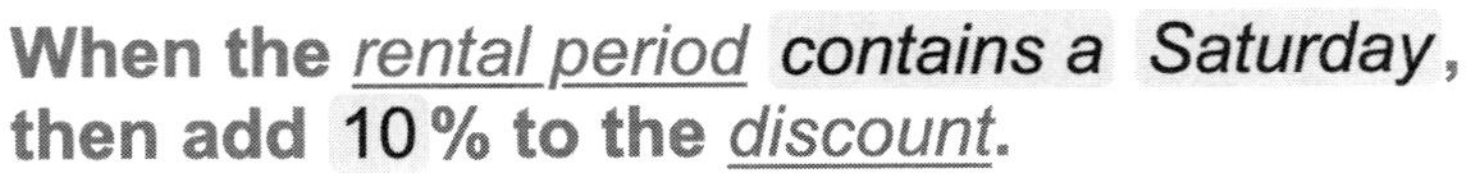

When the rental period contains a Saturday,
then add 10 % to the discount.

Figure 14.1 Some business logic, in the form of a business rule

This business rule expresses that when the rental period contains a Saturday, 10% is to be added to the discount. For a lot of domains, a major part of business logic can be expressed as business rules. Being able to specify business rules with a DSL brings a lot of power, regardless of the domain.

Just from looking at figure 14.1, we can guess that business rule pertains to a rental, as defined by the `Rental` record type. We can also guess that the texts `rental period` and `discount` reference attributes of that record type. We say that this is a business rule defined *on* the `Rental` record type. Having defined this business rule on `Rental` means that we can *compute* the value of the `discount` attribute of a rental, instead of having it set by the Runtime UI's user.

One business rule is virtually never enough to capture all business logic, so a record type usually has more than one business rule defined on it. In chapter 1, we saw another one, shown again in figure 14.2.

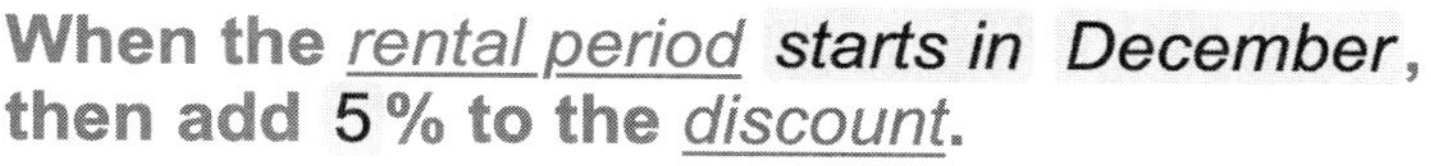

When the *rental period* starts in December, then add 5% to the *discount*.

Figure 14.2   Another business rule (defined) on the `Rental` record type

The general form of such business rules is "When *<condition>*, then *<consequence>*." The <condition> part specifies *when* the <consequence> part of the rule should be executed. The <consequence> part specifies *what* should happen then. Running a business rule means evaluating the <condition> part of that business rule and executing its <consequence> part when the condition evaluates to a `true` value. Figure 14.3 shows this general form, together with some details on the <condition> and <consequence> parts.

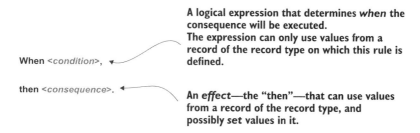

Figure 14.3   The general form of a business rule defined on a record type

In this chapter, we'll evolve our example DSL so the car rental domain experts can specify how to determine a price (quote) for a rental, using business rules. We'll change the Runtime so that it computes the discount using those business rules and displays it accordingly. We'll also expand the code generator to generate the appropriate Runtime code from the business rules.

We don't need to add any new parts to the DSL's architecture (see figure 13.2) for any of that, but we'll be using everything from earlier chapters. While evolving the example DSL, we'll need to make numerous choices regarding the design of the DSL and the implementation of the business rules. I'll discuss these choices to prepare you for making similar choices when working on your own DSLs.

Figure 14.4 shows what kind of concepts need to be added to our example DSL, and which of its concepts need to be extended.

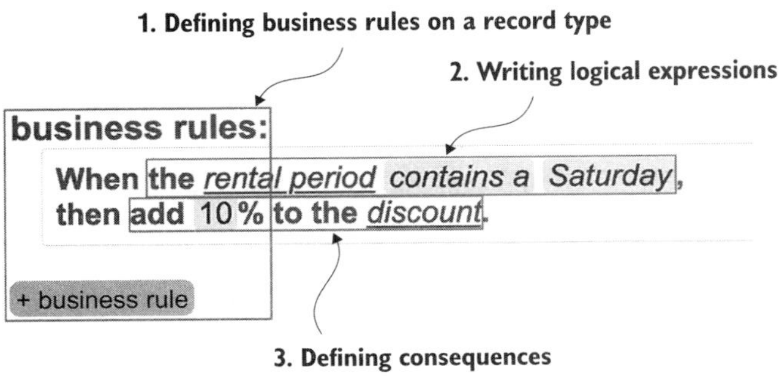

Figure 14.4   The route we'll take in this chapter for evolving the example DSL with business rules

In section 14.1, we'll extend and adapt the example DSL's key aspects of structure, notation, and constraints (including the type system) to be able to write business rules. In section 14.2, we'll learn how to implement the execution of business rules in the Runtime. In section 14.3, we'll extend and adapt the code generator accordingly.

More on business rules

The topic of business rules is broad and complex. It warrants a book of its own, which implies that we can only skim the surface here. For a more general information about business rules, see the Wikipedia article on "business rule" (https://en.wikipedia.org/wiki/Business_rule) and the Business Rules Group (www.businessrulesgroup.org/theBRG.htm).

The form of business rules we'll evolve in our example DSL will provide only basic expressivity. However, the ideas I'll introduce in this chapter generalize to very expressive and sophisticated DSLs. Please keep that in mind while working through this chapter.

14.1   Extending the DSL with business rules

The domain experts have no way of writing the DSL content in figures 14.1 and 14.2 in the example DSL, so it's clear that we need to extend it. The domain experts should be able to do the following:

- Define business rules as part of a `Record Type`.
- Write logical expressions involving date ranges, for the <condition> parts of business rules.
- Define the <consequence> parts of business rules.

We'll go through the items in this list one by one.

Before I walk you through the implementation of the preceding points, you might want to try your hand at doing it unaided. You'll need techniques from all the previous chapters, but nothing more. You'll also have to make a number of design decisions. The chance exists that you'll make different decisions than I will, but you'll probably learn even more if that happens. DSL design is about making tradeoffs just as much as software design in general is.

14.1.1   Defining business rules

For the first item of the preceding list (define business rules as part of a `Record Type`), let's add that a record type can have zero or more business rules attached to it. To achieve that, we'll extend the `Record Type` concept with a `business rules` property that contains instances of the new `Business Rule` concept. Adding a property to a concept requires a migration, which is shown in listing 14.1 and should be added to the src/init/migrations.js file. The implementation is pretty simple because the AST's root is always a `Record Type`.

Listing 14.1   Migration to add a `business rules` property

```
const addBusinessRulesProperty = (recordType) => {        Check whether the
    if (!Array.isArray(                                   business rules property is
        ⮕ recordType.settings["business rules"])) {       already set to an array.
        recordType.settings["business rules"] = []         If it's not, set it to
    }                                                      an empty array.
    return recordType
}

// ...run migration from v1 -> v2 if necessary...          Execute this
doMigration("v2", "v3", addBusinessRulesProperty)          migration.
```

Listing 14.2 shows (with changes highlighted in bold) how to extend the projection for `Record Type` for the `business rules` property, in the corresponding `case` in the `switch` statement in the <Projection> function in src/frontend/projection.jsx.

Listing 14.2   Extending the projection for the `business rules` property

```
case "Record Type": return <UiWrapped>
    // ...existing code...
    <div className="section">
        <div><span className="keyword">business rules:</span></div>
        {settings["business rules"].map((businessRule, index) =>
            <Projection
                astObject={businessRule}
                ancestors={[ astObject, ...ancestors ]}
                replaceWith={replaceInMultipleValue(astObject,
                    ➥  "business rules", index)}
                key={index}
            />
        )}
        <AddNewButton buttonText="+ business rule" actionFunction={() => {
            settings["business rules"].push(
                newAstObject("Business Rule")          ◁────────   We'll add a sensible default
            )                                                      setting for the consequence
        }} />                                                      property later.
    </div>
</UiWrapped>
```

Next, let's add a new concept called `Business Rule`. It has two properties: `condition`,
containing an expression, and `consequence`, containing an instance of a concept we'll
introduce later. Listing 14.3 shows the `case` to add to the `switch` statement in the
`<Projection>` function in src/frontend/projection.jsx.

Listing 14.3   Implementing the projection for `Business Rule`

```
case "Business Rule": {
    return <UiWrapped className="business-rule">
        <div>
            <span className="keyword ws-right">When</span>
            {projectionExpressionFor(astObject, ancestors,
                ➥  "condition")}                            ◁────   Because the
            <span className="keyword">,</span>                        <condition> should be
        </div>                                                       an expression, we use the
        <div>                                                        projectionExpressionFor
            <span className="keyword ws-right">then</span>           function again.
            <Projection
                astObject={settings["consequence"]}        ◁────   Assume that the
                ancestors={[ astObject, ...ancestors ]}            consequence property
            />                                                      always contains an AST
            <span className="keyword">.</span>                      object and is never
        </div>                                                      undefined.
    </UiWrapped>
}
```

We'll ensure that the `consequence` property always contains an AST object and is
never undefined, as follows:

- Instantiate any `Business Rule` with a suitable AST object in its `consequence` property. We'll do that later, in listing 14.13.
- Not providing a `setValue` argument prevents the domain expert from being able to replace the whole consequence. In particular, it prevents deletion, which amounts to calling `setValue(undefined)`.

The code in listing 14.3 will run, even before we incorporate listing 14.13, but until then the projection of any newly added business rule will display "No projection defined for value: undefined" for the <consequence> part.

To make a business rule look visually acceptable, we'll add the CSS in the following listing.

Listing 14.4 Styling for business rules in src/frontend/styling.css

```
div.business-rule {
    margin-left: 1em;
    margin-bottom: 1em;
    padding: 0.75rem;
    border: 1px solid lightgray;
    border-radius: 5px;
    width: 80%;
    font-size: 21pt;        ◁─── Render business rules with a
}                                slightly smaller font size to
                                 make it more readable.
```

Although we're not yet able to write logical expressions, we know that a business rule's condition should evaluate to a Boolean value: `true` or `false`. To be able to compute a type for logical expressions and to type check the condition of a business rule, we'll have to add a `boolean` type to our library of built-in types. The following listing shows the corresponding code changes (highlighted in bold) to src/language/type-system.js.

Listing 14.5 Adding a `boolean` type to the built-in types

```
const builtInTypes = {
    // ...pre-existing built-in types...
    "boolean": typeObject("boolean", "Boolean Type"),
    [untypeName]: untype        ◁─── This is already there.
}

const typeAsText = (typeObject) => {
    const { settings } = typeObject          | Implement
    switch (typeObject.concept) {            | the textual
        case "Boolean Type": return "boolean"  ◁─┘ representation.
    // ...
```

With this `boolean` type, we can add constraints on `Business Rule` that ensure that the `condition` and `consequence` properties are set and that the condition is of `boolean` type. Listing 14.6 shows the `case` to add for `Business Rule` to the `switch` statement in the `issuesFor` function in src/language/constraints.js.

Listing 14.6   Implementing constraints on `Business Rule`

```
case "Business Rule": {
    issueIfNotAstObject("condition",
        ➥ "A business rule must specify a condition")
    if (isAstObject(settings["condition"])) {
        const typeOfCondition =
            ➥ typeOf(settings["condition"], [ astObject, ...ancestors ])
        if (!areEqual(typeOfCondition, builtInTypes["boolean"])) {
            issues.push(`The condition of a business rule
                ➥ must produce a boolean value,
                ➥ but its type is '${typeAsText(typeOfCondition)}'`)
        }
    }
    issueIfNotAstObject("consequence",                    ⟵  Ensure that a Business Rule
        ➥ "A business rule must specify a consequence")       always has a consequence.
    break
}
```

The implementation so far ensures that a `Business Rule` always defines a `consequence`, but it's good practice to make the requirement explicit as a constraint nevertheless.

> **Exercise 14.1**
> - Apply the code changes from listings 14.1 through 14.6.
> - Check whether these changes work. Note that you can't input the business rules from figures 14.1 and 14.2 yet, because we haven't added the necessary other concepts.

14.1.2 *Writing logical expressions*

The second item of the list at the beginning of section 14.1 says we have to extend the example DSL with logical expressions involving date ranges. In particular, the domain experts need to be able to write the following two expressions for the business rules (from figures 14.1 and 14.2):

- The *rental period* contains a Saturday
- The *rental period* starts in December

Let's turn expressions such as these into AST objects. We'll generalize along the way to maximize expressivity.

The notation of both expressions starts with "the *rental period*." It seems likely that both of these are references to attributes, so let's assume they are. That means more general forms of the preceding expressions are as follows:

- <attribute reference> contains a Saturday
- <attribute reference> starts in December

Domain experts probably want to be able to write similar expressions involving other weekdays or months. Let's generalize a bit more:

- <attribute reference> contains a <weekday>
- <attribute reference> starts in <month>

There's no need to insist that the left sides are attribute references, which means we can generalize these forms even more, as follows:

- <operand> contains a <weekday>
- <operand> starts in <month>

For these expressions to make sense, the <operand> must have type `date range`: we'll type check that with a constraint. (Our example DSL currently doesn't have any concepts other than `Attribute Reference` that can produce a value of type `date range`, but that's likely to change in the future.)

To capture such expressions as AST objects, we'll introduce a new concept called `Date Range Operation` with the following properties:

- `operand`—An expression AST object
- `operator`—Either the string value "contains a" or "starts in"
- `time unit`—A string value that's either
  - A weekday (Monday, Tuesday, ... Sunday) used in combination with "contains a"
  - A month (January, February, ... December) used in combination with "starts in"

These operators and time units will suffice for the moment. It's quite easy to add more operators and time units, when that turns out to be necessary. I'll explain and justify my design decisions in more detail shortly.

To work with time units, we'll implement functions that recognize weekdays and months. The following listing shows the code that should go in a new src/language/time-units.js file.

Listing 14.7 Functions to recognize weekdays and months

Import two constants from the Runtime's codebase. We'll add these constants in listing 14.8.

```
const { weekdays, months } = require("../runtime/dates")
```

```
const isWeekday = (timeUnit) =>
    weekdays.indexOf(timeUnit) > -1
module.exports.isWeekday = isWeekday
```
Define (and export) a function that determines whether a given time unit string represents a weekday.

```
const isMonth = (timeUnit) =>
    months.indexOf(timeUnit) > -1
module.exports.isMonth = isMonth
```
Define (and export) a function that determines whether a given time unit string represents a month.

```
const timeUnits = [ ...weekdays, ...months ]
module.exports.timeUnits = timeUnits
```
Define (and export) a constant that contains all time unit strings.

Next, we'll add the `weekdays` and `months` constants to the Runtime's code, in src/runtime/dates.js.

Listing 14.8   Defining the time units `weekdays` and `months`

Define an array with weekday names. The indices of the weekdays match with the getDate() method of JavaScript's Date type.

Export the constant for reuse elsewhere.

```
const weekdays = [
"Monday", "Tuesday", "Wednesday", "Thursday",
"Friday", "Saturday", "Sunday"
]
module.exports.weekdays = weekdays
```

Define an array with the month names. The indices of the months match with the getMonth() method of JavaScript's Date type.

```
const months = [ "January", "February", "March",
"April", "May", "June",
"July", "August", "September",
"October", "November", "December"
]
module.exports.months = months
```

Export the constant for reuse elsewhere.

Sharing code between the Domain IDE and the Runtime

We did a weird thing in listings 14.7 and 14.8: we made the Domain IDE's code *depend on the Runtime's code*. We achieved that by reusing a bit of code from the Runtime by importing it in the Domain IDE's code.

It's quite natural and logical that the Domain IDE and Runtime share some domain-specific functionality, and, therefore, code. In our case, that common functionality is working with dates. Because the Runtime and Domain IDE have different audiences and lifecycles, they (should) reside in different codebases. Shared code should then go in a standalone library or package that you could then use in both codebases.

Having the Runtime and Domain IDE in the same codebase is a matter of convenience for this book, which is why we can share code by importing it. Finally, I put the common code in the Runtime's code because the Runtime is supposed to be a standalone piece of software. The Domain IDE, on the other hand, should have access to the Runtime's codebase: after all, it generates part of it.

Next, we'll implement the projection for `Date Range Operation`. Listing 14.9 shows the corresponding new `case` in the `switch` statement in the `<Projection>` function in src/frontend/projection.jsx.

Listing 14.9   Implementing the projection for `Date Range Operation`

Import the time units definition.

```
import { timeUnits } from "../language/time-units"

// ...other pre-existing code...

    case "Date Range Operation": {
        return <UiWrapped className="inline" showType>
```

```
            {projectionExpressionFor(astObject, ancestors, "operand")}
            <DropDownValue
                className="value enum-like ws-both"
                editState={editStateFor("operator")}
                options={[ "contains a", "starts in" ]}           ◁——
                placeholderText="<operator>"
            />
            <DropDownValue
                className="value enum-like"
                editState={editStateFor("time unit")}
                options={timeUnits}                                ◁——
                placeholderText="<time unit>"
            />
        </UiWrapped>
    }
```

> **The operators available for Date Range Operation.**

> **Use the imported list of time units as options for the drop-down menu.**

We could have filtered the time units shown as options in the drop-down menu based on the "operator" value. To keep things simple, I've chosen not to do so, so domain experts could input an expression such as "contains a December" or "starts in Saturday." We prevent such mismatches using a constraint.

Next, we'll add constraints on Date Range Operation, one of which checks whether its operator and time unit match. Listing 14.10 shows the corresponding code as a new case in the switch statement in the issuesFor function in src/language/constraints.js.

Listing 14.10   Implementing the constraints on Date Range Operation

```
// at top of the file:
const { isMonth, isWeekday } = require("./time-units")

// inside switch statement in issuesFor function:
case "Date Range Operation": {
    issueIfNotAstObject("operand", "The operand must be defined")
    if (isAstObject(settings["operand"])) {
        const typeOfOperand = typeOf(settings["operand"],
            ➥ [ astObject, ...ancestors ])
        if (!areEqual(typeOfOperand, builtInTypes["date range"])) {
            issues.push(
➥ `The left-hand side (operand) of this operation must be a 'date range',
➥ but it is '${typeAsText(typeOfOperand)}'`)
        }
    }
    issueIfUndefined("operator", "The operator must be defined")
    issueIfUndefined("time unit", "The time unit must be defined")
    const { operator, "time unit": timeUnit } = settings
    if (operator && timeUnit) {
        switch (operator) {
            case "contains a": {
                if (!isWeekday(timeUnit)) {
                    issues.push(`The right-hand side of this operator
                        ➥ must be a weekday`)
                }
```

```
                break
            }
        case "starts in": {
            if (!isMonth(timeUnit)) {
                issues.push(`The right-hand side of this operator
                    ➥ must be a month`)
            }
            break
        }
    }
}
break
}
```

Finally, we'll extend the type computation for the Date Range Operation. The following listing shows the corresponding `case` in the `switch` statement in the `typeOf` function in src/language/type-system.js.

Listing 14.11   Computing the type for Date Range Operation

```
case "Date Range Operation": return builtInTypes["boolean"]
```

Exercise 14.2
- Apply all code additions from listings 14.7 through 14.11.
- Add "Date Range Operation" to the list that's the value of the `options` attribute in the call to the `<DropDownValue>` component in the `projectionExpressionFor` in src/frontend/projection.jsx.
- Check that you can now enter the conditions of both business rules from figures 14.1 and 14.2.
- Check that the added constraints and type computation for Date Range Operation function correctly. Hint: Check the tooltip (hover text) for the computed type.
- Do you think the UI/UX of choosing a time unit is satisfactory? Do you see a way of improving it? Try to make that change.

Design decisions for date range operations
Previously, I made a design decision about how to capture these logical, time-based expressions as AST objects, without explaining any alternatives and their tradeoffs to you. I wanted to complete the full implementation first, so that you could have a better appreciation of the tradeoffs involved.

There are two obvious alternatives:

- *Introduce a new concept for each of the "contains a" and "starts in" operators.* We wouldn't have to check that the time unit and operator match, at the expense of having to implement an extra concept. The question is whether it's worth having one more concept just so we can avoid implementing some additional logic in the constraints and possibly the UI.

- *Turn the "contains a" and "starts in" operators into proper binary infix operators.* This means piggybacking on a mechanism that's already there, making it easier to have a consistent editing experience and saving us from implementing a new concept. Despite its advantages, this approach means making more effort in the short term than with the approach I've chosen:
  - Add a built-in type (or types) to represent weekdays and months, so a type could be computed for a time unit as the right operand.
  - Implement a new concept with a `time unit` property, so that domain experts can specify weekdays and months as the right expression of these date range–based operators.
  - Extend the `typeOfBinaryInfixOperator` function for the two new operators.
  - Add constraints that check whether the right operand of a "contains a" operator is a weekday, and that the right operand of a "starts in" is a month.

All in all, the second option involves more work and doesn't necessarily make the resulting code less complex. The binary operation–based approach might be better in the longer run, when the tradeoffs we've discussed have changed, or when you need more date range–based operations. Examples of those are "starts on a <weekday>" or "spans at least <number> days," whose value is an integer instead of a time unit. Fortunately, it's quite easy to migrate instances of `Date Range Operation` to `Binary Operation` instances.

14.1.3 *Defining consequences*

For the third item of the list at the start of section 14.1, the domain experts have to be able to write the following two consequences:

- Add 5% to the *discount*
- Add 10% to the *discount*

Let's turn these consequences into AST objects of a suitable *effect concept*, which we'll add to the example DSL. Like before, we can guess that "the *discount*" is an attribute reference. We can generalize these two expressions to the following common form:

- Add <percentage> to <attribute reference>

For this to make sense type-wise, the reference attribute must have type `percentage` as well. We're going to ensure that with a constraint. We can generalize the preceding form even further:

- Add <operand of numeric type> to <attribute reference>

For this to make sense type-wise, the types of the operand and attribute referenced must match and be numeric.

A consequence such as this, which alters data or generally does more than "warming up the CPU," is often called an *effect*. Let's introduce a new concept called `Increment Effect` that increments the value of an attribute. This concept has the following properties:

- `operand`—An operand that must be of a numeric type
- `attribute reference`—An `Attribute Reference` that references an attribute that has the same type as the operand

We say that the attribute referenced through the `attribute reference` is the *affected* attribute. In general, we can equate "affected" to "determined by business rules." Another way to say that we're executing a business rule's consequence is to *apply the effect*.

The only effect concept we'll implement in this chapter is `Increment Effect`. The projection of the `Business Rule` concept we implemented in listing 14.3 denies domain experts choosing an effect concept, which avoids us having to provide a dropdown menu with only one option and an appropriate `setValue` argument.

It's unlikely that all business rules you'll eventually need to write for a full-fledged Runtime will only have this one particular form of effect for their consequence. You'll need to add new effect concepts or to "widen" existing ones by adding more properties. When that happens, you'll need to complete the projection for `Business Rule` as well.

I chose to have an `Increment Effect` AST object always contain an `Attribute Reference` AST object as a child instead of referencing an attribute directly. That way, we can just use the projection for `Attribute Reference` instead of having to rebuild that projection inside the one for `Increment Effect`. We just saved ourselves from having to write 15 more lines of projection code at the expense of an "extra" AST object.

With these design decisions, implementing the projection for the `Increment Effect` concept is pretty straightforward. Listing 14.12 shows the corresponding new `case` in the `switch` statement in the `<Projection>` function in src/frontend/projection.jsx.

Listing 14.12 Implementing the projection for `Increment Effect`

```
case "Increment Effect": {
    return <UiWrapped className="inline" showType>
        <span className="keyword ws-right">add</span>
        {projectionExpressionFor(astObject, ancestors,
            "value")}
        <span className="keyword ws-both">to</span>
        <Projection
            astObject={settings["attribute reference"]}
            ancestors={[ astObject, ...ancestors ]}
        />
    </UiWrapped>
}
```

Use the projectionExpressionFor function for the expression-valued property value.

Assume that the attribute reference property always contains an Attribute Reference AST object and is never undefined.

The projection of a `Business Rule` AST object (listing 14.3) assumes that its `consequence` property is always defined, but it also disallows deleting the value of that property. Likewise, the projection of an `Increment Effect` (listing 14.12) assumes its `attribute reference` property contains an `Attribute Reference` AST object, which can't be deleted. That means we can satisfy those assumptions completely by providing corresponding sensible defaults when instantiating a new `Business Rule` through the projection for `Record Type`. Listing 14.13 shows the corresponding code changes (highlighted in bold) to the projection for `Record Type` in src/frontend/projection.jsx.

> **Listing 14.13 Instantiating a `Business Rule` with sensible defaults**

```
<AddNewButton buttonText="+ business rule" actionFunction={() => {
    settings["business rules"].push(
        newAstObject("Business Rule", {
            "consequence":
                newAstObject("Increment Effect", ({          ◁─── Instantiate an Increment
                    "attribute reference":                        Effect in the consequence
                    newAstObject("Attribute Reference")      ◁─── property.
                }))
        })                                                        Instantiate an Attribute
    )                                                             Reference in the
}} />                                                             increment effect's
                                                                  attribute reference
                                                                  property.
```

> **Exercise 14.3**
> - Apply the code changes from listings 14.12 and 14.13.
> - Test whether you can now enter the consequences of both business rules in the Domain IDE.
> - Check that you can't delete the consequence of a business rule (entirely), nor the attribute reference inside the `Increment Effect`.
> - Do the projections of the business rules match figures 14.1 and 14.2 entirely?

With the preceding code changes, we're *almost* there: the effects contain number values in their `value` properties, but no percentage signs are displayed, and a type error is reported. To properly display that number value and make the type errors go away, we have to *infer* whether it's a percentage or an amount. (Our example effects all involve percentages, but there's nothing stopping the domain experts from adding an amount to an amount value.)

We can infer the precise type for a number appearing directly as the value of an effect by inspecting the type of the target of the attribute reference. Listing 14.14 shows the corresponding addition (highlighted in bold) to the `typeOf` function that achieves that.

Listing 14.14   Computing the type of a number value inside an effect

```
case "Number": {
    // ...other pre-existing code...
    if (parent.concept === "Increment Effect") {
        return typeOf(
            parent.settings["attribute reference"], ancestors)
    }
    return untype
}
```

The case for **Number** inside the switch statement in the issuesFor function in src/language/type-system.js.

Check whether the number value is directly contained in an **Increment Effect**.

Return the type computed for the referenced attribute. To do that, call typeOf on a "sibling" of the Number AST object, which has the same ancestors.

Exercise 14.4
- Apply the code changes from listing 14.14.
- Check that the projection now displays a "%" or "$" correctly, depending on the type of the attribute referenced.
- Verify that the type errors have disappeared.

Finally, we'll implement a number of constraints on `Increment Effect`:

- `value` must be defined.
- The type of the attribute referenced must equal the type of `value`.

Listing 14.15 shows the implementation of constraints on `Increment Effect` as a new case in the `switch` statement in the `issuesFor` function in src/language/constraints.js.

Listing 14.15   Implementing constraints on `Increment Effect`

```
case "Increment Effect": {
    issueIfNotAstObject("value", "The value must be defined")
    const typeOfValue =
        typeOf(settings["value"], [ astObject, ...ancestors ])
    const attributeRefObject =
        settings["attribute reference"]
        .settings["attribute"]
    if (isAstReference(attributeRefObject)) {
        const reffedAttribute = attributeRefObject.ref
        const typeOfReffedAttribute =
            typeOf(reffedAttribute, [ astObject, ...ancestors ])
        if (!areEqual(typeOfValue,
            typeOfReffedAttribute)) {
            issues.push(
`The type of the value and the referenced attribute
    of this effect must match,
    but they are: '${typeAsText(typeOfValue)}',
    resp., '${typeAsText(typeOfReffedAttribute)}'`
            )
```

Try to follow the reference to the target attribute.

Check whether the types of the value and referenced attribute match.

```
        }
    }
    break
}
```

Exercise 14.5
- Apply the code changes from listing 14.15.
- Test whether these constraints are working.

Exercise 14.6
Can you identify another sensible constraint on `Increment Effect`? (We'll formulate an additional constraint in the next section that probably encompasses the constraint you just found.)

14.2   Implementing the business rules in the Runtime

In the previous section, we extended the Domain IDE so that domain experts can enter business rules like those in figures 14.1 and 14.2. In this section, we're going to implement these business rules in the Runtime. We'll do that first by hand, before we extend the generator accordingly. That way, we can check that the code generator indeed generates the code for the business rules correctly from the AST for them.

We'll need to add the following items to, or adapt them in, the Runtime to compute the discount for a rental period using business rules:

1   Execute each business rule separately.
2   Combine the application of the effects of executed consequences to come up with a definitive value for the discount.
3   Change the UI to use the computed discount value, instead of providing an input field.

14.2.1   Running each business rule separately

We'll start with item 1 of the preceding list, so let's figure out how to code running the business rules. A business rule of the form "When <condition>, then <consequence>" translates well to an ordinary `if` statement.

Listing 14.16   Template for code running a business rule separately

```
if (<JavaScript translation of the condition>) {
    <JavaScript translation of the consequence>
}
```

The value of the rental period is represented at run time as an object of the class `Date-Range`. Let's add a method to that class that implements the "contains a <weekday>"

operation for a date range. The following listing shows the corresponding addition (highlighted in bold) to src/runtime/dates.js.

Listing 14.17   Implementing the "contains a <weekday>" operation

```
class DateRange {                                    Define a method
    // ...pre-existing code...                       that implements the
    containsWeekDay(dayName) {         ◄─────         "contains a" operation.
        const dayNr = weekdays.indexOf(dayName)
        let currentDate = new Date(this._from)   ◄──┐ Make a copy of the from date
        while (currentDate < this._to               │ to increment it day by day.
              ⇒ && currentDate.getDay() !== dayNr) {
            currentDate.setDate(               ◄──┐
              ⇒ currentDate.getDate() + 1)         │ Move one day forward.
        }
        return currentDate.getDay() === dayNr && currentDate < this._to
    }
}
```

Loop over this date range, and stop when the weekdays match or when you run out of days in the date range. (This is not very efficient, but the loop is guaranteed to finish within seven steps.)

With this method, the condition "the *rental period* contains a Saturday" can be translated to JavaScript as

```
this.rentalPeriod.containsWeekDay("Saturday")    ◄──┐ "this" is an instance
                                                      of the class Rental.
```

The consequence of the business rule in figure 14.1 is an "add a <numeric value> to <attribute reference>" effect, where <numeric value> is 10 and the attribute referenced is the `discount` attribute. If we store the numeric value of the discount in a local `discount` variable, this translates to JavaScript as follows:

```
discount += 10
```

Later, in listing 14.21, we'll make sure that the local `discount` variable gets initialized properly. We'll also expose its eventual value on the instance of the `Rental` class, in listing 14.23. In between, `discount` will aggregate the results of applying all increment effects to it.

Combining the translated condition expression and the translated consequence statement in an `if` statement gives us the following code.

Listing 14.18   Implementing the first business rule in the Runtime

```
if (this.rentalPeriod.containsWeekDay("Saturday")) {
    discount += 10
}
```

I'll explain later where exactly to put this code. For now, let's implement the second business rule. To implement the condition "the *rental period* starts in December," we'll add another method to the `DateRange` class. The next listing shows the corresponding addition (highlighted in bold) to the src/runtime/dates.js file.

Listing 14.19 Implementing the "starts in <month>" operation

```
class DateRange {
    // ...pre-existing code...
    startsInMonth(monthName) {
        const monthNr = months.indexOf(monthName)
        return this._from.getMonth() === monthNr
    }
}
```

Define a method that implements the "starts in" operation.

We can inspect the from date of the date range directly—no looping necessary.

We can now implement the second business rule, similar to the first business rule.

Listing 14.20 Implementing the second business rule in the Runtime

```
if (this.rentalPeriod.startsInMonth("December")) {
    discount += 5
}
```

14.2.2 Combining effects

Now that we can execute each business rule separately, we can turn our attention to item 2 of the list at the beginning of section 14.2. Let's figure out how to properly combine the effects of executing the consequences of all business rules.

The code in listings 14.18 and 14.20 relies on the existence of a `discount` variable. Because that variable is not *set* so much as it is *incremented* with a certain number value, it's also necessary to initialize it to a proper value. The `discount` attribute is specified to have an initial value of 0%. I chose to use that initial value for a `discount` variable that is then incremented by the execution of business rules' consequences. This translates to the following.

Listing 14.21 Initializing a `discount` variable to a value of 0%

```
let discount = 0
```

Use the let keyword because the value can be changed.

After we run the code in listings 14.21, 14.18, and 14.20, the `discount` variable holds the discount value determined by the business rules. Because we chose to use the initial value of an affected attribute for sensible initialization, we also have to ensure that this attribute *has* an initial value. Listing 14.22 shows how to adapt (with changes highlighted in bold) the implementation of the constraints on `Increment Effect` in src/language/constraints.js accordingly.

Listing 14.22 Ensuring an affected attribute has an initial value

```
if (isAstReference(attributeRefObject)) {
    const reffedAttribute = attributeRefObject.ref
    // ...more existing code, for type checking constraint...
```

```
if (reffedAttribute.settings["value kind"] !== "initially"
     ⇒ || !isAstObject(reffedAttribute.settings["value"])) {
   issues.push(
⇒ `An increment effect must reference an attribute with an initial value`
      )
   }
```

In exercise 14.6, I alluded to an additional constraint, by which I meant that an affected attribute can't have a computed value. Checking that an affected attribute has an initial value implies it doesn't have a computed one.

We also have to consider whether the *order* in which the rules are executed matters. It's obvious that defining and initializing the `discount` variable needs to happen before running the business rules, but what about the order of the business rules' implementations themselves?

In this case, the answer is "no" for two reasons:

- The evaluation of the rules' conditions doesn't depend on the order in which the business rules are executed. That's because these evaluations do not depend on data that's changed by the execution of consequences of other rules. This property holds for these particular business rules, but domain experts are free to formulate conditions that use data affected by the consequences of other business rules. If that were to happen, things would immediately become much more challenging. To ensure that this property holds for any DSL content, we'd have to implement a constraint.

- The order in which the rules' consequences are executed doesn't matter. That's because our example DSL has only one effect concept, which increments some value. (That's not a coincidence but the result of a design choice.) The addition of numbers is *commutative*: $x + y = y + x$ holds for every value of x and y. As a result, the order in which some initial value is incremented also doesn't make a difference: only the increments themselves matter. Because this is a property of the DSL, it holds for any DSL content, and we don't need a constraint.

Having established that we can choose either of the two possible orders, it's just as easy to stick to the order in which they are defined in the DSL content.

14.2.3   *The execution model of business rules*

The preceding discussion hints at an important notion for business rules: the *execution model*. An execution model is a specification of what business rules implemented by a DSL "mean," or more precisely, how they should be executed. Specifically, it specifies how business rules, specified as DSL content, *work together*. It should answer questions such as the following:

- What effects exist? Can effects always be applied in a combined, or "stacked," way? Or can effects overwrite each other? The latter could happen if an effect sets an attribute to a specific value instead of incrementing it.

- Can business rules always be executed independently of each other? Or is it possible that running a business rule is dependent on running another one first? That would happen if the condition of one business rule depends on a value that's determined by other business rules. In our case, we could formulate business rules whose conditions use the discount value.

- Can business rules be *ambiguous*? That would happen if the conditions of two business rules both evaluate to `true`, but their corresponding consequences produce contradictory effects, such as setting the same attribute to different values. How could we detect that business rules are ambiguous? Is it possible to alert the domain experts to ambiguous rules while they're writing them?

- Does the order in which business rules are executed influence the result? Business rules that are dependent on each other must be executed in dependency order. Do all dependency orders produce the same result? If not, which order would make the most sense?

The DSL's design and the business rules' execution model are two sides of the same coin. The DSL's concepts determine which of the preceding questions need to be answered. The way that those questions are chosen to be answered can lead to additional DSL constraints.

It's a good idea to develop the effect concepts at the same time as the execution model. That allows you to make careful tradeoffs between the expressivity of the DSL and the complexity of running the business rules. We did that for our example DSL: because we chose to have an `Increment Effect` increment the value of an attribute, we effectively avoided (or likely only postponed) having to answer many of the preceding questions, at the expense of having to add one constraint.

This explanation represents the tip of an iceberg that involves many intricacies and subtleties, and which warrants its own book.

Exercise 14.7

Implement a constraint to check, for every business rule, whether its condition references attributes that are also referenced by the `Increment Effect` in a consequence of any business rule. The phrasing "any business rule" is used to include the business rule whose condition we're looking at, to avoid creating infinite loops. (This constraint is necessary to ensure that business rules can be executed independently of each other.)

Exercise 14.8

The business rules in figures 14.1 and 14.2 seem to imply that we can just add up discounts that apply simultaneously, but does that make sense business-wise? Giving a discount d over an amount x means calculating $x * (1 - d)$. Giving two discounts, d_1 and d_2, in a row would then mean calculating: $x * (1 - d_1) * (1 - d_2)$.

- Work out whether that gives the same answer as adding up the discounts and *then* using the formula $x * (1 - d)$ for calculating the discount.

(continued)
- Do you think that conclusion is problematic? How do you perceive stacked discounts being calculated in practice?
- Think about how you could design the DSL, and specifically the effects that can be used as a business rule's consequence, to calculate discounts "properly." Could an effect specifically for stacking discounts help, and what would it look like? Would it help to introduce domain-specific types for discounts?

14.2.4 *Changing the Runtime*

Finally, we can take care of item 3 on the list at the start of section 14.2. We'll change the Runtime so that the discount is computed from the business rules, rather than being input by the user.

We already have all the ingredients for determining the correct value for the discount using business rules, in the form of listings 14.21, 14.18, and 14.20. To use those, we'll implement the `discount` field of the `Rental` class in src/runtime/index.jsx with the getter method from listing 14.23, instead of as an ordinary field (with an initialization).

Listing 14.23   Computing the discount value using the business rules

```
get discount() {
    let discount = 0
    if (this.rentalPeriod
          ⮡ .containsWeekDay("Saturday")) {
        discount += 10
    }
    if (this.rentalPeriod
          ⮡ .startsInMonth("December")) {
        discount += 5
    }
    return discount
}
```

Replace the field initialization discount = 0 with a getter method with the same name. MobX turns this into an observable computed property of Rental.

Execute business rule 1.

Execute business rule 2.

The only thing left to do is to turn the input field for the discount into a simple display field. The original code in src/runtime/index.jsx looks like this:

```
<FormField label="Discount">
    <Input type="number" object={rental}
        ⮡ fieldName="discount" /> %
</FormField>
```

The following listing shows the required code changes, highlighted in bold.

Listing 14.24   Displaying the `discount` computed using business rules

```
<FormField label="Discount">
    {rental.discount} %
</FormField>
```

> ### Exercise 14.9
> Apply the code changes in listings 14.23 and 14.24. Check whether the Runtime functions as desired.

14.2.5 *Generalizing the implementation*

Implementing these two simple business rules seemed easy enough—deceptively so. They translate quite obviously to statements in the getter method for the discount value in the Runtime's code. Plenty of mitigating factors contribute to that impression:

- Only two business rules are defined.
- Both rules only affect the `discount` attribute.
- Their consequences are effects that happen to be commutative.
- Only one effect concept exists.

Some or all of these factors might change as the number and complexity of business rules grows. The following questions crop up:

- What would happen if the business rules don't translate nicely to a bunch of statements in a getter method for an affected attribute?
- Is it always possible to group business rules by affected attributes?

Even without having definitive answers to these questions, or about the tradeoffs involved with them, it seems wise to generalize our implementation a bit in anticipation of increasing complexity. We'll do that before expanding the code generator for business rules, to avoid losing time and effort.

The generalization we'll be making is to not group business rules according to their affected attributes. Instead, we're going to execute *all* business rules in succession. To do so, we'll add a new getter method called `rulesEffects` to the `Rental` class.

Listing 14.25   Running all rules inside a `rulesEffects` getter method

Define a new getter function inside the Rental class.

The initialization statement and the two statements corresponding to the two business rules are the same as in the discount getter function before.

```
get rulesEffects() {
    let discount = 0
    if (this.rentalPeriod.containsWeekDay("Saturday")) {
        discount += 10
    }
    if (this.rentalPeriod.startsInMonth("December")) {
        discount += 5
    }
    return {
        discount
    }
}
```

Construct an object with key-value pairs for all attributes affected by the business rules.

This shorthand JavaScript syntax is equivalent to: "discount": discount.

The `rulesEffects` method executes all the business rules and returns an object with the values for all of the affected attributes, as computed from the business rules. Because all our example business rules affect the `discount` attribute, the difference from listing 14.23 is minimal. That will change as soon as more than one attribute is affected by the business rules defined in the DSL content. Listing 14.26 shows how to use the result of the `rulesEffects` getter method in the getter method for `discount` inside the `Rental` class.

> **Listing 14.26   Using `rulesEffects` to implement the `discount` getter**

```
get discount() {
    return this.rulesEffects.discount
}
```

MobX turns the getter methods from listings 14.25 and 14.26 into observable computed properties that are only reevaluated when their input values change. Effectively, the result object of `rulesEffects` is cached, so we don't have to worry about performance. (In this case, the `rulesEffects` method is only called once anyway, but that may be very different in general.)

Decoupling the running of business rules from the attributes they target with their consequences' effects seems like a sound, generic approach. The code in listings 14.25 and 14.26 is also a good starting point for extending the code generator for business rules.

NOTE   When implementing templates, you'll often find alternatives for the original handwritten code that achieves the same thing but makes for simpler templates. It's a good idea to reduce the complexity of template code, rather than trying to recreate the handwritten code verbatim. After all, the handwritten code serves as a throw-away artifact, whereas you have to maintain (and hopefully expand!) the generator.

> **Exercise 14.10**
> Apply the code changes from listings 14.25 and 14.26. Check whether the Runtime functions as before.

14.3   *Generating the business rules' code*

In this section, we're going to generate the code in listings 14.24 through 14.26 from the DSL content defining the business rules in figures 14.1 and 14.2. To do so, we'll extend the code generator to use the business rules in the AST representing the DSL content. To that end, we have to

1   Compute which attributes are affected.
2   Generate the `rulesEffects` method, and use it to compute the values of affected attributes. (To achieve this, the generator will have to handle instances of the `Date Range Operation` concept.)

3 Change the generation of the fields in the Runtime's UI for affected attributes so they become display fields instead of input fields.

TIP   Before reading the rest of this section, you might want to try to extend the generator for business rules on your own. You can work from the preceding list and listings 14.24 through 14.26.

14.3.1 Identifying affected attributes

We'll start with item 1 of the previous list, so we need to figure out how to compute which attributes of a record type are *affected* by the consequences of the business rules defined on that record type.

First, we'll implement a function to inspect the consequence of a particular business rule and see what attribute is affected. The following listing shows the implementation of that query function, which should go in src/language/queries.js.

Listing 14.27   Determining attributes affected by a rule's consequence

> Define a function that returns an array of all unique attributes affected by the given business rule's consequence.

> Handle the situation where a business rule's consequence is not defined at all.

> Use referencedAttributesIn to follow the (single) attribute reference in an Effect.

> Print a warning on the JavaScript console for the Domain IDE developer.

> Return an empty array by default instead of throwing an Error.

```
const affectedAttributesInConsequence =
        (consequence) => {
    if (!isAstObject(consequence)) {
        return []
    }
    const { settings } = consequence
    switch (consequence.concept) {
        case "Increment Effect":
            return referencedAttributesIn(
                settings["attribute reference"])
        default: {
            console.warn(`affectedAttributesInConsequence(..)
                doesn't handle instances of the
                concept "${consequence.concept}"
                - returning []`)
            return []
        }
    }
}
module.exports.affectedAttributesInConsequence =
    affectedAttributesInConsequence
```

Currently, at most one attribute can be affected by a business rule's consequence, because that's always an Increment Effect that references at most one attribute. However, we return an array for two reasons:

- It's easier to disregard empty arrays (using the flatMap function defined on arrays) than it is to skip over a null or undefined value.
- It leaves open the possibility for effects that affect multiple attributes at the same time.

This function's code looks a bit tedious. That's in part because we want to be able to handle more effect concepts in the future. For the most part, though, it's due to having to handle faulty situations gracefully, to avoid having the code generator crash outright.

Using the `affectedAttributesInConsequence` function, we can figure out what attributes are affected by any of the business rules. Listing 14.28 shows the implementation of a query function (in src/language/queries.js) that computes the attributes affected by the consequences of any of the given business rules.

Listing 14.28 Determining attributes affected by all consequences

The JavaScript expression [...new Set(<array>)] returns <array> with the duplicates removed.

Define a function that returns an array of all unique attributes affected by at least one consequence of the given business rules.

```
const attributesAffectedBy = (businessRules) =>
    [ ...new Set(
            businessRules
                .map((businessRule) =>
                    businessRule.settings["consequence"])
                .flatMap(
                    affectedAttributesInConsequence
                )
        )
    ]
module.exports.attributesAffectedBy = attributesAffectedBy
```

Get hold of the consequences of the given business rules.

Use the flatMap function to concatenate the results of calling affectedAttributesInConsequence into one array.

Finally, listing 14.29 shows the changes (highlighted in bold) to the `indexJsx` template function in src/generator/indexJsx-template.js that adapt the generator to use the `attributesAffectedBy` function.

Listing 14.29 Using the `attributesAffectedBy` function in the generator

```
const { attributesAffectedBy, ... } =
    require("../language/queries")

// ...pre-existing code...

const indexJsx = (recordType) => {
    const name = ccNameOf(recordType)
    const Name = withFirstUpper(name)
    const { attributes,
        "business rules": businessRules } =
        recordType.settings
    const affectedAttributes =
        attributesAffectedBy(businessRules)
    const isAffected = (attribute) =>
        affectedAttributes.indexOf(attribute) > -1

    // ...other pre-existing code...
```

Import the attributesAffectedBy function from listing 14.28.

Retrieve the business rules from the record type, using a renaming destructuring.

Store the array of affected attributes in a constant, for efficiency.

Define a convenience function to recognize whether the given attribute is affected.

Exercise 14.11

- Apply the code changes from listings 14.27 through 14.29.
- Add the statement `console.dir(affectedAttributes)` in a suitable place in the generator code, run the generator, and check whether the affected attributes have been computed correctly.
- Remove the `println`-style debugging statement again.

14.3.2   *Generating and using the rulesEffects method*

For item 2 of the list at the beginning of section 14.3, we'll generate code for running all the business rules inside a `rulesEffects` method after first taking care of proper initialization. We'll use that method to produce the values of the affected attributes as the result of a `rulesEffects` getter method, such as in listing 14.25. Listing 14.30 shows the corresponding changes (highlighted in bold) to the `indexJsx` template function in src/generator/indexJsx-template.js.

Listing 14.30   Generating the `rulesEffects` getter method

```
class ${Name} {`,
    // ...existing code for generating class fields...
    `    get rulesEffects() {`,
    indent(2)(affectedAttributes.map((attribute) =>
        `let ${initializationFor(attribute)}`)
    ),
    indent(2)(
        businessRules.map(businessRuleAsStatement)
    ),
    `        return {`,
    indent(3)(affectedAttributes.map(ccNameOf)),
    `        }
    }
    constructor() {
```

Generate a getter.

Generate initialization statements for all affected attributes.

Generate statements for running each business rule. We still have to add the businessRuleAsStatement function.

Generate code for returning a plain JavaScript object with the values for all affected attributes, as determined by the business rules.

Generate a shorthand key-value pair for each affected attribute.

The missing ingredient is a `businessRuleAsStatement` function that generates a JavaScript statement that executes a given business rule. The general form of such a statement was shown in listing 14.16. We can identify three separate parts in that form:

1 The overall `if` statement
2 The translation of the condition
3 The translation of the consequence

Those parts correspond to the following implementation details:

1   The new `businessRuleAsStatement` function

2   The existing `expressionFor` function

3   Another new function—let's call it `consequenceAsStatement`

Working from listings 14.18 and 14.20, it's not too difficult to implement the `business-RuleAsStatement` function and the `consequenceAsStatement` function it depends on. The next listing shows the associated code that's to be added to src/generator/index-Jsx-template.js.

Listing 14.31   Generating code that executes a business rule

> **Most of the code in this function amounts to the usual "defensive programming" style of templates.**

```
const consequenceAsStatement = (consequence) => {          ⟵
    if (!isAstObject(consequence)) {
        return `/* [GENERATION PROBLEM] value "${consequence}"
            ➥ isn't handled in consequenceAsStatement */`
    }
    const { settings } = consequence
    switch (consequence.concept) {
        case "Increment Effect":                  ⟵
            ➥ return `${ccNameOf(settings["attribute reference"]
                ➥ .settings["attribute"].ref)}
                ➥ += ${expressionFor(settings["value"])}`
        default: return `/* [GENERATION PROBLEM] value
            ➥ of concept "${consequence.concept}"
            ➥ isn't handled in consequenceAsStatement */`
    }
}
```

> **Translate an Effect AST object into an increment statement.**

```
const businessRuleAsStatement = (businessRule) => {
    const { settings } = businessRule
    return [
        `if (
        ➥ ${expressionFor(settings["condition"], [])}          ⟵
        ➥ ) {`,
        indent(1)(consequenceAsStatement(          ⟵
            ➥ settings["consequence"])
        ),
        `}`
    ]
}
```

> **Translate the expression in the business rule's condition property to a JavaScript expression.**

> **Translate the business rule's consequence to a nested statement.**

Exercise 14.12

Apply the code changes from listings 14.30 and 14.31. Run the generator, and check the generated code for the `rulesEffects` method: it should be almost correct. We'll handle the remaining problem next.

You'll have found in exercise 14.12 that the generator produces flags to indicate a generation problem. These flags are comments in the generated code whose texts start with "[GENERATION PROBLEM]". The problem is that the expressionFor function doesn't yet handle the Date Range Operation expression concept that we added in section 14.1. Listing 14.32 shows additions (highlighted in bold) to src/generator/indexJsx-template.js that translate the Date Range Operation to JavaScript.

> **Listing 14.32   Translating Date Range Operation to JavaScript**

```
const dateRangeOperator2methodName = {          Define a map from the date range
    "contains a": "containsWeekDay",             operation's operators to the names
    "starts in": "startsInMonth"                 of the corresponding methods of the
}                                                DateRange class that implements
                                                 these operators.

const expressionFor = (astObject, ancestors) => {
    // ...other pre-existing code...              Define a case that
    switch (astObject.concept) {                  handles the Date Range
        case "Date Range Operation": {            Operation concept.
            const { operand, operator,
                "time unit": timeUnit } = settings
            return `${expressionFor(operand)}
                .${dateRangeOperator2methodName[operator]}
                ("${timeUnit}")`
        }
    // ...other pre-existing code...
```

Perform the translation, using the existing expressionFor function and the look-up dateRangeOperator2methodName[<date range operator>].

Map the operator to the name of the corresponding method on the DateRange class.

Perform a destructuring assignment (with renaming).

> **Exercise 14.13**
>
> Apply the code changes from listing 14.32. Verify that the rulesEffects function is now generated correctly, without flags.

Now that we generate the rulesEffects method correctly, we'll adapt the fields generated for all affected attributes to use it. Listing 14.33 shows the corresponding changes (highlighted in bold) to the classField function in src/generator/indexJsx-template.js.

> **Listing 14.33   Adapting classField for affected attributes**

```
const classField = (attribute, isAffected) => {
    const { settings } = attribute
    const value = settings["value"]
    const fieldName = ccNameOf(attribute)
    if (isAffected) {
        return [
```

Add a parameter to the classField function indicating whether the given attribute is affected.

```
        `get ${fieldName}() {`,
        `    return this.rulesEffects.${fieldName}`,
        `}`
    ]
}
```

> Generate a getter method that
> uses the result of calling the
> rulesEffects getter method.

We now have to change the call to `classField` in the `indexJsx` template function to also pass the correct value for the `isAffected` parameter. Listing 14.34 shows the corresponding changes (highlighted in bold) in src/generator/indexJsx-template.js.

Listing 14.34   Adapting the call to the `classField` template

```
class ${Name} {`,
    indent(1)(
        (dependencyOrderOf(attributes, referencedAttributesInValueOf)
⇒             || attributes)
            .map((attribute) =>
                classField(attribute, isAffected(attribute))
            )
    ),
```

Because the `classField` template function now takes two parameters, we no longer can just pass (a reference to) that function to the `map` function defined on arrays. Instead, we have to use an arrow function.

Exercise 14.14
Apply the code changes from listings 14.33 and 14.34. Verify that the code generator is correct in the sense that it generates the handwritten code for the `Rental` class verbatim.

14.3.3 *Adapting the UI of affected attributes*

Item 3 of the list at the start of section 14.3 says to change the affected fields in the Runtime's UI from input to display fields. Let's adapt the template code for all UI involving affected attributes. We'll start with making the template function for forms aware of the affected status of an attribute. Listing 14.35 shows the corresponding changes (highlighted in bold) in src/generator/indexJsx-template.js.

Listing 14.35   Adapting the functions related to form fields

```
const formFieldInputs = (objectExpr, attribute,
⇒        isAffected) => {
    const { settings } = attribute
    const { type } = settings
    const fieldName = ccNameOf(attribute)
    const isComputed = isAffected
⇒        || isComputedFromExpression(attribute)
```

> As before, indicate explicitly whether
> the given attribute is affected.

> The value of isComputed
> determines whether the
> attribute's value is computed
> (true) or can be input by the user.

```
        // ...the rest of the pre-existing code in this function...
}

const formField = (objectExpr, attribute, isAffected) => [
    `<FormField label="${withFirstUpper(attribute.settings["name"])}">`,
    indent(1)(
        formFieldInputs(objectExpr, attribute,
            isAffected                          Pass the isAffected value
        )                                       on to formFieldInputs.
    ),
    `</FormField>`
]
```

Now all we have to do is adapt the definition of the `<<record type>Form>` function for the record type to pass the isAffected value for each attribute.

Listing 14.36 Adapting the call to the `formField` template function

```
const ${Name}Form = observer(({ ${name} }) => `<form>`,
    indent(1)(
        attributes.map((attribute) =>
            formField(name, attribute, isAffected(attribute))
        )
    ),
    `</form>`)
```

Exercise 14.15

Apply the code changes from listings 14.35 and 14.36. Verify that the generated index.jsx file matches the handwritten version perfectly.

In this chapter, we've extended the example DSL so that the domain experts can define a basic form of business rules. We also adapted the Runtime and code generator accordingly.

Summary

- A *business rule* is a piece of business logic with the general form "Given a *<context>*, when *<condition>*, then *<consequence>*." In this form, the *<context>* is a description of the "shape of the data" that the business rule is supposed to be executed in.

    In our example DSL, all business rules have a single record type as their context and are thought to be *defined on* (and as part of) that record type. As a result, the notation of our business rules omits the "Given a *<context>*," part.

- The *<condition>* part of a business rule is a *logical* expression: an expression that produces a Boolean (true/false) value. To be able to put a type checking constraint on a business rule's *<condition>*, the library of built-in types needs to contain a boolean type.

- Typically, there are several ways to capture logical expressions into AST objects. Which way is best depends on several factors and is always subject to trade-offs, both of which can vary across DSLs and over time. It's a good idea to document your *design decisions.*
- The *<consequence>* part of a business rule specifies how to set or change a certain value in the record type the business rule is defined on. A consequence that alters data, or generally does more than "warm up the CPU," is often called an *effect.* Executing a business rule's consequence is called *applying the effect.*
- Business rules generate code in the Runtime. It's a good idea to execute all business rules at once and to gather their effects in a data structure. This is more flexible than trying to execute business rules grouped by the attribute they affect.
- The *execution model* of the business rules part of a DSL is a specification of how business rules, defined as DSL content, should be executed. The design of the business rules part of a DSL and the execution model influence each other strongly.

Some topics we didn't cover

This chapter covers

- What textual DSLs are, and what parsing is
- Why we haven't used the word "model"
- What the prefix "meta" means, and why we haven't used it
- Using language-oriented tooling

Software language engineering (SLE) is the subfield of computer science and software engineering that does what it says on the tin, with DSLs as a subfield. This chapter touches on a number of topics from SLE that you'll likely come across sooner or later when adopting a DSL-based approach. I'll explain each of these topics with just enough detail that you'll be able to recognize when it's being discussed "in the field." I'll also explain why I chose not to treat the topic more in depth, and earlier in the book. Finally, I'll provide some pointers for further reading, in case your curiosity is piqued.

15.1 Parsing, and textual DSLs

Virtually every programming language, the majority of software languages, and a lot of existing DSLs are purely *textual*: the notation of any of their DSL content consists of a string. Another way of saying the same thing is that their notation and serialization formats coincide.

A textual variant of our usual example DSL content—but without business rules—could look like the following listing.

Listing 15.1   A textual variant of the example `Rental` record type

```
record type "Rental" having attributes:
    "rental period": date range
    "rental price before discount": amount initially 0.0
    "discount": percentage initially 0
    "rental price after discount": amount
    initially -> "rental price before discount"
```

The contents of listing 15.1 can be considered to be plain text, but it's shown here with some syntax highlighting: keywords (or "key sentence fragments") are shown in bold, and type names, such as `date range`, are shown in italic.

Some remarks about the syntax itself:

- Usually, textual DSLs use identifiers as names. An identifier is a string that's easy to recognize within the DSL text, such as `Rental`. Often, an identifier consists completely of a certain range of characters (alphanumerics plus _ and $ is a popular choice) and is delimited by whitespace or other "out-of-range" characters.

  Here, I chose to represent names as strings surrounded with double quotes instead. That way we can keep the spaces in the names, without having to worry about clashing with the DSL's keywords.

- The `-> prefix` indicates that the string following is the name of the attribute referenced, not a literal string.

  We use a version of the example DSL content where "rental price after discount" can't have value kind "computed as" yet. This makes the required grammar (such as the one in listing 15.2) quite a bit simpler and more portable. We ignore the business rules for the same reason.

Exercise 15.1

Compare listing 15.1 to the usual form of the example DSL content:

- In what ways do you perceive the one form to be more intuitive, or have better UI/UX, than the other?
- What details are missing from listing 15.1? Do you see ways of adding these back in? What would be the consequences for a possible implementation of doing that?

> - Which form contains the most syntactic noise or visual clutter? Do you see ways of reducing that? What would be the consequences for a possible implementation of doing that?
> - Which form looks the best?

To do something with that textual content, you need to *parse* it. Parsing is the act of recognizing text that is expected to conform to a *grammar* and extracting structured data from it. A *grammar* is a formal specification of the combinations of characters you expect to occur in the textual DSL content. The following is a grammar in the well-known extended Backus–Naur form (EBNF) notation, which recognizes the textual Example DSL content in listing 15.1. (The EBNF notation is explained in depth in the book *Language Implementation Patterns* by Terence Parr, which I'll discuss shortly.)

Listing 15.2   A grammar in EBNF that can parse listing 15.1

```
STRING: '"' [A-Za-z0-9 ]+ '"' ;            ◄─── Specify a grammar rule (also
                                                 called a production) for a terminal
type: 'amount' | 'date range' | 'percentage' ; ◄─── STRING that recognizes strings,
                                                 surrounded with double quotes.

WS: (' ' | '\t' | '\n')+ ;                  ◄─── Specify a rule to recognize the
                                                 type identifier of an attribute,
attributeReference: '->' WS? STRING ;            using the OR (|) operator.

number: [0-9]+ ('.' [0-9]+)? ;              WS is an often-used abbreviation for
                                            "whitespace," meaning any combination
value: attributeReference | number ;        of spaces, tabs, and newlines.

attribute: STRING WS? ':' WS? type (WS 'initially' WS? value)? ;

recordType: WS? 'record type' WS? STRING WS?
   ➥ 'having attributes:' (WS? attribute)* WS? ;
```

Figure 15.1 shows the architecture of a parsing-based—rather than a projectional—Domain IDE. A *parser generator* is a tool or framework that lets you write a *grammar* according to some grammar notation, and that generates a parser that parses text (supposedly) conforming to that grammar. Parsing produces a *parse tree* from textual content: this parse tree is either already an AST or becomes one after some transformation.

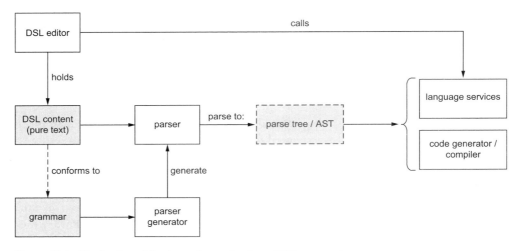

Figure 15.1   The basic architecture of a parsing-based DSL approach

Exercise 15.2
Look at listing 15.2.

- What does it specify, describe, or prescribe?
- What *doesn't* it specify? Hint: How would a parser know where to put all the parsed information in order to extract the structured data into an AST?
- How could a parse tree look different from an AST? What would the transformation mapping the parse tree to an AST look like?

Once a parser has produced an AST, this AST can then be passed on to *language services*. A language service is a small service (you could call it a "microservice") that derives a specific sort of information from the AST for specific purposes. Typical language services do the following:

- Compute a list of possible completions at a specific location in the text: *content assist*.
- Compute what constraints are violated in the current text.
- Compute how to syntax highlight the current text.
- Compute type information for a particular region in the text.
- Compute the contents of tooltips. This may involve calling other language services, such as the one that computes type information.

Such language services typically come integrated into IDEs, often as part of language-specific plugins. The IDE's text editor that the domain expert uses to edit their DSL content calls the various language services. That's usually triggered by some action of the domain expert, such as asking for a list of completions. The parser-produced AST is also used by tools like a compiler or a code generator.

Here's a non-exhaustive list of parser generators:

- *ANTLR* (www.antlr.org)—ANother Tool for Language Recognition. A Java-based parser generator that can produce parsers in many different programming languages from EBNF-style grammars.
- *Peggy* (https://peggyjs.org/)—A parser generator that produces parsers in JavaScript from *parsing expression grammars* (PEGs). (This framework was previously known as PEG.js.)
- *JavaCC* (https://javacc.github.io/javacc)—A Java-based parser generator that produces parsers in Java from an EBNF grammar.
- *Lex* (https://en.wikipedia.org/wiki/Lex_(software)) and *Yacc* (https://en.wikipedia.org/wiki/Yacc)—A parser generator framework that has been the mainstay of parsing for decades, especially in the Unix/POSIX world. I mention them mostly for historical purposes, since they can't be considered state of the art anymore. These two tools also have GNU equivalents: Flex (https://en.wikipedia.org/wiki/Flex_(lexical_analyser_generator)) and Bison (https://en.wikipedia.org/wiki/GNU_Bison), respectively.

To learn more about parsing (outside of the documentation of the preceding parser generators), I can recommend the following sources:

- *Language Implementation Patterns: Create Your Own Domain-Specific and General Programming Languages*, a book by Terence Parr (The Pragmatic Bookshelf, 2009). It provides an introduction to parsing based on Parr's own ANTLR parser generator.
- *Which Parsing Approach*, a blog post by Laurence Tratt (https://tratt.net/laurie/blog/entries/which_parsing_approach.html). It provides a nice overview of various parsing approaches and Tratt's experiences using them.

Exercise 15.3

Hard, and a lot of work: Implement a textual DSL that can at least parse listing 15.1. Do this any way you like: using an existing parser generator, using an existing or self-written parser combinator library (https://en.wikipedia.org/wiki/Parser_combinator), or from scratch by implementing a recursive descent parser (https://en.wikipedia.org/wiki/Recursive_descent_parser). If you're using a parser generator, listing 15.2 will give you a head start on the grammar, although you'll probably have to tweak that a bit still.

- Draw a diagram of the architecture of the end result.
- How does it compare to figure 5.4 from chapter 5? Favorably?

I chose to ignore parsing in this book for the following reasons:

■ *A textual language might not be the best match for non-technical domain experts.* At the beginning of this book, I stated that we were going to focus on implementing DSLs for domain experts in business domains. These domain experts usually are non-technical, so these business-oriented DSLs need to be *user* friendly to them. Even though they probably know their way around a word processor or spreadsheet software, they generally lack a background in software development. That means that they are more used to the user experience provided by apps (web apps or otherwise) than the experience provided by an IDE for software development. Subjecting non-technical users to a textual editor is likely enough to scare them away.

■ *Projectional editing is a good match for non-technical users who are already familiar with apps.* It's also a lot simpler on the conceptual, architectural, and implementation level than parsing-based editing: see figure 5.4.

A technical advantage of the projectional approach is that it's relatively easy to make the projection work sensibly for incomplete or invalid ASTs. That's because the domain experts need to be able to create DSL content from scratch or fix invalid DSL content. If the AST contains a setting that the projection doesn't expect, it can just ignore it. If the AST is missing a setting, the projection can show placeholder text to invite domain experts to provide a value. If the AST is invalid due to constraint violations, the projection just has to show the corresponding issues.

In sharp contrast, parsers need to rely on a mechanism called *error recovery* to "recover" from text that doesn't conform exactly to the grammar. This means that the parser doesn't fail as soon as the first syntactic error occurs—it tries its best to pick up as soon as possible after recognizing bad content. Ultimately, error recovery prevents one wrong character from invalidating all the DSL content at once, so it's a must-have. Unfortunately, without prodigious support from a parser generator, it's very hard to implement useful error recovery.

■ *Parsing is far from trivial.* The fact that parsing theory and parser engineering occupy a good part of the SLE's body of knowledge, as well as its research efforts, is testimony to that. There's a myriad of notions and terms that are important around parsing, such as tokens, lexer/lexing, LL- and LR-parsing, lookahead, backtracking, left-factorization, etc. Learning this topic well enough to implement a parser for a textual version of the example DSL would probably have occupied several chapters of this book alone. After that, we'd still have to implement language services on top of the parser, and integrate all of those with a text editor.

Parsing's main adversary is *ambiguity*: sometimes a text can match a particular grammar in more than one way. We say that such a grammar is ambiguous. A parser for such a grammar would require a mechanism to decide which way to choose before proceeding. You could either implement that choosing mechanism or change the grammar to repair the ambiguity, which might mean that the parser is able to parse fewer texts.

Credit where credit's due: we've left the days of Lex and Yacc (or Flex/Bison) far behind. Listing 15.2 represents the state of the art of more than three decades ago. Modern-day parsing paradigms such as Syntax Definition Formalism (SDF) and scannerless parsing are very powerful and produce performant and versatile parsing. Parser combinator libraries (available for Haskell, F#, Scala, and various other mainstream programming languages) provide a functional programming style of implementing parsers that's more understandable for many people.

Still, coming up with a grammar that parses a particular language is sometimes quite hard. You might even be tempted to fit the language to a working grammar, even if that means the DSL content becomes harder to understand or write. You can find an example in listing 15.1, where I had to prefix an attribute reference with -> to distinguish it from a literal string.

- *Parsing "hides" the AST.* The AST is hardly ever seen explicitly in a parsing-based implementation: it's essentially a by-product of parsing the textual DSL content. That makes it more difficult to explain what an AST is and what its relevance to DSLs is. That's not necessarily an impediment to implementing a text-based DSL, but it is one when teaching about DSLs.

Of course, we do an ample amount of parsing in this book, under the hood: the Node.js and Parcel tools we use, as well as the browser running the Domain IDE, parse all kinds of textual formats, such as JavaScript, JSON, HTML, and CSS.

15.2 *Using the word "model"*

A more commonly used word among SLE practitioners for the somewhat cumbersome "DSL content" is *model.* Technically, a model is an AST, or even a "forest" of ASTs, with a common purpose.

Model-driven software development (MDSD) is an umbrella term for building a software system by encoding its specification as a model. The difference with our "pure" DSL-based approach is that the language used for that specification model doesn't need to be domain-specific. When such a specification language is not a DSL, it's usually a general modeling language. A well-known example is the Unified Modeling Language (UML). You can use a mechanism called *profiles* to add a domain-specific flavor to UML. An example of that is the systems modeling language, *SysML.*

> **NOTE** In addition to MDSD, various other acronyms are also in use that may mean the exact same thing or something subtly different. I like to think

of all of these as *MD**, since the adjective "model-driven" signifies the unifying idea.

> **NOTE** UML is a uni*fied* modeling language, not a uni*versal* one. For more information, see the UML website (https://uml.org/) or Wikipedia's "Unified Modeling Language" page (https://en.wikipedia.org/wiki/Unified_Modeling _Language).

The main reason I didn't use "model" instead of "DSL content" and "AST" is that it's somewhat problematic. In general, the word "model" seems to be understood as "a reductive abstraction of reality." It's also often expected to be a mathematical description. In contrast, it was my intention from chapter 1 that our DSL content was precise enough that we'd be able to generate working software from it: precise enough to make it executable. You'd have to use adjectives like "consistent," "formal(ly defined)," and "prescriptive" on top of "model" to bridge the distance from "abstraction of reality" to our understanding of "precisely represented, executable domain knowledge."

I've also avoided the word "model" because of a number of technical sources of confusion:

- Does "model" correspond to a proper AST, or its notated version, or a parse tree, or its serialization?
- Can "model" correspond to multiple ASTs that may have cross-references? In other words, is there some modularization going on? How is this forest of ASTs managed? How are these cross-references managed and resolved?

15.3 *Using terms with the prefix "meta"*

Another category of words that you'll encounter often within SLE is terms prefixed with "*meta*." The term "meta-*X*" essentially means "an *X* to describe something about *X*s." Figure 15.2 shows a cartoon explaining the term in a very "meta" way.

The most prevalent "meta" combination is probably with the "problematic" word from the previous section: *metamodel*. A metamodel is a model that specifies precisely what the shape and contents of a model are allowed to be. In our case, a metamodel would specify exactly what concepts our AST objects can have, and what properties of which type are allowed in combination with what concept label. In terms of the key aspects from chapter 1, we could say "metamodel = structure = concepts + properties + types." Figure 15.3 shows the key aspects of a DSL but using the words "model" and "metamodel."

Borrowing the class diagram notation from UML for a moment, we could draw a metamodel for DSL content representing a record type—see figure 15.4. (In keeping with our implementation, I made the `value` property of the `Number` concept string-typed, so we can distinguish between numeric values "0" and "0.0".)

Figure 15.2   "Meta"—a comical meta-explanation of "metadata", © Oliver Widder of Geek&Poke fame[1]

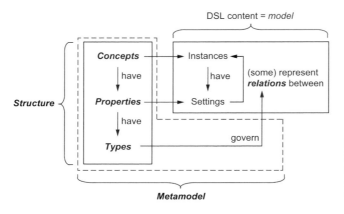

Figure 15.3   A version of figure 1.20 visualizing the notion of a *metamodel* describing the model, which is the DSL content

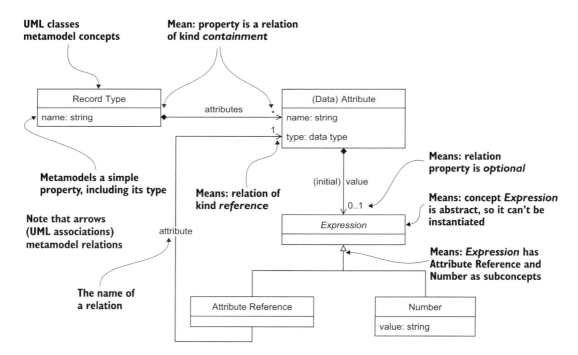

Figure 15.4   A metamodel for DSL content representing a record type, borrowing the class diagram notation from UML

There are a few reasons I didn't make the metamodel for our example DSL explicit before:

- Learning about DSLs is hard enough without "going meta." Introducing the notion of a metamodel is not without danger of me(n)ta(l) overload. Extracting a metamodel from structured data is called *metamodeling*, and it's akin to, and as difficult as, data modeling. ("Metamodel" can be used both as a noun and a verb.)

- JavaScript, being a dynamically typed language instead of a strongly typed one, has no facilities to properly "codify" the metamodel by making our implementation's code type-safe.

  You *can* do that partially in TypeScript, by defining types for the concepts and their properties in the metamodel. (I explained why I chose to not use TypeScript at the beginning of the book, in the "About the code" section.) TypeScript doesn't have particular constructs to define constraints, so you have to do that as we did in chapter 9 anyway.

- The metamodel is changing throughout the book. We saw in chapter 10 that it's convenient to be lenient about the AST, whereas a metamodel is about strictness, which is contrary to leniency. It's certainly possible to use a metamodel and have a lenient AST at the same time, but it takes some work to explain how to do that sensibly. I decided that having an explicit metamodel wasn't worth that extra effort for our small example DSL, which evolves only a little bit.

- An explicit metamodel requires some kind of notation: a DSL for metamodels. A DSL to specify DSLs with (or certain aspects of them) is called a *meta-DSL*. The domain of a meta-DSL is the specification of software languages. In figure 15.4 we used a tiny part of UML as a meta-DSL. By the self-imposed rules of the meta game, the meta-DSL has to have a metamodel as well, which would therefore be a *meta-metamodel*. Not bothering with an (explicit) metamodel absolves us of the need to contemplate such headache-inducing things.

Meta-circularity

To avoid having the meta-metamodel require a meta-meta-metamodel, etc., a meta-metamodel is typically able to metamodel itself. This property is called *meta-circularity*.

It's a very powerful property for a language to have, but it often also detracts from that language being fit for purpose. Meta-circular languages tend to become optimized for meta-circularity at the expense of benefiting the domains they were originally intended for.

Alan Perlis warns about the analogous effect for the similar property of *Turing completeness* of software languages:

> Beware of the Turing tar-pit in which everything is possible but nothing of interest is easy.[a]

This alludes to general programming languages (GPLs), which are usually powerful enough to be Turing complete. Such languages might be used to implement *any* program that solves some problem, and doing so might introduce lots of accidental complexity on top of the essential complexity of the problem. If that's consistently the case, that GPL fell victim to the Turing tarpit. Apparently, the GPL was designed and optimized to be (provably) Turing complete, with usefulness for solving real-world problems taking a backseat.

(continued)

Designing a DSL holds a similar trap: it's often tempting to "enhance" a DSL with constructs that seem "right" to you as the language designer. Those constructs might not be really useful for the domain experts using the language.

---

[a] Alan Perlis, "Epigrams on Programming," *SIGPLAN Notices* 17, no. 9 (Sept. 1982), epigram #54.

A clear advantage of having an explicit metamodel is that we can use it to inform our code about the possible shape of the AST and the types of properties of AST objects. In other words, we'd know the possible type of each setting beforehand. In particular, we'd know whether a relation is a containment or reference relation. While performing a depth-first tree traversal, we wouldn't have to check whether a setting's value is a reference object. Instead, we could just have the algorithm inspect the metamodel to *know* whether a certain property held references or children. (In fact, we wouldn't need reference objects in the first place.) That approach would effectively assume that the AST conforms completely to the metamodel. We've seen in chapter 10 that isn't necessarily always the case.

Exercises 15.4

- Metamodel our example DSL content, including the business rules. Note that I use "metamodel" as a verb here: "to metamodel something."
- Have a look at the types of simple properties in figure 15.4:
  - Could you make those more precise or narrower?
  - What would be the pros and cons of doing that?
- Metamodel the metamodel in figure 15.4. Is the result meta-circular?

Exercise 15.5

Even though JavaScript doesn't have facilities to make our code really type-safe, we can improve our code a little.

- Create a new src/metamodel.js file, and export a `Concepts` object of the following form from it:

```
{
    recordType: "Record Type",
    attribute: "Attribute",
    ...
}
```

- In the rest of the DSL's implementation's code, replace the use of literal strings containing concept labels with property access to this object. As an

example, `Record Type` would become `Concepts.recordType`. (Make sure to import the `Concepts` object from src/metamodel.js.)
- After making this change, find out whether your IDE provides more assistance. For example, does it do code completion after typing `"Concepts."`, giving you a list of all the concepts?
- Can you think of ways to do the same for the names of properties?

15.4 Using language-oriented tooling

We implemented a Domain IDE with a DSL at its core, and we did that with only a mainstream, JavaScript-based technology stack. You might have been wondering, "Isn't there an easier way to do this, where you get more out of the box? Haven't people created tools, frameworks, or libraries specifically for implementing DSLs and Domain IDEs?" The answer is, "Of course, they have!"

15.4.1 Using a language workbench

A tool to implement DSLs and Domain IDEs is called a *language workbench*, a term coined by Martin Fowler in the early 2000s (www.martinfowler.com/articles/language Workbench.html). A language workbench (LWB) is a platform for implementing software languages—in particular, DSLs—in an efficient way. That platform often takes the form of a specialized IDE. The core of such an LWB usually consists of a set of meta-DSLs to specify the various aspects of a DSL: structure, constraints, editors, type system, code generation, etc.

A fair number of LWBs exist, with a large variance in different qualities:

- *Maturity*—The software quality, including whether it is well documented.
- *DSL style*—Textual (parsing-based) style versus projectional, with graphical notation-only as an extreme.
- *Open source*—Most LWBs are open source rather than closed source.
- *Support*—Whether it is backed by a company offering support, has an active community, or both.
- *OS/platform*—Which platform it runs on.

I didn't use an LWB to implement the example DSL in this book for the following reasons:

- To understand how to use an LWB, you need a good working knowledge of what goes into the implementation of DSLs. Implementing a DSL from scratch, as we did in this book, is an efficient way of getting that working knowledge. Trying to learn all of that while using an LWB would essentially put us in a chicken-and-egg situation.
- I didn't want to rely on a specific LWB for this book. Tools change or get outdated, either of which would make this book's content irrelevant. LWBs also tend to adopt their own style of terminology. Using a specific LWB would mean

having to adopt that LWB-specific terminology or to translate it explicitly to more generic SLE terminology.

- Many of the LWBs in the following list already have good tutorials or books written about them.

The following LWBs have attained a level of maturity sufficient to make them suitable for real-world use. This list is certainly not complete, but it consists of LWBs that I'm at least passingly familiar with. They're free to use unless indicated otherwise with a "$" sign.

- *Meta Programming System* (MPS; www.jetbrains.com/mps/)—Running on the JVM and based on JetBrains' IntelliJ/IDEA family of IDEs, it's an LWB for creating Domain IDEs with projectional DSLs. The unabbreviated name comes from the fact that the DSLs run directly in the MPS workbench. MPS is probably the most popular LWB in this list, as it's actively maintained and supported by Jet-Brains, and it has an active community.

  To demonstrate how an LWB is used and what it can provide out of the box, I'll reimplement our example DSL using MPS in section 15.4.2.

  MPS has a number of interesting extensions (plugins):

  - MPS Extensions (https://jetbrains.github.io/MPS-extensions/) is a set of MPS plugins. Many of the features provided by this set have come to be regarded as an indelible part of MPS. That's especially true for the grammar-cells plugin, which provides a convenient way to declare side-transforms. (The "Efficient Development of Consistent Projectional Editors using Grammar Cells" paper by Markus Voelter et al., explaining the theory behind that plugin, can be found here: http://mbeddr.com/files/gc-sle.pdf.)
  - KernelF (https://github.com/IETS3/iets3.opensource) is a functional programming language built on top of MPS. It consists of modules that can be dropped in and configured, modified, or extended on demand. You can use it to get going rapidly with the class of arithmetic, logical, and functional expressions that you'll usually need. You can find Markus Voelter's paper on the design and use of the language here: https://voelter.de/data/books/kernelf-designEvoUse.pdf.
  - Modelix (https://github.com/modelix/modelix) and MPSServer (https://github.com/Strumenta/MPSServer) plus WebEditKit (https://github.com/Strumenta/webeditkit) are two different frameworks that aim to provide cloud storage for MPS models with real-time collaboration, in combination with editors for those models running in web browsers.

  Much more thorough introductions to, and material about, MPS are available in these sources:

  - JetBrains' own resources: www.jetbrains.com/mps/learn/.
  - Dispersed throughout *DSL Engineering* by Markus Voelter (CreateSpace Independent Publishing Platform, 2013).

- The MPS Rocks site is a curated list of interesting material (plugins, books, papers, videoed talks, etc.) on MPS: https://mps.rocks/.
- Two books by Fabien Campagne, which are not in print anymore, can be found secondhand as physical copies and on Google Books digitally .

- *Xtext* (https://eclipse.dev/Xtext/)—Based on ANTLR and the Eclipse Modeling Framework, there are JVM-based LWBs for creating textual DSLs running inside a slowly increasing number of platforms: Eclipse, other popular IDEs that support the Language Server Protocol (LSP), and web browsers. Xtext is supported by several companies (most notably itemis) and has an active community.

- *Sirius Desktop* (https://eclipse.dev/sirius/) and *Sirius Web* (https://eclipse.dev/sirius/sirius-web.html)—Based on the Eclipse and Graphical Modeling Frameworks, Sirius is a JVM-based LWB for creating graphical DSLs for the desktop and web. You can think of it as the graphical opposite of Xtext. It's backed by the French company Obeo and is used by companies like Thales and the European Space Agency (ESA).

- *Intentional Domain Workbench* (IDW)—($) Although the IDW and its creator—the company Intentional Software, founded by Charles Symonyi—don't exist anymore, it's worth mentioning, if only for historical reasons. The IDW is one of the first actual LWBs, possibly predating the term. It has had quite an impact on the field of LWBs, despite almost no one actually having worked with it (see another blog post by Martin Fowler: https://martinfowler.com/bliki/IntentionalSoftware.html).

  IDW could be used to produce *domain workbenches* consisting of projectional DSLs. True to form, the IDW itself was completely based on the projectional paradigm. The IDW was very impressive for many reasons: the extent to which the projectional paradigm suffused the whole tool, its power and flexibility, its performance (especially for the day) in spite of never taking a shortcut, and the way the company seemingly discouraged anyone from using it through exorbitant license fees, lack of documentation, and making it impossible for people with an IQ below 160 to understand or use it.

  The company was bought by Microsoft in 2017, but evidently this was a "human capital acquisition" as Microsoft hasn't released anything like the IDW since. Despite its challenges, I would have loved to see the IDW resurface, but I'm afraid it's not to be.

- *Spoofax* (https://spoofax.dev/)—Running on the JVM, Spoofax is an LWB for producing textual software languages with Eclipse and IntelliJ editor plugins. It started life as an academic research project but is also used in a number of commercial production situations. It's actively maintained by a group founded by Eelco Visser at the Technical University of Delft, the Netherlands.

- *Rascal* (www.rascal-mpl.org/)—Rascal is a general programming language designed for *metaprogramming*: analyzing, transforming, and generating code.

The Rascal language itself has first-class support for lots of SLE-specific aspects: grammars, AST traversal, string templates for code generation, etc. As a consequence, you can also implement DSLs with Rascal.

Similar to Spoofax, Rascal started life as an academic research project but is also used in a number of commercial production situations. It's actively maintained by the SWAT group at the Centrum Wiskunde & Informatica, in Amsterdam (the Netherlands).

- *MetaEdit+* (www.metacase.com/mep/)—($) A closed-source LWB for creating pure-graphical DSLs. It's been around since 1993, possibly making it the oldest LWB still in active use. It seems to be used often for quite technical, "real" engineering-centric domains, where producing a software system is not always the end goal.

- *Whole Platform* (https://github.com/wholeplatform/whole)—Running on the JVM and based on Eclipse technology, Whole Platform is an LWB for creating projectional DSLs. It's not very well known outside SLE circles, despite having been created and maintained by a group of very sympathetic Italians, who have been using it in commercial projects.

NOTE For several years, a group of SLE practitioners organized the *Language Workbench Challenge*. Creators of LWBs (or tools that had much of their characteristics) would demonstrate their tools, and specifically how they could be applied to a particular problem: the "challenge." One of the main outputs of the Language Workbench Challenge is a paper by Sebastian Erdweg, Tijs van der Storm, Markus Völter, et al., *The State of the Art in Language Workbenches: Conclusions from the Language Workbench Challenge* (https://homepages.cwi.nl/ ~storm/publications/lwc13paper.pdf). This paper compares 10 LWBs that were then—in 2013—state of the art on a fairly large number of criteria. Even though it doesn't reflect any new developments during the last 10 years, reading it is useful to get a sense of the field of SLE, and LWBs in particular. It also won the Most Influential Paper Award of the 2023 ACM SIGPLAN International Conference on SLE.

15.4.2 *Implementing the example DSL with MPS*

Let's look at a partial implementation of our example DSL in MPS to get an idea of how that compares to our own from-scratch implementation using JavaScript. I'll demonstrate the implementation as a series of screenshots of MPS in action, showing both the implementation's "code" using the various meta-DSLs that MPS has and the end result running inside MPS. I won't implement the entire example DSL, but just enough to be able to get an idea of how MPS compares to our JavaScript-based approach. You can find the MPS project with this re-implementation (up to date with MPS version 2021.1.3) at https://github.com/dslmeinte/Building-User-Friendly-DSLs -code/tree/main/mps.

Opening the MPS workbench on our MPS project shows the screen in figure 15.5.

Project panel, showing the project's organization

Editor panel—currently empty

"Module" with the DSL content

"Model" within a module

"Language module" containing the DSL's implementation

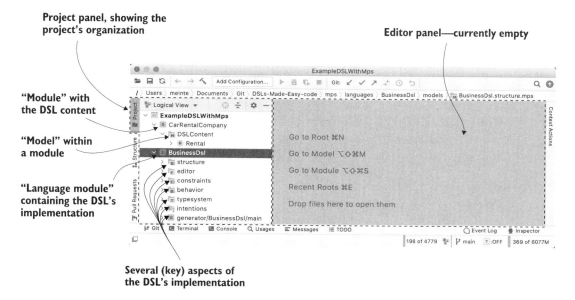

Several (key) aspects of the DSL's implementation

Figure 15.5 An overview of the MPS workbench, with the project's hierarchy shown in the Project panel and an empty editor panel

The Project panel shows the project's hierarchical organization as a tree. The project is called ExampleDSLWithMps, and it has two *modules*:

- CarRentalCompany contains the DSL content.
- BusinessDsl contains the DSL's implementation.

Modules contain *models* of various kinds. The CarRentalCompany module contains just one model, which is called DSLContent and contains the DSL content. That model itself contains one item, which happens to be a *root*: a separately identifiable, named AST. The Rental item corresponds to the usual example record type of the same name, including its business rules (shown later in figure 15.11).

The BusinessDsl module has a number of models in it, which are called *aspects*. Some aspects map to a key aspect of DSLs discussed in section 1.4.1, while others are MPS-specific. Each of these aspects contains root items in one of the meta-DSLs of MPS, specifying part of the DSL that this module implements. Table 15.1 explains the aspects.

Table 15.1 Aspects of a DSL implementation in MPS, with description and mapping to a key aspect from chapter 1 (where that exists)

MPS aspect name	Key aspect (ch. 1)	Role
structure	Structure	As in chapter 1.
editor	Notation	As in chapter 1.

Table 15.1   Aspects of a DSL implementation in MPS, with description and mapping to a key aspect from chapter 1 (where that exists) *(continued)*

MPS aspect name	Key aspect (ch. 1)	Role
`constraints`	n/a	Specifies to which reference properties *scoping* should be applied. (The MPS name is a bit misleading.)
`behavior`	n/a	Defines functions on concepts (among others implementing scoping) and "almost-ordinary" Java classes. MPS provides BaseLanguage, a variant of Java, to implement behavior and code logic within other meta-DSLs.
`typesystem`	(Part of constraints)	Defines a type system and implements all constraints. (Again, the MPS name is a bit misleading.)
`intentions`	n/a	Defines editor actions.
`generator/BusinessDsl/ main`	Meaning	Defines a `main` code generator for the `BusinessDsl`.

Unlike our own implementation, the structure of the DSL (or metamodel—see section 15.3) needs to be defined explicitly through the structure aspect, shown in figure 15.6.

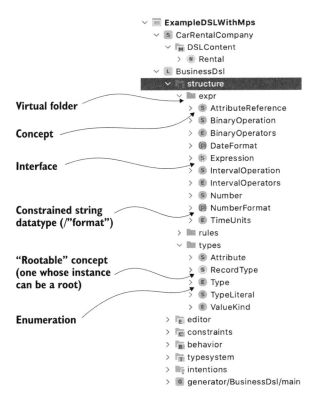

Figure 15.6   The hierarchy of the structure aspect, showing the different kinds of items in it

The structure aspect has a tree hierarchy of its own, which is visible in figure 15.6 as "folders"—which MPS calls "virtual folders"—named `expr` (for *expr*essions), (business) `rules`, and (record) `types`. A leaf on any level of the tree (including the top level) is a separate root item that defines either a concept, an enumeration, an interface, or a *constrained string datatype* (explained shortly). The icon next to the item's name indicates the kind of item.

An enumeration is a fixed collection of textual values. An example is the `Type` enumeration, which defines the types of our example DSL: amount, date range, percentage. An interface is an abstract concept that can't be instantiated, but only specifies properties and behavior, which implementing concepts then inherit. A constrained string datatype definition is basically a regular expression to constrain string values. In our case, we use them to define number and date literal strings, or "formats."

Figure 15.7 shows definitions in MPS for the `Record Type` and `Attribute` concepts, and the definition for the `Type` enumeration.

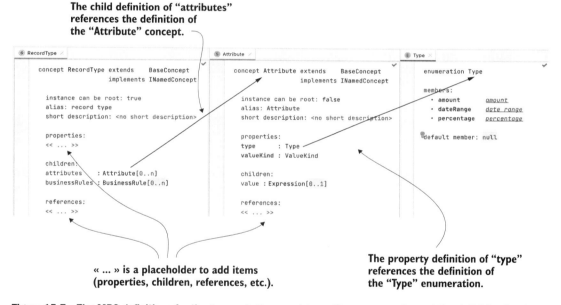

Figure 15.7 The MPS definitions for the `Record Type` and `Attribute` concepts, and the definition for the `Type` enumeration

The definition of a concept contains the following metadata:

- The *name* of the concept, which must be a valid Java identifier.
- A *supertype* of the concept: either a concept explicitly defined in the structure aspect or `BaseConcept`.
- A list of interfaces the concept implements. The `INamedConcept` is a built-in interface that provides a string-typed `name` property.

- Whether an instance of this concept can be a root item, which opens in a separate editor.
- An *alias* for the concept: this is used as a human-readable name by the editor, such as when choosing a concept to instantiate.
- The remaining MPS terms are translated in table 15.2 to terms according to our ORD nomenclature for ASTs.

Table 15.2   Translations of MPS names to terms used throughout this book

MPS name	In ORD terms
Properties	Properties with simple values as their settings, such as strings, Booleans, integers, and enumerations
Children	Properties with containment or parent-child relations as their settings
References	Properties with reference relations as their settings

All expression concepts declare the `Expression` interface as their supertype. The interface type is then used as the type for the `value` child of the `Attribute` concept, which has cardinality `[0..1]` to express that it's optional.

Figure 15.8 shows the definitions of the `Expression` interface and some of the expression concepts.

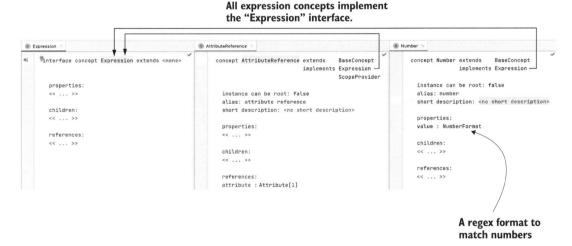

Figure 15.8   The `Expression` interface and two of its concrete subconcepts

Having dealt with the structure aspect, we can move on to the editor aspect and define the notation of each concept as an editor. Figure 15.9 shows the one for the `Record Type` concept.

```
 RecordType_Editor  ×

    <default> editor for concept  RecordType
       node cell layout:
         [/
            [> Record Type { name } <]
            <constant>
            [> ---> [/                                        <]
                    attributes:
                    [> ---> [/                        <]
                            (/ % attributes %      /)
                               /empty cell: <default>
                            /]
                    empty
                /]
            [> ---> [/                                        <]
                    business rules:
                    [> ---> [/                        <]
                            (/ % businessRules %   /)
                               /empty cell: <default>
                            /]
                /]
         /]

       inspected cell layout:
          <choose cell model>

 +   Ⓢ RecordType     Ⓔ RecordType_Editor    Ⓑ RecordType_Behavior   → typeof_RecordType   ○ check_RecordType
```

Figure 15.9   The editor definition for the `Record Type` **concept, defining its notation using a specialized meta-DSL**

You'll see shortly (in figure 15.11) that the editor definition resembles the actual notation quite well. Figure 15.10 shows the editor defining the notation of an `Attribute`.

MPS has an Inspector panel that shows additional properties of the item that's currently selected in the editor. These properties can be used to specify styling, placeholder text, etc., which can even use expressions. In figure 15.10, the Inspector shows how "a" or "an" is shown depending on the first character of the attribute's name.

MPS offers many types of complete UI elements out of the box, each customizable, stylable, and with fully functional UX (user experience). Functionality that comes for free includes navigating around the AST, selection, deletion, copy–paste, and moving content around. This is where MPS tends to shine: implementing DSL notation like this is quite productive—much more so than implementing the projection from scratch.

After building this, we can create DSL content, which then looks like figure 15.11.

In MPS, the type system aspect is used to implement both the type system and the constraints. Constraints are implemented more or less the same way as we did in chapter 9, which is why I'll skip them now.

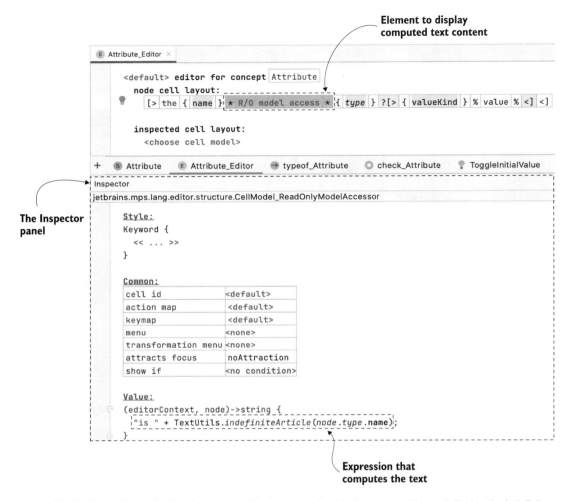

Figure 15.10   The editor definition for the `Attribute` concept, with the computation and display the indefinite article highlighted in the Inspector panel

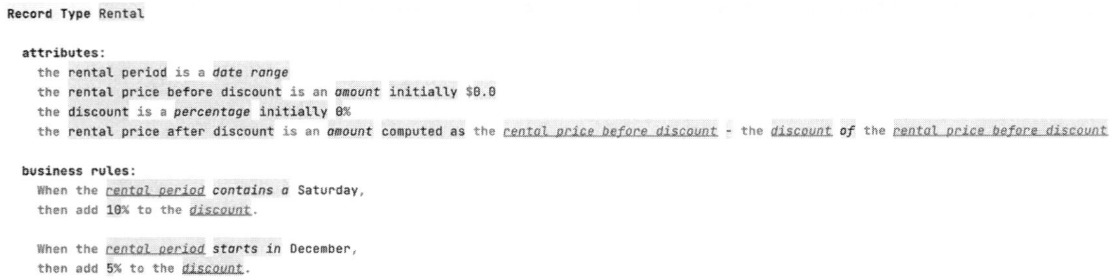

Record Type Rental

attributes:
  the rental period is a *date range*
  the rental price before discount is an *amount* initially $0.0
  the discount is a *percentage* initially 0%
  the rental price after discount is an *amount* computed as the *rental price before discount* - the *discount* of the *rental price before discount*

business rules:
  When the *rental period* contains a Saturday,
  then add 10% to the *discount*.

  When the *rental period* starts in December,
  then add 5% to the *discount*.

Figure 15.11   A screenshot of the usual `Rental` record type as DSL content in the MPS implementation

MPS supports type inference by producing type (in-)equalities, which are then solved algorithmically. That makes it possible to implement a type system that can correctly infer the type in situations where the type computation we discussed in chapter 13 wouldn't do better than producing "untype." The downside is that such an implementation requires more code, which is why I chose not to show that part of the implementation.

Finally, a code generator can be implemented with MPS in the following two ways:

- Implement a *transformation* to map DSL content to JavaScript in JSX syntax. This approach has the advantage that templates are phrased in terms of the concrete syntax of the target language, with "expression-shaped holes" that take values from the input DSL content. That means it's much harder to make faulty templates that produce non-parsable code.

  It does mean, however, that we have to implement a JSX language, encompassing the JSX syntax and enough of the JavaScript language to express the code we need to generate with. That's quite a bit of effort—typically much more than implementing a business-oriented DSL. MPS implementations of a few mainstream target languages are available, but not all of them are complete or even maintained.

- Install a plugin with a template language to generate plain text that happens to be JSX code. That's equivalent in complexity to the approach we took in chapter 8, as well as to using a regular template engine.

NOTE The `plaintextgen` template language plugin originally created by Remi Bosman, Klemens Schindler, and Eugen Schindler is the only usable plugin for MPS (that I'm aware of) that supports generating plain text directly: see https://jetbrains.github.io/MPS-extensions/extensions/generator/plaintext-gen/. Nowadays, it's part of the MPS Extensions.

Because of this unfavorable tradeoff, code generation is the weakest point of MPS, in my opinion. I chose to altogether skip demonstrating a code generator for our example DSL implemented with MPS because of that weakness, and also to save space in the book.

15.4.3 Using language-oriented frameworks

An LWB is not the only instrument that can speed up DSL implementation. A number of frameworks exist that target specific aspects of DSL implementation or happen to be suitable for it. These frameworks don't necessarily cover all the aspects of DSL implementation on their own, so they can only constitute part of a complete DSL implementation.

A framework that simply *must* be mentioned is the Eclipse Modeling Framework (EMF; https://eclipse.dev/modeling/emf/). It's a JVM-based framework created by Ed Merks, so you could say it's the "Ed Merks Framework." It consists of several pieces, the most important of which are

- *Ecore*—A metamodeling facility for describing metamodels.
- *Core EMF*—A facility for in-memory persistence of models that have an Ecore metamodel. That includes serialization to and deserialization from XML, according to the XML Metadata Interchange (XMI) file format standardized by the Object Management Group (www.omg.org/).

Virtually every JVM-based modeling tool uses the EMF. In particular, most implementations of the UML rely on the EMF in some way.

Blockly (https://developers.google.com/blockly) is a framework created by Google for creating block-based visual programming languages. The editors of these languages run in a web browser. Blockly resembles Scratch (https://scratch.mit.edu/), the educational environment targeted at children wanting to learn to program. Blockly powers numerous web-based programming environments for educational use. It supports many built-in constructions called *blocks*, and it's possible to define custom blocks as well. That makes Blockly amenable to building graphical DSLs.

Freon (www.freon4dsl.dev/) is a promising new framework for implementing projectional DSL editors on the web. It's written in TypeScript (but also usable in JavaScript) by Jos Warmer and Anneke Kleppe, two names well known in SLE circles for several books on modeling, as well as for coauthoring part of the UML standard. Freon's specialty is the projection of expressions. It offers several first-class constructs for this, such as declaring operator precedence/priority and an equivalent of cursor positions. It uses that information to automatically add side-transforms (see section 12.4) to the projection, which can then be triggered by the keyboard in a familiar way.

LionWeb (https://github.com/LionWeb-io) is an initiative to create an ecosystem of interoperable components for building language-oriented modeling tools on the web. The name stands for "Language Interfaces on the Web." It provides specifications for communication and serialization protocols, a reference architecture, as well as prototypal implementations conforming to those in TypeScript and Java. (Full disclosure: I'm one of the initiative's founding members.) The goal is to foster collaboration among language-oriented tools—LWBs and frameworks—and their communities.

In this chapter, we looked at several topics that are important in software language engineering but that we haven't covered until now. For each topic, we learned the absolute basics of it and why we didn't discuss it before in this book. You should now be able to recognize those topics when you run into them on the job, and you'll know which resources you can use to learn more.

Summary

- Software language engineering (SLE) is a subfield of computer science and software engineering that contains DSLs as a subfield of its own.
- *Parsing* is the process of extracting structured data from text that conforms to a *grammar*. This can be used to implement (external) DSLs whose content is pure(ly) text(ual): a textual DSL.

- SLE practitioners use the word "model" instead of "DSL content." *Model-driven software development* is the generic term for any software development approach that uses models to build software systems. The models encode that software system's specification.

- A "meta-X" means "an X to describe something about Xs." The most relevant use of "meta" within SLE is for "metamodel": a description of the structure of the DSL, which itself is a model. Having an explicit metamodel is useful, as long as it doesn't hamper evolving the DSL.

- A *language workbench* (LWB) is a platform for implementing software languages—in particular, DSLs—in an efficient way using "meta-DSLs." Several contemporary LWBs exist, with the most popular one being JetBrains MPS. In addition, several language-oriented frameworks exist that can be used to implement DSLs but that are not full-fledged LWBs.

appendix A
Setting up the development environment

This appendix covers

- Setting up a suitable development environment, either locally or online
- Choosing between using a local development environment or a web IDE
- Setting up a repository for JavaScript development
- Learning how to use a JavaScript dependency manager to install libraries and frameworks
- Using the REPL facility of Node.js
- Running development tools

Chances are you're already quite familiar with most of what's in this appendix. Nevertheless, I want to provide the basic instructions you'll need to set up a suitable development environment that's guaranteed to work for the code and instructions given throughout the book. From chapter 3 onwards, we'll be implementing a Domain IDE using this development environment. Along the way, we'll also implement a Runtime based on a reference implementation for it. The reference implementation is introduced in chapter 8.

NOTE   An integrated development environment (IDE) is a piece of software that *integrates* the various aspects of building applications, such as writing code, building/compiling, debugging, versioning, etc.

Figure A.1 is an extended version of figure 1.2 showing the DSL-based approach to developing a Runtime using a Domain IDE—this time including the reference implementation for the Runtime.

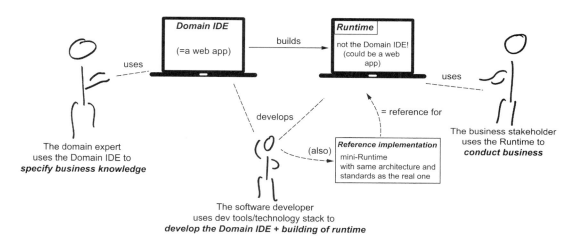

Figure A.1   Using a DSL-based approach to develop a Runtime using a Domain IDE—reference implementation included

TIP   In this book, the reference implementation and the Runtime happen to be the same thing. In general, that's undesirable: I explain this in more detail in section 8.2.

We're going to develop the Domain IDE with a JavaScript-based technology stack that consists of the following:

- JavaScript according to the ES2015 specification (https://262.ecma-international .org/6.0/), running both under Node.js as well as in modern browsers.

  The sixth edition of the ECMAScript specification, which specifies the JavaScript language, adds several features that make JavaScript more useful (and arguably less painful) than earlier. (This specification edition was initially known as ES6.) We'll make explicit use of most of these new features.
- The React framework (https://react.dev/) for building reactive UIs.
- The MobX framework (https://mobx.js.org) for state management.
- The Express framework (https://expressjs.com) for implementing a backend.
- Parcel tooling (https://parceljs.org) for web bundling.

NOTE   In this book, the Runtime (which is also the reference implementation) happens to use the exact same technology stack as the Domain IDE. That's convenient for our purposes, but unlikely in general.

A.1   *Putting together a development environment*

Figure A.2 shows what minimally goes into a development environment for the technology stack described previously.

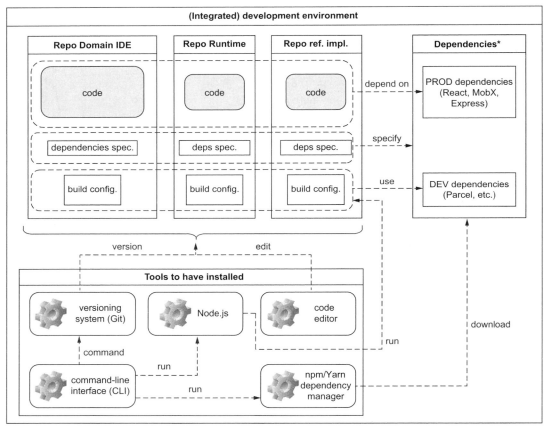

* not drawn to scale

Figure A.2   A development environment with which to implement a Domain IDE and Runtime

Arguably the most important part of the development environment is the three *code repositories* or *repos*. These contain everything related to the Domain IDE, the Runtime, and the reference implementation for the Runtime.

> ### Mono- vs. multi-repo
>
> In this book, I put all of these repos in the same code repository. This is mainly for our own convenience, so we have everything in one place. We can get away with doing that because our Runtime, which also serves as the reference implementation, is tiny compared to a real Runtime. The other reason to use only one repository is that multi-repo setups can be cumbersome—especially for web IDEs (see section A.3).
>
> In general, the Domain IDE, Runtime, and reference implementation should all be in their own, separate code repositories—or at least in separate, isolated, self-contained parts of a monorepo. Having separate code repositories can also help when the technology stacks of the Domain IDE and Runtime/reference implementation differ.

Each code repository contains the following:

- Actual (JavaScript) *code*, with some non-code files (such as HTML, CSS, or image files) alongside it
- A *build configuration* that specifies how to build that code
- A *specification* of the *dependencies* required

A code repository typically is *versioned*. That way, you can tag completed work as such by checking it in (committing it). A code repository usually is distributed, to share work with other software developers. A shared code repository is also a good way to hook up to a Continuous Integration (CI) system.

> **TIP**   In this book, we put any persistent storage of DSL content in the code repository, again for convenience. In general, this is undesirable: a real Domain IDE should use proper persistent storage, such as a database or a cloud-based file storage service. You certainly shouldn't misuse the versioning system for persistence. It's a good idea to exclude files that serve as storage from being tracked.

Another main part of the development environment is formed by the *tools* we'll need to have installed. At the very least, we need the following:

- A *command-line interface* (CLI, or terminal/shell/bash) for running commands.
- A *versioning system*, such as *Git*, to version and share the code repositories.
- *Node.js* for running JavaScript outside of a browser.
- A *dependency manager* (such as *npm* or *Yarn* for JavaScript) to download and manage dependencies.
- A *code editor* for editing the code in the repositories, the build configuration, and the dependencies specification. Ideally, the code editor should understand the things you're editing, not only on a per-file basis, but also in the scope of the entire code repository. It should provide error checking (and quick fixes), content assist, refactoring, documentation lookup, etc. It's probably best to use an IDE that's suitable for developing software using the chosen technology stack.

The final main part of the development environment is formed by the *dependencies*. A dependency is "stuff" that's downloaded from somewhere, and that's either included by the built code or is a tool needed for building it. Which dependencies and which versions are required by the repos is specified in their respective dependencies specifications. It's the responsibility of the *dependency manager* (which is also often called a *package manager*) to manage these dependencies. This boils down mostly to downloading and installing them.

A.1.1 Choosing between a local or online development environment

Nowadays, you essentially have two choices for *where and how* you set up and run your development environment: running locally or in the cloud.

Running *locally* (or "offline") means running under a traditional OS such as Linux/UNIX, macOS, or Windows on a physical or virtual machine. In this case, the tools are installed separately, directly under the OS. The code repositories are situated on your machine's hard drive in a location of your choosing. The dependencies are installed alongside, or often even inside, the code repositories.

One of the tools would usually be a full-blown IDE specifically tailored for developing software using the chosen technology stack: the *desktop IDE*. Its main feature is a code editor that really understands everything in the code repositories. It often integrates the other tools as well (versioning system, CLI, Node.js, dependency manager), to make it a real one-stop shop. Popular examples of useful developer desktop IDEs are Eclipse, Visual Studio (Code), IntelliJ/IDEA, etc.

> **NOTE** It's not absolutely necessary to use an IDE. You could just use vi (or vim) or emacs purely for code editing, and use the CLI to script all necessary development activities through CLI-run tools. But that would beg the following question: if *you* don't (want to) use an IDE, why should the domain experts use the Domain IDE you're building for *them*? After all, an IDE is software that's purpose-built to understand specifications in your domain out of the box and to help you build your own software in an efficient and effective way.

Running *online* in the cloud means running as a web app (in a browser) on any suitable computing device: computer, tablet, or maybe even smartphone. In this case, the web app *is* the development environment and code editor at the same time: a *web IDE*. It integrates all the necessary tools, and even the code repository, into one big web application. The frontend, running in a browser, usually resembles an IDE running as a standalone desktop application. The backend runs in the cloud and manages the code repository, its dependencies, building the code, and the state of the frontend.

Popular examples of web IDEs that you could use for this technology stack are Gitpod.io, AWS Cloud 9, JSFiddle, etc.

> **NOTE** The fine people that made Gitpod have stated that they "are quite allergic to people thinking Gitpod is an *online or web IDE*. Gitpod is an open source orchestration and provisioning platform for automated developer

environments" (www.gitpod.io/blog/gitpod-jetbrains). However, for the purposes of this book I'll conveniently disregard the second sentence of that quote and consider a Gitpod a web IDE. Rest assured that I've taken note of their allergies and associated protests.

Both options have pros and cons, listed in table A.1.

Table A.1 Pros and cons of using a local vs. online development environment

	Pro	Con
Local	• You have full control over the environment. • You are not continuously dependent on something outside your machine. You only need an internet connection for downloading new dependencies and (intermittently) to look things up.	• You face the danger of "configuration paralysis": tinkering around with the development environment instead of doing real work. • Your machine must be powerful enough.
Online	• This doesn't require much local computing power. Scaling up/out should be possible. • Sharing code and integrating with CI is pretty easy. • The development environment usually comes preinstalled with all required tools and pre-cached dependencies. • The frontend is easily updated. • Any development environment setup is easily replicated, also for review purposes. • This option doesn't require local file storage (beyond the browser's cache).	• You need a reliable internet connection all the time. • Your code must be in the cloud (unless you can use the web IDE on-premise). • Integrating with one or more code repositories is not standard yet.

Having a local development environment on your own computer is probably still the default choice for most developers. However, web IDEs are gaining popularity, so they're certainly an option to consider. At the same time, the boundary between desktop and web IDEs is getting fuzzier. Several desktop IDEs are essentially web IDEs running as separate processes on the desktop's OS. It's also becoming easier to "call out" from certain desktop IDEs to online services that perform some longer-running, heavy-weight operations such as CI. Some desktop IDEs now have features to live-collaborate with multiple developers on the same codebase. To do that, the codebase in a "driver" IDE is then live-shared with the other IDEs. Changes made in any of the IDEs are immediately synched back to the driver IDE.

The code we'll be writing easily fits into one code repository, so scalability and multi-repository concerns don't really apply. That gives you the freedom to do it any way you like, including trying to work with a recent web IDE if you haven't done so already.

The following two sections correspond to two sets of instructions:

- Section A.2—Setting up a development environment locally using Node.js, Git, npm, and Visual Studio Code
- Section A.3—Using the web IDE Gitpod.io, which essentially provides the same environment, but cloud-based

The rest of this appendix, from section A.4 on, applies to having followed either set of instructions.

A.2   *Setting up a local development environment*

Let's set up a local development environment. From section A.1, we know we need the following:

- A CLI
- A versioning system
- Node.js

I'm going to assume a suitable CLI and versioning system are already installed. In section A.2.1, I'll provide explanations about and installation instructions for Node.js.

I already strongly advised you to make use of a proper IDE. In section A.2.2, I'll provide explanations about and installation instructions for Microsoft's Visual Studio Code. Visual Studio Code is certainly not the only IDE suitable for our purposes. I'm putting it forward because it's lightweight and free. Here's a short list of other IDEs that I happen to know of, with "$" indicating a paid or non-free one:

- JetBrains' IntelliJ/IDEA family ($) (www.jetbrains.com/idea/), including WebStorm (www.jetbrains.com/webstorm/)
- Eclipse (www.eclipse.org/), especially the Eclipse JavaScript Development Tools project (https://projects.eclipse.org/projects/webtools.jsdt)
- Visual Studio Code (https://code.visualstudio.com), colloquially known as "VS Code"
- Microsoft Visual Studio, without the "Code" postfix ($) (https://visualstudio.microsoft.com)
- Apple's Xcode (free on a Mac, so $) (https://developer.apple.com/xcode)

A.2.1   *Installing Node.js*

Node.js is the platform for running JavaScript outside of the browser. It's essentially the V8 JavaScript engine of the Google Chrome browser, but packaged as a standalone runtime instead of as part of a browser. There are two important differences from the in-browser engine:

- There's no HTML DOM to interact with.
- Node.js can interact with the OS, particularly with the filesystem, and the network.

Node.js is also very popular for creating tools that aim to help with web development.

Node.js comes with a dependency manager called the *Node Package Manager* (npm) out of the box. We'll be using npm to download and install JavaScript dependencies from www.npmjs.com. npm stores these dependencies in a node_modules/ directory inside the repository.

Node.js can be installed on the following operating systems:

- Windows, both 32- and 64-bit, either as a binary or using an installer
- macOS (64-bit/ARM64, which includes Apple's M-series chips), either as a binary or using an installer
- Linux (64-bit, on x64 as well as ARMv7-v8) as a binary

You'll find downloads for the latest current stable version (with the latest features) as well as the latest LTS (Long-Term Supported) version of Node.js at https://nodejs .org/en/download/prebuilt-installer (see figure A.3).

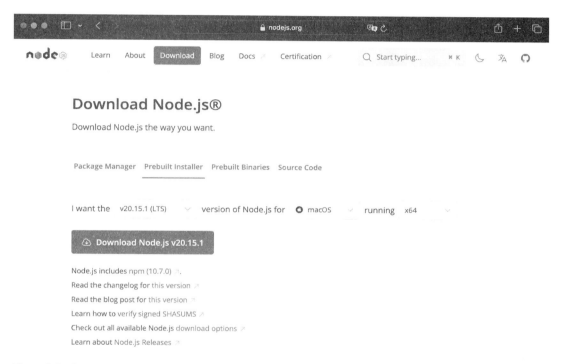

Figure A.3   Download site for Node.js

Node.js version 22.2.0 was the latest current version at the time of writing: in the meantime, we have probably advanced by several major versions. Click a link on that page to get a download for your OS. Using an installer is generally the easiest option, as it will take care of making Node.js executables available across the whole OS and such. Alternatively, unzip the binary and move it to a suitable location on your machine. Building from source is not for the faint at heart and is hardly ever required. In any case, please follow the installation instructions provided.

After installation, you should be able to do the following on the command line:

```
$ node -v
v22.2.0
```

The dollar sign ($) stands for the command-line interface's prompt. It indicates that you have to copy–paste (or type) the rest of the line to your CLI and execute it, usually by pressing the Enter key.

This shows that Node.js with the indicated version is on the common CLI path. Older versions than 22.2.0 should work just as well, although the dependencies we install might insist on a newer version anyway. You don't need to interact with Node.js like this much, but most tools we'll use actually run on Node.js.

Node.js version 22.2.0 is bundled with npm version 10.7.0. We can check whether npm is working as follows:

```
$ npm -v
10.7.0
```

Even though npm is installed along Node.js, it can be updated independently, as you can infer from the CLI interaction previously. When using npm from the CLI, it will usually warn you about updates, including instructions on how to perform an update. It's not a bad thing to keep npm current, as updates often address security issues and come with bug fixes.

You can also choose to use Yarn as a JavaScript dependency manager. This npm alternative has some advantages like speed (because it caches dependencies globally), purported security, and reliability. Yarn is supposedly fully compatible with npm, but every so often some small differences cause stuff to fail when using one, but not the other.

You can get Yarn at https://yarnpkg.com/. Incidentally, Parcel, one of the dependencies we'll be using, uses Yarn internally. Parcel takes care of properly installing Yarn itself, through its own dependencies specification.

Since npm is installed alongside Node.js and still seems to be the more commonly used of the two, I'll provide working instructions for npm only. These instructions carry over to Yarn after tweaking the command-line arguments a little.

A.2.2 *Installing Visual Studio Code*

Visual Studio Code (VS Code) is a suitable, popular, and relatively lightweight desktop IDE. It can be downloaded from https://code.visualstudio.com/Download (see figure A.4).

Clicking the button for your OS downloads an installation package. Opening and running that installs Visual Studio Code. VS Code checks, by default, whether an update is available, which happens quite regularly. It's perfectly OK to let VS Code update itself, as these updates are of high quality and tend to come with many new features and bug fixes. Whenever an update is available, VS Code predownloads the update and prompts you to restart VS Code to accept and install the update. Installing extensions is not necessary for our purposes.

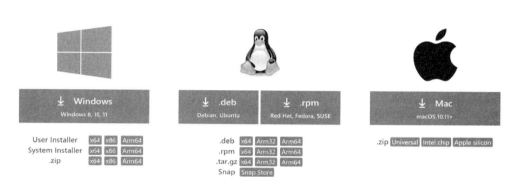

Figure A.4   Download site for Visual Studio Code

A.3   Using a web IDE

A *web IDE* is a web application that provides a complete IDE in the browser, served from the cloud. There are several reasons that this setup might be appealing:

- There's no need to install any tool locally, other than a browser. Updating any part of the development environment is usually quick and easy.
- The development environment can be accessed from any device with an internet connection.
- Development environments are easily replicated and shared, avoiding most, if not all, occurrences of ". . . but it works on my machine!"
- Development environments can be prebuilt, which is especially useful for code-reviewing activities.
- You can scale up/out for the computation-heavy parts of the software development process, such as building the code ("Compiling!") or running a lot of tests.

Several web IDEs exist and are becoming more popular, such as

- Gitpod.io (www.gitpod.io)
- Github Codespaces (https://github.com/features/codespaces)
- AWS Cloud9 (https://aws.amazon.com/cloud9)

- JSFiddle (https://jsfiddle.net)
- Replit (https://replit.com)

I happen to be most familiar with Gitpod.io, which looks and feels a lot like Visual Studio Code—no wonder, because these share a lot of technology. GitHub Codespaces can be invoked from any GitHub repository simply by pressing the dot key (.).

A.3.1   *Using Gitpod.io*

Gitpod.io is a web IDE based on the Eclipse Theia IDE platform (https://theia-ide.org). You can self-host Gitpod, but it's easiest to use Gitpod through www.gitpod.io, which hosts everything other than your code repository in its own cloud for you. Your code repository should be hosted on GitHub, GitLab, or Bitbucket, and you should have a login there. The free Gitpod plan carries a per-account usage time limit of 50 hours/month, four parallel workspaces, a 30-minute timeout, and no further feature restrictions. You might need to sign up for a paid plan with Gitpod.io, which at the time of writing costs €9 (roughly 10 USD) per month per 1,000 "credits."

To use Gitpod.io, you prepend the full URI of that repository with "`https://gitpod.io/#`". Take as an example the repository that contains all the code from this book:

```
https://github.com/dslmeinte/Building-User-Friendly-DSLs-code
```

This becomes:

```
https://gitpod.io/#https://github.com/dslmeinte/Building-User-Friendly-DSLs-code
```

After waiting a couple of seconds for the workspace to spin up, you're presented with a web app that looks like figure A.5.

As you can see from the screenshot, a CLI is provided out of the box. Node.js, npm, Yarn, and Git integration come preinstalled. Finally, specialized editors for all mainstream languages are available.

A.4   *Setting up a repository for JavaScript development*

Let's set up the repository so we can develop JavaScript code. We'll do that in a standard and straightforward way, so it should be easy to configure the tools and find your way around it. In particular, we'll rely on Node.js and a package manager.

I'll assume that you've already initialized a Git repository. If it's a different one, I'll trust that you know how to achieve the same result with it. Depending on how you initialized the Git repo, it may be completely empty or already contain some standard files and directories, such as a README or a .gitignore. To perform the setup, you can use either a (web) IDE or a command-line interface (CLI).

Start by making sure that a directory called src/ exists:

```
mkdir -p src
```

Figure A.5   Gitpod.io in action, with a workspace for the repository at https://github.com/dslmeinte/Building-User-Friendly-DSLs-code

(The `-p` flag ensures that `mkdir` doesn't complain when src/ already exists.) This directory will contain all the JavaScript source files (with extensions .js or .jsx) and some related files. If a .gitignore file doesn't exist yet, go ahead and create it now. This .gitignore file specifies which files and directories Git should ignore, meaning which files shouldn't be version-tracked or distributed. We should ignore all dependencies stored in node_modules/ (because these easily run to 100 MB and beyond) as well as all build artifacts.

The following listing shows an example of the contents of this file.

Listing A.1   Example contents of the .gitignore file

```
/node_modules/
/.parcel-cache/
dist/
```

Ignore JavaScript dependencies downloaded
to and installed in node_modules/.

Ignore directories that are typically generated by the
Parcel.js web bundler (discussed in appendix B).

The lack of a leading / in this file means that these lines match files and directories with these names anywhere in the repository. The trailing / means that this pattern only matches directories.

Next, we'll initialize a package.json configuration file. This file in JSON format is going to contain the following:

- Dependencies specification (production and development, for Domain IDE and Runtime/reference implementation)
- Repository metadata
- Build configuration

Both the npm and Yarn dependency managers understand this file and use it to download dependencies. The easiest way to initialize this file is by running npm as follows:

```
$ npm init -y
```

The y is short for "answer yes, or accept the default, to all questions."

This fills package.json with the contents in listing A.2. Not all of these fields are mandatory.

Listing A.2   Initial contents of the package.json file

```
{
  "name": "<name of repository directory>",
  "version": "1.0.0",
  "description": "",
  "main": "index.js",
  "scripts": {
    "test": "echo \"Error: no test specified\" && exit 1"
  },
  "keywords": [],
  "author": "",
  "license": "ISC"
}
```

If you find that you're often using a particular command on the command line, you can add that to the top-level scripts section, under a name of your choice. You can then run it using

```
$ npm run <script name>
```

Several script names have special status, and their scripts can be run without the `run` argument. Two examples are `start` and `test`. If you have defined a `test` script, you can run that simply as this:

```
$ npm test
```

We'll be adding dependencies to package.json as we need them. There are two kinds of dependencies:

- *Development* dependencies are tools that we use during development, such as a web bundler or a unit testing framework (see section B.1.11 for an example). These development tools are typically installed as executables in the node_modules/.bin/ directory. I'll explain how to run these executables in section A.6.
- *Production* dependencies are dependencies that our application code explicitly relies on, such as the React framework.

Every dependency is specified as a key-value pair, "*<dependency name>*": "*<version range>*" in the `dependencies` (for production dependencies) or `devDependencies` (for development dependencies) top-level section of package.json. Such a key-value pair means that our code is dependent on the *<dependency name>* dependency, and that any version of it in the *<version range>* should work. The *<version range>* uses *semantic versioning* (https://semver.org). A semver version range typically looks like `^x.y.z`, which means "version *x.y.z* or newer, until the next major version *(x+1)*.0.0".

By the end of the book, your package.json file might look quite different. Mine looks currently like this:

```
{
  "name": "Building-User-Friendly-DSLs-code",
  "version": "1.0.0",
  "description":
    "Repo containing all code from the book.",

  "repository": {
    "type": "git",
    "url": "git+https://github.com/dslmeinte/Building-User-Friendly-DSLs-
    code.git"
  },
  "author": "Meinte Boersma (for Manning Publications)",
  "license": "MIT",
  "bugs": {
    "url": "https://github.com/dslmeinte/Building-User-Friendly-DSLs-code/
    issues"
  },
  "homepage":
    "https://www.manning.com/books/building-user-friendly-dsls",
  "browserslist": "> 0.5%, last 2 versions, not dead",
  "dependencies": {
    "express": "^4.18.2",
    "mobx": "^6.8.0",
    "mobx-react": "^7.6.0",
```

I removed the main field and scripts section because there's no single entry point: every chapter has many entry points, which are explained in their respective **README.md** files.

I specified the repository this project "lives" in.

This line forces the Parcel.js web bundler to transpile modern JavaScript into JavaScript code that's understood by the majority of browsers.

```
  "nanoid": "^3.3.4",
  "react": "^18.2.0",
  "react-dom": "^18.2.0"
},
"devDependencies": {
  "parcel": "^2.8.3",
  }
}
```

Note that these contents have diverged quite a bit from the initial, default contents from listing A.2. For more information about package.json, see the npm documentation: https://docs.npmjs.com/cli/v6/configuring-npm/package-json.

Optionally, you can also add a jsconfig.json configuration file to the root of the repository. Giving that file the contents in listing A.3 often helps to convince some IDEs, such as JetBrains' IntelliJ/IDEA, to ignore node_modules/ as much as possible, which saves CPU time.

Listing A.3   Contents of the jsconfig.json configuration file

```
{
    "exclude": ["node_modules"]
}
```

This prevents IntelliJ/IDEA from trying to inspect and reason about the dependencies more than strictly necessary, keeping the IDE more responsive and saving CPU time.

A.5   *Using the Node.js REPL*

Anywhere Node.js is installed, whether that's a local installation or inside a web IDE, you can start Node.js in its *interactive* mode by executing the following on the command line:

```
$ node
```

(Note the absence of any arguments.) This produces a welcome message and a prompt, as in figure A.6.

```
$ node
Welcome to Node.js v22.2.0.
Type ".help" for more information.
>
```

Figure A.6   Starting Node.js from the CLI

You can now type or copy some JavaScript code after the > prompt, press Enter, and Node.js will evaluate that, print the outcome, and loop back to the prompt. This is commonly known as a REPL: a Read-Evaluate-Print-Loop. The REPL of Node.js is especially helpful because it actively tries to help you with content assist.

Let's see how this works by typing in `process.ve` (see figure A.7).

```
> process.version
'v22.2.0'
```

Figure A.7   Using content assist in the Node.js REPL

The REPL tries to suggest a sensible completion of the text you've already typed in, and it shows that suggestion in a light gray color. You can accept such a suggestion by pressing the Tab key. It doesn't always find a sensible completion, especially when the text has invalid syntax.

As soon as the REPL makes a suggestion, it will also try to evaluate the resulting text as JavaScript code, even without you having to press Enter or Tab. Provided that the code doesn't produce an outright error, the evaluation result is also shown in a light-gray color. (The expression `process.version` produces a string with the Node.js version.) The suggestion, or the preview of the evaluation of evaluatable input, is updated by the REPL while you type.

Once you press Enter, the REPL will print out the evaluation result in a pretty, syntax-highlighted way, as shown in figure A.8.

```
> process.version
'v22.2.0'
>
```

Figure A.8   Executing the autocompleted JavaScript code

Exiting the REPL from an empty REPL prompt to return to the CLI prompt is done either by typing `.exit`, pressing Ctrl-D once, or Ctrl-C twice. Ctrl-D issues an end-of-file (EOF) character, which is the traditional way of ending a shell/batch session.

To run code that spans multiple lines, you first have to enable *editor mode* by executing the `.editor` command. Once you are in this mode, press Ctrl-D to run the code you wrote or Ctrl-C to abort the current code altogether.

A.6 *Running development tools*

Development tools are executables that are installed by the npm/Yarn package manager into the node_modules/.bin folder as part of a development dependency. You can run those executables from the CLI from the root of the repository as follows:

```
$ ./node_modules/.bin/mocha src/test/
```

Run the executable from the Mocha test framework to execute tests located in JavaScript files in the directory src/test/.

Some IDEs understand Node.js and npm-based repositories really well. IntelliJ/IDEA's Terminal (its CLI) will automatically have node_modules/.bin on the path. This means you don't need to prepend command-line calls with .node_modules/.bin/.

Another way to run development tools is to use the npx tool. The executable npx is part of the npm installation. As an example, the following CLI invocation achieves the same thing as the previous one:

```
$ npx mocha src/test/
```

In general, this looks as follows:

```
$ npx <executable name> [...<arguments>...]
```

This command runs executables that were installed in the path node_modules/.bin/. If you try to run an executable that's not present there, npx will try to download the npm package with the name *<executable name>*. If that succeeds, it runs the executable in the package with the same name. The npm package will be downloaded to a location *outside* of the repository, and the package will *not* be added to the package.json file. This is a convenient way to run development tools without "polluting" the repository with development dependencies that are rarely invoked.

In this appendix, you learned the basics of setting up and using a JavaScript development environment. We'll use that development environment from chapter 3 onwards to develop a Domain IDE and Runtime.

appendix B
Implementing
a Transparent Functional
Reactive frontend

This appendix covers

- Describing the JavaScript idiom we'll be writing code in
- Setting up a frontend in React and Parcel
- Using React components to structure the frontend
- Using MobX to react to changes transparently

In appendix A, we set up a development environment to develop JavaScript code with. In this appendix, we're going to use that environment to learn how to implement a Transparent Functional Reactive frontend. We'll use that knowledge in chapters 3 through 14 to implement the frontends of the Domain IDE and Runtime.

B.1   *Establishing an idiom for JavaScript code*

You can find JavaScript code written in quite diverse idioms. We happen to be writing JavaScript conforming to the ES2015 specification (https://262.ecma-international.org/6.0), but that leaves quite a bit of wiggle room with regard to coding style conventions.

Let's establish a particular idiom for writing JavaScript, in the form of a list of conventions. I'll stick to this idiom in both JavaScript files (with file extension .js) and in files in JSX syntax (with file extension .jsx). I'll explain what those JSX source files are for in section B.2.

B.1.1   *No semicolons to separate statements*

Semicolons are just syntactic noise to me.

> *Syntactic sugar causes cancer of the semi-colons.*

> —Alan Perlis, "Epigrams on Programming,"
> *SIGPLAN Notices* 17, no. 9 [Sept. 1982], epigram #3

Parsing technology has advanced to the point that any self-respecting parser technology hardly ever requires a terminal to be able to see where one statement ends and the next begins. Practically speaking, the automatic semicolon insertion (ASI) feature of JavaScript essentially works all the time. Therefore, in code listings in this book, you won't find semicolons.

The "usual" exception is an expression statement that follows another statement and starts with an array literal: `[<items*>]`. In that situation, the square brackets of the array literal are recognized to belong to a property accessor rather than to an array literal. This problem could be remedied by prefixing the array literal with a semicolon: `;[<items*>]`. A more elegant fix is to put the array literal inside parentheses: `([<items*>])`.

> **NOTE**   For details about property accessors, see the MDN web docs: https://developer.mozilla.org/en-US/docs/Web/JavaScript/Reference/Operators/Property_Accessors.

B.1.2   *Indentation/whitespace conventions*

In my experience, using spaces for indentation tends to cause fewer problems with tools than using tabs. Four spaces provide sufficient visual separation, while two don't—at least not for me. Three is odd, and five is right out.

Matching "things," such as pairs of parentheses, brackets, and curly braces, that don't occur on the same line should line up vertically whenever possible. Typesetting for book publication demands that lines of code in a listing are rather short, so I've often had to line-break code: this can be gleaned from the ➥ symbol, and possibly extra indentation.

B.1.3   *Using const declarations for values wherever possible*

In ES2015, you can use three keywords to declare local variables: `const`, `let`, and `var`. We'll use `const` whenever and wherever we can, and `let` otherwise. We won't use `var`.

A variable that's declared using `const` can be assigned a value *only once*. This assignment has to happen immediately as the *initializer* part of the declaration: `const <variable's name> = <initializer expressions>`. As soon as you try to assign a value again, the JavaScript engine will throw an error: `TypeError: Assignment to constant variable`. Most IDEs will detect such an assignment in code before running it and will warn you about that:

```
const foo = {}
foo = { bar: 1 }
foo.bar = 1
```
Throws a TypeError with the message "Assignment to constant variable"

Works fine

As you can see, a `const` declaration doesn't make the value held in the variable really *immutable* unless it's not an object or function. If the value is an object or function, you can change it, without the JavaScript runtime objecting, by assigning a key-value pair to it.

In some cases, you'll need to allow for multiple assignments. When a variable is populated as a result of an asynchronous call, it's typically initialized with a value `undefined` or `null`. The value in this variable is most likely inspected multiple times before it's populated with a "real" value. In such a case, you can't use `const` to declare that variable but have to use `let` instead.

The `var` keyword should not be used, mainly because it has "function scope," while `const` and `let` have "block scope." Something that has block scope is visible and accessible within the entire current block. The most-used blocks are a block of statements `{ /* statements… */ }` and a `for` loop. Block scope is less confusing and error prone than function scope. The `var` keyword is still part of JavaScript mostly for backward compatibility.

B.1.4 Defining functions as const declarations using arrow function expressions

Traditionally, functions were defined in JavaScript using the `function` keyword:

```
function <identifier>(<parameter list>) {
    // ...statements...
    return <expression>
}
```

Since ES2015, you can also define functions in the *block statement form*, as follows:

```
const <identifier> = (<parameter list>) => {
    <statements...>
    return <expression-to-return>
}
```

If `return` is the only statement, you can write the function even more concisely, in *expression form*, as follows:

```
const <identifier> = (<parameter list>) => <expression>
```

Both variants produce identical results. The expression form is shorter and visually less "noisy" than the block statement form. However, often it turns out to be necessary to switch from expression form to block statement form along the way. This can happen if you need to introduce one or more local variables or constants that hold precomputed, reused values. It's then quite easy to forget to insert the `return` keyword before the expression to be returned.

It's not required that arrow functions with only one argument surround (the name of) that argument in parentheses. I do always wrap the list of (the names of the) arguments in parentheses, for two reasons:

- If I later find that I need more arguments after all, I can just add `<another argument>` to the arguments list, without also having to add the parenthesis pair.
- For consistency.

I like arrow function expressions for various reasons:

- They use `const` declarations consistently for everything, not just for non-function file members.
- They reduce visual noise/clutter when there are no statements except for one final `return` statement.
- They appeal to my functional programming and mathematics sentiments.
- They don't rebind `this` (as a `function` does).

B.1.5 *Exporting members from files*

To export a member (such as a `const` declaration or a function) from a JavaScript file, we have to put it into a built-in object accessible as `module.exports`. I like to make it clear as soon as possible after the definition that something's exported, like so:

```
const <identifier> = ...
module.exports.<identifier> = <identifier>
```

This feels a bit like prepending the `const` declaration with an `export` keyword. I separate the `const` declaration from the exporting assignment statement, so I can use the function directly in the same file.

You could try to export `<identifier>` immediately as `module.exports.<identifier>` = ... That saves one statement but keeps `<identifier>` out of the file's scope. That's problematic when other members of the same file use `<identifier>`.

B.1.6 *Object destructuring*

Suppose we have an object `foo = { bar: 1, alice: "bob" }`, like before, and we would like to work with the value in `foo.bar`. We can put that value in a variable as follows:
```
const bar = foo.bar.
```
Since ES2015, you can *destructure* the `foo` object as follows:

```
const { bar } = foo
```

This achieves the exact same thing as `const bar = foo.bar`, in the exact same number of characters even, so that doesn't seem useful. I put an extra pair of spaces directly inside the curly braces, for some extra visual clarity.

Destructuring becomes more useful when there are more key-value pairs to destructure from the object. As an example, this

```
const { bar, alice } = foo
```

is shorter and more readable than the equivalent:

```
const bar = foo.bar
const alice = foo.alice
```

You can even do *renaming*. This statement,

```
const { bar: baz } = foo
```

is equivalent to this:

```
const baz = foo.bar
```

Finally, we'll use this construct in the next subsection to select which members of a dependency to import.

B.1.7　Importing members

In JavaScript files that have to run under Node.js, we import members from production dependencies in other files as follows:

**You can't import a
development dependency.**

```
const { <identifiers...> } = require("<production dependency>")
const { <other identifiers...> } = require("./<relative path>")
```

When its argument starts with a period (`.`), the `require` function understands that you want to import members from a local file. The argument then needs to be a valid path to that local file, relative to the file it's in. When its argument starts with a valid identifier character, `require` looks the dependency up in node_modules/.

Node.js doesn't support the syntax `import { stuff } from "module name"` yet, which is why we have to keep using the "old" syntax `const { stuff to import } = require("module name")` for now.

In JSX files, it's customary to use an `import` statement instead of calling `require(...)`. The only difference is the syntax: both variants interpret the string that specifies which dependency to import the same way. The Parcel bundler, which we'll set up as a development dependency in section B.2, turns this statement into something browsers understand. In combination with destructuring that looks like this:

```
import { <identifiers...> } from "<production dependency>
import { <other identifiers...> } from "./<relative path>"
```

You can also do renaming with a destructuring `import` statement, but with a slightly different syntax. This is useful when multiple dependencies export members with the same name:

```
import { <identifier1> } from "<dep1>"
import { <identifier1> as <identifier2> } from "<dep2>"
```

Use as instead of a colon (:)

B.1.8   *Favoring plain objects over classes*

Since language specification ES2015, JavaScript has had proper support for classes. I chose to *not* use classes to represent AST objects in the implementation of the Domain IDE, though. Using classes rigidifies the data to some extent, without really providing so much (type-)safety in return. While we evolve our DSL and the example DSL content, we'll see that there's an advantage to having plain AST objects of the form `{ $concept: "<concept>", settings: { ... } }`, rather than having an instance of a class called `<concept>`. For that reason, we'll stick to using plain objects as AST objects.

I do use classes in the Runtime: date ranges are represented as instances of a class, and the code generator generates a separate class for each record type defined in the DSL content (see chapter 8).

B.1.9   *Using the spread syntax*

JavaScript supports the *spread syntax*. This syntax can be used in three different "flavors"—I use the two array-related ones in this book.

When used inside the parameter list of a function call, `...<array>` turns each member of `<array>` into an individual argument. As an example,

```
foo(arg0, ...[ arg1, arg2, arg3 ], arg4)
```

means the same thing as this:

```
foo(arg0, arg1, arg2, arg3, arg4)
```

When used inside an array construction expression `[ ... ]`, `...<array>` inserts each member of `<array>` separately (instead of as a whole array). As an example,

```
[ value0, ...[ value1, value2, value3 ], value4 ]
```

evaluates to this:

```
[ value0, value1, value2, value3, value4 ]
```

This explains why ... is called the *spread operator*: it spreads the members of an array as if they were individual things.

B.1.10   *Using template literals*

Template literals arrived in JavaScript in the ES2015 specification. They are string literals that start and end with backticks (`) instead of regular single or double quotes.

Their two main advantages over the regular string literals, with the syntax "..." and '...', are *embedded expressions* and *multiline support*. The latter feature saves us from having to write code like this,

```
"this is code line 1\n" +
"    this is code line 2, and it's indented"
```

to output this:

```
this is line 1
    this is line 2, and it's indented
```

Instead, we can just write this:

```
`this is line 1
    this is line 2, and it's indented`
```

> The newline is part of the string resulting from evaluating the template literal, which makes it possible and easy to generate multiline strings.

> **WARNING** Multiline template literals tend to break up code indentation. That's because all indentation inside the template literal ends up as part of the evaluation result, which is probably not what you want. This tends to make the code more difficult to read.

An embedded expression has the following syntax: `${<expr>}`, where `<expr>` is a JavaScript expression. When the template literal is evaluated, every embedded expression in it is evaluated as well. The result of the evaluation of an embedded expression replaces the text `${<expr>}` in the template literal. We say that template literals perform *interpolation*. If the evaluation result is not a string, it's first coerced into a string.

As an example, running this code block,

```
const foo = 3
console.log(`1 + 2 = ${foo}`)
```

prints this:

```
1 + 2 = 3
```

Nesting template literals

Both template literals and their embedded expressions are JavaScript expressions. That means that embedded expressions can contain/use template literals as well, such as in

```
`${`foo${1 + 2}`}`
```

Nesting template literals is powerful, but it also tends to make the code less readable. Avoid too complex embedded expressions by using precomputed values or calling a function that encapsulates the complex logic.

We use template literals to implement a code generator for the Runtime.

> **NOTE**   For details on template literals, see the MDN documentation: https://
> developer.mozilla.org/en-US/docs/Web/JavaScript/Reference/Template_
> literals.

B.1.11 *Unit testing*

In several exercises in this book, I ask you to write a unit test to test code written in the course of the book. Personally, I'm most familiar with the combination of the Mocha JavaScript test framework (https://mochajs.org) and the Chai assertion library (www .chaijs.com).

To be able to use these JavaScript dependencies, we have to download and install them. You can use the npm dependency manager to do this as follows:

```
$ npm install --save-dev mocha
$ npm install --save-dev chai
```

The CLI option --save-dev tells npm that the dependency identified as mocha is a development dependency.

Let's write a unit test using Mocha and Chai. First, we'll create a src/fibonacci.js file and add the code in listing B.1 to that file. This file defines a `fibonacci` function that calculates Fibonacci numbers, which we're going to test using a unit test.

Listing B.1   Calculating the well-known Fibonacci function

```
const fibonacci = (n) => n <= 1
    ? n
    : fibonacci(n - 2) + fibonacci(n - 1)
module.exports.fibonacci = fibonacci
```

Define a function with a const declaration and an arrow function expression to (inefficiently) calculate Fibonacci numbers using recursion.

This proves that we don't need to define functions using the `function` keyword—not even if they're recursive and have to run under Node.js.

Next, we'll create a src/test/fibonacci-tests.js file and add the code in listing B.2 to it. It contains a unit test suite with one unit test, defined using Mocha and Chai. A unit test suite is a convenient way to group unit tests. In this listing, all code bits that make up a general code pattern for unit testing are highlighted in bold. The non-bold bits form the rest that's specific to the unit test.

Listing B.2   Unit testing the `fibonacci` function

```
const { equal } = require("chai").assert

const { fibonacci } = require("../fibonacci")

describe("recursive functions defined as a const declaration",
    (_) => {
```

Import assertion functions from the Chai library—in this case, we only import equal.

Import the fibonacci function to test.

Define a unit test suite by calling the describe function that Mocha will inject into the JavaScript runtime.

```
it("Fibonacci works", () => {
    equal(fibonacci(0), 0)
    equal(fibonacci(1), 1)
    equal(fibonacci(2), 1)
    equal(fibonacci(3), 2)
    // ...&c....
})
```

})

Define a unit test by calling the it function that Mocha will inject into the JavaScript runtime.

Call the fibonacci function that's being unit tested, and make assertions about the result.

The `describe` function's first argument is a string containing a description of the unit test suite. Its second argument is a function that defines the unit tests in this suite. (That unit test–defining function ignores its argument, hence the _ as argument name.)

The `it` function's first argument is a string containing a description of the unit test. Its second argument is a function that actually carries out the unit test.

Often-used assertion functions are `deepEqual`, `isTrue`, `isFalse`, and `isUndefined`. The first argument of `equal` is the actual outcome value, which is then compared with the expected value: the second argument. The `equal` assertion function compares values. To compare the members of objects, arrays, or functions, you can use the `deepEqual` assertion function. See Chai's documentation (www.chaijs.com/api/assert/) for more details.

> **Note**
> The unit test code pattern from listing B.2 can be used if the unit test
>
> - Is completely synchronous, meaning it returns immediately and doesn't call any asynchronous functions. You can recognize such functions either from the `async` keyword or the use of `Promise`s.
> - Executes within two seconds (the default timeout), or Mocha will assume the test doesn't complete at all and will interrupt and kill it.
> - Doesn't need to access Mocha's context, which is passed as `this`.

You can run unit tests from the command line as follows:

```
$ npx mocha src/test/fibonacci-tests.js
```

(See section A.6 for an explanation of what this CLI command does.)

Running fibonacci-tests.js through Mocha this way does the following:

1 Starts a JavaScript runtime using Node.js
2 Injects the `describe` and `it` functions used in listing B.2 into the JS runtime
3 Runs the code in listing B.2
4 Executes all unit test suites and unit tests contained in them, reporting successes, failures, and errors

It will produce the following output:

The text describing the unit test suite: the
first argument of the call to describe

```
recursive functions defined as a `const` declaration
     ✓ Fibonacci works
```

The text describing the unit test in the suite: the first
argument of the call to it. The tick mark in front
indicates this unit test ran successfully.

```
  1 passing (7ms)
```

A count of the number of passing unit tests, plus how
long it took to run all the unit tests (in all suites)

If Mocha doesn't output this, something's wrong. Mocha will then report either

- A *failure*—An assertion detected a difference between the actual and expected outcomes. Chai will show the difference between those in a readable way.
- An *error*—An error was thrown during the unit test execution that wasn't caught by an assertion function. Mocha will show the error thrown, including a stack trace.

In both cases, you'll have some debugging to do, to either fix the unit test itself or, more likely, the code under test.

B.2   *Setting up a basic frontend with React and Parcel*

We'll be using the *React* framework (https://reactjs.org) to implement frontends for the Domain IDE and Runtime. There are several reasons for choosing React:

- React is a well-known, mature framework for building frontends (of web apps).
- React's JSX syntax is a convenient way to embed HTML within a component's JavaScript code.
- React supports the use of *components* to organize and structure a frontend.

I'll explain what you need to know about React to be able to understand the implementation of the Domain IDE and Runtime in this book. If you're already up to speed with that, you can probably skim over a good part of this section.

Let's set up a basic frontend inside the repository in the development environment that we set up in appendix A. First, we'll create three files in the src/frontend path in your codebase: index.html (listing B.3), index.jsx (listing B.4), styling.css (listing B.5).

Listing B.3   src/frontend/index.html

```html
<!DOCTYPE html>
<html lang="en">

<head>
  <meta charset="UTF-8">
  <title>Business Rules Management @Rent-A-Car</title>
</head>
```

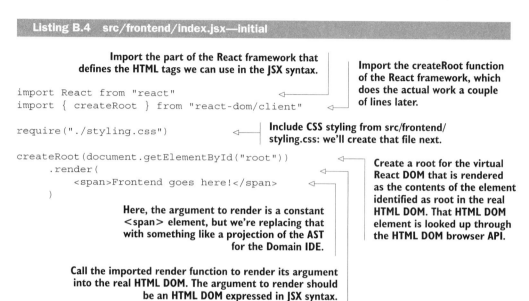

```
<body>
  <div id="root"></div>
  <script type="module" src="index.jsx"></script>
</body>

</html>
```

This line defines an empty HTML div DOM element with root as ID.

This line includes the index.jsx file we'll create next.

Listing B.4   src/frontend/index.jsx—initial

Import the part of the React framework that defines the HTML tags we can use in the JSX syntax.

Import the createRoot function of the React framework, which does the actual work a couple of lines later.

```
import React from "react"
import { createRoot } from "react-dom/client"

require("./styling.css")

createRoot(document.getElementById("root"))
    .render(
        <span>Frontend goes here!</span>
    )
```

Include CSS styling from src/frontend/styling.css: we'll create that file next.

Create a root for the virtual React DOM that is rendered as the contents of the element identified as root in the real HTML DOM. That HTML DOM element is looked up through the HTML DOM browser API.

Here, the argument to render is a constant <span> element, but we're replacing that with something like a projection of the AST for the Domain IDE.

Call the imported render function to render its argument into the real HTML DOM. The argument to render should be an HTML DOM expressed in JSX syntax.

The .jsx file extension indicates that that file is not a regular JavaScript file, but one in *JSX syntax*. JSX stands for "JavaScript XML," and it lets us mix content in XML syntax with regular JavaScript code. This mixing makes it quite easy to write code using the React framework, since we can mix chunks of HTML (in pure XML format) with JavaScript code. We'll see an example of this syntax shortly.

The JSX syntax is not natively understood by any browser, so including a .jsx file from an .html file is pointless. We're going to have set up some tooling that fixes that for us by performing an action called *bundling*. I'll explain what to do after these code listings.

The first import statement imports the whole of `react` and stores it in a variable called `React`. Importing the `React` object seems unnecessary, because we don't—and won't—explicitly reference `React` anywhere in the code. However, the React framework and the bundler need it to translate JSX back to proper JavaScript (again).

The `import { createRoot } from "react-dom/client"` statement is a *destructuring* import statement, explained earlier in subsection B.1.7. This import statement imports *only* the `render` function located inside the `client` submodule of the `react-dom` React npm package and makes it available in this file under its own name.

Normally, the index.html file would use a `<link>` element in the HTML head to include the styling.css CSS file. Now, the `require("./styling.css")` statement causes the bundling tooling to take care of including the CSS in an appropriate place.

Figure B.1 explains what the call to the `render` function in listing B.4 achieves.

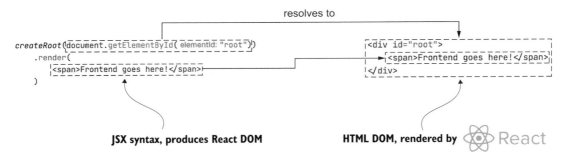

Figure B.1   Calling React's `render` function

We also need some styling using CSS, to make things look somewhat OK-ish.

Listing B.5   src/frontend/styling.css

```
body {
    font-family: Arial, Helvetica, sans-serif;
    font-size: 24pt;
}
```
→ Set the main font to be large and a common variant of sans-serif.

As mentioned previously, just pointing a browser to the src/frontend/index.html file isn't going to work. Doing so results in a blank page and some errors on the developer console. We're going to have to set up some tooling that can turn these three files into something a browser can understand. This "something" is called a *bundle*, and it will essentially consist of one HTML file, one CSS file, and one JS file. The resulting three files contain everything necessary to run the frontend in any modern browser.

Bundling does a lot of things at the same time:

- It aggregates all relevant JavaScript code, including frameworks installed through npm, and puts that in the JS file. That JS file is probably large, but it can be served to the browser in one go, which is more efficient than serving lots of smaller files.
- It makes included frameworks available to JavaScript code, referencing these through `import` statements.
- It "down-compiles" or "transpiles" JavaScript code, possibly in JSX syntax, to JavaScript code that can be understood by and run in all modern browsers. This JavaScript also ends up in the JS file.

- It aggregates all CSS content included by JSX files and puts that in a bundled CSS file.
- It modifies the HTML file to properly include the bundled CSS and JS files.

In essence, bundling turns code that's convenient for software developers to read and write into code that's convenient for browsers to run. Figure B.2 sums up the process of bundling.

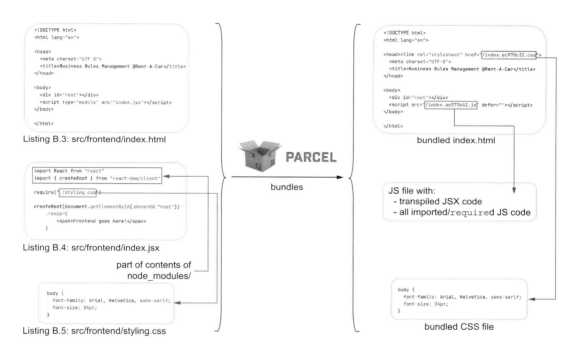

Figure B.2 What bundling does

I've chosen to use the *Parcel* web bundler (https://parceljs.org) to do the bundling. We first have to install the React framework and the Parcel tooling. We'll do this as follows, using npm from the command line:

```
$ npm install react
$ npm install react-dom
$ npm install parcel --save-dev
```

> These lines install the packages from the React framework that we import in the first two lines of src/frontend/index.jsx (listing B.4).

> This line installs the Parcel tooling as a development dependency through the --save-dev argument.

The Parcel tooling is needed to produce the bundled frontend, but should not be part of it, which is why we install it as a development dependency.

Next, we have to add the following line to the package.json file as a key-value pair in the root object:

```
"browserslist": "> 0.5%, last 2 versions, not dead"
```

This configures Parcel to use its built-in transpiler during bundling, targeting a default set of browsers.

After having done this, we can now run Parcel in *development mode*, as follows:

```
$ npx parcel src/frontend/index.html
Server running at http://localhost:1234
✨  Built in 6.29s.
```

In this case, we're running Parcel's executable, aptly named `parcel`. The command-line argument `src/frontend/index.html` points to the entry point of our frontend. When running this command, Parcel bundles the files in src/frontend and starts up a small web server that serves the produced bundle on http://localhost:1234. (You can find the bundle's files in the dist/ directory.)

Not only does Parcel serve the frontend for us, but it also supports *source watching* and *hot module replacement* (HMR) out of the box. When we change files in src/frontend/, Parcel detects that and automatically rebuilds our app. After Parcel has rebuilt the app, this is immediately detected by browsers running the frontend. Each (instance of the) frontend will update itself virtually instantly, without needing to reload. That usually happens within a couple of milliseconds. This keeps the feedback cycle short, focused, and convenient.

The result of clicking on the URL shown, http://localhost:1234, should look like figure B.3.

Using Parcel in production

The way we're using Parcel in development mode is very convenient for coding because it doesn't do any minifying, and it adds HMR support. When deploying a frontend to production, we need quite the opposite. To trigger Parcel's production mode, you add an extra `build` argument in front of the path to the HTML file, as follows:

```
$ npx parcel build src/frontend/index.html
```

You'll find the results in the dist/ directory as well, so you might need to rid that of traces of development activity beforehand.

Projection goes here!

Figure B.3   A screenshot of the browser showing the initial frontend

B.3 *Using React components to implement a frontend*

In section B.2, we set up a barebones frontend. In this section, we're going to see how we can use *stateless React components*. Components let you split the frontend into independent, reusable pieces and think about each piece in isolation.

A stateless React component is a JavaScript function that returns a React DOM. This React DOM looks a lot like an HTML DOM. React *renders* it into an HTML DOM—a process that unfortunately shares its name with the browser turning the HTML DOM into pixels on the screen. Because the stateless React component is a function, it can't hold any state of its own: instead, state has to be passed to it.

> **NOTE** *Stateful* React components are more flexible (in principle), because they can contain state—as the name suggests. In section B.4, I'll explain how we can keep all the application's state in a central place, and how stateless React components can automatically *react* to state changes. This means we don't need stateful React components, which are much more verbose code-wise and are more difficult to reason about and to get right.

As in section B.1.4, the syntax of such a component can have two different flavors. You can use either the expression form,

A React component function must have a certain signature—discussed next.

```
const Identifier = (props) =>
    <an expression returning a React DOM>
```
Sends the record and sets the returned Future to a variable

or the block statement form:

A React component function must have a certain signature—discussed next.

```
const Identifier = (props) => {
    // ...do other useful things first...
    return <an expression returning a React DOM>
}
```
This React DOM expression is typically built up using JSX syntax. That means the React component function must reside in a .jsx file.

A React component function must have a name, `Identifier`, that starts with an uppercase character. React (and Parcel) will complain when that's not the case. This convention distinguishes developer-defined components from built-in ones that correspond to React DOM elements.

A React component function takes a single parameter named `props`, which is short for "properties." This parameter is used to govern, or configure, the appearance and function of the React component we're defining. The value passed in this parameter will be an object containing key-value pairs. I'll explain shortly how this object gets populated.

> **Returning undefined intentionally**
>
> Returning `undefined`, or any other falsy value, from a React component will render a whole lot of nothing, without even giving a warning on the developer console. This behavior is intentional: you don't have to return something like `<div></div>` to tell React to show nothing, keeping the React DOM "clean/unpolluted."
>
> If you forget the `return` keyword in the second block statement form, the component function will always return `undefined` instead of the React DOM you probably intended to return. Because of how React renders `undefined`, it's usually best to use the second block statement form, even if there's initially only one React DOM expression to return. That way you won't accidentally forget to add the `return` keyword when extending the component's code.

Calling a React component is typically done using JSX syntax, as in the following listing.

Listing B.6   Calling a React component named `Identifier`

```
<Identifier
  property₁={value₁}
  property₂={value₂}
  ...more properties...
/>
```

Each $property_i$ is a JavaScript identifier naming the property, and $value_i$ is a Java-Script expression that's evaluated and used as the property's value. The `props` properties object that's passed to the `Identifier` function's body is populated with key-value pairs: each $property_i$ is a key with the corresponding $value_i$ being the value. If a $value_i$ is a string literal, you can drop the curly braces and write $property_i$`="`$value_i$`"`. (The order of the properties doesn't matter.)

In the following subsections, I'll explain more about the idiom that we use in the implementation of the Domain IDE and Runtime frontends.

B.3.1   Using destructuring to receive component parameters

To avoid the body of a stateless React component being littered with expressions like `props.`$property_i$, we can use ES2015's object destructuring again, as follows:

```
const Identifier =
    (({ property₁, property₂, ... })) => {
    return <an expression involving propertyᵢ>
}
```

Replace the props parameter name with the object's structure description with the form { ...properties' names... }. Note the double pair of parentheses on the left side of the double arrow.

Now you can refer to and access any $property_i$, a local constraint within the body of the component, meaning within the last pair of curly braces.

B.3.2 Using application state

State*less* React components can't have state of their own: the only state they can access is received through their properties. So where do these property values come from? The idea is that the application as a whole has a state: its *application state*. The application then passes its state into top-level stateless components, which subsequently can pass the whole application state, or selected parts of it, down into nested subcomponents.

Two kinds of application state

Application state is of one of these two kinds:

- *View* state is associated with the application's UI.
- *Model* state is associated with the application as a whole. This is usually state that's directly derived from the application's *data* and is often synchronized back to that data.

Listing B.7 shows the changes (highlighted in bold) to src/frontend/index.jsx that add state to the frontend and then use it.

Listing B.7 Adding state to the frontend

```
import React from "react"
import { createRoot } from "react-dom/client"

require("./styling.css")

const state = {          ◁───  Define the application's overall state as a single object, held
    ...                         as the value of a const declaration. This object has key-value
}                               pairs that represent parts of the application state.

const Frontend = ({ state }) =>
    <span>Frontend goes here!</span>

createRoot(document.getElementById("root"))
    .render(                         Call the <Frontend>
        <Frontend state={state} />   component, explicitly passing
    )                          ◁──── in the application state.
```

When used like this, React will render a React DOM once and never re-render it. To make React *react* to changes in the application state, we need to use a *state management library*. I've chosen the MobX framework as our state management library. I'll explain how we'll use MobX throughout our codebase in section B.4.

B.3.3 Nesting component calls

We've been calling the stateless React components that we've previously been defining using the *empty tag form*: `<Identifier ... />`. Sometimes, a component needs to receive an HTML sub-DOM that's going to be included in the React DOM that the component is going to return. Let's say we want to implement a component named `WrapInDiv` that wraps an HTML sub-DOM in a `<div>` element. You can use the special React property named `children` for that as follows:

```
const WrapInDiv = (({ children })) => {
    return <div>
       {children}
    </div>
}
```

Include the value of the children property verbatim.

Include a property named children in the properties' object structure description. Where it occurs in the description is irrelevant, but no other property of a React component can be named children.

You can call this component using JSX syntax, as follows:

```
<WrapInDiv>
    <span>...some text...</span>
</WrapInDiv>
```

That call would result in the following React DOM:

```
<div>
    <span>...some text...</span>
</div>
```

B.3.4 *Mapping an array over a component*

Often, we'll want to iterate over an array of items and call a React component for each of them. Naively, we'd do this as follows:

```
{<array>.map((member) =>
    <Identifier thing={member} />
)}
```

When you do this and pull up the developer console, you'll see that React issued a warning that "each child in a list should have a unique "key" prop." React issues this warning when you produce more than one element as the child of another element. You can fix this warning by passing a value for the special React property named `key`. That property implicitly exists on any React component, just like the `children` property does. React will do what it needs to do with the value for `key`, and won't bother you with the warning anymore. You don't have to explicitly receive the `key` property.

The simplest way to produce appropriate, unique values for the `key` property is to use the *index* of each item in the array. The `map` function defined on arrays already provides that index when iterating over an array: it not only passes each array member to the function that we call `.map` with, but it passes its 0-based index as a second argument:

```
{<array>.map((member, index) =>
    <Identifier thing={member} key={index} />
)}
```

B.3.5 Using an and operator for conditional content

Often, you'd like to return some React DOM from the evaluation of an expression if some other conditional expression evaluates to `true` (or another truthy value), and nothing otherwise. An example is when you need to show some value only when it's present. You might be tempted to use an `if` statement as follows:

```
{if (someValue) {
    <span>{someValue} is present</span>
}}
```

Unfortunately, this doesn't work: JSX can only contain expressions, not statements. This code produces a syntax error, so it shouldn't (be) run in the first place.

A common React code pattern for achieving what we want goes as follows:

```
{someValue && <span>{someValue} is present</span>}
```

This works because of the following—admittedly somewhat quirky—behavior of JavaScript:

- JavaScript's logic operators, such as its `&&` operator, operate on values of *any* type, not just on `true` and `false`. The values `undefined`, `null`, `0`, `NaN`, an empty string, and of course, `false`, are falsy. All other values are truthy.
- Not only does the `&&` operator accept values of any type, it can also return any type. If its left side is falsy, it will return that left side without evaluating the right side. This behavior is called *short-circuiting*, and it's often very useful. If its left side is truthy, it will just return the evaluation of the right side. It's then up to the receiver of that return value to decide whether it's falsy or truthy.

In our case, that means that if `someValue` has a truthy value, the JSX expression to the right of `&&` is evaluated and returned. If `someValue` has a falsy value, that falsy value is returned, which React renders as nothing, without complaining.

B.3.6 Combining CSS classes

All HTML DOM elements have an attribute named `class`, which value is a string containing CSS class names separated by whitespaces. The React versions of HTML elements rename that attribute to `className` to avoid confusion with JavaScript's `class` keyword.

Sometimes, you need to build up this string depending on the truthiness of some values. An example is when you need to apply a CSS class named `component` and a CSS class `selected` when the value of a variable `selected` is `true`. That means you have to append the string `"selected"` to the string `"component"` and also make sure there's whitespace between those two strings. That could be done as follows:

```
<div
    className={"component" +
      ⇒ (selected ? " selected" : "")    ⟵
      ⇒ }
>...
```

The leading space in the " selected" string is necessary to separate it from the "component" CSS class name.

The preceding code looks a bit messy, and it gets worse (and more error prone) when more CSS class names are involved. We can improve on this by adding an `asClass-NameArgument` helper function to the src/frontend/css-utils.js file in the Domain IDE's codebase, and exporting it from there.

Listing B.8   Implementing an `asClassNameArgument` helper function

```
const asClassNameArgument = (...classNames) =>
  classNames.filter(
    (className) => typeof className === "string")
    .join(" ")
module.exports.asClassNameArgument = asClassNameArgument
```

From the array with class names, keep all those that are strings (filtering out falsy values like false or undefined).

The parameter list consists of one rest parameter, which declares that this function takes an arbitrary number of arguments (including 0) and that these arguments are passed in as an array named className.

We can use this function as follows:

```
asClassNameArgument("component", selected && "selected")
```

This call will return `"component selected"` if `selected` is `true`, and `"component"` if it's `false`. That's because the `&&` operator shortcuts, so the second argument, `selected && "selected"`, evaluates to `"selected"` when `selected` is `true` and to `false` when `selected` is `false`.

We can now use this function as follows:

```
<div
    className={
      asClassNameArgument("component",
        selected && "selected")
    }
>...
```

Although the code is slightly longer, it looks less messy and is easier to read and reason about.

B.4   *Using MobX to react to changes*

"Anything that can be derived from the application state, should be. Automatically." MobX (https://mobx.js.org) is a *state management library* for JavaScript. Combining React and MobX results in a coding style that is called *Transparent Functional Reactive Programming* (TFRP). Let's break down the adjectives in this acronym:

- *Transparent*, because it requires little coding effort to get working.
- *Functional*, because it encourages the developer to phrase the projection as a pure function of application state to a React DOM.
- *Reactive*, because it reacts to events fired from the rendered React DOM by triggering appropriate actions that in turn manipulate the application state.

TFRP allows us to write code that pretends that everything can be *derived* from the application state. Those derivations are the result of calling functions with some part of the application state. Stateless React components returning a React DOM are the primary (but not only) examples of functions producing derivations. TFRP reacts to changes in the application state by rerunning those derivations automatically and efficiently. Those changes are typically triggered by events that are fired from a rendered HTML DOM. This idea can be visualized as in figure B.4.

Figure B.4   The essence of MobX

TFRP is very useful for implementing UIs that have clear, maintainable, and easily expandable code. MobX is not the only open source TFRP framework out there, but it's one that does it well, and one that I happen to be quite familiar with. The specific use of MobX in this book should carry over relatively easily to other TFRP frameworks.

MobX relies on the Observer and Pub/Sub patterns to do its reactive "magic." React and MobX try to do as little unnecessary work as possible by keeping track of what values a derivation has looked at when run. MobX only reruns those derivations that are likely affected by changes made to the application state.

As a developer, these are the rules you have to follow to achieve TFRP with MobX:

- Mark what constitutes state.
- Mark components that should react to changes in that state.
- Mark functions that change that state: *actions*.

Marking is done by wrapping objects, stateless components, and actions in specific MobX functions.

B.4.1   Installing MobX

Before we can use MobX, we have to install two npm packages. That's done from the command line as follows:

```
$ npm install mobx
$ npm install mobx-react
```

Now we can import MobX functions in JavaScript files as follows:

Import the general MobX functions observable and action from the mobx package.

```
import { observable, action } from "mobx"
import { observer } from "mobx-react"
```

Import the React-specific MobX function observer from the mobx-react "sister package" of the mobx package.

B.4.2   Marking objects as state

You mark a JavaScript object, `someObject`, as state by wrapping it in MobX's `observable` function:

```
const someObservableObject = observable(someObject)
```

As its name implies, the `observable` function returns a version of `someObject` that's *observable*. *Observers* can subscribe to `someObservableObject`, and they're then notified of changes to that object.

Different kinds of changes exist:

- The value of any of the properties of `someObservableObject` may change.
- A key-value pair on `someObservableObject` may be added, or an existing one may be removed. This is important when a setting's value is initially `undefined`.
- In JavaScript, arrays are special kinds of objects, and `observable` has special behavior for arrays. When `someObject` is an array, then array members can be removed or moved around, and new members can be added.

Wrapping objects in proxies

After `someObject` has been used to produce `someObservableObject`, the two don't have any relation with each other anymore. Changes to one doesn't affect the other, so we should forget about `someObject`, using only `someObservableObject` instead.

Technically, `observable` wraps the object passed in a *proxy*. A proxy looks and behaves the same as the object that's been made observable, but it has additional behavior and API. For more details on proxies, see the MDN documentation: https://developer.mozilla.org/en-US/docs/Web/JavaScript/Reference/Global_Objects/Proxy.

A special feature of the `observable` function is that `someObservableObject` is *deeply* observable. That means that any object *reachable* (through JavaScript object references) from `someObservableObject` is made observable itself. As an example, this code fragment,

```
observable({
    concept: "Some Thing",
    settings: {
```

```
        "property1": 1,
        "property2": {
            concept: "Another Thing",
            settings: {
                "property3": [ "foo", "bar" ]
            }
        }
    }
})
```

achieves the exact same thing as the following code fragment (with differences high-lighted in bold):

```
observable({
    concept: "Some Thing",
    settings: observable({
        "property1": 1,
        "property2": observable({
            concept: "Another Thing",
            settings: observable({
                "property3": observable( [ "foo", "bar" ] )
            })
        })
    })
})
```

This holds even for objects that only become reachable from *someObservable-Object* *after* the latter's creation, such as by setting the value of a key-value pair. Essentially, whatever happens inside a deeply observable object doesn't stay in Vegas but is fully observable and on display for interested parties that have subscribed as observers.

B.4.3   *Marking components as reactive*

Now that we can mark objects as state, we want to use those objects in stateless React components so that they automatically re-render their React DOM when changes occur. We do that by wrapping them with the `observer` function from the `mobx-react` package, as follows:

```
const <Identifier> = observer((<parameter list>) =>
    <expression returning React DOM> or {
        <statements...>
        return <expression returning React DOM>
    })
```

This has the effect that the component that's marked as `observer` is subscribed to be notified of changes to any of the observable objects it looks at. Usually, such an observable object is one of the component's arguments. Whenever such an observable object notifies the observing component of a change, MobX reruns the component so that the virtual React DOM is recomputed so that it can get re-rendered. Figure B.5 shows this.

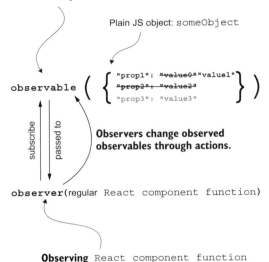

Figure B.5 An observable object and an observing React component

NOTE A component that's been marked as observer reacts to changes to any object it looks at, not just on those objects that are explicitly passed. This means we don't have to explicitly pass application state all the time but can also refer to state that's available globally. However, to keep things clear and explicit, we don't make use of this fact in this book.

B.4.4 *Marking functions as actions*

JavaScript functions that change state are called *actions*. They're marked as such by wrapping them with the action MobX function, which doesn't change their function signature. The following code fragment is an example of a function that most likely should be marked as an action:

```
(event) => {                          ◁——— Define an arrow function.
    state.<property> = "bar"           ◁—┐ Set some property of
}                                         │ the state object.
```

The preceding code fragment defines an arrow function that takes one argument named event, implying that it's the handler for an event listener attached to the React DOM. The state object should be MobX-observable and either is passed explicitly to the component containing this code or is accessed through a global value.

Marking this function as an action looks like this:

```
action((event) => {
    state.<property> = "bar"
})
```

The result of wrapping a function with the `action` function is a new function that behaves identically to the wrapped one but performs MobX-related bookkeeping in addition. We refer to such functions as *actions*. If you fail to mark a function as an action, MobX will complain about that on the JavaScript console. Despite MobX complaining, it will still usually work as expected. You might lose some guarantees regarding performance or transaction boundaries, though, which makes it worth keeping an eye on the console.

The preceding code represents the primary use case for actions: the domain experts interact with the rendered React DOM, which fires events that trigger actions that change the application state. You can see a complete example in section B.4.6.

B.4.5   Marking classes as stateful

In section B.1.8, I explained that we don't use JavaScript classes in the implementation of the Domain IDE, but we do in the Runtime's code. Because instances of these classes are used in the Runtime's UI, and because we want this UI to be reactive, these classes need to be marked as stateful.

This is generally done as follows:

```
import { makeAutoObservable } from "mobx"        ◁──── Import MobX's
                                                        makeAutoObservable function.
class <name class> {

    // (regular) properties:
    <name property_i> =                           ◁──── Define a regular property and
        ⇒ = <initial value property_i>                 (optionally) an expression of
    // ...                                              its initial value.

                                                        Define a computed property
    // computed properties:                             through a getter—discussed next.
    get <name property_j>() {                     ◁────
        return <expression that computes the value of property_j>
    }
    // ...

    constructor() {                               Call the MobX function makeAutoObservable
        makeAutoObservable(this)                  ◁──── in the class's constructor to make this
        // ...more initialization...              instance of the class observable.
    }

}
```

A getter is a no-args method that's prepended with the `get` keyword. It's called as `<instance>.<name property_j>`, so it behaves as a read-only property that's computed on demand.

New instances of this class are made (deeply) observable by the call to `makeAuto-Observable` in the class's constructor. The `makeAutoObservable` function automatically makes any property `observable`. It also makes any property defined through a getter observable. This means two things:

- MobX starts tracking which observable values are referenced in *<an expression that computes the property's value>*.
- When those observable values change, all observers of the class's instance are notified, so they can trigger recomputation of the computed property.

B.4.6   Putting everything together

Using React in combination with MobX to achieve TFRP is visualized in figure B.6.

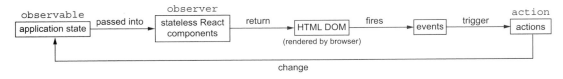

Figure B.6   Using React and MobX to implement a frontend in the TFRP style

The code in listing B.9 implements a simple but complete example frontend in this TFRP style that counts clicks on a button.

Listing B.9   An example frontend in TFRP style

```
import React from "react"
import { createRoot } from "react-dom/client"
import { action, observable } from "mobx"
import { observer } from "mobx-react"

const state = observable({
    counter: 0
})

const CounterComponent = observer(({ state }) =>
    <button onClick={action((event) => {
        state.counter++
    })}>{state.counter}</button>
)

createRoot(document.getElementById("root"))
    .render(
        <CounterComponent state={state} />
    )
```

The event is ignored.

Call the <CounterComponent> directly instead of calling it from inside a <Frontend> component. Following the pattern established earlier, we pass the observable application state, held as an object in state.

The code in listing B.9 should go in an index.jsx file. The src/frontend/index.html file from listing B.3 can be used again. To run this frontend, execute the following on the command line:

```
$ npx parcel src/frontend/index.html
```

This should let Parcel start a development web server on http://localhost:1234 that shows a number that increments when you mouse-click it. This example doesn't use classes, so it also doesn't showcase the contents of section B.4.5.

In this appendix, you learned how to use the JavaScript development environment set up in appendix A to implement a Transparent Functional Reactive frontend.

index